I0161698

OFFICIAL REPORT

OF THE

TWENTIETH INTERNATIONAL

CHRISTIAN ENDEAVOR CONVENTION

HELD IN

MUSIC HALL, THE ODEON AND MANY CHURCHES

OF

CINCINNATI, O., JULY 6 - 10, 1901.

First Fruits Press
Wilmore, Kentucky
c2015

First Fruits Press

The Academic Open Press of Asbury Theological Seminary
204 N. Lexington Ave., Wilmore, KY 40390
859-858-2236
first.fruits@asburyseminary.edu
asbury.to/firstfruits

Committee of 1901.

1. D. B. Meacham, Chairman.
2. S. E. Hutton, Secretary.
3. Rev. A. M. Dawson, Vice-chairman.
4. E. B. Sayers, Treasurer and Excursions.
5. E. P Wilson, Vice-chairman.
6. Miss Cora Gerrard, Official Stenographer.
7. Rev. Justin M. Green, Entertainment.
8. W. W. Warwick, Press.
9. Miss Lottie S. Nichol, Reception.
10. M. Brayton Graff, Vice-chairman.
11. Rev. W. G. Partridge, Pulpit Supply.
12. Rev. A. A. Andridge.
13. W. H. Hutton, Decorations.
14. W. B. Melish, Transportation.
15. Henry Appleton, Juniors.
16. Judge John D. Ellis, Places of Meetings.
17. Melville Ritchie, Printing.
18. C. A. Hinch, Finance.
19. Rev. C. L. Work, D. D., Evangelistic.
20. A. W. Macbriar, Music.
21. J. Albert Miller, Ushers.

OFFICIAL REPORT

OF THE

TWENTIETH INTERNATIONAL

Christian Endeavor Convention

HELD IN

MUSIC HALL, THE ODEON AND MANY CHURCHES

OF

CINCINNATI, O., JULY 6-10, 1901.

Copyrighted, 1901, U. S. C. E.

UNITED SOCIETY OF CHRISTIAN ENDEAVOR,

TREMONT TEMPLE, BOSTON, MASS., U. S A.

1901.

THE COMMITTEE OF 1901.

EXECUTIVE COMMITTEE.

Mr. D. B. MEACHAM, *Chairman.*

Rev. A. M. DAWSON, *Vice-Chairman.*

Mr. M. BRAYTON GRAFF, *Vice-Chairman.*

Mr. E. P. WILSON, *Vice-Chairman.*

Mr. S. E. HUTTON, *Secretary.*

Mr. E. B. SAYERS, *Treasurer.*

Mr. W. B. MELISH, *Chairman of Transportation.*

Mr. C. A. HINSCH, *Chairman of Finance.*

CHAIRMEN OF SUB-COMMITTEES.

Rev. JUSTIN N. GREEN, *Entertainment.*

Miss LOTTIE S. NICHOL, *Reception.*

Mr. W. W. WARWICK, *Press.*

Mr. J. ALBERT MILLER, *Usher.*

Mr. A. W. MACBRIAR, *Music.*

Mr. MELVILLE RITCHIE, *Printing.*

Judge JOHN D. ELLIS, *Places of Meeting.*

Rev. W. G. PARTRIDGE, D.D., *Pulpit Supply.*

Mr. W. H. HUTTON, *Decorations.*

Mr. E. B. SAYERS, *Local Excursions.*

Mr. HENRY APPLETON, *Juniors.*

Rev. C. L. WORK, D.D., *Evangelistic.*

Rev. A. A. ANDRIDGE.

Miss CORA GERRARD, *Official Stenographer.*

MUSICAL DIRECTORS AND ASSOCIATES.

Mr. A. W. MACBRIAR, *Chairman.*

MUSICAL DIRECTORS.

Mr. F. H. JACOBS, Brooklyn, N. Y.

Mr. PERCY S. FOSTER, Washington, D. C.

Mr. H. C. LINCOLN, Philadelphia, Pa.

ACCOMPANISTS.

Miss REBECCA SNYDER,	Mrs. S. D. COCHRAN,	Miss MAY THOMPSON,
Mr. WALTER BERG,	Mr. WINTER WATTS,	Mr. BENJ. DeCAMP,
Mr. ALBERT D. SHOCKLEY,	Mr. IRWIN W. DRIEHAUS.	

CORNETISTS.

Miss GRACE W. BEELMAN.	Mr. BENJ. JELLEF,
Mr. HARRY PUGH,	Mr. ARNOLD C. DRIEHAUS,
Mr. H. CHAMPLIN,	Dr. W. S. LOCKE.

2

INTRODUCTION.

The Great Purposeful Convention.

ADVANCE STEPS AT "CINCINNATI, 1901."

WHAT impressed you most about the Cincinnati Convention?" is a question that has been asked me a dozen times within a week. Let me tell you. There were at least four features that I believe will make "Cincinnati, 1901," memorable.

THE HOME.

First, the emphasis put upon the Home. The four addresses upon this subject were strong, eloquent, and moving. The people in the great audience, too, were quite as eloquent as the speakers, for their hearts were evidently moved, and they felt that the time had come for an advance step, as Mr. Landrith said, and that Christian Endeavor should henceforth stand for Family Worship in the home, as it stands for the Quiet Hour of communion, as it stands for systematic giving and Christian citizenship

Who seconds this motion? Shall we have an enrolment of Christian Endeavorers who believe in and practise family worship? Will you suggest a name for this new Christian Endeavor enrolment of Home Endeavorers who will rally to the family altar to erect it, or re-erect it where it has been neglected? How else can we as Endeavorers help this great cause of family religion? Send me your ideas, or let me know of your interest in this matter; and, if you all say so, in the fall we will begin a campaign which will perhaps be the most important that Christian Endeavor has yet inaugurated.

THE CITY.

Again, tremendous emphasis was laid at Cincinnati upon the duty of the Endeavorers to their own city. Civic righteousness was brought down out of the hazy realm of the nebulæ, and laid upon the hearts and consciences of the young people, especially in Dr. Capen's splendid address, upon Christian citizenship, in which he advocated the formation of clubs or congresses in Christian Endeavor societies for the study of municipal politics and for discussion of matters relating to the life of the city,— congresses with a regularly elected speaker, committees, etc., to meet once a month perhaps, for study and discussion, and that shall meet occasionally the congresses of the other societies in joint debate.

Who says "Ay" to this proposition, and who will form such a congress next autumn when we get back from the summer vacations?

The Christian Endeavor World will have more to say about these two great efforts in the future.

THE WORLD.

"Cincinnati, 1901," will always be remembered for its missionary zeal. How could it be otherwise when such news as Secretary Hatch reported from India was heard, of the probable doubling of Christian Endeavor societies in one year? How could it be otherwise when the thrilling, heroic stories of the siege of Peking and of the African jungle were told? How could it be otherwise when such representatives of Christian Endeavor in foreign lands were present as Ament and Jones and Miyaki and Fulton and Hubbard and Ransom?

But the crowning feature was the raising and pledging of three thousand dollars for foreign work of Christian Endeavor, two thousand of which was pledged by the Congregationalists in their rally to promote the work of Christian Endeavor in China, and to help the union of China to secure a secretary, a Christian Endeavor martyrs' memorial in memory of the heroic Christian Endeavor martyrs of China. There was nothing more spontaneous or "hilarious" about the whole Convention than the raising of this money, and nothing more significant for the future.

THE WORLD TO COME.

If the Home, the City, and the World were remembered at Cincinnati, the World to Come was not forgotten; that is, if the Quiet Hour relates to the world to come any more than to this present world, which I very much doubt. But, because the Quiet Hour has promise of the world that now is and of that which is to come, the attention given to it was most significant.

Two great churches were crowded morning after morning. Though our beloved Dr. Chapman was kept away by serious sickness, Dr. Tomkins and Dr. Woelfkin showed themselves as ever masters of the theme, and Mr. Morgan's meeting and Dr. Carson's were also thronged, while the same high spiritual themes were considered.

After all, the Convention itself was its own most remarkable feature. Undaunted by the awful heat before the Convention, unattracted by special amusement features or excursion advertisements, that those eager multitudes of youth should again come, as for twenty years they have assembled in the hot days of July for a purely religious meeting, shows the everlasting hold of the gospel of Christ on the hearts of the young.

Thank God for "Cincinnati, 1901," in many important respects the crowning Convention of all!

Thank God for this great purposeful meeting!

Thank God that the Home, the City, and the World will feel its influence in all time to come!

Thank God for this new assurance and fresh exhibition of the devotion of youthful hearts to the religion of Christ!

Thank God that the gospel is not losing its power upon the lives of mankind!

Your friend,

FRANCIS E. CLARK

CHAPTER I.

The Twentieth Century Christian Endeavor Convention.

CHRISTIAN ENDEAVOR could not be conquered even by one of the most long-continued, disastrous, and deplorable seasons of excessive heat known in the history of this country. When for nearly two weeks the torrid zone moved northward over all the Eastern and Central States, when men were dying by the scores and hundreds and sickening by thousands, when the country was startled by the passing away of men of national and international fame under the terrific scourge,—when all this continued for day after day and still no prospect of relief came in sight, it seemed impossible that any convention at all could be held, to say nothing of a great one.

Yet the Endeavorers, like good soldiers, proved themselves ready to endure hardness and heat. They gladly made long journeys, they attended the meetings by thousands, the speakers—except those kept home by serious illness caused by the heat—were there to a man, and in the face of the most severe obstacles ever faced by an Endeavor convention the gathering at Cincinnati was a stupendous success, a triumph in which the angels in heaven must rejoice, as well as God's church on earth.

AN AUSPICIOUS OPENING.

Auditorium Endeavor, the main auditorium of Music Hall, is without a peer among International Convention halls, in proportions, architecture and acoustics. Without decorations other than the national and convention colors festooning the arch over the platform, it was a thing of beauty. It was decorated in the most splendid way, with bright Christian Endeavor faces, above the inclined plane of faces on the floor, two balconies brimming with eager, earnest young life.

A gavel of buckeye wood, presented by Dr. Dwight M. Pratt of Cincinnati, gave forth three resounding strokes in Dr. Clark's hand, and the Buckeye metropolis Convention was open, and under the wise and tactful chairmanship of Bishop Samuel Fallows stayed wide open all the evening in enthusiasm and alertness.

Ohio's Secretary of State, the Hon. L. C. Laylin, voiced a welcome that also had a true Buckeye ring.

Chairman D. B. Meacham, of the 1901 committee, spoke but few words in seconding this eloquent welcome; but they were words that condensed volumes of welcome into syllables of sound. He said:

Year after year the invitation of Cincinnati has been extended to the International Convention of Christian Endeavor, but the urgent claims of other cities have taken precedence. The past two weeks have been full of anxiety for us. The intense heat that has swept over other parts of the country we feared would induce thousands to forego the benefits of this convention rather than endure the discomforts of travel.

Disparaging remarks have been made regarding Cincinnati weather by persons who have never enjoyed the refreshing breezes from the gulf that are wafted up our beautiful Ohio. But at last you are here, and we wish by word and by deed to express our appreciation of the honor conferred on us. The United Society has prepared a royal feast for your spiritual needs, and we hope to provide for your temporal welfare in a manner equally acceptable. No features of entertainment have been planned to draw you from the meetings, but every one not familiar with our attractive hill-top suburbs and surroundings should visit them before returning home. Our ambition is that of your recollections hereafter, none shall be more pleasant and helpful than those of the Convention of 1901.

In behalf of the people of Cincinnati and the members of our committee, I give you most cordial greeting.

Vice-Chairman A. M. Dawson dealt in figures numerical and figures of speech. His words of welcome were as follows:

One occupies a place of distinguished honor who is chosen to voice the magnificent welcome that Cincinnati would give to the Twentieth International Convention of Christian Endeavor; a welcome so large and spontaneous, so hearty and generous, so overflowing and enthusiastic, that we say to you, put into our welcome all that you think it ought to be, all that you want it to be, and all that you expect it to be, and write over it all the words, "Cincinnati's Welcome in 1901." Cincinnati is no longer the "Queen City of the West," for the flag of Western empire has moved to Point Barrow, Alaska, and there are other magnificent cities between us and that distant point. But she is the Queen City of the Middle States, and sitting proudly with Covington and Newport upon either bank of the beautiful river, and surmounting the splendid hills of Ohio and Kentucky, with her hundreds of church spires lifted high toward the eternal dwelling-place of God; with her multitudinous factories, teeming with life and power and humming with successful industries; with her temples of commerce, sending their millions of dollars' worth of products up and down the great Ohio River, and across the continent in every direction by her unsurpassed railroads; with her numerous schools of music, and her well-known educational and art institutions,—yes, Cincinnati with her clouds of as beautiful smoke as you ever saw, curling up from thousands of places of industry, welcomes you as heartily as though her many thousands of bells were ringing and all her myriads of whistles were sounding.

Coming to Cincinnati you will find that we make soap enough in one year to make you clean all through your lives. We make shoes enough in two days to supply each of you with a new pair; we make clothing enough to dress you well for the next twenty years; we make suspenders enough in one day to suspend every one of you for years to come; we make enough furniture in one year to furnish every home represented here; and we make safes in sufficient quantities to make you all feel assured of your safety while among us, without having to appeal to the best police force or the model fire company of the nation.

In the name of Cincinnati, I welcome you as the hosts of the Lord God Almighty. With all her breweries, saloons, resorts, Sabbath desecration, Liberal League, etc., etc., Cincinnati has a host of God's children who have not bowed the knee to Baal. As the days set for this Convention pass by, you and they will come close to each other in bonds of sympathy and fellowship, and your presence will strengthen the stakes and lengthen the chords of Zion here. As a great body of trained and systematic servants of the Lord Christ, I welcome you. We shall not only exchange greetings, but we shall exchange with each other our knowledge of practical methods of religious, social and civic work, gained in myriads of fields of service, and we shall each go back to our respective fields, strengthened and made wiser thereby.

In the name of Cincinnati, I welcome the magnificent program of speakers provided for this Convention. Not in the twenty years of Christian Endeavor history has there been a better one. The brightest, brainiest, most thoroughly equipped, most earnestly consecrated men and women on this continent will contribute of their stores of knowledge, gained by traversing every avenue of Christian thought and service, and we shall drink at this great and overflowing fountain until we are filled and then go out to give it unto others.

Finally, we of Cincinnati welcome you as Christian Endeavorers, a great spiritual force, whose presence and uplifting power we need. If your coming shall mean to the ministry and churches of Cincinnati a great baptism of the Holy Ghost; if it shall mean to the unsaved masses of our city, through your evangelistic efforts, the gathering of many into the folds of Christ; and if it shall mean to the 3000 Endeavorers of Cincinnati Union a deeper spiritual life, a thorough consecration, and a mighty impulse to do better work for the Master—if all of the work of preparation for your coming, all the earnest praying during many months, all the hopes and expectations, based upon your coming, shall thus be realized, we shall be blessed indeed, and to Christ shall all the glory be given. And now, friends of Christ, if you will take us at our word, and feel perfectly at home while here; if you will act as though the gates of our beloved city and the cities across the Ohio were thrown wide open to you: if you will enjoy our hospitality as though you believed it to be truly and generously extended; and if you will show that you believe us when we say we enshrine you in our hearts and hold you before the Throne continually for God's richest blessing upon you during your stay with us, you will prove that our welcome has not been extended in vain.

Every year he has occupied the presidential chair, President McKinley has sent a telegram to our annual gatherings. This year's message, forwarded from Canton, was received with prolonged applause, Secretary Baer being authorized to send a fitting response. Said the President:

Canton, O., July 6.

John Willis Baer, General Secretary of the United Society of Christian Endeavor.

Upon the assembling of the International Christian Endeavor Convention this evening, please extend to those present my cordial greeting and best wishes for the success of the associations. I regret that it is impossible for me to be with you on this occasion.

WILLIAM McKINLEY.

Japan was the first to respond to these overwhelming tokens of good will. "Christian Endeavor and I are of the same age," said Mr. Miyaki, the bright little honorary secretary of the Japanese union, as he stood before the audience in his picturesque native costume. "Christian Endeavor is twenty years old, and I am twenty years old in Christ." He presented a silken banner from the Endeavorers of his own city, Osaka. His reception by the audience was an ovation. Among other things the Rev. A. Miyaki, of Osaka, Japan, said:

I am one of the delegates who came the longest distance to attend this Convention. Representing over two thousand Endeavorers in the Sunrise Empire, I bring you our overflowing greetings. I felt very small with only seventy societies in the midst of forty-three millions of people, but I feel big now and greatly strengthened, seeing these hosts. We are a part of this world-wide grand army. It is our prayer and hope that Japan be brought to Christ. Let us go forth with ever increasing faith and energy to hasten the kingdom of our Lord. Osaka Union sends you this banner, and expresses its hearty greeting. I have an official greeting from the president of Japan Union, T. Harada, which I will read:

"The old century has gone. The new century has come. In the first year of the twentieth century, at the twentieth year of the C. E. Society since its first organization, the International Convention is held in Cincinnati. We heartily rejoice at this grand celebration. Our honorary secretary, Mr. Miyaki, representing seventy societies of Japan, expresses our sincere greetings by his presence. C. E. Banzai, C. E. Banzai! never ceasing prosperity to Christian Endeavor, never ceasing growth to Christian Endeavor!"

Once, twice, thrice the applause rung out after Mr. Miyaki had taken his seat, and could scarcely be repressed to give China a chance in the person of Rev. G. H. Hubbard, founder of the first society in China, and president of the United Society of Christian Endeavor for China.

Mr. Chairman, Brothers and Sisters of the World-wide Christian Endeavor, or, as the Chinese might say, "of the nine continents and ten thousand countries, rouse up society, bing-bang:" Every Christian Endeavorer has come here for as much loot as he can get away with and escape visiting the city jail against his will. I, for one, want to thank the secretaries and committees, any and all who have had a share in providing this great feast of good things, thus furnishing us with the looting opportunity of our lives. If we can make it appear in other people's hearts and lives, so much the better, for one of the mottoes of Christian Endeavor is, "Not to be ministered unto, but to minister." As President of the National Society of Christian Endeavor in China, it is proper that I should bring you the salutations of my constituency and wish you peace.

The Queen City of Ontario sent greetings to the Queen City of the Middle States through Rev. Alfred Gandier, trustee of the United Society for the Presbyterians of Canada. He slyly twitted Americans with having a fondness for big things, and suggested that that, perhaps, was the reason for our love for our neighbor of the north, which is the largest country in North America.

Japan's delegate claimed to have traveled the longest distance. China was disposed to scout the claim, but Australia's representative, Rev. William G. Marsh, of Adelaide. boldly swept both claims aside by referring to the splendid commonwealth he represented as the land farthest south, farthest east, and farthest west from America.

And so the Southern Cross joined with the Orient and the Occident, and the Churchman with Puritan's descendants in this visible token of a fellowship that is girdling the globe as fast as are the transcontinental railways and oceanic cables.

The response for the delegates from the United States, was voiced by Rev. W. J. Darby, D. D., of Evansville, Ind. Dr. Darby has been a member of the Board of Trustees of the U. S. C. E. for many years and his splendid statement of Christian Endeavor's principles was heartily applauded again and again.

In nothing did the audience seem more reluctant during the evening than in yielding to the chairman's request not to insist on an encore to Miss Beelman's beautiful cornet solo, that rolled and swelled in billows of seductive sound to the topmost balcony.

CHAPTER II.

President Clark's Annual Address.

For every age God prepares His agencies. As the bee is made for the flower, as the bird's wing fits the air, and the fin of the fish the yielding water, so in the moral and religious world God adapts His plans and methods to the needs of the time.

To the mind of the devout believer there is no surer test of the overruling providence of God. In every great movement in the church of God can be seen God's nice adjustment of time and place and method to the needs of the age.

The Sunday school, begun in the last part of the eighteenth century, had a vast work to do for the nineteenth century in popularizing Bible-study. The nineteenth century was to print a cheap Bible for every one. The Sunday school came just in time to teach every one to study it when printed.

The nineteenth century saw peculiar perils assail the young man. The saloon, the brothel, the gambling-den, commercialism, and materialism laid their traps for him. But God looked down from heaven upon the children of men, and in the middle of the century the Young Men's Christian Association was started to set young men at work for young men in a new evangelism.

Still God's resources were not exhausted. Still He had treasures new and old to bring out of His storehouse. So in the last twenty years of the nineteenth century He developed a new world-embracing plan for the upbuilding of His church among the young in the twentieth century which has just dawned. This plan He called the Young People's Society of Christian Endeavor. Every word is significant. Young—it appealed to the young and enlisted the young. People—the young of both sexes. Society—a thoroughly organized effort. Christian—for Christ and the church. Endeavor—strenuous, earnest effort. For short—a Young People's Society of Christian Endeavor.

GOD'S HOUR FOR CHRISTIAN ENDEAVOR.

God's plans never mature too early. They never delay too long. When the hour strikes, His designs are ready. His clock is never fast and never slow. The hour for the development of new methods and lines of work had come, and today, with the new century only six months old, we can see why the twentieth century peculiarly needs such an agency as the Young People's Society of Christian Endeavor.

In the first place, the twentieth century church needs to cultivate a strenuous, earnest type of religion. The batteries which the twentieth century are already turning on the church of God are the masked batteries of indifference and worldliness,—not persecution and open hostility, and an army that can spike these guns of indifference and worldliness is the most imperative need of the church today. God saw this need and called an army of young people into existence, three million five hundred thousand strong. Who can better overcome these peculiar, insidious evils which threaten the church in this new century than a great company of eager, earnest youth each one of whom has said, "Trusting in the Lord Jesus Christ for strength. I promise Him that I will strive to do whatever He would like to have me do?"

Believe me, my friends. these insidious foes to which I have alluded are the real enemies of the church of God in this new century. The days of martyrdom in Christian communities are past. The days of undue asceticism and religious austerity have forever vanished, and with them have gone in many cases the strong, stern, stalwart characters that made the age of the Puritan resplendent for heroism throughout the world.

THE EVIL OF THE HOUR.

The days of the rampant infidel and atheist are also in the past, as I devoutly believe. No Robert Hume could today greatly influence the thought of the world. No Voltaire or Rousseau could number his followers by millions. Robert Ingersoll today is little but a memory of eloquent bathos and pathos. No thinking man is moved by his "mistakes" of Moses, or his tirades against the Gospels. But something more insidious, more subtle, more harmful a thousand times than persecution or blatant infidelity is the foe of the church of the twentieth century. This infidelity is a scepticism of life rather than of talk. It is the indifference that is born of luxury and fashion.

The nineteenth century has much to its credit. No one shall go beyond me in recognizing its splendid claims upon mankind, but born of its very prosperity and affluence have come these subtle dangers which the church of the twentieth century must meet. Worldliness is an almost certain adjunct of prosperity and wealth. Indifference to divine things is almost sure to accompany unprecedented development in material things. Enormous expansion on the earth does not favor an expansion toward the heavens. "Sure we must fight if we would win," is as true today as ever, but the foes that we must fight are those that weaken our hold on divine realities and substitute earthly prosperity for divine grace.

ON STRENUOUS LINES.

Now I think it is no empty boast to claim that the Christian Endeavor Society was raised up by God for this especial crisis in the twentieth century. It is built on strenuous lines. It appeals to the sense of duty. Its purpose is not to amuse young people, or to tickle them with the entertainment straw, but to call upon them in the name of Jesus Christ to do hard things for their Lord and for His church.

This is the meaning of the Christian Endeavor pledge. Call it what you will,—covenant, affirmation, promise; word it as you choose, so long as you do not take out of it the ring of high resolve and earnest purpose to confess Christ and work for Him. "Love the Lord thy God with all thy heart and with all thy mind and with all thy soul and with all thy strength." "Seek first the kingdom of God and His righteousness." "Make other things subordinate to your religious duties." This is the meaning of the Christian Endeavor pledge, and there is potency in such a promise.

SOME FAMOUS COVENANTS.

Why should we not make such a promise to God? Nothing great or strong was ever done in this world without a pledge. The compact of the Puritans in the Mayflower that founded the American commonwealth was a pledge. The covenant of the Scotch Christians that lies at the basis of the great Presbyterian Church in all the world was a solemn pledge. The Declaration of Independence ends with a pledge. The Magna Charta was a pledge of rights and duties between sovereign and people, and English liberty is founded upon it. Every commercial note is a promissory note. Every marriage compact, every business partnership, every right of citizenship, every home, every united enterprise, every state, rests upon some sure word of promise. This idea has put iron in the blood of millions of young Christians. It has been a tonic for the half-hearted. It has strengthened the weak, and upheld the feeble knees, and put courage into those who were ready to faint. It has been a counteracting influence to the indifferentism of the day. It has offset something of the feebleness of worldly Christianity. It has held up an ideal. It has set up a standard to which the earnest and devoted spirits among the young can resort, and they have flocked to it from all parts of the world. It presents an ideal, to be sure, that is not always reached, but ideals are always above us or they would not be ideals.

THE CHURCH NEEDS THE PRAYER MEETING.

In the second place, the twentieth century church needs the Christian Endeavor Society because it needs the prayer meeting. The influences which I have already alluded to are the microbes which are destroying the tissues of many a prayer meeting. It is too much trouble to go to the midweek service. It is not "good form" in many church circles to give one's testimony to the love of Christ. It is objected to in some quarters as "wearing one's heart on one's sleeve." Any kind of a religious experience is considered "cant" by some people. Some counteracting influence is needed, some antitoxine for these devastating prayer-meeting bacilli. I think I may venture to say that this antitoxine for the destruction of the twentieth century prayer-meeting microbes is found in the twentieth century Christian Endeavor Society. It centres about the prayer meeting. Its beating heart is the prayer meeting. Its life-blood comes back to the prayer meeting every week to be renewed and vitalized as every drop of blood in a man's body comes back to the heart to be revivified.

PRAYER-MEETING CANT.

"I do not see," says Dr. T. T. Munger, "how a church can get on without this free midweek service. I have not heard in the last ten years a word of cant in the midweek service, but I have heard a great deal of cant about it from those who never attend."

I can say the same thing about the Christian Endeavor prayer meetings I have attended for the last twenty years. I have heard a deal of cant about them. I have scarcely heard a word of cant in them.

The Christian Endeavor Society tends directly to keep alive and make more effective throughout the twentieth century the prayer-meeting idea. In these days when this idea is being given up in many churches, when experiment after experiment is being tried, when lectures and Bible classes are being substituted, when the whole trend of the times is to minimize and weaken this service, an organization that stands for it and promotes it and trains for it has been, I believe, born of God for this purpose. It has come to the kingdom for such a time as this.

THE CHURCH NEEDS MORE EFFICIENT ORGANIZATION.

In the third place the twentieth century church needs more thorough-going and effective organization in church life. "Organization is the sign of life," it has been truly said; "the lack of it is death. Enthusiasm and courage are evanescent unless they take on organized forms. Feeling and resolution fade out if not turned into rule and made steady by habit." One of the century's greatest thoughts is specialization and organization, in our business, our factories, our schools, our farms. Shall the church only lag behind in this respect? To decry organization in a church and land it in a factory is the height of folly. Only let this organization never outrun the leading of the Spirit. However many wheels there may be, be sure that the living creature is within the wheels.

Shall we organize thoroughly and efficiently every other department of life, and leave the most important of all, the religious side, unorganized and inefficient? That is a question which confronts the church of the twentieth century, and that is a question which the Christian Endeavor movement will do something to solve, for it believes in minute and thorough organization, in giving every member something to do appropriate to his years and his powers. It practically accomplishes this by placing every one upon a committee, which means that something is committed to him to do. This Society divides the young people into bands according to their mutual sympathies and abilities. It promotes unity by fostering the only kind of unity that God fosters,—the unity of diversity.

EXPANSION IN THE NEW CENTURY.

But let us see to it that this twentieth-century young people's society is a young people's society. Through wise use of the Honorary-Membership plan, by making much of the Junior and Intermediate societies where the latter is needed, by developing the associate members, by dividing the large societies, which, perhaps, is the better plan in many churches, so that the young members shall be brought out and given responsibility for testimony and service. Let us see to it, however old some of us grow in the work, that ours is always a young people's society of Christian Endeavor, and that every young person whom we can reach has a place and a work in the Society. We could not have a better rallying-cry for the twenty-first year than expansion. "The Society for all the young people and all the young people for the Society." Through Junior, Intermediate, Associate, Active, Honorary members—in some way, through some form of membership, the ideal society will sooner or later reach them all.

WANTED—A NEW-CENTURY CHURCH TRUST.

But, once more, the church of the twentieth century needs to be more united. The nineteenth century, though inaugurating these united movements, was a century of individualism and division. Fifty new sects can be counted that sprung up in the United States alone within a hundred years. Starving churches have been formed to perpetuate denominationalism,—a dozen sometimes in a community where one would do the work. I am not decrying a wise denominationalism, an idea for which Christian Endeavor always stands, and which is as wide apart as the poles from a devisive and jealous sectarianism. But I venture to say that if the church of the twentieth century is to do the work of God, it must be more united than was the church of the nineteenth century. This new century will be a century of mighty combinations and tremendous aggregations of material forces. The steel trust, the oil trust, the copper trust, point the way which industrialism is taking. Whether these things are right or wrong I am not here today to judge. But one trust, I venture to say, is needed, and that is a church trust. There should be a religious clearing-house. There should be a combination of the Christian forces of the land to work together in harmony for the advancement of the Kingdom through their own churches and denominations.

PATRIOTISM DEMANDS CHRISTIAN UNITY.

The Christian Endeavor Society does not aspire to be such a trust for the church at large, but it does aspire to promote among the young the spirit of harmony and brotherly love and united service for the kingdom of our Lord and for their native land.

Not only are the great industrial forces of the land uniting, but the devil is marshaling his forces at the beginning of the twentieth century as never before. The saloon-keeper and the distiller are closing up their ranks and combining their evil geniuses to debauch the youth of our land. The spirit of gambling and speculation was never so rampant, and this evil never presented a more united front. Political corruption in some of our States does not even think it necessary to apologize when it steals the people's money, so united, so powerful and brazen, has it become. Who will stem this tide? Who will oppose the united front of evil? Who will offset the fellowship of the work of darkness with the fellowship of the children of light? Surely an organization which has found its way into forty denominations, and into every country beneath the sun, an organization which has united three millions and a half of young people of every kindred and tribe and people and tongue and color and creed, has some reason to think that it was called into being by God for this very purpose.

THE FELLOWSHIP OF RIGHTEOUSNESS.

It was born in 1881, grew strong in the last two decades of the nineteenth century for the sake of the twentieth century, which so sorely needs the united forces of righteousness to oppose the united forces of the Evil One. This union was not the cunningly devised plan of man, but was foreordained of God. As the wheat grows on the prairie, each blade growing by itself, but each one contributing to the unity and glory of the harvest-field, so the Christian Endeavor societies have grown up without man's design or forethought, because God had a harvest of united Christian service to reap in the twentieth century. That our fellowship may be still more complete and our union more for the glory of God and for the overthrow of evil, I again affectionately and heartily invite all young people's societies with the same religious purpose and aim and general methods to come into the world-wide union of Christian Endeavor, that together we may do the Lord's work in the twentieth century as it has never before been done.

The church needs the united prayers of united young people. Every good cause needs their combined and aggregated efforts. The country needs their added forces on the side of Christian citizenship and pure politics. The world needs their undivided zeal to bring the nation under the sway of King Immanuel. Christian Endeavor furnishes a name and a plan of union in which there is no taint of sectarianism, a platform wide enough for forty denominations to stand upon. Who will go with us, that we may each do the other good?

SUBSTANTIAL GROUNDS.

Upon these broad and substantial grounds, then, I claim that God has a use for the Christian Endeavor movement in the church of the twentieth century. There is no magic or legerdemain about Christian Endeavor methods. We have no prophet Elijah or infallible pope or inspired mother in our Israel. I will not refer you to a passing phase or to an exceptional development. I do not point to any past triumphs or ancient history. I do not dwell upon the value of such magnificent conventions as this, or upon any accident or accessory of Christian Endeavor, but rest my case upon these broad, undeniable propositions born of the needs of the twentieth century. First, the church of the twentieth century needs more strenuous religious obligation. Second, the church of the twentieth century needs the testimony and petition of the prayer meeting. Third, the church of the twentieth century needs more complete and perfect organization. Fourth, the church of the twentieth century needs larger brotherhood and more substantial unity. These very things are the things which God seems to have established the Christian Endeavor movement to promote. These are not local and temporary needs. They take in the sweep of the century and the width of the world. They seem to be in accordance with God's plan. When we work with God we cannot fail. Our own plans and schemes and devices may come to naught, but when we humbly seek God's finger-post and follow the way He marks out, we can never go wrong, for we have His spirit to lead us, His Might to strengthen us, His Power infused into every activity, His Word of promise to give us assurance in the final outcome. To Him be all gratitude for the past; in Him all confident hope for the future.

> "Then let us adore and give Him His right,
> All glory, and power, and wisdom, and might;
> All honor and blessing, with angels above,
> And thanks never ceasing and infinite love."

CHAPTER III.

Secretary Baer's Annual Report.

CHRISTIAN ENDEAVOR FACTS AND FIGURES.

In 1891, the close of the first decade of Christian Endeavor, there were 16,274 societies, and we returned hearty thanks to God for what He had wrought. In this year 1901, at the close of Christian Endeavor's second decade, we must employ the same numerals, though differently arranged, to tell our numerical strength, for the 16,274 societies have become 61,427. The nearly one million members have become nearly four millions! This growth is marvelous, and nothing comparable to it can be found in history. The rapidity with which the societies have multiplied is so familiar, having compelled attention around the world, that we have in late years accepted that fact as commonplace. I remind you of this wonderful numerical extension of Christian Endeavor because it proves to me beyond a doubt that ours is not a man-made society, but a broad, interdenominational, international, and inter-racial brotherhood. "Man can organize a society, God creates a movement."

THE NET GAIN.

Each year we have expected that this increase in numbers would be comparatively small, but that time has not yet come. The net increase in numbers of new societies since we met in the great London Convention last July is nearly two thousand, with a total membership of almost one hundred thousand members. In other words, the net increase during the past year equals the total number of societies organized during the first seven years of our splendid history! There have been more than 2000 new societies added to the lists, but the net gain has not been quite that, because we have had to drop from our fellowship societies that have disbanded for various reasons, or that have become exclusively denominational societies. I am glad to say that the number of societies that we have had to take from our enrolment is less the last year than it was the year before. The last year has been noteworthy along this line for two reasons. First, a number of Christian Endeavor societies that left our ranks during the last decade (and in that time there were many that did this) have returned; some with longer names, but just as pleasing to us, such as Baptist Union of Christian Endeavor, or Epworth League of Christian Endeavor. Some have been reorganized on a better and surer basis, understanding our principles, as they did not in the earlier attempt, striving now for quality rather than quantity. Second, a few societies during the last year have given up our fellowship at the request of pastor or church, and in several instances we have found upon investigation that the step had been taken reluctantly, and because of misunderstandings and misapprehensions. Therefore, let it be known everywhere that Christian Endeavor does not insist upon uniformity of constitution or method. I cannot do better than include in this report the action of the trustees taken at Portland, Me., at the time of celebrating our twentieth birthday. The following resolution was then passed:—

"Since Christian Endeavor has become a world-wide movement, it appears to us wise on this, its twentieth birthday, to make plain the flexibility and adaptability of the organization to the varying needs of churches in all lands. The fundamental principles of the Society of Christian Endeavor are the following: First, personal and avowed devotion to our divine Lord and Savior Jesus Christ. Second, the covenant obligation as particularly embodied in the prayer-meeting pledge, to do what Christ would like to have us do. Third, constant religious training for all kinds of Christian service in the prayer meeting and by various committees. Fourth, loyalty to the local church and denomination with which each society is connected. Fifth, interdenominational spiritual fellowship, through which we hope to fulfil our Lord's prayer for spiritual unity, 'that they all may be one.' Sixth, Christian Endeavor makes no attempt and never has attempted, to legislate for the individual conscience, and neither the United Society nor any State or local union regulates, controls, or imposes conditions upon any society of Christian Endeavor. These unions are for fellowship, instruction, and inspiration, and not for legislation or for the exercise of control. If any society is in doubt as to methods of organization and service, it should turn for authoritative instruction to the pastor and church with which it is connected.

"The United Society does not insist upon uniform conditions of organization or a particular form of pledge which shall constitute a Christian Endeavor society. So long as a society holding the fundamental principles of Christian Endeavor enumerated above is working for Christ and the church as its church directs, and is making the young people 'more useful in the service of God,' it is in fact a society of Christian Endeavor, and will be heartily welcomed into the fellowship of this movement."

I hope all will understand the spirit of this statement. It is at once a reaffirmation of the old-time principles of Christian Endeavor, and at the same time an announcement that the United Society does not set itself up as an authority upon the way the local societies shall be organized. Pastors have the fullest liberty to frame the covenant obligation into any form of words they deem wise and call it a covenant or declaration or pledge, and the society is a Christian Endeavor society, and will be enrolled as such.

BIENNIAL CONVENTIONS HEREAFTER.

Another advance step taken at the Portland meeting was the unanimous vote to hold our International Convention biennially, and to ask the States to do the same wherever the plan was practical.

The wisdom of this action has already been shown by the fact that many of the State unions have already taken action which indorses this suggestion, and others are arranging to do so. Many signs and expressions of approval of biennial International and State conventions have been noted, in the press and from the pulpit and the pew.

A FIELD SECRETARY.

Still another recent advance step which merits approval is the election of Rev. Clarence E. Eberman to the post of field secretary, a new position created to meet the onward sweep of Christian Endeavor. For many years the need of such an official to give his whole time to the field has been great. While the executive officers of the United Society will probably spend as much time in the field as ever, it is a matter for general congratulation to know that we can now have the aid of a field secretary.

And especially is it glorious to have such a man to do this work. Field Secretary Eberman is a noble Christian Endeavorer. As president of the Pennsylvania union, he showed his calibre. As trustee of the United Society of Christian Endeavor he has shown himself wise in counsel and zealous in all that pertains to our beloved cause. As speaker at our State and International conventions he has won the hearts of all. As a writer he is thoughtful and uplifting as well as practical. The esteem in which he is held by his brethren of the Moravian Church is indicated by communications from leaders in that honored missionary church. Secretary Eberman's chief work will be the encouragement and development of Christian Endeavor unions, State, district, and local.

OUR INTERDENOMINATIONAL FELLOWSHIP.

The unification of local and district unions during the past year has demanded our admiration. The interdenominational fellowship, which has been from the first a blessed fruit of Christian Endeavor, has during the past year been fostered as never before. There was a time when it seemed that this unique feature of Christian Endeavor would be imperiled, but those days have gone, never to return, we believe. The denominational loyalty of local Christian Endeavorers is seldom challenged, and on the contrary we find it officially and heartily commended by many ecclesiastical courts and assemblies in many denominations. The Presbyterians lead in the United States; then come the Congregationalists, Disciples of Christ, Baptists, Cumberland Presbyterians, Methodist Protestants, Lutherans, in order named, this list supplemented by a large number of other denominations, forty in all. In Canada, with its more than five thousand societies, the Methodists lead, almost all their local societies being called Epworth Leagues of Christian Endeavor; the Presbyterians are next, and Baptists third. The largest number of the more than seven thousand Christian Endeavor societies in Great Britain are Congregationalists, with the Baptists only a few behind, and the Presbyterians coming next. In Australia the Wesleyan Methodists lead in numbers the four thousand societies under the Southern Cross.

OUR INTERNATIONAL FELLOWSHIP.

One of the most gratifying facts to report is steady growth in "foreign" and missionary lands. Secretary Chaplin, of the British section, reported an increase of five hundred societies, particular mention being made of the number of Episcopal Christian Endeavor societies that have been organized the past year in the Church of England. This, and other splendid achievements by our English brothers, show conclusively that the great London Convention was blessed of God.

Indeed, nothing shows the adaptability of Christian Endeavor to every climate and country more than the fact that there are national Christian Endeavor unions in the United States, Canada, England, Scotland, Ireland, Wales, Australia, France, Spain, Germany, South Africa, India, China, Mexico, and Japan, and that Christian Endeavor leaflets and constitutions may now be found in Chinese, Japanese, Malagasy, Persian, Arabic, Turkish, Bulgarian, Armenian, Siamese, German, French, Italian, Greek, Spanish, Swedish, Dutch, Norwegian, Welsh, Australian, Hungarian, Coptic, Mexican, Portuguese, Indian, the many dialects of India and Africa.

Unless you are the closest student of Christian Endeavor expansion, you are not familiar with the progress being made in foreign lands, evidenced by the election of Rev. Franklin S. Hatch, of Massachusetts, to be general secretary of the United Society of Christian Endeavor of India, Burmah and Ceylon. Mr. Hatch is already on the field, and has begun an aggressive campaign. Japan has within a few months elected Rev. I Inanuma its Christian Endeavor secretary. Several other national unions are looking forward to the time when they can have a secretary in the field. May God speed the day.

Unusual as it is to report any backward steps in Christian Endeavor, still it is necessary to do so in South Africa, where the continued hostilities between Briton and Boer have made it seem wise for Secretary George L. W. Kilbon, of the South African Christian Endeavor union, to suspend his work for a time, expecting, however, that, when peace is declared, the work will be taken up with renewed energy and in true Christian Endeavor manner.

We must pause to tell of the cruel blows dealt to our very promising work in China. Hundreds of Chinese Christian Endeavorers forfeited their lives in the past year at the hands of the Boxers, rather than recant. Societies were crushed out in many instances, but I am glad to say that in the last three months particularly there is a most hopeful outlook for Christian Endeavor in China, and the blood of the martyrs is to be the seed of a work that we never expected in the earlier days. China is now calling for a secretary, that her reorganized work may more speedily be accomplished under God's guidance.

THE JUNIORS AND INTERMEDIATES.

Very naturally the increase in Junior and, Intermediate societies continues to be interesting. There are now over 16,000 Junior societies, and 1285 Intermediate societies, the first with 483,000 members, and the second with 38,500. Remember the boys and girls! Christian Endeavor will fail ot its mission in these third-decade days if it does not reach out to every boy and girl, to every young man and young woman in the Sunday school and church, and make them outspoken and active disciples of Jesus Christ.

CHRISTIAN ENDEAVOR IN UNUSUAL PLACES.

There are a number of Mothers' and Parents' Christian Endeavor societies; societies also in unexpected places, such as schools and colleges, asylums, institutions for the blind and for the deaf, among car-drivers and motormen, policemen, traveling men, life-savers on the coast, lighthouse employees, and in schools of reform, and among employees in large factories; among the soldiers in barracks, marines and sailors on men-of-war and in the merchant marine. Indeed, where will you not find Christian Endeavor? It is marvelous how the Christian Endeavor spirit has transformed a dreary Boer prisoners' camp on the island of St. Helena. Deadwood Camp and others have live Christian Endeavor societies. If Christian Endeavor has done nothing else, it is worth these twenty years of effort for the cheer it has carried into such places and into prisons and jails in this country. There is no page of Christian Endeavor history more inspiring than that which tells of the progress made among our brothers in bonds, in the twenty-five and more prison Christian Endeavor societies scattered throughout the great prisons of the United States.

SOME THINGS ACCOMPLISHED.

The societies were asked to state, in short sentences, the best thing that had been accomplished the last year. Here are some of them, and they have been selected with a view to showing the range of Christian Endeavor activity. We give them without comment; they speak for themselves.

"Started a Sunday-school class among the Finns with a membership of forty young men and women." "Active in the Municipal League." "Stopped Sunday ball playing and cock and dog fighting." "Hold a meeting every week in a place where no other religious services are held." "Support a Bible woman in India." "Placed a rack in depot, and keep it filled with good reading." "Organized a reading-room for young men." "Paid for a bed in a floating hospital." "Organized open-air meetings outside the church previous to the regular service." "Bought an invalid bed, which is loaned in the community." "Monthly meeting in county poorhouse and jail." "Entertained in the country twenty-four of the 'Fresh Air' children' from the city." "Gathered 200 books for the prison committee to use in its work." "Held a series of evangelistic meetings." "Furnished our church with a missionary library." "Hold evangelistic meetings at the fire-houses." "Conduct a song service Sunday afternoon at the Home for the Aged." "Educate a Japanese girl and an orphan boy in India." "Helped to put a light plant in Asyut College, Egypt." "Frescoed the entire church and furnished a window for a mission church." "Furnished a double room in deaconesses' sanitarium." "Supporting a bed in the Tibet leper hospital." "Ours is a country society. We pay all the taxes, insurance, and incidental expenses of our church." "Special evangelistic meetings for two months, and twenty-five joined the church." "Furnished a parlor in our new Y. M. C. A. building." "Organized a mission-study class." "Conduct a Bible-study class." "Take charge of the cottage prayer meetings." "Paid our church debt." "Pledged to assist in Sunday evening service." "Organized no-license campaign against the saloon." "Gave Christmas dinners to the poor." "Invitations left at hotels." "Helped to close a gambling-den." "Pay for a special pew for visitors." "Pay our church coal bill."

From among the Junior report-blanks I gleaned the following "best things:" "Clothed and paid board of a crippled boy in school." "Gave a Thanksgiving dinner to thirty-five poor children." "Earned money enough to give poor children an outing in July and August." "Kept a crippled old lady in clothing and food all winter." "Gave a Christmas entertainment at an old ladies' home and a gift to each inmate." "Furnished flowers all winter for our church." "Made scrap-books for hospitals." "Paid toward our vestry chairs." "Bought' a new carpet for our church." "Presented our church with hymn-books." "Increased the membership of our society in three months from twelve to fifty-four." "Educate two colored boys." "Extend the Band of Mercy principles." "Sent Testaments to the soldiers." "Support orphan boy in India," etc.

GIVING TO MISSIONS.

A larger number than ever of our societies have adopted some systematic and proportionate plan for giving money to the cause of missions, to their home churches, and to other benevolences. The two-cents-a-week pledge plan, for each member, works well wherever it has been tried, and we heartily commend it, and wish that the coming year hundreds of other societies might be benefited by its practical and businesslike methods. Over twenty thousand of our members are enrolled in the Tenth Legion, a noble band gladly rendering unto God at least one-tenth of what He has first given to them. God speed the day when many thousands more will have joined the ranks of these Legionaries.

Eight thousand five hundred and twenty-six societies have kindly informed me of what they have been contributing in money as societies to the Lord's work, and the total amount is $504,461.88. Of this amount $200,215.80 went directly to the denominational mission boards, $247,858.37 to their home churches, and $56,387.71 to other benevolences. If 8,526 societies can contribute $500,000, what may not 60,000 societies do when thoroughly appreciating their opportunities and privileges?

And may I at this time remind our societies of one of the principles of our Christian Endeavor platform, which is that all money gathered by the various societies of Christian Endeavor for the cause of missions be always sent to the missionary boards of the special denomination to which the particular society belongs?

And also Christian Endeavor officers and societies are affectionately reminded that appeals to them for money should come through their own denominational authorities; and, when such appeals are addressed to the societies directly, they should be referred to the pastor and church officers for their approval before being acted upon by the society.

The Macedonian Phalanx, the "living link" between the money-earner and the mission worker, has extended its lines into new territory. This Phalanx is an enrolment of all individuals or societies supporting a missionary at home or abroad, or a native worker, or giving at least twenty dollars to their own denominational mission board. Many a Macedonian Phalanx certificate has been sent out to those eligible to membership. The societies deserving especial recognition in this respect are too numerous to mention, but I must tell you that the society in Oxford Presbyterian Church, of Philadelphia, heads the list, with total contributions amounting to $2,766.66. Then comes the Chinese society in the Congregational Chinese Church of San Francisco, whose forty-four members have given in one year $1,521.88. Both of these societies have in past years given over $1000 for benevolences. The Endeavorers of the First Presbyterian Church, Cape May, N. J., are third, with $1445.16; and the First Presbyterian society, of Syracuse, N. Y., next, reporting $1197.89. So far as I know, the Juniors of the Congregational church, Brighton, Mass., have contributed the largest amount of the Junior societies, $232.85. This Junior society has held this enviable record at the head of the roll of honor for several years.

ADDITIONS TO THE CHURCHES.

This year seems to be crowned with another splendid evidence of life. There are now 26,000 Comrades of the Quiet Hour, that have pledged to make it the rule of their life to spend at least fifteen minutes alone with God at the beginning of the day. This spirit, we believe, had much to do with making it possible for God to bless the united efforts of Christian Endeavorers in the closing weeks of the last year to press home on associate members and others the importance of an immediate decision and open confession of Christ by joining the church. February 2, Christian Endeavor Day, was especially signalized as Decision Day, and thousands were born into the kingdom of God.

More and more is Christian Endeavor becoming an evangelistic agency for Christ. In all, 160,000 young people have in the last twelve months joined the church from the ranks of our societies.

Have you ever tried to think of what has been accomplished by Christian Endeavor in the past twenty years? Have you ever attempted to put those thoughts into words? It's a difficult task. Listen to what our lamented and sainted friend and trustee, Dr. Maltbie D. Babcock, wrote to me in January, just before he sailed for his holiday trip to the Holy Land. I do not believe any one could put so much in so few lines, and with Dr. Babcock's words I will close this report.

"The supreme value of the Christian Endeavor Society is, to my mind, its creation inside the church of a normal department, a training-school. The public worship of the church, the Sunday school, the old-fashioned prayer meeting, were all to teach and not to train. All the average young Christian could do was to listen, to think, to receive. This new movement trained the mind to think for others; the lips to speak, to pray; the feet to go on God's errands; the hands to work in Christian ministries. The form of organization, the wording of the pledge, the conventional committees, may be changed; but the idea that the church should have a department for the training of the young Christian to do something more than worship, to witness, and to work for God, has come, please God, to stay."

CHAPTER IV.

A Glorious Sabbath.

CHURCH SERVICES — EVANGELISTIC MEETINGS FOR MEN, WOMEN AND CHILDREN.

The sun shone brightly, the fresh breezes tempered the air to a delicious coolness, every one was smiling and happy on this day of days. The street-cars were bare of Endeavorers, and the streets were full of them, speeding busy feet to the preachers of their choice.

And what a choice! Should it be Sheldon the practical, Henson the scintillant, Morgan the spiritual, Hoyt the Boanerges, Power the eloquent, Hill the thought-provoking, Hall the powerful, Woelfkin the conscience-quickener, Tomkins the uplifting? Were there not such missionaries as Jones, and Ament, and Hotchkiss, and Hubbard, and Fulton? Was not Beach of Denver, to preach, and Pounds of Cleveland, and Landrith of Tennessee, and Bishop Fallows of Chicago? Was there not the possibility of hearing such heroes of the faith as General Howard, Dr. Anna Howard Shaw, Dr. Garrison, Dr. Troxell, Dr. Carson, Dr. Torrey? To listen to Dr. Hamlin would be glory enough for any Lord's Day; or Pope of New Haven, or Moody of Northfield, or Dixon of Hartford, or Willett of Chicago. But the list is too long even to name, and the names of some of the most prominent have been omitted. It was a list sufficient to drive an Endeavorer wild with perplexity; whom should he hear, where all were so desirable?

THE CHILDREN'S MEETING.

A thousand Juniors warbled like canaries, whistling the chorus of a joyful song Sunday afternoon, in the opening of the children's meeting in Auditorium Ohio. It was "the main session of the Convention," as Rev. C. E. Eberman, the leader, put it.

The speakers were all main-line limited expresses. Miss Kate Haus of St. Louis, delighted her eager young hearers by telling off on her fingers four things God wants them to use in helping to save other boys and girls; the strength of a lion, the brains of a man, the sacrifice of a calf, and the swiftness of an eagle. It was so practical, pictorial, and pithy that the ears and hearts of the youthful audience drank it all in.

Mrs. F. E. Clark rapidly painted a picture of a convention she attended last year in a country that they could reach most directly by digging straight down through the earth. At first she could not tell the Chinese boys from the girls, but presently she discovered that the boys had their hair braided down their backs and the girls wore trousers.

She told of the lesson of strength in unity that one speaker taught by means of a bundle of sticks, and applied it to the things the thousands of Juniors can do collectively.

She taught the Juniors to say good-by as the Chinese do, by shaking their own hands and saying, "Pingang."

THE CONVENTION CHORUS.

Treasurer Wm. Shaw exhibited a boy friend of his "Johnny Magnet," who wore the Convention colors, a red jacket and steel-white trousers, and who taught how the selfishness that keeps everything to itself spoils children, and the unselfishness that shares with others gives strength to help them.

Field Secretary Eberman closed with an object-lesson on shining as lights, by means of a pocket incandescent bulb.

It was a short, spicy, satisfying meeting, a model of its kind.

THE MEN'S MEETING.

There is no sound, not even the majestic choral of Niagara, worthy to be compared with the singing of a great company of men. "Crown Him Lord of All!"—how the mighty words rung out in grand Music Hall from the throats of those thousands of men on Sunday afternoon! Men of all stations were there, broadcloth men and shirt-sleeve men and shirt-waist men, laborers and capitalists, men of brain and men of brawn, Endeavorers and those that were not even Christians.

Chairman of the convention's music committee, Mr. A. W. MacBriar, exquisitely rendered a cornet solo which was an appropriate introduction to the hour. President Clark presided and in the deplored absence of Dr. J. Wilbur Chapman, the meeting was conducted by that business man's evangelist, Mr. William Phillips Hall of New York City, whose first utterance was a loving prayer for God's blessing on Dr. Chapman up by Winona Lake.

Mr. Hall caught his audience by telling the story of a large man who was found floating around after a wreck in Lake Erie. They offered to take him into a crowded boat. "No," said he, pointing out another unfortunate, "take that red-headed fellow over there. I'm interested in him." The large man finally got ashore, thoroughly exhausted, and they persuaded him to tell why he was so much interested in the red-headed man. "Well, if you must know, he owed me fifty cents; and I hated to see him go down."

That is the spirit of the world, and Mr. Hall contrasted it with the spirit of Christ, which finds its highest profit in what often brings no money reward whatever. "It pays to accept Christ," was his text. A massive series of examples buttressed his argument, such noble Christian lives as those of Washington, Lincoln, Grant, McKinley. He told many pathetic and moving stories of lives that had gone down in great misery, and then had laid hold upon the Great Deliverance. With a tender power that moved to tears hundreds of the strong men before him, Mr. Hall told his own bitter experience in refusing at his father's sick-bed the surrender to Christ that he rendered at length, in the deepest of sorrow and regret, at midnight over his father's dead body. After a heartfelt appeal for Christian decision Mr. Hall called upon all the followers of Christ to stand, and then he urged all those who were not Christians to stand with them. Not a few, thank God! accepted the earnest invitation, and the men's meeting had won its infinite reward.

THE WOMEN'S MEETING.

Auditorium Williston, on Sunday afternoon was a rainbow of pink and white and blue, for "Women Only" was written over the portal. There was not a seat to spare; not a minute went to waste.

Two happier selections for speakers could not have been made than Miss Margaret Koch, Maine's Junior superintendent, and Miss Rhena E. Mosher, of Westfield, N. Y.

Miss Koch's address on "A National Service" was worthy the scholarly woman she is, and yet it was simple, direct, and telling. She urged on her hearers a concrete religion, the every-day kindliness that does not go about with the snipping scissors of criticism in its hands.

Miss Mosher, representing the Young Women's Christian Temperance Union, speaking of the wonderful opportunities for women, told how the first woman to study medicine in Geneva was ostracized by the women of Geneva, who held aside their skirts when she passed. She showed the relative strength of Christianity and heathenism by strips of ribbon hung from the walls in various lengths, each inch representing ten million persons. The women who are so influential in shaping the expenditures of Christendom must see to it that there is not so awful a discrepancy between the amount spent for luxuries and that spent to redeem the world.

"Woman from the Man's Standpoint" was a theme that gave Secretary Baer a chance to say some wholesome things in a way that drove them home and clinched them on the other side.

If women were given to hurrahing, no doubt every earnest hearer was ready to say, "Hurrah for the woman's meeting!"

CHAPTER V.

Sabbath Observances.

The Sabbath-observance meeting in the Second Presbyterian Church was a notable meeting, considering that it was one of three simultaneous meetings. The audience was a notable one, filling the large auditorium to the walls. There were two notable speakers to help the audience see the question.

Treasurer William Shaw presided over the meeting and added here and there the right word in the right place.

The first speaker was the Rev. F. D. Power, D. D., of Washington, D. C., a trustee of the U. S. C. E.

The Pearl of Days.

Rev. Frederick D. Power, D. D.

The Pearl of Days is the day we call the Lord's. Through the week we go down into the valleys of care and shadow; when Sunday comes we ascend the heights of communion with God. Our Lord's days should be hills of light and joy in God's presence, and so as time rolls by we should go from mountain top to mountain top, till at last we catch the glory of the gates, and enter in to go no more out. It is impossible to estimate the blessed effect upon a nation's wealth and happiness when, on the return of each Sunday, the mills are released from toil, the ledger closed upon the desk, the hammer rests on the anvil and the wheel in the factory, the mine sends forth its crowds into the light of the new born day, the plow stops in the furrow, and the ax, the spade and the hoe are uplifted; men rest their wearied frames; even the dumb cattle partake of the universal blessing, and the sound of church bells and sweet voices of Sunday school children are in the air.

Without the Lord's day the Church of Christ, as an organized body, would cease to exist. The church must hold or lose its spiritual power in almost exact proportion as the scriptural Lord's day is hallowed or profaned, and for this reason all godless forces in the land seek to blot from the calendar this pearl of days. Without it one of the chief cornerstones of our civilization would crumble, and with its desecration would come the degeneration of society. The Oriental legend tells how, when Solomon was on the way to visit the Queen of Sheba, he came to a valley in which dwelt a peculiar tribe of monkeys. On inquiring their history, he learned they were the posterity of a colony of Jews, which many years before settled in that region and had by habitually profaning the Sabbath degenerated into brutes. Our civil Sunday uplifts the race; it is a physical boom; it promotes social and family life: it saves from constant grind, and low groveling in ceaseless toil; it breaks in upon the anxious, restless ambitions and rivalries, and rush of life; it tones down distinctions between rich and poor; capital and labor; it gives breathing time and thinking time, and recruiting time; it, above all, affords opportunities for religious service: it witnesses for God, and the promise of rest.

Historically considered, we have the Creation Sabbath, the Thoecratic Sabbath, and the Christian Lord's Day. The Sabbath is the oldest institution in the world: older by thousands of years than the decalogue: older than the Bible: older than marriage. God blessed the seventh day and honored it, said Moses, which indicates the earliest division of time into sevens. Weekly observance of a weekly day of rest was written in God's physiological and social laws for man, as plainly as in the Decalogue. The fourth Commandment, "Remember the Sabbath Day to keep it holy," clearly reminds men of its previous institution, showing the consecration of the seventh part of time was coeval with creation. "Remember," God said to Israel, as if in course of time, man had forgotten and neglected this institution, and still the word may be spoken, "Remember." Remember thy creator, your origin created in God's image; remember the exodus, God's deliverance from the bondage of sin; remember the victory over death, and the promise of the endless life. "Remember!"

The Creation Sabbath was not an arbitrary appointment without meaning. God rests. Creation rests. The morning stars begin their song. What rest means for Him that fainteth not neither is weary, we may not say. God's rest must be as real as God's joy, or God's love. It was a Sabbath festal celebration, a rest of God in which we may enter. The reason for selecting the day was that the Creator rested. God kept it negatively in a cessation of work, positively in blessing and sanctifying it, and while of every other day Moses speaks of an evening—evening and morning were the first day, or the second day—of this day he names no evening, intimating a day without ending, an eternal Sabbath of the soul. And this Sabbath was made for man, said Christ, not for the Jews only, but for the race. All mankind are interested in the sanctification of this day. It was made for man; that is, his temporal and eternal benefit. God did not create man for the greater glory of the Sabbath; he ordained the Sabbath for the greater welfare of man.

The Theocratic Sabbath begins with the Exodus; the deliverance of the Israelites, on that day led to its consolidation into law. Remember the Sabbath day to keep it holy. This is the only commandment beginning with this word "Remember," indicating both past and prospective application. Here also the purpose was rest. A Sabbath day's journey was less than one mile. It was a day of rest, of delight, of joy, of worship, of holy service. Read the Sabbath Psalm 92. Rest from all servile work, field work, as sowing and reaping, gathering wood, bearing burdens, preparation of food, business affairs, toils and bondage, came to man and beast, and worship, holy convocation, meetings to hear and meditate upon God's word, were the order of this holy day.

But this gracious institution was perverted. The Pharisees made it a burden. Enactments between Ezra and Christ repressed all happy celebrations of it. Rules prescribed, even the kind of knots one could tie on the Sabbath. The camel-driver's knot and the sailor's knot it was unlawful to tie, or untie. A knot which could be tied or untied with one hand was allowed, a sandal or a woman's bonnet. It was forbidden to write two letters, or write in different inks or different languages. The quantity of food to be carried must be less than the bulk of a dried fig. To kindle or extinguish a fire was desecration: to give an emetic, set a broken bone, or pull into place a dislocated joint. To wear one kind of sandal was carrying a burden; to wear another was not: wooden sandals one must not wear, nor shoes with nails. One could not on the Sabbath day pick up and eat fruit fallen from a tree. Even the wicked in Hades were said to rest on the Sabbath; and the one thing on account of which the whole universe was created, said the Pharisees, was the Sabbath day. No wonder Christ rebuked them, and they sent spies to detect him, and on the charge of Sabbath breaking the Sanhedrim determined His death.

Do these things seem absurd? We have had similar laws. "No one shall run on the Sabbath or walk in his garden or elsewhere, except reverently to and from church. No one shall travel, cook victuals, or make beds, sweep houses, cut hair, or shave on the Sabbath. No husband shall kiss his wife, or mother, her child." This was the law in Connecticut. "No one shall fire a gun on the Sabbath, except to shoot an Indian." This was a law in Virginia. So men brought Judaism, and a false Judaism at that, into the religion of Christ. The truth is we are no longer under a theocracy. We keep not the Sabbath of the old law. We are not under Moses, but under Christ. We have our own day, our day of holy rest and worship, more sacred even than the day which typified it. We have the Lord's day forever blessed and sanctified as the resurrection day.

The Christian's Lord's day is now the Pearl of Days. Our Lord has made this His own day by rising from the dead on the first day of the week. On this day he appeared to Mary Magdalene, to the women, to Peter, to the ten disciples, to the two on the journey to Emmaus, and then again to all the disciples. The Holy Spirit seven weeks later came to the apostles on Pentecost, and the Church was born. On this day the early church assembled for worship, for we read, "On the first day of the week when the disciples came together to break bread, Paul preached to them;" and "upon the first day of the week let everyone of you lay by in store as the Lord hath prospered him." On this day John was in the spirit and caught the vision of unutterable things; and this day they called not the Sabbath, but the Lord's day, forever holy unto the Lord, a new day belonging to a new dispensation, a season of loftier joy as it commemorates a more august event than the creation of the world or the deliverance of a nation. As the sunflower turns from morning till evening to the sun, so did the early church turn to her Lord.

How is it to be observed? "In the spirit." The first principle involved is the consecration of one-seventh of time. Remember that you keep holy one day in seven. Consecrate this day as the Lord's unto the Lord. Let it be unlike other days. Sanctify it. Setting apart this day brings the existence and claims of God upon all our time before us and before all men. It is the sinner's day for feeling after God; it is the saint's day for fuller communion with God; it is the worldly man's day for remembering God; it is the Christian's day for enjoying God. "On that day," said Christopher North, "to our hearts the very birds sing holily, a sacred smile is on the dewy flowers, the lilies look whiter in their lovliness, the blush rose reddens in the sun with a diviner eye, and with a more celestial scent the hoary hawthorn sweetens the wilderness."

The second principle is the suspension of labor. To make room for the acknowledgment of God on this day ordinary occupations are suspended, and this in the interest of labor itself. When in the French Revolution they abolished the Sabbath, they found it would not work. France must have the Sabbath, or she is ruined," said De Tocqville. "The keeping of one day in seven as a time of relaxation and refreshment, as well as of public worship, is of admirable service to the state, considered merely as a civil institution," said Blackstone. "From a moral, social and physical point of view the observance of the Sabbath is of absolute consequence," said Gladstone. "While industry is suspended, the plow lies in its furrow, the exchange is silent, no smoke ascends from the factory," says Macauley, "a process is going on quite as important to the wealth of the nation; man, the machine of machines, is repairing, winding up, so he returns to labor on Monday with clearer intellect, livelier spirit, renewed corporeal vigor." "I find I can drive a horse eight miles an hour six days in the week to more advantage than six miles an hour for seven days," said Bianconi, before the British Association for the Advancement of Science. "I discovered by not working on the Sabbath I make a saving of twelve per cent." So great an instrument as the Constitution of the United States recognizes the need of Sunday rest.

A third principle enters into this Sunday observance, the principle of worship. We are to be "in the spirit on the Lord's Day." Do you ask may I do this, or may I do that, on Sunday? I answer, "Be in the spirit on the Lord's day." Come to Christ. Lift up your heart. Behold higher and everlasting realities. The Lord's Day is the day of days on which the Lord has the first claim. The first duty, as in the case of the women, as in the case of the disciples, is to hold converse with the risen Lord. The early Christians came together on this day to remember the sufferings and death and resurrection of Jesus. It is a holy day. Physiologists, political economists, practical business men demonstrate the necessity of a cessation from toil. Pictures with much pathos are placed before us describing the hard fate of those on whom dawns no day of rest. True enough, but confine your argument to that, and you leave man on a level with the brute. Of the old Jewish Sabbath it was said, "In it thou shalt not do any work, thou, nor thy son, nor thy daughter, nor thy man servant, nor thy maid servant, nor thy cattle." A traveler passing a coal mine in Pennsylvania saw a field full of mules. "Those are the mules," said another, "that work all the week down in the mine, but on Sundays they have to come up into the light, or else, in a little while, they go blind," but how much better is a man than a mule?, Something more is wanted than rest. Sundays are the happiest, purest, richest in blessing in which the spiritual nature is considered. Not only on which business has been put aside, profane literature unopened, ordinary occupation suspended, but the Bible opened and the worship of God performed; in which, as in the temple of Solomon, the sound of the hammer has not been heard in the temple of the soul. Keep men buried in business for the whole seven days, give Sunday to picnics, excursions, base ball, Sunday races, bull fights, or the prize ring, the Sunday bicycle or the Sunday newspaper; rob the Lord of the service the soul owes Him in his sanctuary, and as the mules go blind in the pit, so will men lose the very faculty of spiritual vision, having neither eye nor ear, nor heart for divine things. "To golf, or not to golf, on Sundays," is one of the burning questions in our eastern press, and a leading preacher of New York city declares, "I affirm that every man has a right to play golf on Sundays or to ride his horse on Sunday if his conscience approve. He has a right to follow his conscience in any wise recreation, or re-creation of his faculties." Can we believe it? May a Christian violate the laws of the state and the teachings of Christianity if his conscience approve? Is this day to be as any other day devoted to pleasure, desecrated by secularism, broken into fragments, by the iconoclastic spirit of our time, leaving no monument of the resurrection of the son of God, no prophecy of the general awakening of all to judgment and eternity? God forbid. God preserve to us this perfect legacy. God save us from the continental Sunday. God keep us mindful of the duty we owe our Creator, to have ever before us the new and eternal creation in Christ.

The tourist among the Alps climbs one of the great mountains in dense and dripping mist until he has passed through the clouds and stands on a lofty peak in the clear light of the sun. Beneath him lies the fog, a waveless sea of vapor. He hears the sound of labor, the lowing of the cattle, the voices of little children, peals of the village bells, coming up from the vales below. But there he stands on the tall summit, far above all the vexed, troubled, broken life of the vales with only heaven's blue above his head, and the glorious mountain peaks about him. Such a true Sunday experience is to every devout life. Week days we dwell in the low vales amid the mists. Life here is full of struggles, failures, disappointments, burden-bearing. Then the Lord's day comes, and we climb out of the low places of care, toil, and tears, and spend the day in the sweet, pure air of God's love and peace. We get near to the heart of Christ; we have wider views. We see life from its heaven side. We see God's face and hear his voice. Without this vision the people perish.

General O. O. Howard, the next speaker, said that he was born again forty-four years ago among the Methodists, and one thing he learned of them was to say, "Amen," which has since been changed to "Ahmen." He wanted to say, "Amen," or "Ahmen," according to whether his hearers were Low Church or High Church, to Dr. Power's splendid speech. His mother said, "No, Oliver," when he wanted to take his gun and go to the woods on Sunday. There was a wholesome restraint in those words.

Men, he declared, cannot afford to lose the Sabbath because they moved from New England to Ohio.

General Howard believes strongly in preserving the Sabbath by inculcating in the children a realization of the presence of God. His conversion was at the age of twenty-six, and he felt now that it ought to have taken place twenty years earlier, perhaps twenty-six years earlier.

What is needed for a revival of Sabbath sanctity, he thinks, is less criticism and more positive belief in Christ, the Lord of the Sabbath. We must not trade the positive commandments of God for theories. He was taught in school a theory of sound that has since been swept off its feet. If we trust in the positive truths of God to change the hearts of the people, they will then cheerfully obey the commandments, and more will be accomplished for Sabbath-preservation in a year of positive preaching than by two hundred years of theoretical education.

The Sabbath observance meeting was one of those meetings that run quiet and deep, and fix purposes and make character.

CHAPTER VI.

The Temperance Meeting.

"How many can you get into one of these seats, Mr. Harvnot?" Secretary Baer asked at the opening of the temperance rally on Sunday afternoon. "That depends upon the size of the Christian," replied the quick-witted pastor of the large Central Christian Church. "I don't believe you can fill this church." continued Mr. Harvnot, addressing the Endeavorers as they crowded in; "I've been trying to do it every week for five years, and I haven't succeeded yet." But the Endeavorers did it, sitting on pulpit platform and perched in every available cranny.

The first speaker, Col. George W. Bain, made a masterly plea for individual temperance. The following is an abstract of Col. Bain's address.

The Safe Side of Life for Young Men.

By Col. Geo. W. Bain.

I do not assert that every man who drinks intoxicating liquor as a beverage will become a drunkard, but I do hold up total-abstinence as safer and better for practice, and if confined to but one moment of time I could prove this claim. Moderate drinking leads to drunkenness; total-abstinence leads away from drunkenness—then total-abstinence is the better. Drunkards are made of moderate drinkers, drunkards are never made of total abstainers; then total-abstinence is the better. I give as the Bible definition of temperance, "Moderation in regard to things useful and right, total-abstinence in regard to things hurtful and wrong." I know drunkenness comes from drinking intoxicating liquor, therefore I plead for total-abstinence. "But," says some young man before me, "I will not go so far—I can control myself." You do not intend to go beyond the danger line, nor did they who sleep in drunkards' graves. Do you suppose Edgar Allan Poe ever dreamed when he took his first drink of intoxicating liquor that it would ever weave for his tongue a bitter wail? Do you suppose Thos. F. Marshall, our great Kentucky orator, imagined when he stood at the foot of fame's ladder that his last words would be: "And this is the end. Tom Marshall is dying, dying on a borrowed bed, under a borrowed sheet, and without a decent suit of clothes in which to be buried." Don't you think if alcoholic liquor had been a good beverage, God would have made a few springs of it? Bore into the earth; you can strike oil, but nowhere whiskey; plenty of springs of water are up and down the earth, but nowhere in nature a beer-brewery. It is water, water, everywhere. "But," says one, "this is a free country, and if a man wants to drink and become a brute it is his privilege." Drunkards are not brutes. Who was the man shot, twenty years ago, in a saloon in Louisville at midnight? The gifted grandson of Henry Clay. At the same time, in the same city, a great-grandson of Patrick Henry lay drunk in the station house. Richard Porson the Scholar, Richard Brinsley Sheridan the Wit, and Robert Burns the Poet were not brutes. But while intemperance drags down the gifted and noble, temperance will build up the humblest and lowliest. Bring me the child of the tenement district in this city. Let him pledge me he will never touch intoxicating liquor, add industry and honesty to his sobriety and in twenty years he will walk your streets honored, respected and loved. "Again," says another, "this is a free country, and if a man wants to drink let him, and take the consequences." The trouble about that is, a man takes the drink and some one else takes the consequences. All over our land bruised and blackened bosoms heave above hearts that are broken, and wives and mothers go down to death because men take the drink and women take the consequences. I can understand how young men are tempted to take a glass of wine from the jeweled hand of a beautiful young woman, but I cannot see how a young man who loves his mother, whose mother loved him first, loved him best and will love him to the last can go out of his mother's home into a saloon. Young men, have any of you done this is the past month or six months? Promise me today, in the name of home and mother, you will never do this again. What a grand meeting this would be if all the young men of this audience would make this promise and keep it to the end of life. If you would keep in the safe way of life, make the Bible the "man of your counsel and guide of life." I have now passed the sixtieth milestone of life, I have studied life's problem and without faith in this book, human life is a failure and a farce:

Col. Bain had a worthy successor in that renowned lady, Rev. Anna Howard Shaw, D. D., of Philadelphia. Erect, stately, with a face expressive of nobility and character, her words were as impressive as her bearing. She pleaded for lofty ideals, as against the specious arguments of expediency in the temperance reform. She urged that all Endeavorers place themselves on the double platform of total abstinence for the individual and total prohibition for the State. She showed how the first is useless without the second, how under the terrible temptation of the fiendish appetite no amount of pledge-signing avails so long as the open saloon can spread its snares around the poor fellow who yearns for a clean life again. She told how as a young college girl, in the early days of the Woman's Crusade, she had obtained the temperance pledges of one hundred drunkards, and was so happy over the results. But by eight weeks, ninety-eight of the one hundred were drinking again. "The power of the saloon," she declared with an emphasis which the Endeavorers emphasized with hearty applause, "does not rest upon the number of men employed in the business, or the amount of capital invested in it; it rests upon the attitude of government toward it. Our hope as a nation is upon you Christian Endeavorers more than upon any other body of young people in the land."

Oliver W. Stewart, of Chicago, so widely known in connection with the National Prohibition party, was for years an active worker in and at length the president of the Illinois Christian Endeavor union, and he was thoroughly at home in that Christian Endeavor audience.

Salvation From the Saloon.

An Abstract of an Address by Oliver W. Stewart.

The subject on which I am to speak naturally raises the question, "salvation for whom and how is it to be obtained?" Perhaps the first one who comes to your mind now as needing salvation from the saloon is the drunkard. The chains of the slavery of drink have been forged upon hundreds of thousands of men. Under the influence of habit they sink lower and lower. All efforts to save them seem unavailing, or nearly so. Yes, drunkards need salvation from the saloon. But it is not my purpose to discuss the question from the standpoint of the drunkard's need, for he is not the only one who is being lost on account of the saloon, nor is he the most important.

Others will say that we need salvation from the waste and extravagance of the liquor traffic. Attention is called to the fact that over one billion dollars are spent annually over the bars of the saloons of the land. To save the country from this fearful waste certainly would be worth while. If we could put into the legitimate channels of trade the money that is wasted for drink, business would have a revival that would be permanent. Such a thing as hard times would be almost unknown. Important as this is, however, I do not consider it the most important salvation.

Others ask, "how can we save the government from the saloon?" and well may that question be considered. Our politics has become corrupted by the presence of the saloon. Politicians court its favor, legislators think of the interests of the liquor traffic and do its bidding. The day is rapidly approaching, if not already here, when no legislation of any kind for the interest or benefit of the people, can be passed except by the consent of saloon keepers through their agents, the public officials. One of the certain results from this must be that conscientious, godly, Christian men will turn away from political service, refusing to attempt to serve their country, when in doing so they must, first of all, serve the liquor traffic. But there is something still more important for you than to save the country, and to save the country would not be unimportant. It would be well worth the sacrifice for all of you, to lay down your lives that your country might live, and that her government might continue and her institutions be saved; but, the salvation from the saloon about which I wish to speak, comes much nearer each of you than anything I have yet mentioned.

As a basis for my argument I submit this, that the salvation from the saloon that is most needed now is the salvation of Christian voters from complicity in the legalization of the liquor business. I intend to make this so clear that I cannot be misunderstood.

Let it be remembered, speaking broadly and generally, that the traffic in alcoholic beverages is a legal traffic. The saloon business is a legal business. It may violate some of our laws. Undoubtedly it does. But the fact remains that there are other laws which relate to the saloon and that it can exist without violating those laws; that the government, state and national, recognizes the traffic to protect it and does protect it. The supreme question confronting the government and the saloon is "what shall be the attitude of the government toward the liquor traffic." The supreme question for the individual is "what shall be my attitude toward the sinful policy which my government pursues with reference to the traffic. Shall I approve that policy and thus become equally guilty not only with the government, but with the saloon itself, or shall I disapprove that traffic, and if I am to disapprove it, how may that disapproval be so expressed as to leave me guiltless in the presence of the sinfulness of the saloon and its legalization by the government?"

I need waste no time on the question of the policy of the government toward the saloon, for it certainly is well understood by this intelligent audience. Nor need I take much of your time to point out the fact that prohibition, if it were a failure, so far as putting an end to the liquor traffic is concerned, would still be a success so far as freeing the government from its complicity in the business. The government, like the individual, is bound to do right. The question is not whether it will pay most to do right. The question is not so much what is the effect of doing right, but what is right? For example, some people contend that under prohibition we would have many low dives and disgraceful, disorderly saloons in violation of the law, but that under high license these places would give way to orderly, decent saloons that would not be such a disgrace to the community. I do not for a moment believe that this is true, but assuming it to be true, what has a Christian government accomplished? It has made the temptation greater and it has made sin seemingly respectable, and I have a conviction to the effect that no Christian man, and no group of Christian men and no Christian state have any business attempting to make bad things look good. Ours is a fight, not a compromise.

But I must discuss the question which I have announced to be my theme, that is "how can you save yourself from complicity in the sinful policy of your government?" A discussion of this question, of course, takes us dangerously near the political arena, and there are some people who are never so badly frightened as at the advance of a thought or an argument that has to do with political duty. But an audience of Christian people is certainly brave enough to face anything that has to do with Christian duty and this question is of that kind.

In this country we have government through political parties. I do not say it is the best kind or the best way, but it is the kind of government we have, or it is the way that we govern. Our voice in government is heard through the medium of our political party. Of course some of us are more independent than others. Some would never think of scratching a ballot, but always vote a party ticket straight. Others would scratch a ticket occasionally, leaving off some particularly bad candidate. Some others would go so far as to stay at home occasionally from an election, and others even to the extent of now and then voting another party ticket. Underneath all this, however, is one law of which we must not lose sight, and that is that when we vote a party ticket, whether we do it once in four years or once in twenty years, we vote for the things that party stands for. You may not believe in the things it stands for. You may vote its ticket because you believe in only one of the things that it stands for, whereas it may stand for nine other things that you do not believe in at all, but when you vote a party ticket, you vote for all the things that it stands for, without regard to what your belief in them may be.

Nor does the question of your prayers enter into this matter. You may pray for one thing and vote for the opposite, in which event, so far as your citizenship is concerned, it would be your vote that would count. You would lose your prayer.

The saloon policy predominates in this country. The license of the liquor traffic is the plan generally adopted. That mere announcement of itself, necessarily means that this country is governed by saloon parties, for the country can have no policy except it gets it from parties that rule. The only question then left for consideration is what is you relationship to the political parties that stand for the license of the liquor business. That brings me to the question of your need of salvation. Any Christian man who votes the ticket of a political party that stands for the license of the saloon, votes for the saloon. The Christian man who votes for the saloon is in need of salvation from the saloon. The fact that the saloon is in power, and that this government is committed to it and to the license of it, proves that there are thousands, I might say millions, of Christian men who need to be saved from the consequences of their own acts in supporting that policy. It is not necessary that I should point out what you are to do. I feel that the road in that direction is plain, but it does seem very necessary for some one to point out what we ought not to do. We ought not to give our votes and our support to political parties that stand squarely opposed to what the church and Christian people long ago have declared to be the proper policy for the government to pursue with reference to the saloon.

It is our very lack of independence that defeats us. It is our slavery to party that in turn enslaves us to the saloon. Why should the men engaged in the liquor business have more influence in party councils and more power as to party action than the Christian men of the country? They are not wiser than we. They are not more patriotic than we. They do not control more wealth than Christian men do. They are not better educated. There is not one thing in their favor which we do not possess to a greater degree, except that they have real political independence. No party, no politicians, can control the votes of saloon men except on the basis of doing the bidding of the saloon. But the disgrace of our Christian civilization today is that we Christian citizens who love God supremely and who would die for the church and count it a joy to do so, can be chained to the chariot wheels of the saloon business if our political party need seems to demand it. If one-tenth of the Christian voters of America would walk up to one election as independently as the saloon-keepers approach the ballot box, we would have the politicians and parties of this country at our feet begging for the slightest indication as touching what we want, and we would find them quick to do the thing we wanted as soon as they ascertained what it was. As it is, no politicians of any note in this country, outside of the handful of men who really vote their convictions on the saloon question, concern themselves in the slightest degree as to what Christian men want or what the church resolves about the saloon. They go on their way giving it license and protecting it. And they do that because they dare to. They understand perfectly well that they can violate the teaching of the church and spit upon her resolutions and that her people will not resent it This would not be specially alarming, certainly would not be worthy discussion before this assembly, were it not for the fact that our support of parties and politicians who serve the saloon first and give the church the crumbs that are left, is the support that makes us guilty. The question is not what can you absolutely prevent? You, perhaps, cannot prevent the any great amount of evil in this world. Certainly you cannot prevent the evil that others do, to any large extent. But you can right yourself, and to do anything else than right, is to do wrong, and by the thousands the Christian voters of this country are doing something else than right about this thing.

Salvation from the saloon. Who needs it? The drunkard needs it. Who needs it? The business man needs it from the sinful waste of the liquor traffic. Who needs it? The government needs it from the peril of saloon rule and control of its institutions. Who needs it? More than all others the Christian man needs it. He needs salvation from his own guilt and complicity in the sinful policy that his government now pursues Who can save the Christian man from this guilt? He alone can save himself. He must save himself. He must save himself if it breaks up every party in America. He must save himself if it dethrones every whiskey politician in power. He must save himself if it requires him to build a new party. He must save himself though it takes him into a party that he long has ridiculed and has never even dreamed that he would ultimately support. He must save himself or he will be lost and with him will go our institutions, our commerce, our prosperity, all swept away in one tremendous ruin.

Will he save himself? Yes, he will. The gospel of Jesus Christ is yet a motive to hold men true. Faith in God and in the right is yet in the world to inspire men to noble, higher living. Yes, the Christian manhood of the country will save itself and when it does the saloon will die.

Secretary Baer, who presided, closed this powerful meeting in a most impressive way. "No saloon in here," he reminded us. "Everything is calm and peaceful here. The struggle is outside those doors, on the street. What are we going to do with this meeting out there?" And the temperance hour closed with a period of prayer, a genuine temperance consecration.

Gen. O. O. Howard.

Rev. A. A. Fulton, D. D.

Rev. Charles M. Sheldon, D. D

Rev. Robert Johnson, D. D.

Rev. J. P Jones, D. D.

Rev. Edwin S. Shaw.

Col. George W. Bain.

Rev. Ira Landrith.

William Phillips Hall.

Miss Margaret Koch.

Dr. Charles L. Thompson.

Rev. Anna H. Shaw, D. D

SOME OF THE CONVENTION SPEAKERS.

CHAPTER VII.

The Sunday Afternoon: A Missionary Meeting.

The missionary rally on Sunday afternoon was universally agreed to be one of the very finest sessions of the kind Christian Endeavor has ever held. Dr. Samuel B. Capen of Boston, President of the American Board, presided with so much tact that the speakers were actually grateful for being stopped. And the session moved from stirring beginning to climacteric conclusion.

No one has done more to introduce the Christian Endeavor movement into India than that strong-hearted missionary, Rev. J. P. Jones, D. D., who from the first and through all the years of Christian Endeavor growth in that vast empire, has been its self-sacrificing friend. This ardent Endeavorer was heartily welcomed, for his worth's sake, and because of what he could tell us about the progress of missionary work in the land to whose salvation he has devoted his life.

India, The Land of Wonders.

Rev. J. P. Jones, D. D., India.

To the Christian of America India stands pre-eminent as a land of wonders. It covers an area one-half that of the United States. Its population is four times that of this land, and a fifth of that of the world. More nations are found there than in Europe, and they speak at least seventy languages and dialects. When thirty centuries ago our ancestors were groveling in primitive savagery, the Aryans of India were rejoicing in a civilization of their own which was unique and distinguished.

In this great land there is progressing a wonderful conflict. Christianity, the mightiest of missionary religions, is engaged in a struggle with the greatest of ethnic faiths. Never before did our faith meet so doughty and subtle a foe. Neither Roman law and rule nor Greek philosophy and ideals were comparable to the mighty powers which Hinduism is putting forth today in order to arrest the progress of Christianity in that land. But they cannot discourage the Christian worker in that land nor blind him to the fact that already the people are gradually transferring their allegiance from Krishna to Christ. The two thousand missionaries and the twenty thousand native Christian workers represent a mighty force with which to produce a grand revolution. The million Christians in our Protestant mission churches are rapidly growing numerically, and in intelligent, religious zeal and power, and in social position and influence. Three hundred thousand scholars in our mission schools are studying God's Word. It is a land which presents a wonderful opportunity to Christian workers. India is now our close neighbor. Modern appliances have brought her to our very door. The community of life and interests with our antipodes furnishes us a great opportunity. God has, in a remarkable way, joined the destiny of India to that of the Anglo-Saxon race. Moreover, they are today much more accessible to Western influence than they were ever before. They study our philosophies, are largely ruled by our laws, their life is touched at all points by our civilization. Their sentiments are increasingly shaped and animated by our Christian principles. Young India is keenly sensitive to all influences which breathe a Western spirit, and is becoming increasingly restless. In times of famine, as at other times, youth sees that hopefulness, helpfulness, brightness and progress are of the West; and that stagnation and death, selfishness and gross superstition characterize the East. The condition of the masses in India is still more cheering. There is a movement among the lowest classes towards our faith. In some missions the gathering into the Christian community is limited only by the want of means and suitable instructors. Coupled with all this is the high privilege of laboring for Christ under that strong Christian government, under whose protection are enjoyed freedom of speech and religious liberty.

All this enables us to see in India a land of wonderful promise. The greatness of present opportunity is the assurance of future triumph. Protestantism alone has gathered a community of one million natives. And what is of more importance, it is developing in strength more rapidly than in size. Considering the educational progress of the women, as well as of the men, it may be said that the Christian community is the best educated of any in the land. The native agency of our missions is a source of much cheer. This great army of Christian workers is growing more efficient. India is to be saved by God through the agency of her own sons and daughters. In the societies organized for work among the young we see a large blessing. The Y. M. C. A. is doing a noble work. The Christian Endeavor Society also has spread over the land, and is stirring up thousands of young Christians to give themselves up to a self-denying, outgoing life for others.

Endeavorers all over the land remember with delight a former return to this country of the Rev. A. A. Fulton, D.D., Presbyterian missionary to China. At that time he stirred us all to a zeal for missionary giving, setting up a minimum standard of beneficence, the two-cents-a-week plan called by his name.

Dr. Fulton is a fervent and fascinating speaker, and his address, "And Who is My Neighbor?" was an eloquent plea for the 350,000,000 of Chinese, with their Confucianism, which is agnosticism and does not pretend to be a religion, and their Buddhism, which is a mass of mummeries and idolatrous superstitions.

"And Who Is My Neighbor?"

Rev. A. A. Fulton, D. D., Canton, China

A man was going from Jerusalem to Jericho, and fell among thieves. In this prostrate victim of man's inhumanity I see a type of the 350,000,000 of Chinese stripped and helpless so far as any true religious beliefs are concerned. The Chinese are a marvelous people. Commercially considered, China is the greatest prize on the earth. Numerically regarded, it is the mightiest nation ever held together under one ruler. In industry and economy they are excelled by none, and they have the elements that go to make a great nation.

How do these Chinese stand related to the truths of the Bible? The greatest name in Chinese literature is Confucius, a transmitter, not an originator. His writings have exerted an influence of transcendent importance, and have been one of the strongest factors in giving homogeneity to the vast empire. But it is to be borne in mind that Confucianism is not a religion, but a political-ethical creed, and meant to be that. Religiously considered, it is agnosticism. There is in it no priesthood, no sacrifice, no temple worship and no immortality. Look next at Buddhism, which is responsible for the burden of idolatry in China for two thousand years. With its mass of mummeries and idolatrous superstitions, Buddhism added nothing to the creed of Confucius. Millions in money are spent every year by working people in building and repairing lying temples, where husks are offered to the worshipers, and to the troubles which they have is added the sin of idol worship. In times of famine and flood and plague Buddhism suggests no relief. Ancestral worship has been practiced from remotest ages. Confucius found this, and inculcated the binding obligation of the rite. The worship of ancestors adds millions to the burden of idol worship.

Such is the condition of China in the face of the Christian religion, stripped, smitten and helpless, the only, solitary hope an empty refuge of idolatry, the mummeries of Buddhism and the superstitious follies of ancestral and spirit worship. He must be a most unfeeling Christian who can contemplate this condition without being moved. But Christian sympathy was never intended to be a close corporation article. We must go to the heathen, or send. The great work of saving the Chinese must be done by their native preachers and evangelists, but for long years they must have foreign missionaries to lead, instruct and equip native helpers. The Samaritan not only went to the man, but bound up his wound and supplied medicine. Medical agencies are of vast importance in introducing the Gospel. Nothing more effectually disposes of prejudice than unselfish kindness. Everywhere the hospital and dispensary are potent agencies in preparing for the Gospel. The Samaritan made provision for a permanent cure; he brought the man to an inn, and paid the bill, and said: "Whatsoever thou spendest more I, when I come again, will repay thee." We are to continue our help until idolatry disappears from the face of the earth. We are predominantly Christian and Protestant. Billions of money are in Christian hands—now is the opportunity. The United States is held in highest esteem by the Chinese. More than one hundred thousand converts have been brought out of darkness; thousands of these suffered death as proof of sincerity. We have a magnificent plant in China. We need more power. Through the influence of a native Christian Church will come China's regeneration, and a Christian Emperor will sit upon the throne and the night of idolatry will forever disappear.

A missionary of the Friends was Rev. Willis R. Hotchkiss, of East Central Africa, whose address had the deep eloquence of heroic experiences. He had been one of seven devoted missionaries who went up into the Dark Continent; three he had buried and three he had carried sick to the coast and the home-bound vessels. For eighteen months he did not see a single white face. He told in a thrilling way about his search in the native tongue for a word signifying "Savior," and of his joy when one day a native told him how he had saved another man's life, and in the recital used the long-sought word, a word used by the missionary with great effect in his preaching.

Dr. W. S. Ament of Peking, closed the meeting magnificently. With characteristic modesty, he made no reference to his own work, and of course none to Mark Twain. An ignorant hearer would never have thought that the speaker had been one of the most influential actors in the historic scenes described. Perhaps the most thrilling portion of his address was the account of the faithfulness of the native Christians. Of course, some were unfaithful, but so were some of the early church when Nero and Domitian persecuted them. Many hundreds, however, sealed their faith with their blood.

Dr. Ament's own Christian Endeavor Society held the first meeting that was held after that fateful siege at Peking. Before the massacre, the society had contained forty-seven members. At that meeting only twenty were present; twenty-seven had become glorious martyrs.

CHAPTER VIII.

The Twentieth Century Home.

THE PARENT'S RESPONSIBILITY. — THE HAPPIEST PLACE ON
EARTH. — ITS BEST BOOKS. — FAMILY WORSHIP. —
THE HEART OF THE HOME.

In opening the important session on the home, Monday morning, Dr. Clark said truly that Christian Endeavorers will have much to do with the making of the homes of the new century, and they should be thinking about how to do it well.

The first speaker, Rev. Edwin Forrest Hallenbeck, is vice-president of the New York State Christian Endeavor Union. His address was a faithful presentation of the parents' great and blessed responsibility for the Christian training of their children.

The Parent's Responsibility.

Rev. Edwin Forrest Hallenbeck, Albany, N. Y.

As the drop of dew which hangs upon the morning grass faithfully mirrors the sky, be it azure, or be it darkened with clouds, so will the life of the child reflect the home.

As the little scarlet thread is woven into every piece of cordage in Britain's navy, so will the influences of the home be worked into the character of the child.

There are some things which may be torn from a life when it has reached the years of maturity, but it is not possible to root out the germs which have been planted and nurtured in the home.

The child may journey to the ends of the earth, he may find for himself an abode far away from the dwellings of men, but he will never be able to get from under the shadow of his father's house.

He may live an hundred years yet to the very end the impressions of youth's fireside will cling to his soul.

This is one of the themes of today. Poets have dreamed dreams concerning it; philosophers have formulated principles with reference to it; preachers have uttered stirring words about it; yet with all our dreaming and formulating and preaching we have scarcely begun to comprehend its importance.

The home is the rudder which gives direction to the life of the child. It is the training school where he learns his best lessons. It is the armory from which he draws ammunition for the battle.

It goes without saying that the parents are the architects of the home. Others may have some part in the building, materials may be brought from various sources, but father and mother will make the design. Their ambitions, their ideals, their conduct will largely determine its character and shape its influence. To the parents, then, belongs a tremendous responsibility. God has laid it upon their hearts—laid it there with the hand of love,—laid it close beside the sweetest privileges of life. It may not be disowned. It can only be measured by the issues which are at stake. These are high as heaven, deep as hell, broad as the boundless eternity.

Not long ago a mother in New York City shut her children in the rooms which she occupied on the upper floor of a tenement, placed a padlock on the door and went off to market. During her absence the apartment took fire. The neighbors, aroused by the screams of the children, endeavored to go to their rescue, but the door was locked. At length the mother returned. She was frantic when she saw the situation. She tried to find the key; in her agony she almost tore the clothing from her body, but the key had been lost. Then she leaped against the door, seeking with her hands to tear away the lock. When at last the door was battered in, and the flames extinguished, the children were dead.

I know parents who by the influence of their lives are shutting their children up to a fate more dreadful than that.

I could tell you of other parents who are building their homes after the pattern which God has shown in the mount. Every day the household is catching more of the Spirit of Jesus. Its sunlight is love. Its atmosphere is peace. Its melody is praise. To its firesides the angels come with the benedictions of God. Within its holy walls the children learn the beauty of a Christlike life, and out from its gates they go to carry the blessed stores of such a life to a weary, sinsick world.

Such a home doubtless rose before the sacred writer's mind when he made mention of two noble-hearted saints and sent greetings to "the church which was in their house."

It is not enough for us to lay the precepts of God away in our own hearts. He commands us, saying, "Ye shall teach them to your children, speaking of them when thou sittest in the house, and when thou walkest by the way, when thou liest down and when thou risest up. And thou shalt write them upon the door posts of thine house and upon thy gates."

The best thing God ever said of Abraham was this: "I know him that he will command his children and his household after him, and they shall keep the way of the Lord." No higher tribute could be paid to any parent.

But if this momentous obligation rests upon us it were well to honestly and earnestly seek how it may be met. Will you permit me to speak a few homely words of counsel?

First, you must know Christ yourself. The home where He has no place will never fulfil its sacred mission. Its equipment from the world's standpoint may be complete. The artist, perchance, has exhausted his skill in its decoration. The furnishings are magnificent. The work of the masters hangs upon the walls. The wardrobe contains the richest fabrics. The larder is stored with luxury. But if the Son of God is not there, the most important item has been overlooked. The home is the place for Christ's throne. He is to reign there with His sceptre of love, and God expects the parent to lead Him to that throne..

Without Him our homes are not safe. On the Passover night in Egypt, when the destroying angel went through the land upon his mission of death, the only homes which had no cause for fear were those which had been marked with the blood of the lamb. Destroying angels are going up and down the land today seeking for unguarded doors through which to enter, and no household is safe except the blood-marks of Calvary be upon it.

You may call me an extremist, perhaps I am, but I do not hesitate to say that it is criminal for a father to keep himself from the fellowship of Christ; he is defrauding his children, robbing them of the most precious portion of their heritage.

For a mother to lock God's Son outside her heart is a fearful thing; she may be blocking the path to heaven for those she loves.

The influence of motherhood is one of the most potent forces of life. It would be impossible to overestimate its power.

> "The mother in her office holds the key
> Of the soul; and she it is who stamps the coin
> Of character, and makes the being who would be a savage
> But for her gentle cares, a Christian man."

This is her mission, but how may she put the touch of Christ upon her children's lives if she has not surrendered her own heart to that touch.

Our children may go out into the world and find some stranger hand to lead them to the cross, but the chances are the cross will not become a stopping-place in their lives if they do not catch glimpses of its glory in the home.

Second, dedicate your child to God. Mingled with the first cries of the new born life should be the voice of holy gratitude with which the parents yield back to God the precious gift which has come from Him. Before the little one nestles for its first sleep against the mother's breast, let the hands of parental faith lay it upon the heart of hearts.

In the long ago a man and his help-meet gave their child to God. They did not fear the king's edict which promised death to every male child of the Hebrews. They did not falter when they must deposit the little life in the bulrush ark and lay it in the flags by the river's brink. It was safe. Parental faith had laid it in the everlasting arms.

Hannah said, as she carried her child to the sanctuary: "I have lent him to the Lord: as long as he liveth he shall be lent to the Lord." That simple act contained the prophecy of Samuel's greatness.

Then, once the surrender has been made, believe that your child is God's. We fail to make the Divine ownership real. If the voice from above bid him to the sacrifices of some far away service, we murmur. If he is asked to take up some humble task, we rebel. And if the chariot of gold come from the Celestial City to take the loved one into a brighter glory, we say with our actions, if not with our words, "God has no right to rob me of my child." Thus we prove that we had never honestly yielded the precious life to Him.

Be sincere about it, friend. Lay your treasure, once for all, upon the altar, then believe that love divine will overshadow it, messengers from the throne will guard it; infinite wisdom will indicate its course; and one day you may expect to see it—a jewel of redemption, in the Savior's crown.

But this is not all. We must prove the sincerity of our offering. If the child is God's, then to train it is a sacred trust, and with all the strength of our being we shall devote ourselves to the work.

Third, give your child the fellowship of your better self. Lock not the stores of your love against him. Open your heart to his gaze.

Here is the supreme blessing of the Divine Fatherhood. God gave Himself to His children. He came down into their need. He linked His life to theirs with the bonds of a hallowed fellowship. Thus He sought to woo them toward holy things.

You owe this to your child.. It is one of life's most sacred debts.

Your fathers are toiling early and late, bearing burdens that are heavy, fighting battles that try men's souls. What for? I hear you answer: "To make a living for my family." But, man, living does not consist in bread to eat and clothes to wear and dollars to spend. Living is high ideals, and noble aspirations, and unselfish ministries. Living is holy friendships, and heavenly joys, and the peace of God. Money will not purchase these. Toil cannot win them. If you would help your child to know them you need to make your life the link between him and God.

Heaven pity the children whose father believes his duty is ended when he has put coal in the cellar and clothing in the wardrobe, and bread in the larder. They may be admired and envied of men, but it does not require the vision of a seer to behold the shadows gathering about their lives, shadows whose gloom is painted in the coloring of despair.

God pity the home whose mother is so occupied with novels and dinners and dress that she has no care to take her children into the fellowship of a love which will touch the deepest springs of their nature and lead them to reach out for the best in life. That home may have every equipment that money and pains can give, but through its chambers we can almost hear the bells of eternity as they ring the death-knell of its hope and joy.

A prominent man in relating the story of his conversion from infidelity says that his first impulse toward God came to him in the revelation of his father's love. He had grown up through boyhood with no idea that the man who presided over the home cared for him. There was no companionship between them, no expressions of confidence, no words of affection. But one day after he had reached the years of manhood the father opened his heart, and poured out its treasures of love. He told him how it grieved his heart that he had not more of temporal blessing to give, how gladly he would go hungry himself if thereby his son might have bread. Then he reached into his pocket and drew out the last coin which it contained and laid it in the hand of the boy. No wonder the young man's heart was melted and that unconsciously he began to reach up for that love of which a father's affection is only the feeble type.

Your child needs you more than he needs your gold. Nothing short of a pure, true comradeship will help you to meet your obligation. To fail here may be to strike the knife to his eternal weal. What shall it profit a man if he shall gain the whole world and lose his own child.

Fourth, pray for your child, not with the formal petitions of a listless heart, but with the fervent prayer that will not let God go. Pray as the ruler prayed when he threw himself at the Master's feet crying, "My little daughter lieth at the point of death. I beseech Thee, come and lay Thy hands upon her." Pray as the Syrophenician woman prayed when she prostrated herself before the Lord and pleaded for her devil-possessed child a few crumbs from His table.

You have a closet, of course. No parent can meet his responsibility without one. You have your quiet hours of fellowship with God. Let no one be oftener mentioned in these seasons than your child. Talk with the Father concerning his dangers, his sins, his ambitions, his companions. Thus shall he be

"Bound with gold chains about the feet of God."

There is a marvelous power in the parent's prayer. Prison officials tell us that the last influence with which the hardened criminal breaks is his mother's prayers. When everything else has failed to affect his life, and in his degradation he almost seems to be sealed for perdition, the memory of the petitions which ascended from his early home will often fan into flame the spark of longing for a better life.

A prominent preacher bears witness that when he had plunged into the very depths of sin and seemed to lie a hopeless wreck upon the edge of the bottomless pit, the prayers of his Christian parents saved him. He was among strangers, hundreds of miles away from home. So great was his loathing of life that he was ready to summon death with his own hand, when those holy petitions reached across the gulf like mighty arms of love and power to lift him up to Christ. And when the awful stains of the guilty past had been washed away, the same prayers led him up the steps of a pulpit and touched his lips for the proclamation of God's gospel.

Augustine was saved because his mother besieged the throne on his behalf.

John G. Paton became one of the heroes of modern missions with a story which has won the admiration of the Christian world because his parents dared to claim Heaven's blessing on his behalf.

O pray for your child! Give God no rest by day or by night! Keep his interests continually before the throne of grace:—thus you shall build up hedges along his way and keep his feet from many a sin.

We come to the fifth and last consideration—you owe your child a godly example. Precept is good but practice is better. The words of counsel which you speak may drop out of his memory, but your child will never be able to get away from the grip of your life.

When Phidias carved the famous statue of Minerva in Athens he so wrought his own image into the shield of the goddess that it could only be removed by destroying the work. Thus the parent engraves his image upon the soul of the child. It will not be effaced, he will find its outlines in eternity.

Have you ever noticed how frequently in the story of Jewish kings it is said of some young ruler "he walked in the ways of his father." Of course he did. So will your child. You are paving the path for his feet.

A man was leaving his home one winter morning. The ground was covered with snow. As he walked down the street he heard behind him a baby laugh and looking back beheld his boy trying to put his little feet into his own great footprints. "I'm coming, papa," he cried, "I'm coming, right in your tracks." When a bit later that man was tempted to gratify an evil desire suddenly he stopped and turned back, for he seemed to hear that childish voice as it cried, "coming, papa, right in your tracks."

O friend, be careful how you live, for down the path of life your child is coming right in your tracks. You may plead with him not to walk in the ways of his father. You may command him to turn his steps toward worthier goals, yet in spite of all, on he will come, led by the hand of your example over the same path which you have chosen for your feet. If you are a careless citizen you may expect him to be. If you are an inconsistent Christian you may expect him to be; either that or none at all. If gold is your god, you are training him to worship at the same shrine. I know there are exceptions to the rule, nevertheless it holds "like parent, like child."

I think the saddest picture of fatherhood which the Word of God paints is that scene at the city gate where David weeps for Absalom. David loved his son. He doubtless counselled him aright, but his example was unrighteous. This was the awful mistake. By his own life he had led his son toward ruin. Now as he goes up to the chamber over the gate we hear him sob, "O my son Absalom, my son, my son Absalom! would God I had died for thee, O Absalom, my son, my son." But it was too late, the prodigal would never come back!

If there is power for evil in an ungodly example there is a wonderful incentive toward righteousness in a pure strong Christian life.

Richard Cecil the great English preacher tried in his early days to be a sceptic, but he could not get past his mother's holy life.

That was a beautiful tribute which a lad in the Sunday School paid to his mother. The teacher described the character of Jesus without mentioning His name. She told them of His love and His kindness, His patience, His unselfishness. Then she said, "Can you tell me who this wonderful person is?" Without a moment of hesitation the little fellow answered, "Why, that's my mother." Beautiful answer! Happy child! He had seen these traits so strikingly revealed in his mother's life that he thought the teacher must be speaking of her.

O woman, mother! Is the light of God shining in your face? Is your life breathing out the sweet fragrance of Jesus Christ? O father! Are you preaching the gospel of God's Son in the conduct of every day? It should be so; and if it is not, you are withholding from your children that which is of greater value than caskets of jewels and bars of yellow gold.

In these days of dazzle and glitter we are tempted to feel that the home is a narrow sphere for a life, but only God is able to bound the influence of such a ministry.

Susanah Wesley was wielding a mightier sceptre than many a queen on her gilded throne when in the humble parsonage she trained her boys for Christ. The world had no appreciation for her work. It did not even know her name till she was gone, but the sound of her voice is heard today whenever a Methodist church-bell calls worshipers to the house of God; the fruitage of her life is seen whenever a penitent kneels before a Methodist altar. Take heart, O ye weary ones, as you toil on amid the perplexities and cares and trials of the home, and one day the grandeur of your work shall appear.

During the building of one of the old world cathedrals a man came one day to seek employment. For the humblest pittance he offered his toil. They gave him a large stone to cut. He could do no harm and his work might be useful in some insignificant place. With rare devotion he toiled on day after day. He seemed to forget himself and the ordinary comforts of life were often denied him. They gave little heed to the old workman and his task until one day they found him cold in death. He had completed his work. The tools of his craft were in order by his side. His countenance seemed to wear even in death an expression of rapture as it turned toward the face which he had cut in the stone—the image of Jesus Christ. As they looked upon it with uncovered heads they whispered, "In all the building there is no work so wonderful—it is the work of love." And they gave it a prominent place in the great structure.

O parents, give yourselves to this sacred trust. Win your children for Christ. Train them for noble ministries. Write the precepts of God across their hearts. Set them a pattern of holiness in the home. There is no more exalted work than this—it is the work of love. The daily round may keep you back from the notice of men. The world may not even know your name. But you shall have the smile of heaven. You shall have the joy of establishing the church in the home, and building the home into the church. And in the day of unveiling it may be told that the faithful influence of your life had part in chiseling upon the souls of your children the likeness of Jesus Christ.

Rev. Ira Landrith, the splendid chairman of the Nashville Convention committee, the new Cumberland Presbyterian trustee, was the next speaker, treating the beautiful theme, "The Happiest Place on Earth." He urged a revival of family worship, and that in every home a family Christian Endeavor service should be held every week. "Christian Endeavor has transformed our churches. Let us now give it an opportunity to transform our homes. I haven't a bit of sympathy with the sneer that says that C. E. means Courting Everywhere. Why not? Under what better than religious auspices could young folks marry? If there were more altars in the homes there would be fewer skeletons in the closets."

One of the most forcible portions of this brilliant address was the protest against the tendency of women, that do not need to work, to go outside the home for money-earning. "No woman is too good to be set down in a nursery. The new woman? That's a passing fad. Every time the new woman becomes somebody's old woman the thing is over." No address of the entire Convention was more full of wit, gracious humanliness, and sturdy common sense. It will be found, printed in full, farther on in this report.

A novel topic for our Convention was Dr. John E. Pound's "Read the Best Books." The address was packed full of Dr. Pound's witty aphorisms.

Read the Best Books.

Rev. John E. Pounds, D. D., Cleveland, O.

The mood of my subject is imperative. The law of progress and the spirit of our time say read, and the voice of conscience and the instinct of self-preservation say read only the best. Reading is becoming daily a more important source of education, and education a greater necessity of life.

We boast of the speed of our express trains and ocean liners and automobiles, but the fastest and safest means of travel is by books. Literally in the twinkling of an eye one can be exploring with Livingstone in Africa, and without danger of the Congo fever, too, or be campaigning with Kitchener and learning the experiences and issues of war without coming in range of the bullets. One can meditate with Socrates without fear of disturbance by either Xantippe or the police, conspire with Cataline without any prickings of conscience, steal the Stratford deer with Will Shakespere without thought of game laws, swim the Hellespont with Byron without fear of wind or tide, weigh the earth with Newton without scales or climb the heavens with Herschel without so much as borrowing Jacob's ladder. Truly your book is your greatest magician.

A library is a veritable storehouse of riches. The young man scarcely appreciates the wealth of his literary inheritance. He does not consider how many men have counted their lives as not dear unto themselves if they might track the stars along their paths and harness the lightning to the heaviest of human burdens. The thoughtless boy says, "Books are cheap." Aye, because some one else has paid the price. It costs little to see the vision of a "Paradise Lost" because a Milton paid the price of blindness. The progress of a Christian Pilgrim is easy and free, for a Bunyan was content to sit behind the prison bars. George Eliot read a thousand books that one more book might be worth the reading. A great book is a vessel into which a great man has poured his soul.

He misses much of life who does not make friends with books. They are companions as good as people in that they are always ready to give advice, and better in that they can be "shut up." They are neighbors that tell you all about other people, and tell other people nothing about you. They are teachers that govern without the rod and impart wisdom without arrogance. They are superiors that associate without condescension and bestow help without patronage. True, some books are worthy of only a nod as you pass by, and others to be dined with on occasion, but the best books are to be lived with. No one stood with Paul in the hour of his need, but he knew some friends who would not desert, and so he asked Timothy to "Bring the books."

It is imperative that one read the best. Science tells us that the body changes every seven years and at the end of that time is composed of the things that have been eaten meanwhile. May this not also apply to the mind? Animals are classified by what they eat, being called carnivorous, herbivorous or by some other long name. Could we not classify minds in the same way? Some feed only on fads. Like the men Paul found in Athens they do nothing else but seek for some new, literally some newer, thing—the very latest. They would not read an article in a yesterday's paper, even if it were a reprint of "The Deserted Village" or the "Holy Grail." But if a thing is new or seems to be, they devour it greedily. Even a new name is as a sugar coating and they will swallow what is as stale and nauseating as Buddhism under the new name of "Theosophy."

Some feed on excitement. They fear the Giant Despair less than the Sloth Monotony. One of the worst symptoms of the times is that many young people can neither contain nor entertain themselves. They find no joy in an hour's quiet meditation or a stroll through the fields or woods. They crave external excitement every moment. Such books as "Reveries of a Bachelor" and the "Sketch Book" they find stupid. They find freedom from care only when the hero of the story is imprisoned on a false charge and forget their headache only when the heroine is raving with brain fever. They judge cooking entirely by the amount of salt and vinegar and pepper used.

There is one class of animals that I hesitate to mention because it is so revolting—the scavenger. It feeds on decay and refuse. Yet I know no other fit companion for those who feast themselves on the record and detail of moral decay. That there are such is evidenced by the fact that such obscenity is printed. And the readers decide what shall be published as certainly as the customer determines what the merchant shall keep upon his shelves. They who like scandal have none of the spirit which rejoices not in iniquity, and they who devour the record of violence and murder are akin to those who applauded the battle of men and beasts in the arena of old.

The application of Endeavor principles will go far toward solving the problem of how to read.

One important principle is definiteness. Have a purpose in life and make your reading subserve it. Not that one should read only books that bear directly on his life work, but most of his reading should have some reference to it. One must know at least enough of what he wants to go to the water for fish and to the woods for squirrels. Learn where to go and for what. There is danger enough of missing even if you take aim.

Another Endeavor principle that should be applied to reading is regularity. One book a month is better than twelve books in one month and nothing during the rest of the year. It is only once in a lifetime, and then when God has special work as he had for Elijah, that one can eat or read enough to go in the strength of it forty days and nights. If one should take five minutes with the poets every morning his mind would be inspired and stimulated for the work of the day. It would be like going to the organ for the proper keynote of song. It is better to get the keynote for a day's thinking and living from Tennyson or Longfellow than from the conversation of the street car or the work shop. You could take no more helpful pledge concerning your reading than this: "I will read something of the best every day I live."

The selection of books is most important. Man may be the architect of his own fortune, but the best of architects cannot build without materials. There cannot, then, be too much care in selecting books since they will be built into one's very character and destiny.

Every young man is a young Solomon, not in wisdom, but in the opportunity to choose it. When he stands in a library there is set before him whatever his heart could wish. Strange things, however, are chosen. If I should say that the dust is gathering on Bacon and Emerson and even Macauley, the pretty librarian might think I was bringing a charge against her housekeeping. The wise man of Israel did not choose riches, but our young man always journeys to "King Solomon's Mines" in search of the true gold. An eminent college professor says sensational novels are read in the spirit of the gambler. The gambler seeks excitement· and profit. It is passing strange that any one should expect to find either in a book with a title that sounds like; "The Shearing of Billy the Butter, or, the Villain Uncovered," or like this: "The Nine Lives of Thomas the Rambler, or, Come Home to Die." How many mistake mere glitter for gold and gather it, as the explorers carried shiploads of mica from Virginia to England.

How shall we know the best books? By what test shall the young people try them? I think rather by their fruits than by their artistic beauty. The best books will cause certain results in the minds and hearts of the readers. Try them by these tests:

The best books are instructive. Imparting information is a most important function. Facts are entities, so the more a man has in him the larger he is. Education is the power behind the man behind the gun.

By information I do not mean historical or scientific facts alone. There are truths concerning motives and morality that are not less important to life. Poetry and fiction may teach these and one must not refuse instruction because of the form in which it comes. History records the actions of men, fiction interprets them. History dissects realities, fiction incarnates motives and passions. The historian is the chemist who analyzes, the novelist is the artist who creates. Nor is the message of the one more essentially true than that of the other. One learns more of Scotch character sitting "Beside the Bonnie Brier Bush" than tramping over the fields of Bannockburn and Culloden. It may be that William Tell never lived in the flesh, but he is Switzerland's truest and best known son for all that. It is possible that Mark Anthony did not deliver his funeral oration in English, using such words as "I come to bury Caesar, not to praise him," but I pity the man who can not feel that he did. One can scarcely fail to love the knights of King Arthur's Court better than those of King Richard's, and feel them to be more real. Books that teach us to understand life teach us well.

The best books make an impression. They stamp themselves upon the memory. It is no great sin to forget a book if you can. But who can forget the Bishop in "Les Miserables" or the experiences of Shylock or Lady Macbeth? The scenes of Squeers' school remain with some as vividly as those of their own school life. No one can read Robertson and ever again preach from his texts without more or less preaching his sermons. Those pesky ancients have not only stolen all our best thoughts but are always present. like Banquo's Ghost, to exult in the theft.

Good books develop good taste. Taste is, or ought to be, in our reading what intuition of purity is in living. Speaking morally taste is as conscience, speaking artistically it is as ear in music and as eye in color. And like all delicate faculties it may be perverted or cultivated, dulled or quickened. Tastes differ but no normal palate likes poison. If any question arises in your mind or heart as you read give yourself, not the book, the benefit of the doubt.

Form your literary taste on the classics. Fortunately they are in reach of all, for, unlike congressmen, the best can be bought the cheapest. Do not be discouraged if you are not thrilled by them at first. The lamented Isaac Errett said he did not like "Paradise Lost" until he was sixty years old and had read it six times. Be sincere with yourself, too. Do not exclaim with rapture over a book with a great name unless you feel it. I admire the honesty, if not the taste, of the young lady who said, "No doubt Milton is great, but for my part I prefer the Ladies' Home Journal." The taste will grow right if one feeds it on the right stuff. I commend the wisdom of a friend who said, "I am going to read Dickens through this winter if it kills me." To be sure Garfield said, "Dickens will kill me yet," but he meant it in a different way. You are reading the best books if they cause you to like only the best.

The best books inspire the readers. They help to overcome human inertia. Knowledge may not be power but it is the fuel which produces power. A book has done you good when it makes you want to do good. The best missionary books are those which make the most missionaries. The final test of a book is not admiration but imitation. The Gospels surpass all other writings in that the Character which they hold up draws all men unto Himself. When other orators spoke the Greeks applauded. but when Demosthenes talked to them they said, "Let us go and fight the enemy." We do not need the voice of critics to tell whether a book like "Uncle Tom's Cabin" is great, after it has been applauded by the cannon of Chickamauga and Gettysburg and hissed at by the answering shell.

The best books inspire a man to think. Bacon says reading makes a full man but it is even more important that men be made strong and active. The chief purpose of reading is not to fill the mind with facts as a storehouse is filled with grains of wheat which can be taken out again at will, but rather as an engine is filled with coal and water that it may give out power. We read that we may produce rather than reproduce. It is said that Senator Depew always reads something from Macaulay just before going to make an after-dinner speech, that he may get his mind above the commonplace.

The best books inspire to service a gracious result. "Nicholas Nickleby" passed the death sentence upon Yorkshire schools, "The Bridge of Sighs" opened doors to the homeless like a key, the prayer of "Tiny Tim," "God bless us every one," was the "open sesame" of many an English pocketbook, Mrs. Browning's "Cry of the Children" has been heard in earth as well as in Heaven, and "Oliver Twist" is as a living stone built into the walls of every orphanage.

The best books inspire us with noble ideals. While reading them we see visions that allure us up the mountains. I cannot give my consent to the modern idea that the whole purpose of a novel should be to tell a story.

The sage of Elmwood says of himself:

"There's Lowell, who's striving Parnassus to climb,
    With a whole bale of isms tied together with rhyme.
He might get on alone, spite of brambles and boulders,
    But he can't with that bundle he has on his shoulders.
The top of the hill he will ne'er come nigh reaching,
    'Till he learns the distinction 'twixt singing and preaching."

Thank God, he never learned it, else we must have buried one of our best American poets out of our hearts. The "Elegy in a Country Churchyard" was not written to amuse nor the "In Memoriam" to entertain, any more than the Angelus was painted to adorn a wall. "John Halifax" not only defines a gentleman but incarnates the definition in the reader. A book that creates great aspirations is great. For ideals are a component part of manhood. To properly judge a man you must add what he wants to be to what he is and divide by two.

There is another effect of books, by which they must be tested, although I do not know what to name it, unless it be projection. I mean the ability to put one's self into the place of another, than which there is no harder thing to do. We can not do it by a simple act of the will. We may weep at those who weep but scarcely with them. We learn by experience,' as a mother who has lost a child knows how to sympathize with another mother in a similar bereavement. But no one can experience all the joys and sorrows and passions and aspirations of all men, so cannot thus learn how to be a real friend and priest to them. But we are not left without resource. Books make us to know what the thrill of joy and the pain of heart-break are. A book that brings a tear to the eye has interpreted some great emotion of the human heart, or made one understand the vital spring of some noble action. Charity began in Heaven with Him who said of Israel, "I know their sorrows." How literally Jesus spoke when He said, "Father forgive them for they know not what they do." The mob thought they were putting a hated one to death and that He would suffer physical pain. But what did they know of the bitterness of rejected love, the sadness of a misunderstood teacher, the loneliness of leadership, the burden of a world's sin borne for those who did not comprehend its weight or care that He bore it for them. He is the world's great Friend because He knows the great world's heart. And the more we come to understand men the more we can befriend them. "The Scarlet Letter" makes us to understand remorse, and he who understands is able to minister. Shakespeare was not trying to make us hate Othello or love Hamlet so much as to understand them. Books that do this are great.

I leave to your own hearts to suggest the value of devotional books, and the necessity of reading the one great Book of all. A light above the brightness of the noonday sun shines into every window that is open toward Jerusalem. Go into the closet to read as well as to pray, and when you have shut the door it will be the lightest room in the house. For he who enters therein needs no light of the sun by day or the moon by night, for the Lamb is the light thereof. So in building the library of your home be sure to make the Stone which the builders of old rejected to be the head of the corner, and the joy and peace and light of that home, being the Lord's doing, will be marvelous in our eyes.

A most vigorous and effective speaker is the Rev. W. G. Marsh, of Adelaide, Australia. With strong words he treated the practical topic, "What Can Christian Endeavor Do for the Home?" "Be honest," he pleaded. "If you don't put your Christian Endeavor into your home life, you are no Endeavorer." He urged unselfishness, patience, obedience,. self-denial, love, and sympathy; and his address left us all more determined that our consecration should be no meaningless word, but should blossom into fruitful service of our dear ones.

The most important of all these necessary themes was that treated by the tall man from Canada, Dr. Robert Johnston,—family worship, "the heart of the home," as the program called it. For many years Christian Endeavor has set before it the steadfast purpose to promote family worship.

The Heart of the Home.

Rev. Robert Johnston, D. D., London, Ont.

It was my privilege four years ago at our great gathering in that city of the west whose Golden Gate is washed by the tides of the Pacific, to speak of the Sabbath in its relation to National life. I venture then to refer to the Sabbath as one of the two great foundation stones upon which God intended all human organization to be built. This morning it is mine to speak of the other of those divinely laid Edenic corner stones of human progress and human success—the family. Permit me to say in a single sentence that I know of no conception which, if it could but possess the minds of the men and women of this generation, would do so much to purify, enoble and glorify our National life as this—That the Sabbath and the Home are the two great trunk lines originating in God's Will in Eden which it is His purpose should run down through all human organizations and around which and in due accord with which all these should be associated; and this further that only those features of social, national, and, I will add, religious, life which move in harmony with and in loyalty to these divine thoughts for man can make for true and permanent blessing. This conviction, Sir, I assert, possessing with a mastering power' the minds of the Christian men and women of this generation would be more valuable to our age than the discovery of diamond mines or the multiplication of the inventions of an Edison or a Tesla.

It is not within my province this morning, to speak of the home in general, but rather of that particular feature of its life that stamps it as Christian and recognizes it as dependent for success and happiness upon God's favor—Family Worship.

It would be easy to multiply reasons why family worship should be an established and unfailing custom in every home, but I content myself with mentioning only two.

First, It is seemly and right that God should be recognized as the God of the family. It is impossible to read Scripture without being impressed with the fact that the family, the household, occupied a large place in God's thought for His people. He dealt as we know with nations and individuals. For them He had His purposes and to them He uttered His promises, and as nations and as individuals it was the part of those to whom these were spoken to claim them. He asked for recognition in national life and in individual life. So also for the family apart He had His gracious purposes and to it He spoke promises of grace; from the family therefore He claimed and ever claims recognition. There are blessings that can only be described as family blessings; events, providences, occurrences that effect us not alone as individuals but as families, evils too that threaten our homes, against which we seek protection and help. Surely if we realize this, and who that knows what true home life means can fail to realize it, we will not be content to call upon God in secret devotion or in the public congregation of God's people, but conscious of family needs, rejoicing in family joys, trembling in the face of family perils, shrinking with dread from family sorrow, we will as families, surround the altar of the home and as families join in recognizing God as the Author of all our good and our Help in trouble.

The home and heaven should surely not be separated. The lower should be but the vestibule of the higher. Daily should the face of the family be turned toward that Father's house in which we trust at last to gather. Daily should He be honored in the unbroken home circle before whose throne as an undivided family we pray at last to meet. I have heard that on one occasion when an ancient temple in Rome was suffering at the hands of vandals who were carrying away the carved pillars and works of historic value, the reigning pope erected in its midst a cross to preserve the ruin and protect it from the ravages of ruthless hands. So when there is set up in the family an altar where the name of Christ is daily honored, a protecting power and gracious influence is established to ward off the ruthless hands of the destroyers of family peace and family joys, and precaution is at least taken that the peace and quiet of the home circle may be preserved.

I urge as a further reason for the observance of family worship, that It Proves a Bond for the Cementing of Family Fellowships, and As An Anchor to Bind the Members of the Home to the Throne of God.

It is a truism, and we learn that it is such, as the days go by, that home joys are not only the sweetest and purest, but they are the most enduring. What to any one are financial triumphs, professional successes, social adulation or the plaudits of the nation, if the home life to which the hero of all this must return is barren of those sweet fellowships, those trustful confidences, which more than aught else of earth bring rest and quiet and content to life? Now, if these are to exist and flourish in the luxuriance and strength possible to them, it is only in the warmth of home religion that such is possible. Strange it is but true that the very circumstances of kinship often prove a centrifugal force rather than one centripetal; they separate rather than unite. The birthday festivals and Christmas and Thanksgiving celebrations do much to fuse the different dispositions and to unite around a common centre various ambitions and desires. But the most powerful force of all to this end is family worship. when from day to day the hearts of all bow before the throne of grace and join in common petitions for one another; when hearts of parents and children, of brothers and sisters, of husband and wife, of masters and servants, grow tender for one another as together confessing their sins they humble themselves before God and seek his grace and favor.

And this bond, need I say, will not cease in its cementing power when the unavoidable separations of life occur. One of the mightiest influences of family worship, one of the most emphatic reasons for its observance is found in the enduring character of the impressions which it makes upon the members of the family circle. Imagination carries me to a far off land and to a slave's hut, where at the dead of night, while a babe sleeps, a mother is putting the last touches to an ark woven of the bullrushes that have been gathered from the marshy banks of the Nile. The hour has come when the babe can no longer be hid. Tenderly he is lifted and placed on the soft lining of that strange cradle; gently the coverings are adjusted; again and yet again the mother bends to kiss the parted lips; but while the brother and sister stand expectant, ere the father lifts the precious burden, they kneel around the cradle and in tones subdued so that the slumbers of the babe may not be disturbed, the father pours out his soul to Israel's God for the babe so precious and so threatened. And then the mother and father go forth and lay their treasure not on the bosom of the Father of Waters but in the everlasting arms of Israel's covenant God.

Not an old picture is that but an ever new one. The lad is ever going forth, no longer to be hid by loving care and tender counsel within the barriers that love erects around the home, but forth into the great Egyptian world he goes, to its dangers, its attractions, its pitfalls and its lurking emissaries of the pit. I had rather send him forth from such a scene as that than send him forth without it, heir to Golconda's mines or to Klondyke's treasures. Well for the lad who goes forth with his heart, bound through the years during which he was sheltered within the home, by the golden chains of love around the feet of God. As for Moses, so for him; the path from the river bank to yon far mountain height where God shall kiss away the soul of his servant to eternal rest, may be long and winding, but it shall end at last before the throne of a covenant-keeping God, and they who took him to nurse for God shall stand with him in the home from which they shall go no more out.

Considering the manner of family worship, circumstances must direct. Assuredly it is best when the picture drawn by Burns of the Scottish Cottar, so familiar to many of us in its every detail is realized, when the father is the priest for his own family circle;

> "The cheerfu' supper done, wi' serious face,
>   They, round the ingle, form a circle wide;
> The sire turns o'er wi' patriarchal grace
>   The big Ha' Bible, ance his father's pride:
> His bonnet rev'rently is laid aside,
>   His lyart haffets wearin' thin and bare;
> Those strains that once did sweet in Zion glide,
>   He wales a portion with judicious care,
> And 'Let us worship God;' he says with solemn air.

> "Then kneeling down to heaven's eternal King,
>   The saint, the father and the husband prays;
> Hope 'springs exulting on triumphant wings,'
>   That thus they all shall meet in future days;
> There, ever bask in uncreated rays,
>   No more to sigh or shed the bitter tear,
> Together hymning their Creator's praise."

Well may the poet add

> From scenes like these old Scotia's grandeur springs,
>   That makes her lov'd at home rever'd abroad;
> Princes and Lords are but the breath of kings,
>   "An honest man's the noblest work of God."

Mr. Chairman, I am not a Scot, nor the son of a Scot, and I may be pardoned the eulogy when I say that Scotland stands and has stood in the forefront of nations in all matters of progress and moral truth, and for that proud position she is indebted not alone to her splendid system of education, not alone to her magnificent scenery that has had so great a hand in moulding national character, but more than to all these to the Bible and to the place it has held in the family circle.

If I might offer a prayer for my land it would be that that scene might be reproduced in every home within her borders, and this thought comes to me; May not Christian Endeavor be the means in effecting that end so desirable? Sir, we recognize in this great movement one of the mightiest agencies that God has used in these trying times for righteousness and for spiritual life. We thank God for the man upon whom the spirit of God fell, as upon Gideon, so that blowing a trumpet there have been gathered to him the young and eager hearts from a hundred lands. We praise our God for the devotion of a membership three millions strong, for the heroic committee work, for the fires kindled in many a consecration meeting, for the sacrifice of the Tenth Legion, and for the devotion of the Quiet Hour, but, sir, I venture to suggest another work and I throw out another watchword for the Twentieth Century Christian Endeavor, "A Family Altar in Every Home." Let Christian Endeavor address itself to this and under God's blessing accomplish it, and it will crown all its other services to the nation, to the Church, and to Christ. with the grandest and the most fruitful of all its splendid achievements. Oh, that it might be in our day and in some measure through our agency, that God would fulfil to His Church His closing promise of Old Testament Scripture to "turn the hearts of the fathers to the children and the hearts of the children to the fathers." Where shall this be done but around the family altar?

CHAPTER IX.

Some Junior Workers' Ideas.

The Junior school of methods, over which Secretary Baer presided, was just what it is labeled. Short, sharp, telling work was the word. Mrs. F. E. Clark mentioned the mothers' meeting, the ministers' sympathy, and superintendents with hearts in touch with God, as open doors of opportunity for the Junior Society.

Miss Frances LeBaron, of Chicago, Ill., thought that a good way to interest the parents is to have one of the Juniors announce their meeting in the Sunday school. One society found that if the parents are invited to eat pop corn and taffy with the Juniors in a social, they are likely to have a sticking interest in the society. Sometimes it works splendidly to have a social, the price of admission to be one parent.

Rev. G. W. Montgomery of Oak Mount, Pa., told how the pastor can help. He would have him an active member of the Junior society, no matter how gray his head. Of the pastor who thinks himself too busy to attend the meetings he asked, "What is the pastor there for, if not to be worn out in the service of the Master's little ones?" Mr. Montgomery's ideal of a pastor is a man who can call his Juniors by name, and to whose coat-skirts the Juniors will cling.

Some of the best suggestions from the floor were: A romp with the Juniors once a week, illustrated blackboard sermons, and Junior songs in the morning church services.

"Without a Junior committee no Christian Endeavor society is completely organized," said Miss Clara L. Boyer, Ohio's State Junior superintendent. This committee should attend the Junior meetings and superintend the committees of the Juniors. Junior graduates make good Junior committees.

"In the first place, do you keep the pledge yourself?" was the question Miss Kate Haus of St. Louis fired at the superintendents present in discussing the topic, "How to Secure Faithfulness in Keeping the Pledge." She also flung out a few don'ts." Don't give prizes for keeping the pledge. Don't be forever talking about the duty of keeping the pledge; emphasize the privilege of keeping it,—the joy.

Mrs. M. L. Hageman of Muncie, Ind., suggested that outside the meetings the Juniors may save scrap-iron and old rubber for missionary money, form anti-cigarette clubs, and have a Junior Christian Endeavor World committee to see that each boy and girl has a copy of the paper.

John W. Logan of Meriden, Conn., told how to conduct a Junior meeting. He said: "Do not make your meetings girlish. The superintendent must be a boy, even if she is a young lady." Mr. Logan would use the members of the Junior committee to fence the noisy boys and the giggling girls apart. If there is a tendency to thoughtless praying, it is better to have less prayers in order to have more prayer.

Again it was the floor's turn, and suggestions rained; a pledge-signing meeting, a fresh-air society, a Junior monthly paper, and a Bible sword-drill. A number of public-school teachers testified as to how the Junior society helps to make more obedient pupils.

Miss Elizabeth W. Olney's paper on Bands of Mercy left no excuse for thoughtless cruelty on the part of Juniors. She would have rescue homes for summer cats in the summer, and sand on the icy pavements in winter. The Junior superintendent that gets Miss Olney's paper in the official report will have a magazine of suggestions that will last for years.

That connecting link between Juniors and Seniors, the Intermediates, had a worthy representative in Miss Ida Cook, of Pittsburg. Allegheny County, Penn., is the citadel of Intermediate work.

"Get within reach of the boy," advised Mr. William Shaw in telling how to get hold of boys. Get his love. Don't be forever saying "Don't" to the boys. Give them something to do. Boys are hero-worshipers. That is why Buffalo Bill is a saint with some boys. If they could be given John G. Paton, Jacob Chamberlain, and Dr. Ament to read, they would idolize them. Mr. Shaw pleaded for the freckle-faced, pug-nosed, out-at-the-knees boy.

If all Junior missionary meetings were conducted according to the ideas of Rev. George W. Pollock, president of the West Virginia Union, our Juniors would be on fire with missionary zeal. He would have the Juniors study countries. He would have the Junior superintendent read missionary books, and tell the Juniors about them in such a way as to make them fall in love with the romance of missions.

Ammunition for Junior workers was hoisted on deck by Mr. George B. Graff, publisher of the United Society. It must have been a surprise to many to learn what a wealth of printed material there is for Junior workers.

From the floor, again, came a volume of bright suggestions. Rev. G. H. Hubbard, of China, told of a good-roads committee that picked loose stones out of the roads. The illustrated lectures on birds, furnished free by the Audubon Society, were heartily commended for humane work.

Shall we go back to the catechism? The trustees have expressed a desire that the Juniors get the benefit of the catechetical drill that made their grandfathers brawny saints. Field Secretary, Clarence E. Eberman told how to do it. Set apart five minutes, and study to make it the brightest five minutes of the meeting. The memory is the biggest faculty a child has between certain ages; employ it in this way. Mr. Eberman would have the pastor take charge of the catechetical period. He would have the boys and girls in separate classes, and set each to emulating the other by answer contests, stimulated by prizes.

In another meeting, Miss Margaret Koch, Maine's gifted Junior superintendent, gave splendid suggestions for training our successors, among which were the following: The Junior superintendent can give to her Juniors nothing greater than herself. The boys and girls will learn more through her personally than through what she may say. How shall we train the boys and girls? Teach them to listen. Get them to sit straight. If you get them to listen with the chest you will be sure then that you have got hold of the heart, and life. Get each one of the society all round to tell what good thought they got out of the meeting. In that way you create a generous spirit, and an atmosphere that will help them to grow. Teach them to feel. Get hold of their heart.

THE JUNIOR ROUND TABLE.

At the Junior headquarters, the First English Lutheran Church, Mrs. Clark conducted on Monday afternoon a delightful and most instructive discussion of live Junior themes. Two hundred earnest Junior superintendents were there, and every one took part in answering the questions printed in the programs, or in propounding new ones. It was a free-and-easy affair. Every one could talk as long as she desired, and no one desired to talk longer than two minutes.

How to secure reverence was one of the subjects discussed at some length. "Get the pastor to preach upon it," suggested some one. "And he might well preach to the older Christians on the same subject," added another.

Ways of signing the pledge so as to make certain that the children know just what they are doing, were helpfully told. Many encouraging testimonies were given in answer to the question, "How has the pledge helped the girls and boys?" It had led some of them to read the Bible regularly. Others are behaving better in school. Others that were reported had been able to bring about a better religious life at home.

Of course the boy question came up; it always does. Probably the majority sentiment was, that to win and hold the boys a young man is needed for Junior superintendent or as assistant, or at least to come in occasionally to talk to the society; but many of the Junior workers thought it easily possible for women to "be boys with the boys," and win them by hearty sympathy with their boy natures.

These are only samples of the very practical themes discussed, and the very practical way in which they were treated.

CHAPTER X.

Catechetical Instruction.

Field Secretary C. E. Eberman.

The Board of Trustees, of the United Society of Christian Endeavor, composed of representative men from the various Evangelical Churches, at a meeting nearly two years ago, unanimously adopted the resolution which commended the introduction of the Catechism into the meetings of the Junior Society.

This resolution, however, involved more than the Question and Answer method of teaching the Bible, for the evident purpose was to suggest the training of the children in Christian doctrine, and especially to familiarize them with the Catechism of their individual Church denominations.

We are coming to see, more and more, that the method of inculcating Christian doctrine, as devised and pursued by our fathers, had very much in it to commend, and that the neglecting of it in our present day, has weakened Christian culture.

Foundation work cannot begin too soon, and we can easily find instances today, of strong and stalwart Christian character, the beginnings of which reach far back to the time and the methods when the children were taught in the home and in the Church to memorize Bible texts and truths, and the doctrines of the Church, whether in Bible language or in words and expressions covering those truths.

The resolution adopted by the Trustees of the United Society suggested that five or ten minutes of each weekly meeting be devoted to the work of training and drilling the children in the Church Catechism, not, however, to the exclusion of other essential features of the Junior Society.

That this suggestion was a wise and timely one is proven by the commendation which it has received from different Churches, especially from those who have distinctive Catechisms, and who use them in connection with Bible Study and Confirmation Classes.

Personally, I have felt the need of just such early work, for in my own Church, we have a Catechism which forms the basis of Bible study and the study of Christian doctrine, in the weekly meetings, at which are gathered those who have signified a desire to confess Jesus Christ, and to join His Church. We certainly would have better results if these young persons came to the meetings, already familiar with these truths, and the work of the pastor would be to enter upon a fuller and more personal explanation of the questions and answers.

The practical question then is, "How to use the Catechism in the Junior Society?"

1. Introduce the Catechism into the Junior Society meeting, by setting apart five or ten minutes for this purpose, and have the time regular and bright, so that the children may know when to expect the period, and to eagerly look forward to it.

2. It might be well to begin with some simple record of Bible truths and history, especially of the life of Christ. Such primal Question-and-Answer books are usually issued by Church publication concerns. The United Society, I think, publishes such a booklet. This introductory method would not be found as difficult as the usual Church Catechism, and it will serve to fix the general knowledge and the historical features of the Bible as a basis for subsequent study.

3. But the introduction of the Church Catechism would speedily follow and the study of it should be made as interesting and attractive as possible. The pastor has, here, an opportunity, which is invaluable, that of coming in close and vital relation with the children of his congregation. Of course in the selection of the proper Catechism, the pastor should be

consulted, but, in addition to this, I knew of no one better qualified to conduct this period, than the pastor, who adapts himself to the needs of the smallest member of his flock, for he can begin a training, which he may follow up, until the child becomes the confessing Christian, asking for admission to the communicant Church-fellowship.

4. It may be necessary for some churches to adapt their Catechisms for use among the youngest children, or to abridge them, but this need can only be met by the action of the individual Church authorities. It might also be well to incorporate a brief outline of Church history, so that the future men and women of the Church may be familiar with the history of their own denomination. Intelligent Church loyalty can be based upon the knowledge of what the Church stands for, what it has done, what it teaches, and how God has honored it in the past.

5. I believe that it is also good to expect positive memory-work, as a basis for future intelligent conception of Christian doctrine. Memory-work is certainly not the ultimate object but it is an aid in acquiring and holding knowledge. Things learned by heart may also find permanent lodgement in the heart, and truths acquired in childhood are the last to be forgotten.

6. I am not at all averse to some moderate system of reward, merit or honor, for those who show studious and careful attention and effort. If a youthful member shows special interest, or some mastery, a little commendation, even if it is tangible, will do no harm, and will stimulate him to increased activity.

7. Arrange some system of review, quarterly or half-yearly, so as to gather up the results. A public meeting might be held, to which parents and friends could be invited, and the review can take place at this time, together with other Junior exercises. Such a meeting would emphasize the work which is being done in the Junior Society, and serve to create a wider interest.

8. In order to vary the period, I have also found it helpful to divide the Society into two parts or companies,—the girls and the boys,—in order to ascertain their relative proficiency. This always leads to a healthy rivalry, and serves to arouse flagging interest and to awaken emulation. The questions may be asked either individually or in concert.

Thus by wise and everlasting patience on the part of the superintendent, or the pastor, for, again let me say, that this is the pastor's great opportunity,—by repetition, and reiteration and judicious use of tact, illustration, and interesting explanation, we will add another helpful and blessed function to the Junior Society of Christian Endeavor, and again prove it an efficient ministering servant of the Church.

CHAPTER XI.

The Twentieth Century Society.

One of the most practical of the Convention sessions was the School of Methods, held simultaneously in Endeavor and Williston. At the first meeting Mr. George B. Graff, head of the United Society's publication department, was the appropriate and skilful presiding officer.

"A Century More of the Christian Endeavor Pledge," the first topic, was admirably handled by Rev. C. Lee Gaul, of Philadelphia.

The soldier who was to march under the Roman Eagle was inducted to his martial responsibilities and honors by taking the "sacramentum"— the solemn oath of allegiance to Caesar's cause. Marvelous courage was cultured and sacrifice endured to extend a material and military power. A Gibbon inevitably wrote "the decline and fall of the Roman Empire."

During the last 20 years of the century just closed, an unusual and unprecedented spectacle has been witnessed in the great host of Christian Endeavorers who have gathered about the standard of the Cross, to spread peace, truth and righteousness over the whole earth, to extend the reign of a spiritual and eternal kingdom.

These legions of Jesus Christ are under the obligation of "the Pledge."

WHAT IS ITS CONTENT?

This in measure ought to determine its perpetuity through the century. It is the confession of trustful dependence on Jesus. And above all our endeavoring (all our machinery never so perfect and our planning never so comprehensive) there is heard the sober voice of the God-man saying to all laborers, "without me ye can do nothing."

Note also by the analysis, the profession of an implicit obedience to the Master. The strongest life that ever devoted its successful energies to the kingdom of God said in the beginning of its service, "Lord what wilt thou have me to do?"

Do we all earnestly sing, "I'll go where you want we to go, dear Lord"?

The promise is made to daily commune with the Lord—the individual soul is exalted to that atmosphere in which the Man of Nazareth lived, whose life breathed benedictions on all its surroundings.

An important item of the contract is to "read the Bible." The spiritual babe finds milk and the strong man meat.

Instead of dallying, doubting and being ensnared by the tempter, the knowledge of the blessed will of God in the truth prompts the quick and foiling response, "It is written."

Many are being captured by erroneous doctrines and science falsely so called, but the Endeavorer by daily reading is kept in the comfort of a sound mind, and in the assurance of a strong faith. These holding aloft the torch of truth guide many into the pathway of life and will shine above the brightness of the stars for ever and ever.

A bright line in the spectrum of the Pledge is "Loyalty to the church," the vow to attend the services of the sanctuary and to personally participate in the worship. Month by month the roll call witnesses the remembrance of my solemn vow made unto the Lord.

It is worth our while to ask additionally, "What is the product of the pledge? To whom do pastors look when works of mercy and help are to be wrought—the aged sick, straying, imprisoned are to be visited and strangers are to be made welcome?

To whom do the grave officers of the church point when selection of associates or successors is to be made?

THE CHRISTIAN ENDEAVOR MUSEUM.

AUDITORIUM ENDEAVOR AT THE OPENING SESSION.

To whom does the business world pay compliment when young men are applicants for responsible position?

To whom are we looking to build homes over our land that anticipate the very happiness of heaven? Who will bring to us that higher type of Christian Citizenship our nation now needs?

To whom is Jesus looking to carry forward his great missionary enterprise and splendid evangelistic movements that mean all the world for Christ?

To Christian Endeavorers.

Shall we have a century more of Christian Endeavor pledge? Thousands of hearts in unison reply—Yes!

Dare we say "Follow me as I follow Christ?"

You who have not taken the pledge don't ask me to bring back my colors to your standing. Bring yourselves up to the Standard.

The peculiar aggressiveness and power of Carthage came as all such products do, from her leaders. Among the many proud generals who led the Punic forces against the Romans was Hamilcar. He knew the influence example and oath and brought his noble hearted son Hannibal before the altars of the national gods and made him swear eternal enmity to Rome. Against all forms of sin—the rum power, the social evil, political corruption, every enemy of the coming kingdom of God we bring ourselves and our youth. We mean to take the world for Jesus. Give us a century more of the C. E. Pledge if that time is needed to bring all in tribute to his feet.

"This is an open parliament," said Mr. H. H. Marcusson, of Chicago; "you are to open it and I am to shut it." His parliament called for "New Committee Ideas for the New Century." Some of the plans discussed were these: the Christian-citizenship work of the Providence union, which is making a hand-to-hand canvass of the voters for better citizenship; loyalty to the church; training the Juniors; late comers amazed by finding the society turned around, the leader sitting at the rear, so that as they came in they confronted faces and not backs; the emphasis of the honorary membership, the honorary members in one church serving as leaders of the mid-week prayer meeting.

President W. L. Darby, of Missouri, handled the very necessary subject of honorary membership, advocating the sensible plan that gradually withdraws the older Endeavorers from the society as they have received its training, and transforming their pledges to the work of the older church-membership.

The Point in Honorary Membership.

Rev. W. L. Darby.

Honorary membership in any organization carries with it the suspicion of age—attained or approaching. It hints that the day of active service is passed or is swiftly passing, unless, of course, some rule or circumstance forbids the activity that might otherwise be seen. Now that we have celebrated Christian Endeavor's 20th birthday it will not be thought strange that some who joined the movement in its earlier days should be near the meridian of life, and nobody's feelings will be hurt if I say that this is so. In view of this statement, which none will dispute, several serious questions arise for settlement, and about them the older East is naturally more insistent than the newer West. Among the number is one that comes before us because there is no age limit in Christian Endeavor. It was felt, and rightly, too, that the matter could well be left to itself and the good judgment of those who make up our membership. In our Constitution there is a provision for certain ones who shall be termed honorary members," but not much use has been made of it in the past. However, the time has now come when the scope of that section can be so widened as to bring inestimable benefit in its train.

Who shall constitute our honorary membership? Previously only such among the older Church members as did not care to assume the active duties of the Society, and yet wished to be identified with it in some way in order to give the younger people the assurance of their interest in its principles and purposes. That was an excellent idea, and it has no doubt been productive of good in some places; but the plan has not been tried extensively, because, perhaps, its basis was not sufficiently practical to make it of much real value. But time has now brought the question to the front, and with a larger and weightier aspect than it had before.

Dr. Clark, in one of his delightful and suggestive "Familiar Letters," has called this "The Neglected Continent of Christian Endeavor," likening it to South America. But it will soon be such no longer, for we have been compelled to explore it in order to ascertain its possibilities. It seems about to afford the solution of a vexed problem of colonization! What shall the older workers in the society do—those who have been its mainstay for so long, but who are now getting past the period of youth? Shall they withdraw or shall they remain? There is danger in either course, and we do well to recognize it. The question is a delicate one, and requires the most careful handling. The first danger is that if they keep themselves prominently to the front the younger members will be embarrassed by their constant presence or discouraged by their superior ability, so that the training that is now most needed is not secured. When this is the case is it not better for these older ones to step aside and allow their younger brothers and sisters to have the same opportunities that they have had? Is it not both selfish and wrong for any other course to be taken? The other danger is that when they do cease their connection with the society their interest in its future success will also cease. Going out into the larger work of the church (as they should) they forget about those who now need their prayerful sympathy and continued support (as they should not). Just here is the point of the honorary membership, and here its constant opportunity. If an older member feels that for the good of all he should no longer keep his name on the active roll, it will be an easy matter, indeed, for it to be transferred to the honorary list, and he can still feel that he belongs to the organization and that it demands the performance of such duties as come to him in view of the changed relationship that he holds. If such a member shows no signs of giving up his active connection, and rather clings the more tenaciously to the honors of office-holding he can be given the gentle hint that the "honorary membership" is the place for him! If he has any judgment or worth he will take the hint. If not—well! With the same marvelous wisdom and insight that he has shown from the time that the society was founded until now Dr. Clark has perfected the plan by which the dangers mentioned may be avoided. It is his idea that "honorary membership should mean something distinctive as truly as active or associate membership," so he has proposed this form of pledge:

"Trusting in the Lord Jesus Christ for strength, I promise Him that I will strive to do whatever He would like to have me do, that I will make it the rule of my life to pray and read the Bible every day, and to support my own church in every way. I promise to give aid and sympathy to my brothers and sisters in the Christian Endeavor Society in their work for Christ and the Church. As an honorary member of the society of Christian Endeavor, I promise to attend the mid-week prayer meeting of the church unless prevented by a reason which I can conscientiously give to Christ, and to enter into some definite church work to which I may be called."

This pledge is as significant for what it leaves out as for what it puts in. It is truly "the logical and natural outcome of Christian Endeavor," and it furnishes to one who does not think it best for him to remain an active member an honorable way of leaving the society and entering into the wider service of the church. The conditions imposed are not burdensome, and there is no reason why this plan of procedure should not occupy an important place in our work hereafter.

The necessity of keeping in the closest possible touch with the members of the church, and especially with its officers, should always be remembered. In some quarters the society has been accused of trying to run things according to its own sweet will in the particular church of which it was a component part. There may be an element of truth in the accusation (to which we should never lay ourselves open), but no doubt if some churches ever do get out of a slow walk it will be because the young people could not rest content at that pace, believing that "the King's business requires haste." If the officials of the church can be brought into full sympathy with us by the method of honorary membership a distinct point will have been gained. We should assure them that we not only recognize their right of control, but wish also the benefit of their assistance in whatever way it can be given. As among the hosts of armed Greeks who surrounded ancient Troy there was a place for aged Nestor with his wise advice, so we should make a place for our elders and welcome their suggestions. "Old men for counsel; young men for war" is as true in the church as anywhere else. Special favors should be shown the superintendent of the Sabbath school. He is our worthy fellow-laborer in a most noble cause, and as such deserves our cordial co-operation. By all means include him in the list, and make his place a prominent one. Once or twice a year have a special meeting for these earnest friends, and give them the opportunity of testifying in whatever way they wish. If they grow reminiscent, do not stop them; profit by their experiences. Bear ever in mind the fact that we ourselves are hastening toward the day when we shall be eligible for such membership. Let us not expect to leave the society in which God has so richly blessed us by any other way. Plan for the future. Keep the organization always young—full of youthful life and enthusiasm, ready for every good word and work. If we do not our whole purpose will not be accomplished. It is not an end in itself; it is a training school for the larger sphere of service that lies just beyond it. As such it should have your unceasing prayer and effort even though you do not maintain your active connection with it. Indeed, it will be better if you do not; let the honorary list be your goal, and honor it and God by faithful effort.

You see the point, I am sure. A right use of the plan will emphasize one of the society's chief purposes; yea, more, it will make of this class of our members a source of power and inspiration through all the days to come, and through the genuine helpfulness that it brings all our service for Him shall be made sweeter, nobler and better.

A California Endeavorer, Mr. J. M. Warren, led the open parliament on "What Are the Elements of a Strong Society?" A prayerful, spiritual atmosphere. The five-minute prayer service with the leader before the meeting. A faithful executive committee. Good officers. Systematic beneficence. Every member on some committee, and every member faithful to his committee work. A committee of young men to work with the young men and bring them into the society. Go out into the highways and hedges, doing city-missionary work. The officers train their successors. These are only a few of the wise suggestions.

"A little boy," said Mr. Graff, "was once asked what his eyes were for, and answered, 'To go to sleep by.' Now the lookout committee is the eyesight of the society; but it is not at all to go to sleep by." He was introducing the able address on "Lookout Committees that Look Out," by Ernest Edwards Brown, M. D., of Cleveland.

"Lookout Committees That Look Out."

Ernest Edwards Brown, M. D., Cleveland, O.

In all departments of Christian Endeavor work one fundamental idea is, or ought to be, predominant; namely, the training and proper development of characters unfolding in our midst. The strong, gray strand in the hand of the weaver appears now upon the surface, then is buried under threads of brighter hue; but is everywhere essential to the strength and very existence of the fabric. So character building forms the underlying, though sometimes underestimated, principle controlling all the various activities of the organization, but is plainly the one direct aim of the Lookout Committee, whose duty as laid down by the Model Constitution, is but a restatement of the object of the society.

With so broad and vital a topic it would be as impossible as it is unnecessary to attempt, in the brief time allotted, a complete synopsis of Lookout work. Those two sources of strength, Prayer and Bible Study, can receive but passing notice. Their tremendous importance has naturally, and very wisely, made them the subject of many earnest and learned discourses. We shall today merely suggest a few points which demand the frequent attention of the Lookouter who would truly lookout.

First, we must make a careful study of the individual needing assistance, learning his strength and weakness, discovering the subtle influences that have contributed to his present condition; always bearing in mind that true character study measures a man by the best within him, not by the attainments of another. This is happily accomplished if we can think his thoughts as he thinks them; scanning life, present and future, from his view-point, with little reference for the time being to our own ideals. Let us plan our spiritual maneuvers as practically and carefully as does the admiral in time of war; ever ready to change or abandon an unwise course, never willing to drift. We may be strong in faith, yet fail of the victory.

Having, then, made our study of the individual and his needs, the question always arises, "How may we best approach and influence?" The way dearest to the heart of the Christian, who has within him an unquenchable yearning for souls, is a personal conference, in which everything may be talked and prayed over; where the different standpoints may be discovered, and placed in their proper perspective; where we may ask "What would Jesus do?" This, however, may be just the wrong course to pursue. Good intentions counteracted by poor judgment have caused the alienation of many a sensitive soul. Want of tact on the one side and distorted vision on the other often result in aggravated injury. The usual avenue of approach will sometimes seem, and be, unwise. We shall not lower but raise the standard of our work if, the tried way proving unavailable, we promptly break a new path. It may be by persuasion or authority, tenderly or with force, bluntly or with the adroitness of a diplomat, personally or through an influential agent, at home or quite removed from familiar surroundings! Whenever, wherever, and however the opportunity arises to become an embassador, we must bring to bear all the power of a God-given personality; all the wisdom and judgment of a broad education; then, in trustful dependence upon the King of kings, may we lead a younger or weaker brother, though we be but humble followers.

Perhaps new emphasis given in the prayer-meeting causes the vibration of chords long silent. Or we may seek the assistance of close companions, earnest perhaps, but blind to the fact that one of their number is falling behind spiritually. Cannot a lookouter awaken these chums, thus securing the co-operation of that grandest human element, the influence of a personal friend?

Effective, but seldom recognized, is the method of stirring a dormant nature by sending the weak member, together with one strong in the work, to another society. Here a different atmosphere and manner of thought-expression is often more impressive than would be the case in the home meeting, where the whole program is so stereotyped that it can almost be predicted.

Sometimes, too, a diffident nature loses self-consciousness in the enthusiasm of the broader Christian fellowship; and, once having experienced the blessing of confessing Christ before men, the act becomes a habit.

Many an Endeavorer hesitates to speak his noblest thoughts, because his life's record, known to the listeners, is inconsistent with the utterance. Away from home, freed from these restraints, the thought is put into words; and his own words, if sincere, mean more to him than the most eloquent sermon. He now has a new standard for future actions. instead of allowing, unconsciously, his past history to control what he dares to say.

These are not theories without foundation, but practical points demonstrated time and again. Not infrequently members have been transformed by such a process, mediocre workers becoming the best that our great system of Christian education develops.

Of course this department of Lookout work is most easily carried on in conjunction with a Union Committee, such as Lookout, Fellowship, or Visiting; but the absence of Union assistance need not dampen the ardor of the local Committee. It is an easy matter to make a general survey of the societies in a neighborhood, whether city or country, and arrange visits accordingly. Energy and perseverance are necessary here as in every department of life, but the results certainly justify a large expenditure of both.

This train of thought closes naturally with a danger signal. Take care! Be on the Lookout, as well as on the Lookout Committee! Pardon a personal illustration.

While passing a newly opened street after nightfall, I noticed a red lantern casting a distinct shadow in the gleam of the strong electric light overhead. The thought came, "Do we sometimes by our imperfect equipment interfere with the pure light from above?" The next morning I directed the sun's rays across a common gas flame, and again found a well defined shadow, on the wall. Are we not, as Christian workers, in danger of intercepting some rays from the Sun of Righteousness, by the very flicker of the candle with which we are striving to illuminate our neighbor's path?

An idiosyncrasy or personal bias sometimes casts a shadow. This, however, is as nothing compared to the obscuring 'inconsistency of a life that shines in the prayer-meeting but not at home. If only we will put aside the imperfections and impurities of this earth-made light, and reflect or transmit the pure light, heaven-born, we shall be one step nearer the foot of the Cross, where alone we may look out for a fellow being.

Pastors That Lead.

Rev. Edwin S. Shaw, Wahpeton, N. D.

This does not mean, I take it, pastors that lead the meetings, for that is contrary to the spirit and purpose of Christian Endeavor. The pastor should not do anything that he can get anyone else to do, first, because he will still have enough to do, and second, because he will thus best fulfil the purpose of Christian Endeavor by training Christian workers.

It does mean pastors that lead their Young People's Society in their efforts to realize their motto, "For Christ and the Church."

Three points suggest themselves; driving, guiding, leading.

1. It is not worth while to stop long on the first. You may drive a horse, but you cannot long drive a Christian Endeavor Society made up of intelligencies—individuals with reason and freedom of choice—who think and act for themselves. The pastor who undertakes to drive his society. will find it like David Harum's horse. It will stand without hitching. I once had an experience with a man, who was intrusted with some business matters in which I was interested. He would not act. I reasoned

with him; I coaxed him! all to no avail. At last I threatened to apply the law, and he replied with considerable feeling: "I won't be druv." The twentieth century Endeavor Society won't be druv, and it ought not to be. If it will, I should say of it, as one man said of another, who was being pitied because he was hen-pecked: "If a man will be hen-pecked, he ought to be."

2. Among teamsters, this expression is used: "A teamster is worth his weight on the load." Not riding, but guiding; not idle, but every faculty in use. He can guide the team, avoiding the rocks and the ruts, so the pastor is worth his weight as a guide to the young people. He sees beside the Christian Endeavor Society all the other departments of work, their relation to each other, and their relation to the whole, and with a steady, guiding hand, he avoids the rocks of offense, and the ruts of disaster. The guiding process is for the ordinary road. At times he may wisely "give the horse his head."

3. But there comes a time when the horse will neither be driven nor guided. He is at a standstill. The way is dark and untried; the footing insecure. Then the teamster must get down from his load, go around to the head, explore the path—if he know it not—then gently holding the rein, lead the way. Few horses who know their leader will refuse to follow where he leads. Jesus, the great leader's strength, lies in the fact that he asks us to follow him. "Where he leads, I'll follow," is the response of every truly surrendered life.

The Student Volunteer Movement revolutionized missionary work because Student Volunteers went from college to college, and said to the young men and women, not "Go" to the foreign field, but: "Come with us."

Like priest, like people is true in Christian Endeavor as elsewhere. The twentieth century pastor-leader, will lead by setting his Endeavorers an example in:

(a) Piety—a devotional life.
(b) Righteousness—right living and right dealings.
(c) Intelligence—investigating, proving all things, holding fast that which is good.
(d) Enthusiasm—a holy zeal, born of the Spirit.
(e) Steadfastness—"Stickability."
(f) Thoroughness—whatever is worth doing, is worth doing well.

Then he will be, as the first letters of the Christian Endeavor words indicate: a true priest, a true leader.

Colonel E. G. Osgood, President of the Vermont Christian Endeavor Union, discussing "Prayer-Meeting Committees that Plan," advised that prayer-meeting committees organize with a vice-chairman to take the chairman's place in his absence, and a secretary to keep careful records; also, that each member of the committee should be given one or more meetings in his personal charge. Very wisely, also, he urged that the Endeavorers plan also for the church prayer meeting, and help in it all they can. He described a chain meeting, carefully planned so that the members should take part in a regular order, with an arranged progression of thought.

For his own sake, and for the sake of his noble father, the Endeavorers gave a hearty welcome to Mr. William R. Moody. His topic was "Your Testimony in the Meeting." He reminded the Endeavorers that upon each one of them rests Christ's command to His disciples that they should be living witnesses to the truth, and he went on to develop the character of the true witness.

One point he emphasized was the avoidance of cant, "that abomination in the sight of God." The first thing to which a witness is sworn is to tell the truth. "I find it very hard," said a young man to an old one, "to express what I feel." "As you grow older," answered the old man, "you will meet a greater difficulty,—to feel what you express."

The closing half-hour of this most profitable session was occupied by a new feature, a "Christian Endeavor Round Table," conducted by Dr. Clark. Five pages of questions were printed in the back of the program, and the Endeavorers answered them, asking other questions prompted by them, maintaining a brisk fire of discussion, in the course of which a host of valuable plans were pithily described. This animated form of open parliament will undoubtedly be permanently adopted in our Conventions.

CHAPTER XII.

More Practical Methods for the Twentieth Century Christian Endeavor Society.

It was "Twentieth Century" day in Williston auditorium, too, and with Prof. James Lewis Howe, of Lexington, Va., in the chair, and the watchwords "Expansion" and "Development" put in the fore by Dr. Clark, both audience and speakers vied with each other in suggesting betterments for the society.

No more vital topic could be named than that on which Miss Margaret Koch spoke, "Training Our Successors." It was a wise saying that, first of all, we must train the Juniors how to listen. We must teach them to sit erect and listen with their spines and chests and eyes. We must teach them to feel what they say and pray and sing, and to do this we must ourselves feel what we say to them.

Ex-President W. H. Ball, of the Philadelphia Union had the important task of coaxing the audience to tell what improvements they would like to see in the Endeavor Society. That Endeavorers want lots of improvements argues well for the future. "A larger use of the word of God," spoke up a voice. "Less reading, and more speaking and praying." Said another, "I would rather hear a member speak one word out of his own heart than read a page from the best author." "More definite aims and less shooting in the air," was the last suggestion to get through before the time gates were closed.

If Mr. E. G. Routzahn's good advice had been taken literally, in regard to "What Can Be Done with Good Literature?" the Christian Endeavor and denominational literature tables in the hall would have been cleaned out as by a horde of grasshoppers, and the agent for The Christian Endeavor World would have worn his pencil to a stub recording new subscriptions.

What Can Be Done with Good Literature.

E. G. Routzahn, Dayton, O.

We have ten minutes in which to discuss a phase of Endeavor activity which affects the efficiency of every officer, every committee-member, every Endeavorer.

In considering so extended a field we must take it for granted that you understand the why and wherefore, and that you appreciate the intimate relationship between the printed paper and cardboard on the one hand, and the Endeavorer and the Endeavor Society on the other. Believing that any lack in its use in the past was due to limited information as to materials and methods we confine this paper strictly to a simple working outline. With no effort to be original or unique, ideal or eloquent, we offer a specific and workable plan of campaign for general acceptance during and following the convention.

Literature or printed matter serves a three-fold purpose in the provision of ideas and inspiration for the worker, of information and instruction about the work, and of implements and ingredients for use in the work by the worker.

Some societies have no committee in charge of this work, and others have but names—shadowy and mournful suggestions of what has been or what might have been.

In either case we urge somewhat the following programme:—

First, and by all means, be yourself a committee on investigation and exploration. Travel up and down the fronts of the two booths facing Hall Endeavor examining every book, leaflet and card so that you may learn its nature and scope. Buy if you choose, but do not fail to examine. Accept as personal conductor one of the willing attendants, or plunge in boldly without invitation, permission or further persuasion.

Second, make a similar visit to the denominational exhibits on the second floor. If your own church is not represented avail yourself of the opportunity of locating a few nuggets of value for use in the future.

Third, make a persistent, systematic effort to get every delegate from your Society and your Union to do likewise.

Fourth. If not already a subscriber, or a regular reader of the Christian Endeavor World, surely the next step is to turn to page 64 of the official programme and obey the injunction of the first line, so that you may be sure to receive the Endeavor World, a great wealth of material so complete in itself that, added to your Bible and your own denominational paper, you possess practically all of the information, inspiration, instruction absolutely necessary for the highest degree of efficiency in church, Sunday School, Christian Endeavor, and other lines of effort.

Fifth. Go home and organize or re-organize a Literature Committee, or be a Committee till a working organization can be secured in your Society and your Union.

Sixth. The Society literature work may be cared for by a regularly authorized Committee; or the Vice-President may be placed in charge of the press, literature and information work; or the Information Committee may have its field of labor enlarged in this direction; or one member in every Committee may be selected to make up the Committee; or the Missionary or some other existing Committee may care for the work; or see that your own Committee does its own proper share of literature work—every Committee can and must do some of it; or the President or some other interested worker—this means you—the delegate in the Convention from your Society—will take up this work till the time when such a Committee can be duly organized.

Seventh. Turn to page 57 of the Convention programme and accept the dictum of the two lower lines. When you receive the response, read it, and pass it on, and on, and on, till it falls to pieces and refuses further service.

Eighth. Decide to spend five cents, ten cents, or better, thirty-five cents a month, a quarter, or even every year, in buying choice printed helps for your personal use as officer, committee-worker or member. Present yourself once or twice a year with one of the Workers' Library series at thirty-five cents, or one on the Christian Endeavor Booklet series at ten cents.

Ninth. After reaching home be sure to write to your own church Sunday School and Mission Boards for lists and samples of leaflets and periodicals, offering to co-operate towards securing a larger circulation of the same.

Tenth. And in brief, do something—do it now—keep on doing it—get some one else to do something—keep them doing it—then add another to the number of active helpers in this work.

Time will not permit of reading a detailed classified list of the splendid array of material edited by Dr. Clark, Caleb Cobweb and others, but mention will be made of a few choice bits selected here and there.

For the Prayer-Meeting Committee secure "Our Crowning Meeting" and the leaflets "How to Lead" and "Hints on Taking Part." These leaflets should be placed in the hands of every member.

The Lookout Committee should be provided with "On the Lookout."

Hang up a big-type copy of the pledge, and see that every member possesses a copy of the pledge card.

Co-operate with the Missionary Committee in using the missionary reading slips, arrange a simple circulating library of leaflets and pamphlets, purchase one of the missionary libraries, work out a series of scrapbooks classified by countries and topics, and so on. Note the series of two-cent leaflets, "Home Life in Lands Not Christian," to be seen at the missionary exhibit.

For the Junior Committee no better service can be offered than to contrive in some fashion to provide a library of helps—at least get the Junior Manual at seventy-five cents.

Citizenship, Temperance and Sabbath Committees should possess "Weapons for Temperance Warfare" and "Citizens in Training." Address Rev. W. F. Crafts, Washington, D. C., for suggestive material. Gather leaflets and clippings, place in envelopes and loan to your members. For citizenship work in which both young men and young women may share, which will not "get you into politics"—till you are prepared, which is elementary and preparatory to bigger things, and which will really show results, see "The Work of Civic Improvement" and "The How of Improvement Work" at the literature booths (National League of Improvement Associations, Springfield, Ohio, for twenty-five cents).

The Tenth Legioners have a rich literature from which to select. Write Layman, 310 Ashland Avenue, Chicago, and your Mission Boards.

Provide the Relief Committee with readers for the sick and the "shut-ins." Follow the example of the Cuban tobacco workers and send readers to work rooms where such a plan is feasible.

Back up the Sunday School Committee in making the Sunday School library a success. See that helpful Bible study and other reference helps are secured. Enlist the boys as King's Messengers in connection with the Home Department, sending out missionary and choice secular reading.

Insist that the Executive Committee study the Officers' Handbook—and many problems will no longer puzzle your Society.

The Social Committee cannot have an unsocial social if "Social to Save" and "Social Evenings" are applied with fair proportions of sanctified common-sense and good hard work. Have a literature social, a book show, a press reception.

Humane workers will of course write to Miss E. W. Olney, Providence, R. I., and to Geo. T. Angell, Boston, Mass. "Pets and Animals," Springfield, Ohio, is well worth sending for.

Tell the Mothers' Society of the Mary Wood-Allen leaflets about boy-life, and of the material prepared specially for mothers' meetings.

For evangelistic work no better plan can be followed than to send twenty-five cents to H. B. Gibbud, Springfield, Mass., for samples of his varied and novel "weapons."

For the disposal of good magazines and other periodicals—which should never be sold as old paper—get "Pass It On" for two cents at the literature booth, ask Y. M. C. A., New York, how to direct matter to reach the soldiers and sailors, address your Church Boards, or write to Literature Exchange, C. E. Union, Chicago. Be sure to use some of these papers in your home town.

Solicit subscriptions for your church papers and for the C. E. World. Circulate samples and circulars, read extracts in meetings, mention special offers.

Suggest to some local dealer that at least the more important C. E. and mission supplies be carried in stock, promise to buy some yourself, and urge others to do the same.

This last is also work for the local and county Union. Every Union officer should own and study "Our Unions," which tells all about them.

The Union may also inaugurate a traveling library, send one leaflet a month to every Society in the Union, and place one of your most reliable workers in charge of the Union press work.

Plan to co-operate with your local public library, place the C. E. World in the public reading room, and if you have no such institution set about getting one. In almost any State you can secure a choice traveling library for the express charges two ways. Push the Book a Month plan and otherwise aid in directing the secular reading of the young people.

Include the Press Committee with the literature management. Get some High School young people to care for this, if possible securing some newspaper man as advisory chairman. Watch for real news—the items people want to read—make them bright, brief and breezy. Write on one side of the sheet, and double the chances of acceptance by using the typewriter. Study your papers and shape matter accordingly. Seek personal acquaintance with reporters. Get the news bulletin from the United Society. Send news items and samples of all printed matter issued by your Society to your denominational papers. Send five cents to Woman's Temperance Publishing Association, Chicago, for six leaflets, and another five cents to Miss Reed, North Pennsylvania Street, Indianapolis, for "Points for Press Workers."

A few don'ts:—Don't give a paper, leaflet or book when it can be loaned. Don't waste any legitimate printed matter—loan, send or give to some one. Don't fail to buy all you can of your own denominational publishing house. Don't use tracts—use leaflets, or pamphlets, or extracts, or —anything but "tracts." Don't fail to do something.

Social Committees That Are Social.

Mr. Alexander E. Matheson, Janesville, Wis.

In speaking upon the subject, "Social Committees That Are Social," there is a suggestion that there are Social Committees that are not "social"; and, if this be true, there are Social Committees that are not doing the work for which they have been appointed. Our purpose is, briefly, to make some observations upon the importance of the Social Committee and the means for increasing its effectiveness as a factor in Christian Endeavor life.

We are all more or less social by nature. We all long for companionship, and our characters are largely indicated by the quality of our companionship. We are made better or we are injured through our social relations, and we are constantly influencing others as we meet them.

The Young Men's Christian Association makes a great deal of its comradeship. Indeed, this is the principal method for making the forces of this Association useful in the service of Christ.

Effectiveness in Church work depends upon fellowship and sociability. The minister may prepare and preach the finest sermons, but, unless he comes into close social contact with his hearers, little or no fruitage will result from such preaching. It may seem to some that the minister does his most important work in preaching his sermons. The sermons may take a considerable part of his time in preparation and delivery, but the real work of the preacher is done as he meets men and women and children in homes, at Church gatherings, and generally throughout the community.

We make our lives useful and effective through this spirit of sociability and neighborly kindness, by friendly greetings, and by acts of sympathy and love. These are the means by which we make ourselves helpful in the best way. Such things may not be widely heralded; they may not be accompanied by shouts, the blare of trumpets, and great eclat; but they are no less serviceable in Christ's growing kingdom.

This spirit must be in the Young People's Society of Christian Endeavor. If the meetings are to be other than cold and formal, if the work is not to be stereotyped and characterized by spiritual inertia, the spirit of fellowship and comradeship must predominate in all the gatherings of Endeavor activity.

Let us not delude ourselves with the thought that our success, socially, depends upon the quality of our ice cream, the color of our lemonade, or the abundance at our suppers. "Angels' Food" is not always evidence of the presence of angels. These things may be necessary as means to an end, but of greatest service is the spirit of the gatherings, and that spirit must be the spirit of love, or no permanent results will follow.

Formality should not in any way enter into the socials or other meetings of a society. Formality is deadening; it is without heart and, therefore, cannot reach the hearts of the young people. It is hardly necessary to add that Social Committees must aim to break up the gathering of young people into cliques, and they must see to it that there are no lines of social cleavage. Any tendency to condescension is quickly recognized by a man or woman of character. In other words, Social Committees cannot hope for success, "Social Committees cannot be social," unless all their plans and all the gatherings under their auspices are without hypocrisy, dissimulation, or insincerity, and are characterized by real fellowship.

I shall not say that the Social Committee is the most important, but I will say that it is as important as any other Committee. Formal rules are apt to be injurious. The moment we commence to prescribe formal precepts, we are becoming heartless and unsocial, and we are losing the spirit of social fellowship and brotherly love. The real gentleman need spend but little time in the study of rules of etiquette, and the real lady is prompted to act the part of a lady without the help of these published suggestions and talks for their benefit. The real gentleman, with common sense, with the spirit of love, need not fear to enter the ranks of any society. Thus it is with those who plan for the social work of an Endeavor Society. They do not need formal rules; they need the spirit of Christ, and, having this, they will know what to do.

Christ, as He went and came on earth, was bound by no formalities. He despised cant, pretense, hypocrisy, insincerity, and formalism. He needed not the rules of etiquette, for His pure spirit was an absolute guide to Him. Wherever He mingled He was at ease and assumed the place of true leadership. Let us, as Social Committees and as members in general, study this rich life that we may catch Christ's spirit, and, with that spirit, go forth with faith and hope, and absolute assurance of success.

The saying, "Money talks," was exemplified in a new way in the conference on "How Do You Raise Your Money?" The first response seemed to meet with general approval,—"We raise our money by giving it." On the question, "How do you use it?" the answers were more various, and some of them astonishingly good. One society gave one thousand dollars to missions, and another thousand for local church-work. Another supported workers in India and China, and gave five hundred dollars toward a parsonage.

It was not enough to glance into the twentieth century with the naked eye; so a telescope was brought into requisition, and President Kirbye of the South Carolina Union was the first to tell what he saw the pledge might mean in the new century.

What Our Pledge May Mean in the New Century.

Rev. J. Edward Kirbye, Charleston, S. C.

A delightful story is told concerning the best known of Raphael's famous Madonnas. Bernardo, a pious hermit lived in one of the quiet valleys of Italy. He was greatly loved by everybody. He taught the children to read and write, and was kind in sickness. His cabin was near a large oak that sheltered him from the heat of the summer and from the blasts of wind in the winter. He claimed two friends. One was the vine dresser's daughter who lived near, and the other was the shading oak. He called the little girl his talking friend, and the oak his mute friend. A great storm swept over the valley one day and the little cabin was threatened with destruction. While the wind was swaying the branches of the tree, and the little cabin walls were creaking, it seemed that he heard a voice. The oak seemed to say, "Come up among my branches and you will be saved." It seemed prophetic and he heeded. The cabin was swept away, but in the huge branches of the tree he was safe. The vine dresser's daughter came soon after the storm and took him to her home and cared for him tenderly. The last wish of the old man was, that both these friends might be glorified together.

The pledge is the mute friend of the Christian Endeavorer. The winds of criticism may blow against it, but the young Christian is safe if he follows what it seems to say. The other friend of the old man finally became a woman and the mother of two boys. Raphael passing them one day stopped to gaze, and then taking a piece of a board that had been sawed from a limb of the old oak, produced a sketch which soon after became the celebrated Madonna.

We are all weak at the beginning of the Christian life. Our two friends then help us in the way. The pledge of the Christian Endeavor stimulated me to give my first testimony, Christ helped me in giving it, and that sent me into the ministry.

What May the Pledge Mean in the New Century?

The pledge may mean more of an emphasis on the daily Christian life. The complaint is far-reaching that family worship is becoming a thing of the past; that this mighty spiritual force that moulded the home-life into symmetry and strength is now pushed aside because of the cares and responsibilities of an active business career. The prophetic warning is undoubtedly sane.

But it cannot be true in Christian Endeavor ranks if the spirit of fidelity possesses its membership. And the accumulated experience of some years confirms my conviction that loyalty to the pledge was never stronger or more potent than now.

The pledge opens a great opportunity to the discouraged pastor. If it is true that young people are not as devout as were their fathers, an obedience to the requirements of the pledge in the spirit of love will solve the perplexing problem. Nothing can be more specific and far-reaching that the words, "I promise to pray and read the Bible every day."

The pledge may mean a solution to the problem of the Sunday evening service. Pastors are discouraged everywhere. Churches with large memberships have a scattered handful at night. There is a church within a few blocks of the church which I recently served that has a membership of nearly six hundred. The Sunday evening congregation will average about fifty or seventy-five, perhaps. A recent pastor became so discouraged that in the morning service he would announce that if it rained or threatened rain at night the service would be dismissed.

The case is not exceptional. The complaint is widespread. Occasionally a denominational journal will tell you of a successful Sunday evening service, perhaps one in New York, Brooklyn or Chicago, but they only do this about once per year, for the discouragement of the hundreds who are not so successful. I think that Sunday evening services are largely failures because the preachers think they must attract the multitude, so that standing room will be at a premium. God should have his way. If the preacher cannot attract the multitude, he can with a Christian Endeavor Society make his Sunday evening service delightfully helpful to the spiritual life of the membership and the church. The pledge may mean a solution, if the pastor is willing to work with the comparative few instead of seeking to impress the absent multitude by prolonged discussion and sighs of regret. The author of Black Rock says, "One value of work is not that crowds stare at it."

The pledge may mean an intelligent Christian testimony, the Christian Endeavor has always stood for this.

Our machinery is such as will produce this result. The subject for a meeting and consideration of it by thought and prayer, tends toward the production of an intelligent type of piety. The helps and suggestions given in our representative paper are indispensable if we wish to obtain the best results.

We believe that friendship with God is absolutely necessary. Prof. Henry C. King in a recent book says, "A condition of any deepening friendship is expression. The psychological law is unmistakable. Consciousness is naturally impulsive; every idea tends to pass into act. Only through expression does any psychical state get its full significance. And on the other hand that which is not expressed dies." Do you wonder at dwarfed spiritual lives, when expression of Christ is discouraged or denied?

One of the great spiritual needs of our age is an emphasis on Christian testimony. I have but very little sympathy with the idea that you can make intelligent Christian piety by a relief of all responsibility. We hear it said, that the pledge tends to make religion a matter that you wear upon your sleeve. What do the objectors mean when they cry for an open door and large liberties? Generally they mean nothing at all. It means that young people are to be admitted to our ranks without conception of what trust in Christ means. Now I believe that the door of the church should be as wide as the gate of heaven, but I do not believe that anyone has a right to say that the pledge is a barrier. The specific requirements are a help. The pledge like the oak of Bernardo shelters when you are weak. The society will lose its vitality when honest, earnest testimony ceases to be given. It is the best leaven in the church today.

Christianity has made its greatest strides when there has been an emphasis on testimony. The efficacy of the preaching of the disciples in apostolic times was not due to the syllogism. Religion was a matter of experience. They demonstrated its truthfulness by unselfishness and the pouring out of love in praise. Study any great revival period. You have never heard of one while the church was indifferent. I have never seen a revival except where fervent Christian testimony was given. What was the secret of the Wesley's movement in England? Wherever these preachers went they organized classes, and the condition of membership was evidence of a regenerate heart by a fervent testimony. England was literally afire with the enthusiasm. Salvation became the chief topic of conversation. The spirit is illustrated by an anecdote related by Alfred Tennyson. He had gone to visit the home of a Methodist family. On arrival, he asked for the news when the old lady replied: "Why, Mr. Tennyson, there's only one piece of news that I know, and that is that Christ died for all men." Mr. Tennyson replied, "That is old news and new news and good news." One of our best interpreters of history has said that the Wesleyan revival saved England from the experiences of the French Revolution. I trust that the time will never come when we discourage Christian testimony. If we want to produce the most intelligent type of piety that the world has ever seen, let us insist on fidelity to the requirements of the pledge. Faithful obedience to the pledge is the seed that will cause beautiful flowers of holiness to blossom in the gardens of our lives.

The Christian Endeavor pledge is on probation no longer. Pastors and workers have had time to test its practicability. We have noted whether it was a barrier or a blessing to the young people. As a worker the pledge has my unqualified endorsement. I have seen young men and young women without Christian stability, timid, scarcely able at first to read a verse of Scripture, learn to pray and speak intelligently, and it was plainly evident that there was a development of the spiritual faculties as well, and more of a likeness of Christ. If we would strengthen Christian Endeavor from within, we have the means at our command.

When William the Conqueror was about to go on some important campaign, it is said that he called his officers around him and lifting his hands above his head, would ask them to place their hands between his own and say, "We place our hands between your hands to be your true men and loyal for this campaign."

The pledge has taken the hands of many a timid disciple and placed them between the King's hands where they have promised to be loyal and true. And as we stand here today under the benediction of this mute friend, let us remember that it is to the Christian Endeavor Society what the majestic oak was to Bernardo. Oh, that our mute friend with Christ might be glorified in this new century.

The second eye to look through the lenses was that of a skilled expert in solving Christian Endeavor and Christian-citizenship problems, and competent, therefore, to tell how Christian Endeavor can make good citizens—President R. V. Hunter, of the Indiana Union.

How May We Manufacture Christian Endeavor Citizens?

Rev. R. V. Hunter, D. D., Indianapolis, Ind.

To be an Endeavorer is to be a follower of Jesus Christ. A citizen is one who has a right to participate in the affairs of government and a right to its protection and privileges. By changing the form of our title, but not the meaning, we may state it thus: We may have a citizen who is a follower of the Son of God by having Christian homes. We need something of the old time family religion. Parents frequently turn the religious instruction of their children over to the Sabbath school. This instruction ordinarily is of a diluted form; often inferior persons, intellectually, are employed as teachers. Others fairly intelligent along other lines, have little knowledge of God's word, and have a limited Christian experience to draw from. There are conscientious and superior teachers, but they are the exception. In order to manufacture "Christian Endeavor citizens" it will be necessary for more parents to erect, or resurrect, the family altar and give personal supervision to the religious instruction of their own children.

We may "manufacture Christian Endeavorers" by raising the standard of Sabbath school work. The International Sabbath School Lesson plan has become a back number. It is unscientific. We need to re-organize the methods of Sunday school Bible study, so that intelligent teachers may be attracted. Some sort of normal training is in order. The church must contemplate the children more in its services. Let the Biblical standard of citizenship be intelligently, proportionately and patriotically preached to the young and to the old alike. The Christian Endeavor societies themselves ought to make more of practical Christian citizenship. The obligations of right thinking men to attend the primaries and to vote for the very best candidates for office regardless of party lines sometimes, is essential; they must insist upon the fearless enforcement of law. A good citizen will remember to keep the "Sabbath Day holy;" to curtail the debasing influence of liquor and to stand like a rock against enterprises which injure his fellowmen and dishonor his Master.

If our young people are thoroughly indoctrinated in the principles of the Christian religion, and in the fundamentals of an enlightened patriotism, then given practical exercise along the lines of good citizenship, we will have a generation of "Christian Endeavor citizens." In proportion as we train up young men and young women to become such, will we have multitudes willing to go into the by-paths, both at home and abroad, to bring about that condition when "all shall know Him from the least even unto the greatest."

Mr. Baer's "round table" was a unique feature. The questions were printed in the program, with blanks beneath for answers. Judging from the way in which the answers sparkled, they had been hewed out and planed down and sandpapered.

This liveliest of round tables was followed by a fitting climax to such a practical session, Rev. Richard W. Lewis's address on "An Arm Like God's."

CHAPTER XIII.

The Forward Look of Christian Endeavor.

Rev. R. W. Lewis, Denver, Colo.

I.—OUR TWENTIETH CENTURY BATTLES.

If in the twentieth century the battle of Gog and Magog is not to be fought, nevertheless the moral battlefields of this hundred years will go down to posterity as unsurpassed for valor in previous human history. And who knows but that Christian Endeavor has come to the kingdom for such a time as this? We believe that it has, and by a most wise Providence.

But if the greatest battles are to be fought, the best soldiers, with the best arms will be needed, for we are to undertake that of which the Psalmist speaks in Psalms 10: 15, "Break thou the arm of the wicked and the evil man: seek out his wickedness until thou find none." Before undertaking so great a task we may well enquire of ourselves with the patriarch of Uz (Job 40: 9), "Hast thou an arm like God?" In response to this text-question let us make a show of arms—Endeavorers, up with every right arm in this vast assembly. Arm inspection, if you please! Thank you; now down. What did we show? Arms of flesh. Some strong and muscular, others weak and withered. Some plump and round, others long and lean. But are these the arms to be like unto God's, and with which we are to fight our twentieth century battles? Nay, verily. Jeremiah (17: 5) declares, "Cursed be the man that maketh flesh his arm." The arms with which we are to fight our great moral battles of this century are unseen. We can hardly exhibit them here in fleshly form. But again, the arms which we have just uplifted were covered, whereas God told Ezekiel (4: 7), when He sent him to lay symbolic siege to Jerusalem, "Thine arm shall be uncovered." Can it be that Christian Endeavor arms are too much covered to enter the great struggle now confronting us? May I ask, What is that on thine arm? O you say, this is muslin, or silk, pique, or some other summer fabric. Ah, well enough for bodily comfort and ornament. But go yonder into the blacksmith's shop and see that great brawny muscled man with his sledge hammer upon the red hot iron. Is his arm covered, even with these light textiles? No, indeed. It is bare, giving it every advantage. Recall the Grecian races, or see the modern athletes,—how bared their arms that muscles may do the best work. What is that on thine arms,—on thy fighting arms, O Endeavorers? Do I not see some sleeves of worldliness? On another the fabric of levity? On another the cumbering cambric of superficiality? On another the fine linen of lack of spirituality? And alas, do I not see on some arms the gauzy garments of inaction? Should the Master come today and say to us, stretch forth thine arms, would He find them withered or covered and cumbered so that the battle could be easily turned against us? Certainly not so in every case. The magnificent work performed by the society in reaching its majority, forbids any wholesale charge of hindered arms. But the very putting of our topic suggests the possibility of better things in the future than in the past. This means that our arms are to be barer than ever before and that God is to empower and employ them as never before.

The exigencies and emergencies of the times call for the strong arm of the "Quiet Hour," in the words of Isaiah (33: 2), "O Lord, be gracious unto us: we have waited for thee: be thou our arm every morning, our salvation also in the time of trouble." This arm of the Lord has been the stay and the prop of His people in all perilous times of the past. The Psalmist tells of that arm in driving out the Canaanites, in these words (Psalms 44: 3): "For they got not the land in possession by the sword, neither did their own arm save them, but thy right hand, and thine arm . . ." Again we hear the Psalmist exultantly exclaim (Psalms 8: 1): "O sing unto the Lord a new song; for He hath done marvelous things: His right hand, and His holy arm, hath gotten Him the victory."

Abraham was a member of the "Quiet Hour" Circle of the Patriarchs, else he never could have lifted his arm with that glittering steel gripped, ready to obey God in plunging its point to the heart of his only son. Sampson had a "Quiet Hour" arm, else he never could have slain 1000 men with so simple a weapon as the single jaw-bone of an ass. Had not David possessed a "Quiet Hour" arm he never could have routed a whole army of proud and defiant Philistines with an insignificant sling. So in the twentieth century conflicts of Christian Endeavor we must be equipped with a "Quiet Hour" arm of strength and skill, or we shall be inadequate to cope with the combined forces of evil now confronting us.

II.—OUR TWENTIETH CENTURY VICTORIES.

1. With arms like God's we shall behold a triumphant Christianity in the twentieth century. But let us not be deceived: An arm like God's will never be attached to an evil life. Such an arm will ever be associated with a clean, strong, heroic personal life. No wonder Paul, the finisher of a good fight, should have said to Timothy, "Keep thyself pure." If the partaker of the divine nature be the possessor of a divine arm, he must be pure. Our labors can never rise above our lives. Our lives advertise our Christ. We are epistles known and read of all men. To accomplish any new and great work in this century we must fight evil with arms reinforced and supported by lives of purity. The object-lesson sermon of our lives is worth far more than the theoretical sermon of our lips in influencing the world for Christ. Or, as Emerson expresses it, "What you are speaks so loud I cannot hear what you say." Thus let us see to it, that whatever others do, we, Christian Endeavorers, shall in this new century maintain a higher standard of practical, personal life, (a) in keeping the Sabbath day holy; (b) in attending divine worship regularly and punctually: (c) in properly deporting ourselves in the house of God and before the world; (d) and in loyalty to Christ and the church at whatever cost or sacrifice. Private, personal victory must prepare the way for public conquest.

2. Arms are given to us for service. The fact that we have an arm like God's means that we should use it as Christ used His—to help others. Great are the privileges of Christian Endeavorers. Many a middle-aged Christian has regretted that Christian Endeavor did not exist in his youth so that he might have enjoyed its training. Even young people may in some ways help and stimulate these older Christians, so that in not a few instances they can yet develop their neglected gifts. Even the old, wrinkled and nearly worn out arm may be aroused to action by association with vigorous young arms. Thus Isaiah cries aloud (51: 9), "Awake, awake, put on thy strength, O arm of the Lord; awake as in the ancient days, in the generations of old." Of course God's own arm has never been asleep, but too often the church member's arm is, and that is the arm of the Lord to be awakened. By our zeal may we not "provoke very many" to an aroused service? Indeed, we may. But being younger we should be careful to do our provoking humbly and inoffensively,—be "as wise as serpents and as harmless as doves." Our cheerful, animated songs should comfort and encourage the older Christians of our congregations. Let us sing in the choir or in the pews, as called upon; in the chorus, or as soloists, as requested. Let us be unlike some other Christians and the world, in that we shall not take offense about the music, whatever the provocation. When a leader in prayer is needed, let us pray. When money is called for, let us pay,—at least the tenth of our income. Does the opportunity offer, let us exhort one another to the highest and holiest living. Wherever we are let us witness for Christ.

Thus the young Christian may inspire even older Christians to stand up for Jesus and spend their remaining years in a better service.

3. A still more victory-inviting field for the Endeavorer's bare, brave arm in the twentieth century is to be found in service for and with the children. There are few, if any, more charming prophetic descriptions of Christ's great work in the world than Isaiah's in the 40th chapter, 11th verse: "He shall feed his flock like a shepherd; he shall gather the lambs in his arms, and carry them in his bosom." Are we Christ's? Have we his spirit? Are we continuing the work he started? Have we an arm like his? If so, in our arms the little lambs are borne.

Surely every Bible student has been struck with Christ's tender regard for the child. Others said, take the children away, they trouble the Master. Jesus said, suffer them to come unto me, and took them in his arms and blessed them. Ah, did he not put a child in the midst of adults and pronounce him greatest in the kingdom of heaven? Did he not even say the child's conversion was to be a standard for the adult life? "Except ye be converted and become as little children, ye shall not enter into the kingdom of heaven." (Matthew 18: 3).

Truly child-salvation is the hope of this century. The ripest wisdom and the purest consecration of the last century were exhausted on the problem of saving adults. The failure was great and heart-rending. Then God called out, in the closing days of the century, the Christian young people of our young nation into Christian Endeavor activities as a stepping-stone towards reaching the children for Christ eventually. (It would have been too great a shock to our conservatism to have begun the work among the children at first.) The next step was the organization of the Junior Endeavor. Then primary work in the Sunday school took on new life and has come to have new meaning. "Decision Day" is next announced, and at last we are beginning to work on that end of humanity which God has even intended should be worked on first, and which yields most readily, namely, childhood. It takes at least ten times as long to reach the average unsaved adult as the unsaved child. If we would be successful in our twentieth century evangelization of the unsaved masses, let Christian Endeavorers, as do Foreign Missionaries, turn their attention to God's beginning point in saving souls—the child-life. Then when we shall have secured the salvation of a child, there is a longer probable life of service for the Savior. Mr. Torrey says, "A man converted at 60 is a soul saved plus 10 years of service, a child saved at 10 is a soul saved plus 60 years of service." How long will it take us to decide where we can do the most economical work?

But do you ask, How and where can we work for the child's salvation? The answer is: (1) in the home; (2) in the Junior society; (3) in the Sunday school, as teachers; (4) with the individual child, and (5) in the community, endeavoring to generate an interest in the salvation of children.

Finally, winning the lost world to Christ should absorb us and engage the strongest and most skilful Christian Endeavor arms,—arms like God's arm, as never before. Isaiah (53: 1) asks, "To whom is the arm of the Lord revealed?" and we are forced to reply, Unto very few, savingly. Many know of his saving arm in a general way, but few know experimentally of its power to save. In the home-land and in foreign fields that great divine arm of salvation must be revealed. Shall we not resolve that as a part of our twentieth century service for Christ and the Church we shall say to the Lord, "Here am I, send me?"

We who are Christians know the strength of that almighty arm to save, to bless, to guide and protect. Such an arm all the world needs. the arm of flesh will fail. All men need to become "partakers of the divine nature," and to have the help of a divine arm. God holds us responsible for witnessing to the world as to his mighty arm. Even in his old age David prayed, "When I am old and grey-headed, O God, forsake me not, until I have showed thine arm (margin) unto this generation, and thy power unto every one that is to come." (Psalm 71: 8.)

Philip and Andrew were not satisfied to know the Christ selfishly.

They hastened to find Peter and Nathaniel to whom they declared the power of Christ's arm. The woman at Jacob's well left her water pot,— for the time lost sight of her secular duty, and became a home missionary of marked success. "Hast thou an arm like God?" Go tell another of God's arm, and demonstrate the likeness of thine to His. Go, bearing in mind that the Holy Spirit will gladly go with thee and bear willing witness to the arm of the Lord which thou dost seek to reveal unto the unsaved. In the mouths of two witnesses shall the truth be established.

Do not let us lose sight of the fundamental fact in the propagation of our Christianity, namely, that so far God has generally used saved people through whom to reach the unsaved. That He could employ other seen and unseen agencies, no one will question. But in order to conform to His plan, personal workers must offer themselves. But if God needs men and women to declare the might of His arm in salvation, shall not we who have been reached by that arm hasten to our neighbors, and even to our enemies, with the joyful testimony, "Jesus saves, Jesus saves?" To this end were we born as an organization—let us fulfil our mission.

It is gratifying to note how large a part Endeavorers have taken in the church's witnessing for Christ throughout their minority. Now that we are "of age," shall we not come to an understanding, namely, that our United Society and all our component societies exist primarily and principally for the purpose of rescuing the perishing? We have already claimed this as our highest and holiest aim in the past, and we have fulfilled that noble aim largely. But shall we not now go forth into the mighty conflicts of this new century with arms so much like our Master's that the success of the past in soul-conquests shall be as nothing compared with our new victories?

On all sides sin is seen marshalling its forces, strengthening itself and fortifying its territory. Common attacks with ordinary arms will never defeat our mighty foes of this intense century. The arm of flesh can never win the day.

Then let us examine our arms, first, as to the arm itself, whether or not it be like God's; and second, as to its freedom for service.

To your tents, O Endeavorers, for the requisite Quiet Hour arm that God gives, and then spring forth into the battle against the giant forces of darkness. Christ is our Captain General, and He leads us in the interest of immortal souls. God will give us the victory through the strength of His right arm. "Hast thou an arm like God?" Use it.

CHAPTER XIV.

The Twentieth Century City.

"Seats in Williston only," was the salutation one received from the ushers as he entered Music Hall on Monday night. Auditorium Endeavor presented a brilliant spectacle as the eye swept its unbroken tiers of compact humanity.

For such an audience and such a theme as "The Twentieth Century City," it was meet that such a speaker should be forthcoming as the chairman of Boston's '95 committee, the president of the American Board of Commissioners for Foreign Missions, and, as Dr. Clark introduced him, "the leading layman of New England, the man to whom we in Boston turn when we want anything done, municipal or religious."

The Christian Endeavorer's Duty in Municipal Politics.

Hon. Samuel B. Capen, LL. D., Boston.

The greatest political problem in America is the problem of the cities. Throwing out of our discussion this evening the questions growing out of our recent war with Spain, it can be said that there have been before the American nation three great questions. The first had to do with our independence as a nation, and was settled at Yorktown more than a hundred years ago. The second had to do with the unity and integrity of the nation, and was settled at Appomattox Court House nearly forty years ago. The third has to do with the purity of our municipalities, and in some respects the latter is the greatest question of them all. Wendell Phillips prophesied before his death that there would be sometime on this American continent a conflict greater than that through which the nation had just passed in the overthrow of slavery,—the question of the government of our great cities. We are in the midst of that conflict to-day, and the importance of it no one can over-estimate. DeTocqueville has well said that "municipal institutions are to liberty what the primary school is to science." The problem of the city, I repeat, is the supreme question of the hour.

CONDITIONS.

We have been passing through a period of civic neglect. It seems to be the law of the universe that one extreme shall follow another. Winter follows summer; night follows day; business depressions and panics follow periods of great business prosperity. During the time of the Civil War it was an era of intense patriotism. The heart of both the North and the South was with the army; every family had several representatives at the front. But when the war was over, the pendulum swung to the other extreme and we entered a period of apathy and indifference in civic matters.

The first reason, and perhaps the greatest one, for this condition has come because of our rapid increase in wealth. This has become, as is well known, almost fabulous in its amount. Seventy citizens in the United States are said to be worth about three thousand million dollars. One great reason for this great increase in wealth has come about from the wonderful inventions in machinery. A girl working on a loom today can

F. H. Jacobs.

H. C. Lincoln.

Percy S Foster.

Rev. Edwin F. Hallenbeck.

Rev. F. D. Power, D. D.

Hon. S. B. Capen, LL. D.

Rev. J. E. Pounds, D. D.

Rev. David N. Beach, D. D.

Rev. P. S. Henson, D. D.

Rev. George Darsie.

Rev. James Chalmers, D. D.

Marion Lawrence.

SOME OF THE CONVENTION SPEAKERS.

do in ten hours one thousand times as much as her great-grandfather could do a hundred years ago. One man with a steam engine can do the work of two hundred and fifty men. It was three days before the king of England knew the result of the Battle of Waterloo ninety miles away. Now, a man has sat in his office in London, sent a cablegram to British Columbia, and got an answer back (thirteen thousand miles) in ninety seconds. Under these new conditions, the possibilities of acquiring wealth have been very great, and men have been willing that anybody should care for public interests, if only they could be allowed to go on with their money-getting. Of course some of this wealth is in the hands of those who are making a splendid use of it for humanity, but too much of it is in the hands of those who care nothing for the public weal, and use it selfishly, and oftentimes recklessly, against the public interests. Too much of our legislation, we all know, is shaped and controlled by these supremely selfish men who live only for themselves. And it ought to be noted that this great wealth is found largely among the residents of our great cities.

Second: Over against this tremendous massing of wealth in our cities is the other extreme, namely, most Wretched Destitution and Want. We have the crowded tenement houses with their poverty and vileness. In New York forty-five people have been known to sleep at one time in a single room. Can any one paint in too dark colors the wretchedness of such conditions, especially for the young? Bishop Smith says, "A child has a right to be born and not damned into the world." It is in these conditions of extreme poverty that the corruptionist and the demagogue find their opportunity. We all know the restraining force where people largely own their own homes. In the country districts it is said that sixty-six per cent. of the population do still own their own dwellings. I was startled recently to see the figures that in cities of one hundred thousand and more, only twenty-three per cent. own their own homes, while in Boston this is still further reduced to eighteen per cent. and in New York to six per cent. These figures may not be strictly accurate, but they are sufficiently so to show that the vast proportion of our city population own no real estate, and feel that they have little or nothing at stake in civic matters.

Third: We have in the city with all the terrible evils that grow out of it, the saloon, which is the headquarters of all the worst elements of vice, and which are, to a certain extent, often controlled largely by a few wealthy wholesale dealers. The forces that centre in the saloon always work together against the forces that make for righteousness. We quite understand the truth of the remark of an ex-United States Senator who said he would rather have the support of five saloons than twenty churches. The man who supports the saloon can always be depended upon to be at the caucus and the polls.

Fourth: We find in the city, using the influences that are right at his hand, one of the most dangerous enemies of the Republic, the "political boss." He is in politics for what he can make out of them and has no scruples as to his methods. We have not only the big boss who tries to control the city, but we have the ward boss who controls a group of smaller bosses. There is in most of our great cities in all the lower wards what is called the "gang," composed at the start of very young men who have a rendezvous, sometimes a cheap room, more often a favorite saloon. They are perfectly unscrupulous, and by the use of a little money, can be made to do all the filthy work of the lowest politics.

Fifth: The worst and more dangerous, almost, than any of these, are the well-to-do citizens who have everything at stake in the government of the city, and who seem to be perfectly indifferent to its highest interests. The "heelers" and the ward politicians get their power largely on account of the indifference of this class of men. They are really the most dangerous of all classes, for while they might be leaders in righteousness, they shirk and skulk and do nothing.

DUTIES.

If this is a fair picture of the conditions and tendencies in our great cities, and I believe it is, it certainly is true that the Christian Endeavorer has some very positive duties he owes to his city. First, he is in duty bound to have an intelligent opinion upon all questions which relate to the well-being of his city, and such knowledge can be acquired as other knowledge is acquired, only by study and patient effort. There is more ignorance to the square inch at this point than at almost any other. I talked with a gentleman who is at the head of a corporation of a million and a half dollars, and I asked him a few elementary questions about the government of his city, and he finally admitted that he knew nothing about it whatever; the man is simply an illustration of the majority of the community. I wonder how many young men in this audience tonight ever read the charter of the city where they live, or the reports of the School Board, or in fact know anything very definitely about the practical workings of their own municipal government. Our young men are reading David Harum and Richard Carvel, and books of this class, and wholly neglecting literature that bears practically upon the life of their own community. I think I ought to make as an exception one class in many of our cities. I refer to the Irish Americans. I was talking a short time ago with a gentleman who had been a Trustee of the library in one of our cities, and he told me that the Irish Americans were reading history, biography, constitutional law, and the American young men were reading novels. It seems to me the time has come fully to call the attention of our Christian Endeavorers, not only to their bounden Christian duty, but to their glorious privilege, of making a study of the questions which have so much to do with the welfare of the cities where they dwell.

As a means to this end, I wish there might be a movement begun at this Convention to organize in all our cities, grouping Christian Endeavorers together, if you please, what I would call in such community a Congress of Christian Endeavorers. This would be in all respects, so far as possible, copied after our National Congress, or our State legislative bodies. There should be a Speaker chosen, and committees of various kinds having relation to certain definite subjects. There is literature in abundance bearing upon various political points. This Congress should study also Parliamentary law, understand rules of order and Parliamentary practice, and thereby fully equip its members to take their place later in governing large assemblies. In this Congress they should discuss the various problems of the city and the nation, questions which have to do with the best organization of the city government, with regard to the care of paupers and criminals, great questions of arbitration between capital and labor, and the broader question of international arbitration. To illustrate, there is one question which might well be discussed all over our country, and that is the question of making the Caucus an "initial election." Instead of having the ward primaries held, as in most of our cities, in the few closing hours of the day and on different days by the parties, the polling booths should be open all day, and both parties should hold their caucus on the same day. Such a plan would abolish nomination by delegates in Conventions, for the people would vote directly, and the ward politician would be at a discount. Discussion of such questions as these would make sentiment rapidly towards a reform of this kind, a reform which is opposed by all the bosses for they see in it a deadly blow to their power. Let this Congress be held once or twice a month, and the young men fit themselves thus by honest and persistent work to become intelligent citizens. We do not want any more "goody-goody" young men, and certainly no more "cranks." We want young men who by study and intelligent consideration of public questions are not in danger of bringing a reproach upon Christian Endeavor by doing foolish things. We want them sane and well-balanced in whatever they do, being willing in all these things to be influenced by those who are older so that every step taken may be wise and helpful. We should ever remember that the good man who is weak and easily influenced may do more harm than one who is really bad. We watch the latter and his power for mischief therefore is limited; but a weak good young man who is used as a tool, can do incalculable mischief. There is something in this study of municipal problems in preparation for service which will be most attractive to our young men who sometimes drift out of our Christian Endeavor Societies. It is time for us to stop singing so much about Heaven and the life that is to be, and sing and think very much more about the life that now is. Too many of our young people are considering altogether too much how they can be amused, but I believe all this will be changed if they can be shown the splendid possibilities along these lines for training themselves for the noblest Christian citizenship.

There certainly can be no more imperative duty at the present time than for our young men to train themselves in this way for the largest usefulness. With the steady drift of population from the country to the city in about twenty years at the present rate of increase, the great cities of the country will throw a larger vote than the country, and will then absolutely control the nation. It is for us, therefore, to hold the cities for righteousness, and this must be done by our young men.

And while I am laying especial emphasis upon this organization in the form of a Congress of our young men, I would not by any means exclude from it the young women. They ought to be as eager as the young men to study these problems. While they may not have the same right to vote, they may, if they will, influence the young men who are to cast the vote. There is a good incident told by ex-Mayor Schieren of Brooklyn. A young drummer met him soon after his election, and introduced himself by the remark, "I voted for you, but I didn't mean to." On inquiry as to the reason, he told the Mayor that he went home Saturday night in order to be at home Monday to vote, and he put on his best clothes and went to see his best girl, and, "Well," he said, "I voted for you!" We have not forgotten the Christian Endeavor girl in Florida who said some time ago, "if she could not have a vote, she could have a voter." The young women have it in their power to influence the young men as no one else can, for the best things, and the young men will be inspired to do better work if they are entering fully into sympathy with them in it all. Let us have the Christian Endeavor Congress started all over the country that we may have young Christian Endeavorers who will have an intelligent opinion in all municipal matters.

Second: Every Christian Endeavorer, besides having an intelligent opinion, as soon as he becomes of age, should make it a Christian duty always to attend the caucus. He must make his knowledge of practical value to the community.

We all know the importance in everything of the first step. It is that which counts most, and this is nowhere more true than in our political caucuses. Government in America is practically shaped in the caucus. Yet while this is true, multitudes of men seldom, if ever, are seen in the gathering where the future is so largely shaped. We ought to keep before the eyes of our young people that popular government in the cities of America is still in the experimental stage, and unless the citizens arouse themselves, the selfish interests will have complete sway. Conditions, as they have existed in the last few years in the city of New York and the city of Philadelphia, are a reproach to our nation. For the Christian man the primary meeting should be as sacred appointment as the place of prayer, and if the Christian men of the community at almost any election would take the interest, they might get good men nominated. May I repeat two instances which will be better than any argument? Some years ago in one of our great cities, the caucus was appointed on the evening of the regular church prayer meeting. It was said that this evening was selected in order to prevent the attendance of the prayer-meeting men. But in one community at least, the scheme miscarried. In one of the churches the brethren went to the prayer-meeting at 7.30, and a little later almost every man left the prayer meeting in the hands of the pastor and the women and went to the caucus. The presence and action of these Christian men helped to prevent a wrong that was threatened. In marked contrast with all this, in an adjoining ward at about the same time an important caucus was held, and the good and the bad were so evenly balanced that the latter triumphed by only one vote and thereby nominated a man who was a tool of the saloon. Within a few rods of that caucus a temperance prayer meeting was being held in one of our churches where there were forty men gathered, any two of whom, if they had gone to that caucus, might have nominated the good man. There is a time to pray and a time for the caucus, and when the prayer meeting and the caucus are appointed for the same night, the caucus is the place for the Christian man.

And may I speak a word to the young women who have an important work that they can do here, even if they cannot themselves attend the caucus? If I was a young woman I would not let any young man come to see me who neglected his duty in this respect, and if I was a married woman, I should be very much inclined to give my husband a very poor supper, if he had not attended, or did not propose to attend, to this first duty as a citizen. The young women certainly can have large influence here in holding the young men up to their sacred duty.

Third: No Christian Endeavorer should ever forget to cast his ballot on the day of election. After doing our best to nominate good men, then it is our still further duty to do everything in our power to elect them. It is a sad fact, but a fact nevertheless, that in many of our cities only about two-thirds of the registered citizens cast their ballots at the municipal election; and the trouble is that in the best wards, so called, where we would suppose men had the most at stake, the neglect is the greatest. You will often find in a ward where there are perhaps four thousand voters, that only about twenty-five hundred of them appear at the polls. More than one-third have not interest enough concerning those who are to rule over them to turn aside a few rods and cast a ballot. Such neglect is only one stage removed from the criminal. For a Christian Endeavorer to neglect his ballot is to be false to the flag that covers him, and to the city that protects his home. It has been well said that "the citizen who does not vote ought to be court-martialed and drummed out of the camp of citizenship to the tune of Rogue's March."

Fourth: Let every Christian Endeavorer place first in his thought the moral character of the man for whom he votes. Government in America is now, and always has been, by parties; these are a necessity, and a man's influence usually counts for the most who is identified with a party which most nearly represents his political belief. But a man is released from all obligations if his party selects some candidate of doubtful character. Let us make our protest at this point by "bolting the ticket." We want not so much better methods in our political life as better men. Carl Schurz was right when he said years ago, that he would rather have Lucifer make the laws if Gabriel was to execute them, than for Gabriel to make them if Lucifer was to execute them.

Fifth: Every Christian Endeavorer ought to be willing to accept public office if it is offered to him, even at great personal sacrifice. Of course at the first such positions will be those which are sometimes called of small importance,—positions on ward and city committees and in the lower branches of our municipal legislature; but however small the place may seem to be, remember that it is a place of public trust and may be used for great public service. I recognize that a man who accepts such positions must do it at great cost to himself. He must expect to receive criticism most severe, for partisanship in this country often runs very high. Personal abuse is the penalty which men have to pay when they accept any public office. For a young man of keen sensibilities this is oftentimes most painful, but if he views it right as a place of trust, he will be willing to bear whatever is necessary while in the discharge of his duty. The unwillingness of so many men to accept any public position is a serious peril to the Republic, and every Christian man is in honor bound to take his place and do his part, as he is bound to do jury duty or to serve as a soldier in times of national peril. I am sure no young man will shirk from his duty because it is a place of sacrifice. Mazzini was right when he said, "No appeal is quite so powerful as the call, 'Come and suffer'." At Valley Forge when Washington's army was suffering from hunger, with their feet bleeding for lack of shoes, he asked them to die with him for their country, and they responded most quickly for such sacrifice. And the young man who will not in this crisis in the municipalities respond to this call of duty is no Christian, but a coward; he is not a saint, but a shirk.

Sixth: While it is true that parties in the state and nation are a necessity, in municipal matters, the municipality should be governed along broader lines. The State is a sovereign power. A city is a corporation with limited power, and to manage municipal government along the lines of national party politics is an absurdity. Prof. Fiske has put this point admirably in his remark that it is as foolish to select municipal officers along the lines of national parties, as it would be to choose them because of their belief in homeopathy or because they had a taste for chrysanthemums. Christian Endeavorers ought to be willing in any city to join organizations which are trying to help towards the better government of cities; such municipal leagues or citizens' organizations, by whatever name they may be called, should be open to all without distinction of party, race, or creed. It must be that in all our cities the number of persons who really are selfishly benefited by bad municipal government is very small. It must be for the best interest of the great majority to have pure, clean government. The poor man has often more at stake than the rich. If the schools in the city where he lives are poor, he has no alternative but to have his children attend them, while the rich man can send his to some private instructor. If the drainage or sanitary conditions of the city are wrong, the poor man must submit, while the rich one can take his family to the mountains or the sea during the unhealthy season of the year. The trouble is to get the unselfish to work together. Men are so prone to cling to their party that it is difficult to make headway. Practically the result is that the good men of the city divide off among the parties while the bad men are sure to keep together. Goethe has well said, "Piety is a close bond, but ungodliness is a closer." It makes us shudder to think of this, but is it not true that in most of our cities the saloons are in closer touch for evil than the churches are for good? We must organize in our cities to meet combinations of evil with combinations of good, and there is nothing more amusing than these hysterical attempts that are made from year to year a few weeks before election. We shall never have decent government in our great cities until the good are willing to get together through some organization which is persevering and fearless. There is all the difference in the world between a "league" and the "machine"; one has moral convictions and the other has none; one is a fountain and lives to bless, the other is a sponge and likes to soak everything to itself; one is light and the other is darkness. Let Christian Endeavorers be at the front, eager to bring together the forces which make for righteousness in the cities where they live. I know there are difficulties in the way, but I submit that it is not yet time to read the baby act. Oliver Wendell Holmes has said, "There are two classes of people in the world; one who goes ahead and does something, and the other that whines and wonders why it was not done some other way." Let Christian Endeavorers all of them join the first class.

As said at the beginning, we are in our cities face to face with evil, and the destinies of the Republic depend, humanly speaking, upon rescuing most of our cities from misrule and extravagance. Christian Endeavorers should more and more study these great municipal problems and be willing to give their service without stint in this holy war. What we need now is not men to fight for our country, but men who, in our great cities, year in and year out, will live for the public weal. It has seemed to me for many years that the only way we can save our cities and our nation is to make this a religious movement of Christian men of every sect, without any distinction whatsoever. This is but a return to a part of our religion which has been most sadly neglected. The old prophets from Elijah to Malachi were civic reformers, and denounced with burning words those in public places who were unworthy. Moses, the great statesman of the Hebrews, who shaped the first constitution of a free people, lived three thousand years before Thomas Jefferson.   And the great movements of history from that time to this have been religious movements. We glory in the story of Lexington and of Concord, the brave deeds of the men of that generation, but who was it that suggested the organization of the "Minute Men" of Lexington? Who was it that all through Middlesex County was the controlling spirit? Read the records of these early times and you will find that it was Rev. Jonas Clark, the village pastor.

I know, with evil entrenched as it is in our great cities, it seems sometimes like an almost hopeless task to try to dislodge it, and place men of sterling character and unselfish purpose all through our cities in positions of high trust. But have you ever stood at Lexington before the belfry that held the bell that rang out the morning alarm 126 years ago? Have you ever stood on Lexington Common and thought of the helplessness of those seventy minute men facing seven hundred of the best trained soldiers in the world in that early morning? Have you tried to listen to the words of Capt. Parker preserved on the monument, "Stand your ground; don't fire unless fired upon; but if they mean to have a war, let it begin here"? It seemed almost like recklessness, but that morning skirmish gained time, and the alarm was given and the farmers came rushing across the fields to fire from behind stone walls and wherever they could get a chance until victory was won. That early skirmish was a part of the day's work; and that day's work was a success. So this movement to save our cities looks helpless, but these movements that are going on now all over our country in so many of our great cities are calling attention to the greatness of the struggle, and these are to increase until everywhere we shall drive out of places of high power those who are prostituting these positions for their own selfish interests. Christian Endeavorers, let us step out upon the skirmish line, like the Minute Men of '76, and help to rally the forces in this battle for righteousness. Let us remember that there can be in this crisis in the cities of America no piety without patriotism. No matter if the odds are against us at the start. Any coward can fight when he is sure of an easy winning. Give me the man who will fight for the right when he knows for a time at least he must be beaten. No matter if we are misunderstood and abused. Spurgeon's remark is always in order in such case, "I never try to brush off the mud that is thrown at me; most of it will come off when it is dry." Heroic souls in the past had no more opportunities than we have, but they used them. There were daring deeds to be done then; are there none now? Sacrifices to be made; are there none now? Let Christian Endeavorers move into the very thickest of the fight in this effort to redeem our cities. Courage and earnestness will be contagious. Our young men will be heroes moving to the attack and as we are fighting the Lord's battle we know we shall be on the winning side. "God is not dead."

In our late Civil War, in one of the battles near Richmond, the brave Gen. Birnie was mortally wounded; while dying in his tent his lips were seen to move, and as they gathered about him and bent over his form, they caught this whisper of the dying man, "Keep your eye on the flag." May I change that expression a little, and say to all Christian Endeavorers, "Keep your eye on the flag and on the Cross," the one the emblem of the nation, and the other the symbol of the Christian church, the hope of the world? May God help us to be faithful to both!

Dr. Capen's utterances were like an injection of salt into the veins. They set heart-beats going that will yet burst bonds of political shame. The echoes of the hand-claps that punctuated his sentences will yet be heard where misrule shall tremble at them.

There was a song in the new book that just fitted this patriotic address,—there were fitting songs for all the themes,—and no music ever thrilled that hall with such prophetic fervor as did this magnificent burst of song, led by Percy S. Foster.

A dramatic feature of the evening, not on the bills, was the introduction of Field Secretary Eberman. When Dr. Clark asked, "Where should the United Society turn when it wanted a man for this important work?" from the front centre section of seats came back an answer, almost a chorus of shouts,—"Pennsylvania!"

If there was any mystery about this response, it was dispelled when, as Mr. Eberman arose to reply, suddenly this whole block of the audience rose to its feet as one man, and Pennsylvania's delegation voiced a greeting to Pennsylvania's beloved president.

But that was not enough. The whole audience must have a share in that God-speed. So, at the suggestion of Wayland Hoyt, D. D., five or six thousand voices answered the question, "Will you stand by me in this responsible work?" with a stentorian "I will," that sounded like reverberating thunder.

Never was a sweeter solo than Mr. F. H. Jacobs's that followed.

Then Dr. Clark expressed the pleasure it gave him to introduce a second personal friend, Rev. Charles M. Sheldon, D. D., to speak on the daily papers of the twentieth century.

The Daily Paper of the Twentieth Century City.

Rev. Charles M. Sheldon, D.D., Topeka Kansas.

This discussion is necessarily along the lines of ideals. That is what the Christian Endeavor movement stands for. It does not stop with what has been done nor with the average goodness in any case but is always reaching out after something better. By the ideal we do not mean what is beyond our reach, but rather, something to reach after with the expectation of getting it. The discussion does not start out with the assumption that there are no good daily papers today. Neither does it assume that the press is hostile to suggestions which simply have for their object the possible bettering of journalism, but it does assume that there is a very large and undeveloped field open to the daily press which is not at present cultivated. It is, therefore, pertinent to this article to ask this question—what have we a right to expect a daily paper in the twentieth century city will represent, that is, a daily paper that Christian Endeavorers would publish and buy and read? To make it practically personal, if the Christian Endeavor Society organized a daily paper in a large city sometime during this century, what would probably be its policy? What sort of a paper would it give to the city? This question involves the other question; what kind of a paper ought the twentieth century city to have if the great movements now going on in the world, especially in the great cities, are movements which are at the foundation distinctly religious? What phase of this progress would the daily press assume if it were conducted on an ideal basis?

In answer to these questions the very first statement of all that it seems necessary to make is this: the daily paper of the twentieth century, that is, the daily paper of the kind we are considering, will no doubt have, as a marked feature of its policy, an open discussion followed up day after day by editorial and printed matter of all kinds against the saloon as perhaps the greatest curse in the life of the city that is known today. In other words the policy of this twentieth century daily paper, that the Endeavor Society would publish, would be the policy of prohibition against the liquor traffic in all its forms.

1. To say that the saloon is the greatest curse resting on this nation

is to utter a platitude. It is not necessary any longer for the temperance orator to deluge his audience with statistics in order to prove the monstrous extent of crime, insanity, and poverty that are the direct outcome of the saloon. We have gotten past the period of statistics. We do not need to have the case against the saloon proved. It has already been proved and found guilty and sentenced and ought to have been hung by the neck until it was dead long ago. Why it is out on bail, after receiving sentence from the highest tribunal in the land, is a mystery to God, angels, and all good men and women, but it is also a mystery that after being found guilty of all the crimes on the calendar after it has had proved against it more misery, wrong, heartache and human woe than have ever been proved against any other institution—it is a mystery, I say, why the greatest of all civilized agencies for printing human events is so profoundly silent on the subject. There is scarcely a daily paper in all this country that openly and for principle's sake takes up the cause of prohibition against the greatest curse on the earth. The largest moral issue in America today receives less space for discussion in most of the great city dailies than base ball or Sunday golf and right here is the opportunity for the twentieth century daily, such as the Endeavorers would probably publish. If any great daily in America were to begin tomorrow morning to make the prohibition of the saloon one of the most prominent features of its policy, if it were to begin to print whole pages of illustrations showing what drink does, if it were to make the editorial column prominent every day with positive utterances calling attention to the need of abolishing the great enemy of humanity from the cities, that daily would suddenly spring into prominence as the champion of the people and would receive support unmistakably. Is it any secret that the conscience of America is awaking every minute more and more to the seriousness of the drink curse? Is it news to be told that within the next ten years the question of the prohibition of the saloon will be the most prominent issue in political campaigns? It does not require a prophet to say that in less than ten years every political party in this country will be obliged to reckon very seriously with the numbers of Christian votes that are going to be cast only for those candidates in any office who are known to be for principle's sake against the saloon and all it represents. On that account the first great daily that openly, with determination, with set purpose and for principle's sake espouses this cause will be the most influential daily in the United States. The strength of the voting possibilities of the next ten years that will grow out of the Christian citizenship of this country is underestimated by the professional politician. Some day in the very near future he will wake up to the fact that he must reckon with moral factors which hitherto he has scorned. Twenty years of Christian training in the citizenship represented by this great Endeavor movement will put into the field of political action, within the next ten years, an army of voters who will compel attention and the time is very swiftly drawing near when the daily in the city that does not make the saloon an issue and one of the first issues of its policy will be a back number in every sense of the term. Any newspaper man who sees anything of the signs of the times ought to see that an issue as great, as profoundly serious as this, cannot be ignored very much longer. The Christian vote in this country has not heretofore been counted. I am very much mistaken if in the next decade it will not prove to be as formidable as the non-conformist vote in England has been whether allied to any political party or not. The young voters that come out of our churches in the future will be in some way or other a solid union against the whiskey power. The old parties will no longer be able to line them up, and the greatest opportunity before journalism at the present moment is to ally itself, heart and soul, with the rising Christian sentiment which will undoubtedly express itself in votes against the brewer, the distiller, the jointist, the licensed saloon and every other form of corruption that grows up with these enemies to humanity.

2. Another distinctive feature of the daily in the twentieth century city would be the prominence it would give to the distinctive work done

by the Christian missionaries of the world. Not in special editions when some great missionary gathering centers in the city to talk over its work but in every day numbers making a specialty of the religious life of the world, its romance, its adventures, its wonderful history of triumphs and heroism. The common people the men on the street know practically nothing concerning the march of Christ's kingdom in foreign lands. The history within the last twenty-five years as given by the religious papers, which, however are read by only a part of the church members, is a history which for human interest and a display of versatility, courage and heroism has not been equaled in all human history. In the hands of competent writers the missionary annals of the last twenty-five years could be made as intensely interesting to the average reader as any account of present crime or sport. It is safe to say that a majority of the readers of newspapers in the United States are practically ignorant of the wonders that have been accomplished by the missionaries of the cross. These wonders are certainly of far more value to society than the discussion of the dinner given by Mrs. Millionaire or the great wedding between the English Lord and the American heiress. Just as in the case of the espousal of prohibition by the daily so the taking up of the subject of missions as a human event of tremendous importance would be a distinctive feature in journalism which would command general and universal interest.

Allied to this as a feature would also be the prominence given by the twentieth century daily to the problems of the city itself viewed especially from the religious and social standpoint. Take for example a city of thirty-five thousand people which has over twelve thousand church members, over a third of the entire population. Add to that the numbers of men and women who do not belong to churches but who are practically in sympathy with them and more or less connected, add to them a large number of children in Sunday school who are not yet church members but who will be very soon and the entire number of the people in the city who are favorably inclined towards religious interests and personally interested in what the churches are' doing would easily make two-thirds of the entire city. Now the twentieth century daily would take instant account of this fact and publish fully as much at least for two-thirds of the city as it did for the other third that might be indifferent to religious things. I know scores of families that would welcome as the most interesting reading matter that could come to them in the daily press, purely religious information of what the churches in the city are doing, not only the churches but all the religious organizations and they would read with much more interest the paper that had in proportion two-thirds of its columns filled with items of the good things that men are doing, than to read the same paper that has two-thirds of its columns filled with accounts of crime or political affairs or commercial events. In one town that I know where more than two-thirds of the people are genuinely interested in social and philanthropic interests the local papers will print day after day entire pages devoted to base ball, horse races and crime. Why should the minority of a reading population be catered to with the kind of news it would like to have and have it in excess? In another town are perhaps one hundred men who are interested in a boxing contest, who are professional sports but why should the paper published in that town the morning after a pugilistic contest, devote three columns to these one hundred men and ignore the three thousand men in the town who do not care anything about such an event, but on the other hand prefer to have something of an entirely different character? If the papers are going to give the public what it wants it might not be a bad plan for the papers to call for an expression of public opinion in the matter. It would be very interesting, if answers could be obtained from the constituency of the daily paper to know what the majority of the reading population wants to read. But it would seem as if it would be a fair inference to make that two-thirds of the population of a city are believers in Christianity and more or less followers of Christ, who would prefer to read matters which have to do with the progress of Christ's kingdom in the earth. If the objection is made to this kind of journalism that it would be simply a religious symposium it would be also fair to say that if a community is Christian, then it is Christian news which it is mostly interested in, which it wants to buy and read. The vicious elements in any community in the United States are at least in a minority and if anything must be given at all to that class of readers it ought to be the smallest possible quantity.

3. In addition to this the twentieth century daily, such as the Endeavorers would probably publish, would take very large account of the social movements of the times and especially those movements as registered in the great centres of population. The city has become the place where human destinies are being shaped. It is already becoming a feature in very many publications to advance the ideas of municipal ownership of public utilities. A daily paper that ten years ago reported a series of sermons on "Christian Socialism" to be exceedingly dangerous, the other day published and followed up with an editorial a series of articles advocating much more than the sermons advocated and all that under the same business and editorial management that condemned the preacher a decade ago. The twentieth century daily that will boldly for principle's sake, because it sees the signs of the times, advocate all necessary measures of reform in the city and give prominence especially to all forms of Christian progress which curtail the selfish monopoly of the few for the social service of the many will be the coming influential daily of the country. I do not say there are no such papers today; there are some but they are not yet typical in number of the journalism of the city life. Money interests still sway the policy of many great dailies rather than human interests; dollars count for more than duties, and commercial interests figure first before the rights of the common people in very many large and influential daily papers. The twentieth century daily, of the kind we are describing, will have a standing question in its business and editorial management—What is the best thing for the best interest of the city? What will promote the welfare and happiness and morality of the entire family? What is for the best good of the city brotherhood? The literature of social problems is becoming exceedingly rich and valuable. Instead of publishing photographs of the leaders of fashion with long accounts of the dresses they wore on fashionable occasions, instead of long Sunday editions devoted to the monstrous mixture of all the ends and oddities and abnormal actions of humanity, the twentieth century daily, that we have in mind, would publish the results of social problems, laying rightful emphasis upon intelligent philanthropy, social settlement work, give the reader an outlook on the brave, unselfish, heroic side of humanity as it is actually known in all great cities today. It would not hurt any daily paper in this country to exclude from its columns for an entire month every account of human depravity and fill its columns up with the optimism of human unselfishness. The crimes of the cities do not amount to anything compared with their acts of goodness. I assert that goodness is "news," and can be made to be intensely interesting news to the average man. All this the twentieth century daily would attempt in some large measure to do, seeing again for its own advantage the signs of the times which point unmistakably to the upheaval that is going to be caused by social regeneration.

4. Another large cause that the daily we are considering would champion, would be the question of the Sunday that America ought to have. In place of the vast amount of printed matter which has to do with purely commercial transactions where money figures as the great thing, the twentieth century city daily would publish broadsides calling attention to the fact that unless America preserves a Christian Sabbath there will come a time when the possession of money and all that commercial interests stand for will be of no account. If we do not have the Christian Sabbath, if the day is going to be a copy of the continental Sunday of Europe, the amassing of great fortunes, the putting up of great buildings the manufacture of immense quantities of products, the planning and building of gigantic railroads will be of little use in the summing up of

that which is the final standard of success of any nation, and that is, character. Cash without character is poverty; and the nation will not have any character unless it preserves among other great institutions a Christian Sabbath. Dr. Hillis never made a truer or more pertinent statement than this: "The problem of the pulpit today is in the Sunday question. The problem before America today is whether it will keep Sunday in the calendar and relax into paganism or observe a Christian Sabbath and become Christian."

A daily which really has at heart the good of this nation would call vivid attention to the facts of Sunday desecration, to the slavery imposed on a great army of railroad employees by the railroad corporations. It would make as one of the prominent features of an avowed policy, illustrated with living illustrations, the question of the relation between a Christian Sabbath and a Christian nation. One of the great dailies of this country the other day, devoted three solid pages to an account of the building and launching of a battleship. It was an interesting article, fully illustrated but in comparison with the value to the nation of a Christian Sabbath there is no comparison. Another large daily a few weeks ago gave four pages to a description of the oil fields in Texas and gave optimistic forecast of the immense wealth which the oil fields represented, but in comparison with the real wealth of the nation which grows out of a reverence for God and observance of His rule of the Sabbath rest, the wealth of the oil fields of Texas is the sheerest poverty to any republic. The commercial interests of this republic are playthings to the tremendous interests that are at stake in the matter of character and moral growth of the people, and I say that the daily paper that acknowledges this fact and makes it prominent in its daily publication will be the paper that shall hold the place of the highest honor in the republic among the people who love the republic and pray for God's blessing to rest upon it.

Such a paper as we have in barest outline described, would of necessity be under the management and control of the most profoundly patriotic consecrated Christian men and women. It could not be owned by any selfish individual, it could not be controlled by any political faction, it could not be run in the interests of any commercial power; it would stand for love of the people, love of truth, love of common every day righteousness, love of justice, belief in the value of principle over against policy, it would be of necessity a religious paper but none the less in the largest and truest sense, a newspaper. Recognizing the fact that this nation was born in the most intense religious atmosphere and that it is full of religious instinct, this paper of the twentieth century would not be afraid to rest upon religious foundations. I do not know how it may be with this State but one of the things that makes me proud of my own State of Kansas is this, that when we want the biggest convention of Kansas people that can be gathered together we call a Sunday school convention. More people will attend a Sunday school convention in Kansas than any other kind. The politicians have never been able to call together, in the most exciting times, as large and enthusiastic a crowd of men and women and children as will come together to study the Bible, the child, and the best method of carrying on the fundamental work of religious child training. The daily papers of the future will take account of these facts. May I, as I close, venture to express the hope that some way or other this great Christian Endeavor organization will be the means of establishing such an organ for righteousness in more than one great city in this great country. The possibilities for such journalism are big with Christian ambition. If the Christian young people of this country will unite their efforts they can establish such papers in every large centre of population, and they will prove to be, under the hand of God, one of the mightiest sources of real power in shaping the future destiny of this republic which we all love.

CHAPTER XV.

The Twentieth Century City.

ITS SALOON PROBLEM.—THE POWER OF THE PEW.

Auditorium Williston was crammed on Monday night, and there, owing to the sickness of so many of the speakers and their necessary absence, were given the condensed programs prepared for both Ohio and Williston.

Here, too, as well as in Endeavor, the Twentieth Century City was the theme. The first speaker was that keen, pointed, eloquent orator, Rev. Frank Dixon, of Hartford. He discussed the saloon problem, and without gloves.

The Saloon Problem of the Twentieth Century City.

Rev. Frank Dixon, Hartford, Conn.

The saloon is a curse. It has been such to the nineteenth century; it promises to be such to the twentieth.

I do not believe that the saloon is the one hindrance to the millennium. It is as much the product of vicious forces as it is the producer of moral and economic evils. To strike at it, without attacking the conditions out of which the saloon grows spontaneously, would be folly. While it is impossible to detach the saloon problem from the general problem of progress, it is allowable for purposes of analysis to focus all possible light upon this one point, and discuss it for a while as if it were distinct. I desire to be candid and fair in all I say. It is not my purpose to denounce men, however unworthy I may hold their occupation to be, but to discuss certain great principles which furnish the basis of a solution of the saloon problem.

What is this problem? Let us clear the ground of certain prevalent misconceptions. The saloon problem of the twentieth century is not how to abolish the saloon by direct legislative action. This method does not commend itself to a free people. The problem is not how to persuade a thirsty public to withdraw its patronage voluntarily from the saloon. The public has never yet given evidence of so great self-restraint. The problem is not to persuade the man who can drink beer moderately to abstain from the use of stronger beverages. The man who can do that will settle his own problems. The problem is not to heap maledictions upon the saloon-keepers until no man can be found callous enough to engage in the business. Had that method been effective, the saloon would have disappeared already. The problem is not how to convert the present army of drunkards to Jesus Christ, leaving the same forces operating unchecked which have produced these drunkards. The problem is not how to introduce instruction into the public school system of such a harrowing nature as to terrify the youth. Physiology goes to the wall when brought into collision with appetite. The boy who studies the deadly effects of alcohol upon the human system will have his faith in physiology shaken when he next sees an old toper who has defied physiology for three score years, or four. He will drink whenever he wants to unless he has strong moral convictions which forbid him. The problem is not how to use the saloon as an agency for raising the largest revenue for national and municipal governments. It is here that the saloon is most strongly intrenched. The man who thinks that the saloon is paying his taxes may be himself a sober man, he may be a zealous churchman, but that man will be among the last to drop into the temperance ranks. Nothing so blinds a man to the facts of a case as financial interest in it.

The failure of temperance reform to accomplish any very substantial or permanent results along the lines hitherto pursued is thus explained: We have failed to locate the enemy and force him into open battle. He has fought under cover, and used smokeless powder. Our manoeuvers have been brilliant and spectacular, but harmless. We have excoriated the saloon-keeper, we have hurled invective at the rum politician, we have invoked the wrath of heaven upon the brewer and distiller, but the business goes right on. These men are not the enemy we need to fight. The saloon-keeper is a hireling who would often prefer another job. The rum politician is a petty demagogue, ignorant and feeble in himself. The brewer and distiller are but the visible representatives of an invisible host of men who have their money invested in corporations which are engaged in the manufacture and sale of liquors. These stockholders are the real enemies of temperance reform. They are enriched from the profits of the business. Until we train our guns upon them, we are merely wasting ammunition. But who are they? We do not know them. They may be among the "best citizens" of our communities. They may be members of our churches. They are always conservative men. If a preacher uses severe language in his denunciations of the drink traffic, they are scandalized. They are deeply pained at his extravagant utterances. They are lovers of the "old gospel." They abhor agitation. Who are these men? Nobody knows. They know, and they creep into their vaults and cut their coupons, and smile at the charity of a long-suffering public. It is impossible to drive these men out of their hiding, and compel them to fight in the open. Conscience has made cowards of them all, but while cowardice is profitable, they will endure the scourge of conscience. You cannot drive him from concealment, you cannot locate him, but you can refuse to pay the expenses of his business. That thrust will pierce his heart, for it will damage his income. The attacks commonly made upon the drink traffic have confused the issue, and forced the saloon to assume the role of defender of personal liberty. This has been a fatal tactical blunder. While the friends of temperance are willing to appear as enemies of personal liberty, the saloon can never be dislodged from its present position. No principle is dearer to the American people than that which the saloon is permitted to champion. If the public be forced in the future, as it has been in the past, to choose between the destruction of popular rights and the continuance of all the evils issuing from the saloon, the decision will be in favor of the popular rights. With this decision I am wholly in sympathy. Man may choose ignorantly, foolishly, wickedly, nevertheless God says he must have the privilege of choice—he must have personal liberty. Whenever I undertake to prescribe for my neighbors what their food and drink shall be, they have a right to say "Who are you, that you usurp authority which God Almighty Himself did not exercise?" It is a fact, that my neighbors differ from me in matters of taste, as well as conviction, and, if I begin to coerce them, they are likely to retaliate. Some genuine comfort is left me in the reflection that God did not make me the keeper of the consciences of my fellow-men. Possibly I might have kept them safely, but that was not His method. Under the circumstances, I find my attention pretty well occupied in keeping my individual conscience in a fairly healthful state.

What is the real saloon problem of the twentieth century, and what shall be its solution? The problem is this: How Shall the Burden of Expense which the Saloon has Hitherto Imposed Upon the Sober Element of the Public Be Bound Directly Upon the Back of the Saloon Itself? The great regulative principle of responsible existence in the universe of God is this: evil carries within itself the seeds of its own destruction. Sin is suicidal. To eradicate any evil, it is only necessary to establish direct, immediate, infallible connection between that evil and its consequences. To do this is to array all the forces of the universe, into whose structure God has wrought righteousness and truth and justice, on the side of reform. Evil must nourish itself forever upon the good. If it be denied the privilege, it starves. Drunkards could not exist in a community where all men were drunkards. There must be sober men and women who are willing to furnish the drunkards subsistence. The saloon could not exist in a community where the industrious, wealth-producing classes were unwilling to pay its expenses. The saloon produces no wealth. It is a parasite, and its existence is possible only so long as the public bears its expense. The saloon cannot renew its life from internal sources: it must devour the wealth which industry and sobriety have created. Whenever they refuse further supplies, the saloon perishes inevitably. It never has a year's supplies in store. The one argument which the saloon cannot resist is this—the withdrawal of its supplies. We cannot afford to treat the saloon unfairly. Give the saloon-keeper the same chance that you give the grocer, the butcher, the merchant, the manufacturer. Impose no burden upon him that you would not impose upon them: show him no favor that you would not show them. If his business is as legitimate as theirs, it is tyranny to compel him to pay heavily for the privilege of conducting it. The license-tax imposed upon the saloon is either a gross injustice to the men engaged in that business, or it is a betrayal of the interests of the community that does not patronize the saloon. Why is not the grocer who gives food to the public compelled to pay for that privilege, the same as the saloon-keeper who supplies the demand for drink? Why this discrimination? The law recognizes that the saloon inflicts injury upon the public. The tax imposed upon the business is intended to reimburse the public for expenditures made from the public treasury on account of the saloon. The grocer adds nothing to the burden of public taxation by his business. He does not create the necessity for additional courts and almshouses. If he incurs liabilities in the conduct of his business, he is compelled to meet them himself: he cannot appropriate the profits and turn the expense account over to the public. The saloon-keeper ought not to be taxed to pay the expenses of the grocer. When conditions are normal, and justice is meted out impartially to all, every business that cannot pay its own expenses must go to the wall. If the saloon cannot bear the burden of expense which it creates, the grocer, the merchant, the manufacturer ought not to be compelled to assume it. The people who do not patronize the saloon have some rights that must be respected. Give the ordinary business man a chance. We cannot all engage in the saloon-business. Let a man be permitted to serve the public as a merchant, or mechanic, or physician, without having the burden of the saloon bound upon him. The ordinary honest man must pay his way as he goes—honor his views if he thinks he should not be called upon to pay the saloon-keeper's way, too. Give the sober man a chance. The license system is a betrayal of the public interests, because it is based upon no rational estimate of the injury which the saloon inflicts upon the public. It is necessary for a company to meet its liabilities as they occur, or go out of business. I believe that I am within the bounds of moderation when I say that for every dollar the saloon pays to the national or local government it imposes a burden of ten dollars upon the community in the maintenance of police, courts, jails, penitentiaries, almshouses, insane asylums and widows' homes and orphanages. The principle for which I contend is rational and just. It is this: Find out by Patient, Scientific, Impartial Investigation the Burden of Taxation and Charity Entailed by the Saloon Upon the Community, and Bind That Burden Upon the Back of the Saloon, Even Though it Breaks It. If the present license is too high, if the saloon pays more into the public treasury than it takes out of the pockets of the sober people of a community, the saloon-keeper is suffering injustice. His tax ought to be reduced. If the license is not sufficient to pay the expenses which the public now bears through taxation and charity, let it be raised to the requisite point. This will have an elevating effect upon the saloon-keeper. He will acquire greater self-respect by paying his own expenses. Our plan of taking the consequences of his business, while he takes the profits, has tended to pauperize him, and retard his moral development. It is mistaken philanthropy. The saloon-keeper has had things his own way for a long time, and he ought now to be willing to grind at his own mill.

This will be the solution of the problem of the twentieth century city. It will be effective, because it avoids the difficulties which have rendered temperance reform hitherto so largely nugatory. It demolishes the strongholds within which men have hidden themselves. It will not drive them into the open, but it will compel them to part with the spoils they have wrested from the hands of sober industry.

This solution will preserve the principle of personal liberty, and give it universal application. The liberty of the citizen who wishes to indulge his appetite is not restricted, but the liberty of the sober man who does not wish to pay the bill of the drunkard is protected. It may seem revolutionary to assert the rights of the sober, industrious man, but this man will make himself heard in the twentieth century. This solution conforms to the law and wisdom of the Eternal, and enlists all the forces of the universe on the side of reform. It was an ancient decree which enacted that "whatsoever a man soweth, that shall he also reap," but there is no appeal from it. Whatsoever the saloon soweth, that let it also reap. The twentieth century will see to it that this law is respected. Let no man think that because interest in temperance reform languishes, and the saloon is the most powerful single influence in national and local politics, there is, therefore, no hope of breaking the bondage in which the sober man is held. Any solution of the saloon problem which commends itself to practical wisdom, which proposes measures of relief that do not threaten society with evils worse than those the saloon creates, will be welcomed by the great majority in this country. The solution I have urged must evoke the enthusiasm and satisfy the reason and sense of justice of intelligent citizens. I believe that it places victory within our grasp. It does not propose absolute justice, yet it suggests the nearest approach to exact justice possible in this world.

At this point, as already in Auditorium Endeavor, Secretary Baer introduced the new field secretary, Clarence E. Eberman, who was enthusiastically received, and spoke a few earnest words of lofty ambition for Christian Endeavor.

Dr. W. H. McMillan, the chairman, quietly remarked: "We shall now have the privilege of listening to an address by Rev. P. S. Boanerges," and Dr. Henson received a warm welcome. "The power of the Pew" was his happy theme. His introduction was a comical account of the descent of the pulpit, from its lofty position formerly among the rafters, down, down, till in some of the twentieth century churches the pulpit is actually the lowest thing in the house. The pews are rising in influence in the same way.

Dr. Henson told what the pews could do to help the preacher,—by their eloquent hearing, for instance. He had a deaf auditor once who sat in the front seat and turned up at him his "gospel trumpet" and an eager face as if he thought that the speaker would really say something sometime; and often the preacher would lean over and fill that trumpet full of truth, and hear it gurgle, gurgle, gurgle, down to his soul.

"Praise your pastor. Lay it on thick. He can stand it, so long as your consciences can. I had a dear old deacon once that always came up after my sermon and said, 'I praise you, pastor.' Even when I kerflumuxed, as the boys say, and covered myself with mud instead of glory, he would come up at the end and say, 'I praise you, pastor; you did as well as you could.' I believe in having your trumpeters about you. I came from Chicago. Have you ever seen a watch-spring burning, flashing, coruscating in an atmosphere of oxygen? O what a difference it makes to the preacher when the atmosphere in which he speaks is charged with the ozone of faithful and expectant prayer!

"And the pew can help mightily by its living. It isn't the higher critics that are destroying the influence of the church,—and I have no more sympathy with the destructive critics than you have; but the trouble is not with the higher critics, but with the lower living of Christians. The fog of higher criticism is not to be dissipated by firing great guns at it. That only adds to the fog the smoke of the powder. You can dissipate the fog only by the sunbeams of Christian living. I'll wear myself out preaching the evidences of Christianity, and some cross-grained old representative of Christianity in the pews will spoil the whole inside of ten minutes after I get through.

"Then, by giving. It's the business of the pews to make the money. It isn't a sin to be rich; it is a sin not to be rich, if a man might have become rich by a wise use of God-given opportunity. I bless God for the power of the pews to hold up the hands of the pastor by their financial support.

"Finally, by preaching. I deprecate the division of things into secular and sacred. This making a shut-up cold-storage warehouse of the church is a sin of the day. It is the business of all Christians to preach the gospel. The Lord never meant that the preaching of His truth should be left to a little company of men. You can't hire a substitute. Rockefeller, with all his millions, couldn't. A business man can preach better than a preacher in one point,—no one suspects that he does it because he is paid to do it. We haven't preachers enough to go around. It is the business of the whole church to win the world for Christ."

CHAPTER XVI.

The Power of Christian Endeavor.

Prof. Amos R. Wells, Boston.

When I was a small boy, I used to tell folks what I wanted for my birthday presents. I do so still, but in a less transparent way. And this year I got a birthday present for Christian Endeavor by asking for it. The present was letters from pastors, one thousand, eight hundred and ten of them, and each answered eighteen questions about our society. If anything can prove the power of Christian Endeavor, it is these eighteen hundred letters from busy men, every one of whom paid his own postage. The questions covered all debated points. They gave abundant opportunity for criticism; and though, as the percentages I shall give will show, some pastors criticised, yet I received very few critical letters, because the critics really are few. The letters came from 45 states and territories; they came from 39 denominations; and they constitute the noblest testimony yet given to the power of Christian Endeavor.

There is no power like the power of an idea. Steam power must have its rails, but an idea can run over any road. Electricity escapes at a touch, but an idea grows stronger the longer it is used. They have storage batteries now—a kind of current jam—but nothing can confine an idea.

The power of Christian Endeavor is the power of an idea. The idea C-E-zed upon Dr. Clark first, and then he C-E-zed the rest of the world with it. Yes, all the world; for if you had hands big enough to grasp the globe, you couldn't take hold anywhere without being pricked by a Christian Endeavor pin.

Now there are one-power organizations. The stock exchange moves by water power. The political party that I don't belong to moves by gas power. But Christian Endeavor is a compound engine that utilizes for good all kinds of power. It's an electric motor and a steam engine and a tide mill and a water wheel, with a treadle for the foot and a handle for the hand and a lens for focusing the power of the sun. Born in the heart of Yankeedom, it has Yankee versatility.

And yet there are some powers that even this engine will not use. Gas power, for instance. We'll let others use that. Those, for example, who declare it to be an insidious peril to promise to pray and read the Bible every day and take part in prayer meeting.

Compressed air. Christian Endeavor doesn't use that, either. Christian Endeavor doesn't work under pressure; it works from love, from desire.

Liquid air. That's the coldest agent known. It freezes mercury so that you can drive a nail with it. But there's nothing cold about Christian Endeavor. We can run our engines without liquid air.

Gunpowder. They are using that, nowadays, to propel automobiles. A cartridge explodes and the wheels turn a few times; then another cartridge, and so it keeps going, just like some jerky people I know. But Christian Endeavor doesn't go by jerks.

Well, what is the power of Christian Endeavor? In the first place, it is steam power. And the steam power of Christian Endeavor is our covenant. It is our practical, pointed, purposeful, pertinacious, pugnacious, persistent, persevering, perennial pledge!

I asked those 1800 ministers whether they believe in the Endeavor pledge, and ninety-one per cent. of them gave an enthusiastic yea. I asked them whether the young people are as faithful to their Christian Endeavor pledge as the church members to their vows, and ninety-two per cent. of them declared that they are. I asked them about the effect of the pledge, especially its promises of daily prayer and Bible-reading, on the heart life of the Endeavorers, and ninety-four per cent. of these 1800 pastors thought it helpful. I asked them whether the Christian Endeavor prayer meetings in their churches are well attended, enthusiastic, and spiritually uplifting, and ninety-three per cent. testified that they are. I asked whether the Endeavorers are as faithful in their church attendance as the older church members, and ninety-six per cent. of these 1800 pastors gave a hearty testimony that they are.

These pastors recognize the power of promises. Whatever is worth doing is worth promising to do. No one objects to pledges in practical life. Take a railway time table. That is just such a promise as our Christian Endeavor pledge. The time table doesn't promise to get passengers to a certain place at a certain time, but it promises to endeavor to, to "make it the rule of its life" to. Imagine a theorist, with one of these railroad pledges in his hand, talking with an engineer. "Don't you see what a moral wrong you are doing with your time table?" asks the Theorist. "As how?" growls the engineer. "Why, you might not reach Columbus at 10.42. You might break down. There might be a collision. And then, don't you see how foolish it is to bind yourself? You might not want to go to Columbus; you might prefer to go to Indianapolis. Furthermore, my good Engineer," says the Theorist, "don't you see how formal your time table makes all your movements, how it destroys your freedom and spontaneity of action? The very steam in your boiler, that might spout with the picturesque independence of a geyser, is tied down to a humdrum cylinder. Abolish your time table, my good Engineer," says the Theorist, "or your railroading will become dead and pharisaical. We are not under the law, but under grace."

What the Theorist would like, probably, is a time table that reads as follows: "Train No. 10 on the Big Four will start from Cincinnati, if it can do so without forcing its inclinations, at 8 a. m., more or less, and will head in a general way north east. It makes no promise to reach Cleveland, since it is better not to vow than to vow and not pay (Eccl. 5:5), but it may find it convenient to look in on the Cleveland station some time in the course of the afternoon, provided it can do so in a modern, informal, and wholly unpharisaical manner. Andrew Easy, Passenger Agent." That is the kind of time table our Theorist would enjoy,—for other folks to travel on.

But Christian Endeavor believes in time tables, believes in pledges. The time table is not strictly carried out? Very well; Christian Endeavor doesn't believe in abolishing it, but in oiling up the engine, using better coal, getting a more efficient fireman and engineer and a more business-like conductor, or perhaps lengthening the schedule a trifle if it calls for too rapid runs; but a time table it must have. It believes in progress, and it knows there is no pro-gress without a pro-gramme.

For our Christian Endeavor is not a stationary engine, it is a loco-motive. When a Christian Endeavorer spells "gospel," he emphasizes the first two letters,—"g-o." "Thy Kingdom go," he prays, as well as "Thy Kingdom come." We call him "Father Endeavor Clark," but it's about time we stopped doing that, for he's proving himself the youngest of us all. Let us henceforth interpret the F. E. of his name in a better way and call him "Forward Endeavor Clark."

So much for the pledge, our Christian Endeavor steam. But I said that our society moves by many kinds of power. It moves by hand power also.

All Christian Endeavorers are handsome. I mean it. For "handsome" means, literally, handy, good at doing things. With all our machinery, we do not believe in machine work, but in handiwork, and this hand-work is done in our committees.

How we exult in committees! Some time there will be a German society that will start out with only one committee to do all these various works, and after the logical German fashion they will give that committee a name expressive of its complex functions, and the name will have forty-five syllables. It will be called the:

prayermeetinglookoutmissionarysocialmusicflowerSundayschoolinfor-
mationtemperanceJuniorgoodliteraturecitizenshipexecutivewhatso-
ever committee.

And the Germans will smack their lips over that word and call it good.

Now no Endeavorer can pass through that list of committees without coming from the experience remarkably handsome, that is, handy, in the work of the Kingdom. He will have as many hands as an octopus, and he will be "all hands at it."

I asked those 1800 pastors for testimony. I asked them whether our Endeavor committee work is training the young in church activities. Ninety-three per cent. of them declared cordially that it is. That is praise worth having.

So let us cherish our committee work, Endeavorers. Let us expand it, invigorate it, advertise it, instruct it, consecrate it, till the hand power of our society grows strong for any tool God may present and any task He may set before us.

The power of Christian Endeavor is the steam power of the pledge and the hand power of the committees. What else is it? It is foot power. I do not mean that it is a tread-mill affair; O no. To say that Christian Endeavor goes by foot power is to say, nowadays, that it goes by bicycle. And when I say that Christian Endeavor goes by bicycle, I do not wish to be understood as remarking that it is cranky. It is a modern bicycle, with a tire that cannot be punctured by criticism; it is chainless, except in the matter of prayer chains; and it has coaster brakes that hold it under control on any hill. On this bicycle the girls have no difficulty in keeping up with the boys, for the wheel is a great equalizer.

It is easily converted into a water bicycle. It crossed the ocean long ago. Hindus have learned to ride it, Chinese and Japanese, Zulus, French, Germans, Armenians. In every land its bell rings, and its lamp is lighted, at about half-past six. It will discover the pole before the explorers. "Go ye into all the world," said our Master; and Christian Endeavor is obeying the command—on a missionary bicycle.

I asked the pastors about this also. The question was, "What effect has Christian Endeavor in promoting the missionary zeal of your young people?" Eighty-seven per cent. of them replied that it has a notable and glorious effect.

But our missionary bicycles have yet many miles before their cyclometers. Here we are, at our first meet in the nineteen hundreds, just setting out for a century run. What great missionary goals are before Christian Endeavor? They are five. First, more mission study; second, more missionary prayers; third, better missionary meetings; fourth, more missionary money; fifth, more missionary workers. Study is the frame; prayers, the wheels; meetings, the handle bars; money, the oil; workers, the pedals; and if we can better the wheel in all these points, we shall win the race for the prize of our high calling, and the race we shall win is the human race.

Well, we have found that Christian Endeavor moves by steam power, the pledge; and hand power, the committees: and foot power, its missionary zeal. Does it not also make use of electrical power? Ah, have you ever felt the electric thrill of Christian Endeavor fellowship? It is· like the good old days when you were studying physics at school, and you all joined hands around the room in a scholastic union meeting. You took particular pains, you will remember, to happen accidentally to stand next to pretty Margaret Lamson. Then there was a Leyden jar shock or a Bunsen battery tingle, and you all dropped hands with a laugh. How much closer together you all were after that, and how much better your lessons went, and what a jolly good fellow the professor seemed!

Now some do not want anything like this in young people's religious work. No hand-clasps. No electric circuit. Do you know what their ideal is? They have just realized it,—wireless telegraphy! In wireless telegraphy, you know, the cold, aerial, ethereal radiations all emanate from one centre, and there must be no other radiating centre within a hundred miles, or it throws everything into confusion. That is the ideal, each denomination with its young folks isolated, and one authority in the centre throwing out its orders through the air.

Do you know, on the contrary, the Christian Endeavor ideal? It is a telephone exchange. Hullo, Central! This is Presbyterian. Give me Lutheran. Hullo, Lutheran! What's your best prayer-meeting plan? Ting-a-ling-a-ling! That you, Baptist? This is Congregational. Want to tell you what a good missionary meeting we had the other night. And say, Baptist, call up Disciples, won't you, and both of you come around tonight to our social! That's the way our Exchange works.

I asked the pastors about this Christian Endeavor fellowship. In the first place, I wanted to know about its effect at home. I asked, "Does Christian Endeavor work diminish or increase your young people's loyalty to the church? Ninety-four per cent. of these 1800 pastors asserted with positiveness that Christian Endeavor increases their young people's church loyalty. Then I asked an important question: "What proportion, do you think, of the accessions to your church have come from Christian Endeavor ranks?" The answer was a magnificent tribute to Christian Endeavor: forty-one per cent. was the average. Of course, Christian Endeavor does not claim the entire credit for this; and yet it is a noteworthy fact that, the pastors themselves testifying, nearly half of the accessions to these 1800 churches came from our society.

Then I asked for their opinion in regard to the influence of our union work, our electric fellowship. Again ninety-four per cent. of them declared that this influence is noble, uplifting, inspiring. That is what the pastors think about our telephone exchange.

Now there's only one religious telephone exchange in all the world, and that is Christian Endeavor. It works by union meetings, by society visits, by committee conferences, by conventions great and small, by reports in the papers, by letters, by union prayer-meeting topics, by a great undercurrent of mutual understanding and good will and sympathy and helpfulness and love, that flows from young hearts to young hearts back and forth among the denominations, back and forth among the sections of our own land, back and forth among the nations and races of the globe.

Is it worth doing? Why, the world is belted with cables, its continents and oceans are caught in a mesh of secular business, interlacing, thrilling and throbbing, bound inextricably by electric communication. And shall the units of Christ's church remain coldly and feebly isolated? Shall the forces of Christ's Kingdom be less subtle and pervasive? While the worldlies are drawing mightily together shall the heavenlies dwell in sullen separation? Where is the Cyrus Field of the Christian churches? Has he not come already? And the cable they began to lay at Portland twenty years ago shall yet, please God, reach the haven of every Christian heart.

Christian Endeavor, then, runs by steam power, hand power, foot power, and electrical power. How about water power? Yes, that also. No power is so majestic as the power of waterfalls, rivers, and tides, because it is the vast power of gravitation. Were it not for that mysterious force, which draws with imperative hand every atom of the universe, no Niagara would leap headlong toward the sea, and no tides would lift themselves toward Niagara. Put a machine, like a tide mill or a 'dynamo. in the way of that force, and you have power enough to do the vast world's work.

It is a great thing to be in line with one of God's powers. And Christian Endeavor has done this great thing. It has set itself in line with God's providences, God's tidal waves. Everything is moving its way. The tendencies of the times are with it. Even criticism has helped it along. Definite and unmistakable in its covenant, it has come at a time when the world has grown tired of invertebrate religion. Daring and aggressive in its methods, it fits in with this courageous and out-reaching era. Full of faith, it meets the need of an age of doubt. Within two decades, this gravitative current of divine providence has carried our society from Portland, Maine, to London, Paris, Berlin, to Cairo, Constantinople, Jerusalem, to Cape Town, Calcutta, Kioto, and Peking. This tidal wave of Christian Endeavor has steadily risen, till we number three and one-half million members, found everywhere among Christ's churches, till young people's religious work has become thoroughly established, as a permanent feature of the church.

The very first question in my list for pastors was this: "Do you believe that the Christian Endeavor movement marks an advance in Christian work among young people?" The answer was almost unanimous. More than ninety-nine per cent. of the 1800 pastors shouted Yea! Now this advance movement is not an accident, it is the advance movement, the tidal wave, of God's providence. Nothing else can account for it. With fewer paid workers than ever before led a work of this magnitude, with the expenditure of a mere handful of dollars, Christian Endeavor has attained its present position of influence by the power of God alone. It will continue as long as it is obedient to the will of God; never for a moment fear the contrary. All we have to do is to keep in the providential current whereon the movement has been launched.

Steam power, hand power, foot power, electrical power, water power,—and now one power more. Christian Endeavor goes by sun power. That is the power of the twentieth century. Some day the last forest will have become a government reservation or an issue of a Sunday paper. Some day the last coal mine will have turned out the last slag and shale. Some day the last gas well will have flickered out, and the last oil well will have ceased to gush and even to simper. But still over that world of dismayed factories the sun will rise with power in his wings. Still every foot of earth where the mighty rays fall will be a possible factory site. And then the Rockefellers and the Vanderbilts will migrate to the tropics, and the hottest desert will became a New England, and sun engines will rival the bicycle in variety of patents, and the world, out of that age of unlimited energy from sunlight, will look back to the ages of coal as dark ages indeed.

But Christian Endeavor has already invented a model sun-power engine. The Juniors have not a monopoly of their sunshine committees. Every Christian Endeavor committee is a sunshine committee. The first sunshine song instantly became a favorite with Endeavorers, and so have all the ninety-nine sunshine songs that followed. Some people call the pansy our floral symbol; but no; we borrow from Kansas Endeavorers, and ours is the generous sunflower. The sun never sets on Christian Endeavor. Somewhere beneath its cheery rays there are always societies meeting and committees working.

Now the only thing that many people get out of sunshine is wilts. But Christian Endeavor gets its supreme power from the sun. Not from that fiery ball, the big, flame-faced servant of the planets, around whose puffy waist the astronomers have already flung their girdle of calculation, and guessed how soon he will die into coldness and uselessness; but our light is from the Sun of the sun, the Centre of all universes, the Light that in the Genesis days lighted the candle of light itself. Shot through with this sunshine, what room have we for croakers and pessimism? Cleansed by its healthful rays, what lurking place remains for the deadly microbe of doubt? Touched by the gentle flame of this new Pentecost, dividing itself from the gracious sky upon our heads, what tongue can remain churlishly silent? The highest power of Christian Endeavor is its cheerful consecration. The power is from above, and the heavens are an infinite reservoir. Without price, without stint, with no asking but the willingness to use, our God pours upon us the sunshine of His grace. And as we receive it reverently, and as we use it faithfully, this one power becomes manifold powers. The light transforms itself to heat, to electricity, to sound, to motion. The sunshine vaporizes water and sets the steam engines puffing. The sunshine lifts the ocean and sets the rivers flowing and the cataracts falling, and the water wheels whirling. The sunshine thrills the dynamos into fierce activity. There is no agent or power used among men that does not rest back upon the sun. There is nothing done in earth's busy factories that will not be easier done when we have learned to extract from the sunbeams their secret of power. And there is nothing done in the Kingdom of God that will not be easier done when men have learned the power of sunshiny endeavor, of cheerful consecration. Banish the clouds, and whatever barrier lies between our lives and the Sun of our souls! Reach up your hands of willingness, and God will fill every palm with power! Go forth into the darkness of the world, and the sunlight will follow your steps! Yours is a might irresistible, for it is not yours. Yours is a wealth unimagined, for you are not your own. You are a child of all the future, Christian Endeavor, for you are a child of God, and His is the Kingdom, and the glory and the power, forever and ever.

CHAPTER XVII.

The Twentieth Century Church.

It is impossible that summer weather could be finer than greeted us on Tuesday morning. Clear skies, cool air, fresh breezes,—weren't we sorry for the thousands that stayed home for fear of the heat?

It was a day for courageous forward looks, and what theme more suitable than "The Twentieth Century Church?" In Auditorium Endeavor a pastors' symposium on the power of the pulpit fittingly introduced the fruitful discussions, and Rev. A. L. Phillips, D. D., of Nashville, was the first speaker.

The Power of the Pulpit.

Rev. A. L. Phillips, D.D., Nashville.

Let the first word be this, the power of the pulpit depends on the power in the pulpit. When the man in the pulpit depends chiefly on logic, or rhetoric, or elocution, or ecclesiastical gymnastics, or music, or what not, then his power will be as that of any other man in like conditions. But when the minister of Christ is filled with the Spirit of Christ, then shall he be clothed with victorious, with irresistible force.

He is the Mouth-Piece of Jehovah, and is commissioned to speak upon one subject only—the soul in its present and eternal relations. From the back-ground of the highest and broadest culture of our times he steps forth to proclaim the inspired word of the Almighty,—cleansing for the sin-polluted; healing for the soul-sick; for the guilty, pardon; a heaven-birth for the earth-born; a sure hope of freedom for the sin-enslaved; a life at once enriched and adorned by the fruits of holiness; peace in this world and hope for the world to come and overflowing joy forever. He is the advocate of the only true optimism of all time, because he speaks a message that came only from God and which alone can draw men up into fellowship with Him. The engineer in his good work of setting bounds and habitations, speaks by the chain and compass and is forced to make corrections because of the variations of the magnetic pole; the lawyer in defending the right argues and persuades upon the acts and decrees of good and wise men; the physician in his Christ-like ministry of healing prescribes out of his own experience and that of others equally skillful; but the minister speaks with God's authority God's message to God's own children, calling them to God's own fulness. Truly the pulpit's power lies in the message which it delivers.

The power of the man in the pulpit is largely the power which emanates from personal holiness. The requirements laid by Jesus on His apostles were undoubtedly intended to distinguish them sharply from those amongst whom they labored and prayed. In the organization of the church under the guidance of the Spirit, Paul puts its standard of living very high. Successive ages of culture have brought the common standard of mankind's morals far above that of a century ago. It is not enough that the minister shall live up to the rule of decency and respectability which controls men about him. He must be emphatically and distinctly a marked man, known not only by the absence of certain flagrant sins, but also by the presence in overflowing abundance of the gracious fruits of the spirit. In our day there are two manifestations of holiness that need emphasis. On every side the Lord's prophets are warning us against the deadening power of worldliness which is surely making its way into the church. The minister's testimony against it must be re-enforced by a life of glad and real self-denial. The enormous activities of the church, the meetings to be attended, the addresses that must be prepared and delivered, the simply endless demands upon his time, tempt the preacher away from his daily, private, face to face communion with God. Prayerfulness is absolutely essential to his personal holiness and to the life of his people. Surely the pulpit must be holy, living in positive separation from the world and in unbroken prayer to God.

The minister's power is largely measured by his ability to love men. Most men love here and there according to certain elective affinities. They pass by the false and deformed and mean and give themselves to the strong, and the beautiful and the good. But upon the ambassador of Christ rests the imperative obligation of loving all men everywhere. Black and white and yellow and red men he must love, whether they live under the blazing gorgeous "Northern lights," or roam at will over the vast prairie, or hide themselves in the dark recesses of our African forest, or crowd the great cities of travailing China. Love must be his chief motive to action, his inspiration in doubt and difficulty, the inward regulator of all his life. It must be the chief means of introduction to men's hearts and his mightiest weapon in their conquest. It is his soothing balm for wounded hearts and the universal solvent of hardened spirits. Some ten years ago a young minister became pastor of a scattered and discouraged congregation of poor people in a growing Southern city. One minister after another had labored there and departed in hopelessness. It was called a "hard field." With a heart fairly aflame with Christ's love, this young man began to preach simply and plainly of the love of God for men's lost souls. Day and night he visited them in their homes. His loving heart brought sunshine and gladness to old and young, rich and poor, alike. On the street, in the workshop, on the cars, in their homes the people heard of the Savior from his lips. He was not handsome, nor learned, nor eloquent, but he knew how to love the people, and so they came and were taught to love, and a multitude have been saved through him. Men who know the apostle of the South Sea Islands, John G. Paton, can never forget the tenderness and reverence shown by his pronunciation of the name of "Jesus." His unsurpassed power over the hearts of the most degraded cannibals can be understood only in the light of his yearning, irresistible love for their souls.

> "And a viewless thing is love,
>   And a name that vanisheth;
> But her strength is the wind's wild strength above,
>   For she conquers shame and death."

Combine the power of his message of his holy life, of his resistless love into one force and the result is the most valuable of all earthly qualities— Constructive Power. The minister is essentially a builder, and the pulpit's chief title to the gratitude of men is that it lifts up toward the loftiest ideal, "the measure of the stature of the fulness of Christ." If at times he must be a severe critic it is only that the false and unlovely may give place to the true and beautiful. The power is at once the test and proof of his efficiency, and must ultimately command the respect and support of all honest men.

Am I not right then in saying that the "power of the pulpit" lies in its commission to proclaim the pure Word of God to sinful and struggling men; in its holiness begotten and nurtured by the Holy Ghost; in its power to love all men into loving; in "its power to build men into some real likeness to the son of God"?

President C. D. Crane, of Maine, comes from probably the only county in the United States that has a parson for a sheriff, who is making it so hot for the rumsellers that they are getting their beginning in this world. Sheriff Pearson sent a message to the Convention, telling how he had been offered $70,000 if he would permit the sale of only three kinds of liquor in Cumberland County; and Mr. Crane bore brave testimony to the reality of prohibition in Maine, and declared it to be ten times more effective than license in Cincinnati, which he declared should be pronounced "Sin-Sin-Naughty." Sheriff Pearson is a concrete example of the possible power of the pulpit. "When God wanted to save Nineveh, he didn't send a pulpit bird of paradise down there to warble."

President W. S. Danley, D. D., of Kentucky, spoke of the power of the pulpit as reflected from sympathetic pews.

It is said that Dr. Knox used to say to his divinity students, "Young gentlemen, when you wish to preach a good sermon, first get a good audience." The pew makes the pulpit. The people throw an atmosphere about a minister, and sometimes it is an atmosphere of winter. Some pulpit orators have preached in churches that were cold-storage rooms. These preachers have found it hard in such conditions to operate their vocal apparatus. A sacred proverb declares that ministers are like their people; but that true old saying has been turned end about in popular parlance. It does happen sometimes that while the preacher preaches the gospel up, the pew preaches it down.

To be a power, the pulpit must stand for culture and intelligence. The people demand that their preacher shall be a leader in intellectual matters. A preacher wields small power over those who are ashamed of his literary acquirements. Though literature is not his profession, and no one demands that he shall be an expert in literary criticism, a minister who is a power in the pulpit must possess decided literary tastes and accomplishments. He must know books as well as men.

Pulpit piety is no apology for ignorance. There ought to be no place for one that says, "I'll be a lawyer, or a doctor, or I'll teach, and if I can do nothing else, I'll preach." No preparation, previous or immediate, can be too careful or extensive for the pulpit of real power.

Strength of moral character is an element of pulpit power. The preacher of true power must be a good man as men see him, of course, but also as God sees him. God works through a minister who is good all the way through. A preacher can have power only over people who believe him a true man. Character tells. Of Dr. Stuart Robinson it was said by one who knew him well, that his most eloquent sermon in Louisville was his life of a quarter of a century in that city.

Great faith is an essential element in pulpit power. A man who asks others to believe, must himself believe. A shaky pulpit is a weak pulpit. The antidote for the doubt of our day is a preacher who believes the truth he preaches with all his might, and preaches without if's or and's, or but's. In pulpit affairs, the grip of faith insures mental grasp and spiritual vigor. Strong faith makes a strong man and a strong pulpit.

Hopefulness is a power in the pulpit. A doleful preacher has as little power as a dull one. It is the business of the pulpit to send out light into the dark regions around. No cloud of gloom envelops the preacher who is brightening the lives of his people. He is as optimistic as the gospel itself, which sees a new heaven and a new earth evolving from present conditions. His face, therefore, is set forward, and the light of heaven and the future falls upon his head.

Earnestness is necessary to pulpit power. No powerful pulpit was ever without zeal. Spurgeon said it is the first, second and third thing in preaching. It was the first thing people observed in Moody. Some said he was great in one thing, and others said he was great in another thing; but all said he was full of life. He was a fire, and set people on fire. He rushed like a cyclone, and carried all with him. The best things said in a lifeless manner fall flat. As Cecil said, there is more in the manner than in the matter. Simeon kept a portrait of Henry Martyn, "The man who never lost an hour," hanging in his study, and whenever he felt himself lagging in his work he would look up at the picture and say, "I will be in earnest, I will not trifle."

Under all pulpit power, and source of it all, is the power of the Holy Spirit. It was this power Christ spoke of when he said to his disciples, "Ye shall receive power after that the Holy Spirit is come upon you." Then they would be able to carry the gospel to the world's end. When God works through us we can do his work. The spirit gives all kinds of spiritual power—power of feeling, power of vision, of knowledge, of utterance, power of faith, love, courage, success.

The man of pulpit power is always a man of prayer. Only a praying man has connection with God, and receives the power of his spirit. A self-reliant preacher may have fox-fire, and the semblance of success; but that is all. Prayer is a sign as well as a means of communication with God. Whoever prays to God has God's help in God's work. That means power and success. It is not that ministers need so much to pray that the heavens be opened and the Spirit be poured out; the heavens have been opened, and the Spirit has been poured out; but we should pray that our hearts be opened, and the Spirit poured into them. The outpouring is secure, let us make way for the infilling.

The final speaker of the symposium was the Rev. Allyn K. Foster, President of the Connecticut Christian Endeavor Union.

One of the most essential powers in the pulpit and of the pulpit is its bare existence. An institution's existence is its power oftentimes. A certain institution may not in itself be a good thing; officers may not be as efficient as they ought to be, but the fact that there is in existence the institution that is exercising its function has a restraining influence, and a civilizing and an uplifting force beyond the power of words to describe. For example, the fact that there is a police force in Cincinnati means a great deal. Of course all policemen are not what they ought to be, but the very fact that there is a police force is enough to restrain criminality in the largest degree. The fact that there is an institution known as Christianity, the very fact that there are exercises in our churches Sunday after Sunday, and week after week, is enough of itself to extend the Kingdom of God.

IN WILLISTON ALSO.

"The Twentieth Century Church" was the theme that was also presented to the wide-awake church-members in Auditorium Williston.

In a symposium on the Sunday evening service, Rev. J. S. Henderson, President of the Ontario Christian Endeavor Union, said:

The Second Service is one of the serious problems of church life. Three things have helped to make it such: The indifference of church members who, on the slightest pretext, absent themselves from the service. The experimenting of ministers who try every questionable method of attracting the crowd. The desecration of the Sabbath. In proportion as the rein is given to greed of gain, pleasure, and selfishness, and the holy Sabbath is degraded into an opportunity of gratifying these, to that extent have we full parks and crowded pleasure resorts—and empty churches. The great question is, "What are we going to do about it?" The Christian Endeavorer has only one answer to that question—"We must continue it." Every suggestion for its discontinuance can be used with double force as a reason against giving it up; and usually where it is most difficult to maintain, there it is most valuable. The church members who do not support it need it most. They need to be bound more tightly to the church. They need the instruction the Church gives, in order to counteract secularity.

How shall we make it a success? By awakening the Church to a sense of its importance. Bring the members to see, feel and believe that it is "the" service of the day for reaching the indifferent, the careless, and strangers. It is a great evangelistic opportunity. Let the ministers give more personal and practical attention to the service. The preacher who trusts to spontaneous combustion to make the Sabbath evening service interesting will have seats to let in his church. If the minister is so indifferent as to leave the preparation for it to the fag end of the week, he must not be surprised if he is left to thunder to wooden forms. By ministers and churches combining to put a period to adventitious, secularizing methods. Quackery is the last resort of men who have failed in legitimate practice. So this continual experimenting to draw the crowd is an acknowledgment of failure. The Twentieth Century church is too intelligent, too spiritual, too much alive to her high mission to place a substitute for good old gospel preaching.

Let the whole church life and work and worship revolve round Christ as the planets round the sun, and the Second Service will no longer be a problem.

How to improve this service was Rev. H. W. Sherwood's subject. He did not claim to have a panacea, but he believed in blood-transfusion. The service must be vitalized by pouring into it the best talent and heart the church has.

A great difficulty presents a great opportunity. The question is not to give up the evening service but make it what it ought to be. At the evening service a large proportion of men and women have first met Jesus Christ. Working people cannot always attend the morning service as these people must have a little rest. The difficulty must be met and that which seems to be a doubtful matter will become a blessing to us all. It is not fair to leave the building and maintaining of the evening service to the pastor alone. Vitalize the service by large attendance, by a large attendance of young and old members, especially the young. First vitalize, then energize and spiritualize the evening service. It will either become sensational or spiritual. If you intend to make it spiritual, you will find that more and more the people that attend will expect to receive good from it, and if it is spiritual, they will receive good.

Dr. Charles M. Sheldon had one prophecy to make concerning the evening service,—that it would become largely a devotional meeting and training-class for service. This would mean not less evangelism, but more; for those so trained would go out into business and journalism and the profession to exalt Christ and bring men to Him.

THE PLACE OF THE CHURCH IN THE COMMUNITY.

Rev. James Chalmers, D. D., of Elgin, Ill., speaking on the place of the church in the community, likened human nature to the three elements that compose sugar, salt, alcohol, and vinegar alike; namely, oxygen, hydrogen, and carbon. The work of the church is so to change the combination in human nature that the sour will be made sweet and the poisonous wholesome.

Dr. Chalmers told of the result of his experiments in Elgin, Ill., in getting all the members of the church to go to work. Each member promised to give two hours a week to visiting and inviting and helping; and as a result between two hundred and three hundred members have been added to the church since last December. Let the members of the church all lift together as the stevedores loading timbers all lift together at the "He-o-heave!" of their leaders. And the church will lift together when its leaders ask.

Dr. Johnson Myers, of Chicago, thought that while the church of the twentieth century has gained vastly in numbers, as compared with the church of the first century, it has lost in power.

The Church's Supreme Need.

Rev. Johnston Myers, D.D., Chicago, Ill.

The spirit of the church today is weaker than the spirit of that first church. We are larger in numbers, but in proportion we are far less effective. If the same efficiency pervaded the church of today which was characteristic of those first disciples, the whole world could be won to Christ in a decade. No one can question but that the church is growing, according to statistics; but go into any community and you are conscious that whatever the number of Christians may be, there is an air of weakness and the consciousness of inefficiency. The church does not grip, conquer, overthrow. The fact is that the church of the closing days of the nineteenth century and of the opening of the twentieth century, despite its numbers, is passing through a struggle. We are meeting reverses. The remedy, to my mind, in this hour, is to be found in a return to certain fundamental principles of the first church. They will succeed as certainly now as they did then. If we read the words of Jesus, and more certainly if we enter into their spirit, we cannot fail to see that he intended his followers to be of heroic, self-sacrificing spirit. They were to be cross-bearers, sufferers for his sake. They were to count not their own lives dear if need be to offer their bodies as living sacrifices. Those early disciples caught that spirit from their Lord's life and teaching. Whatever could lead men to such unselfishness, to such consecration, drew the love of humanity. It was not the philosophy of their religion, it was not the teaching, but the life which impressed itself upon the people of that first century. Wealth and power have come into our Protestant churches, millions for church edifices and for the comfort and training of the ministry. There is no question but that the church of today stands in striking contrast to those little bands which constituted the first churches. The heroic element has faded out. When an example of Christian heroism is found, it is advertised and used as an illustration for the inspiration of other Christians. It is so rare that it is remarkable and noteworthy. What the few missionaries did recently in China should be the regular life of the church. This element must come back, and will come back into the church of the twentieth century.

The church of the first century had but one message. The great pioneer thus gives us the spirit of his life and ambition: "I am made all things to all men, that I might by all means save some." Grant that Paul's teachings are largely for instruction; these Christians are instructed not for their own sakes, but that they might save. They lived, they suffered, they preached to save. Salvation to them was the definite thing. We today are absorbed with a variety of useful, honorable, worthy occupations. We are educating, refining, protecting humanity. It is well that we should do all that the church is now doing along these lines. But the successful church of the twentieth century will be a church of salvation. All the agencies will take their subordinate places, and that church will exist to save. Our work has lost in some measure its intensity because there is so much to do besides saving men's souls. That coming church will clear away the criticisms and the reproaches, and will stand among the wreck and ruin of souls as their Savior. That church of the first century had one object. One being filled their thought: "I count all things but refuse that I may win Christ." To glorify his name was the master passion.

We spend a large part of our time in considering the needs of humanity. Philanthropy is the great work of the church today. We have lost our bearings. We have forgotten that the whole life of the church finally is the glory of Jesus. The clamors of the world that we help them, that we relieve them, that we attend to their demands, have drawn us away from that to which we must return. As the church of the twentieth century approaches the close of the age, it will partake more largely of the spirit of the perfect church which bows before the Lamb, saying, "'Thou are worthy to receive honor and power and glory." The test question about a gift or an act or a message will be "will it glorify Christ?" Every Christian life will shine to glorify him. That will bring before the world a view of his kingdom. Giving, living, serving for his glory. I believe in the church and her final victory, but all her efforts must be pointed toward Jesus. The kind of church we will have must be determined largely by you. Let us not be cowards or fools. If we are seeing signs of weakness, let us acknowledge them. Let us face them. Let us overcome them. Let us go home to make our own church the heroic, soul-saving, Christ-glorifying church it should be. The present church with its present spirit will never conquer this world for Christ. But the signs are clear that we are going to see it changed.

CHAPTER XVIII.

The Power of the Twentieth Century Church.

THE BIBLE. — PERSONAL WORK. — EVANGELISM. — ITS SUNDAY
SCHOOL. — ITS CONVENTIONS.

No one could better treat that magnificent topic, "The Power of the Bible," than Dr. A. J. Lyman. He began with a noble tribute to Christian Endeavor in the form of a promissory note to Dr. Clark for the beautiful service done in his church by our society. "The Bible is not a book," said he, "but an incarnation; it is God in a literature. Its power is intellectual, the power of genius. Its power is ethical. The Bible has mastered the masters. 'Jesus is amiable, but not strong,' said one to Wendell Phillips. 'Jesus not strong?' replied that man of might. 'Test the strength of Jesus by the men He has mastered!' The biblical writings are the supreme articulation of the conscience. Its power is supernatural. I might as well expect a sheaf of Syrian lilies to burst from a stack of Roman spears as seek in the first century world the source of the Gospel of John." The whole of this admirable address will be found farther on in this report.

The Power of Evangelism.

William Phillips Hall, New York City.

In the natal days of the Christian Church every Christian engaged in the work of Evangelism, and it was largely because of this fact that, despite extraordinary opposition, the cause of Christ advanced with such remarkable rapidity the first century of its history; when over 500,000 persons were led to confess Him as their Savior and Lord. The Church itself was born through the agency of Evangelism; and today it may be truly said that all the magnificent structure of Christian civilization rests upon the foundations laid, under God, by the evangelists of the cross of Christ. The late Wm. E. Gladstone once said, "Talk about the questions of the day, there is but one question, and that is the gospel." That can and will correct everything, or, if I may be permitted to express the same thought in other words, talk about the questions of the day, there is but one question, and that is the evangelization of mankind, that can and will correct everything. The chief, God-commanded mission of the Christian Church is the evangelization of men; and should the church of the present time realize not only the spirit, but the enterprise and works of apostolic evangelism the millennium would not be far away! For a number of years, the speaker, in connection with many others, has prayed and labored for a revival of primitive evangelism in the Church of Christ. He has endeavored to exemplify in his own life the spirit and works of such evangelism, but at one time in the past he felt very much as he has imagined how he who is now an honored President felt when he was personally advertised as the "advance agent of prosperity," when all the country was suffering from financial depression. The story is told of how, about the time in question, one day in the city of Canton, in this State, two sons of Erin were discussing the general situation when the then noted nominee for the Presidency of the United States walked by on the other side of the street, whereupon, noting the attention the honored gentleman seemed to be attracting, Mike said to Pat, "Phy, Pat, who is the gentleman over there?" Pat replied, "Phy, don't you know who that is? that gentleman is the advance agent of prosperity." "The advance agent of prosperity is he!" said Mike. "Well, upon my wurrerd he's a long way's ahead of the procession!" But conditions and times have changed both commercially and spiritually, and today, while enjoying material prosperity unparalleled, we are also being blessed with a foretaste of spiritual prosperity that I seriously believe will prove in its larger manifestation to be the desired result of a revival of primitive evangelism, unparalleled in power and results in all the history of the Christian Church! Never before in the World's history has such an opportunity like the present offered for the advancement of the Kingdom of our Lord and Savior Jesus Christ, and never before in all the history of the Christian Church has she been so fully equipped for the evangelistic conquest of the World as at the present time. The extraordinary prevalence of sin and doubt in almost every department of human life, the widespread assailments of the citadels of our most holy faith, the questioning of the reality and stability of the very foundations of the Christian Church, all point to the present as a time for the fulfilment of the Divine promise that "When the enemy shall come in like a flood, the Spirit of the Lord shall lift up a standard against him." And God is now raising up the standard in the spiritual quickening of His ministers and people, and in the creation of a holy expectation in the hearts of a vast multitude of believers of the imperative need and certainty of realization of the greatest spiritual revival of the ages! In olden times there were periods of "no open vision," when although God was present with His people, as now, He did not manifest Himself in other than ordinary ways to and through His own, and then afterwards there came other periods when God bared His arm in extraordinary exhibitions of saving and delivering grace, and thus made more manifest His presence.

We believe, to a certain extent at least, there has been a recurrence of the former periods of late years, and that we are now entering upon a recurrence of the latter periods when God is manifesting, and shall yet more abundantly manifest Himself in wondrous power and love to and through His loved ones. This statement is based not upon fancy but upon facts.

Across the Atlantic, our brethren in Great Britain have recently entered upon what has already proved to be one of the greatest and most important evangelistic arousements of the Church and of the Nation ever experienced in the history of that great people. God has given them, as He has also given us, a broader vision than has hitherto obtained Pentecostal days of the evangelistic responsibilities and opportunities of all His ministers and people.

In our own beloved country the Twentieth Century opens with such a revival of interest in the work of Christian evangelism as promises in the near future to practically revolutionize Christian conviction on the subject. Only those who have made a careful study of the matter can even in part realize the great change that has taken place in Christian thinking in this regard. But a few years ago it was generally believed that the work of evangelism should concern and engage the ministry only; in this year, 1901, a very large and rapidly growing percentage of Christian people believe that the Christian Church is entering upon an evangelistic era never before equaled in her history, and in which not only the ministry but all the laity are Divinely called to engage. Moses' prayer, "Would God that all the Lord's people were prophets, and the Lord would put His Spirit upon them" is being answered, and Joel's prophecy that "in the last days, saith God, I will pour out My Spirit upon all flesh: and your sons and your daughters shall prophecy" is being fulfilled more completely than ever. These facts appeal to every Christian believer for immediate consideration. Extraordinary development and advance seem to be the order of the day. This is true not only in the fields of science, literature and art, but also in that of the Christian religion. God, through His Word, His Providence, and the awful spiritual and moral needs of mankind, certainly

seems to be calling upon His people to "Go forward" in evangelistic conquest, as never before in all the history of His dealings with men. One
of our poets has very truly and thrillingly written:

> We are living, we are dwelling,
> In a grand and awful time;
> In an age of ages telling;
> To be living is sublime.
> Oh! Let all the soul within you
> For the Truth's sake go abroad!
> Strike! Let every nerve and sinew,
> Tell on ages! Tell for God!

And God has given us this, His work, to do! Shall we respond to His
call as we hear the sweet accents of the voice of His dear Son as He
once more calls upon us to "Go ye into all the world, and preach the
Gospel to every creature!" He has promised that if we would but "Come
and follow Him, He would make us fishers of men." The humble, ob-
scure Galilean fisherman listened to that appeal, and responded to it as
well. Today his name shines out in immortal brightness from the pages of
God's word, and we recall him now as the great evangelist who on Pentecost's glorious day had no small part in winning three thousand souls for
His Redeemer's Kingdom, and Peter will never be forgotten of God or
men.

One day, some forty-five years ago, a layman of one of our Eastern
cities, being strongly impressed with a sense of his evangelistic responsibilities to God and to his fellowmen, called upon one of the members of
his Sunday School class, then engaged as a clerk in one of the city stores,
and placing his hand affectionately upon the shoulder of his scholar he
told him of the love of Jesus Christ for the unsaved, and plead with him
to yield to Christ for the salvation of his soul. The earnest message was
graciously blessed of God to the young man's salvation, and being thus
led to Christ through the work of Christian evangelism, he resolved to engage in the same blessed service. He carried his resolution into immediate effect, and although ignorant of the classics of men, he speedily acquainted himself with the classics of God, and drawing his ammunition
from the same magazine of Divine truth as had his Master 1900 years before, he soon became mighty in the Scriptures, and in the things that per-
tain to the Kingdom of God. The years passed by, and with constantly
increasing power he witnessed to the truth as it is in Jesus. Soon famed
for phenomenal effectiveness in evangelistic service in his native land, he
responded to the Macedonian cry of his brethren beyond the sea, and although those who had extended the invitation were all dead when he arrived on English soil, he, nothing daunted, still pressed on in his chosen
work. Commanding but an extremely limited hearing at first, this humble
unordained servant of God soon found tens of thousands eagerly hanging
upon his every word. In a short time his personal influence and message
for Christ were felt throughout all Britain, and then all around the
world. After many days he returned to his native land, and spent the
remainder of his time on earth in constant and strenuous efforts to lead
his fellowmen to Christ. Something over a year ago he passed from
earth to heaven, and all Christendom rejoiced in his triumphant death
and wept over his departure. But being dead yet speaketh, and the
Christly eloquence of his magnificent personal influence and works was
never more effective in the arousement of evangelistic effort and enthusiasm than at this moment, and the name and work of Dwight L. Moody
the Apostle of Christian Evangelism will ever be held in the most affec-
tionate and glorious remembrance by the Church of God.

On the third day of December last, in pursuance of a call issued by the
speaker, a notable conference of Christian leaders, representing over ten
million Christian believers, gathered in New York City to consider the
advisability of voluntarily organizing for the promotion of a national revival of evangelical Christianity through existing organizations and agencies. The conference appointed a National Central Committee to promote

such a revival. That Committee, consisting of many representative Christian leaders of our country, including our honored leader in Christian Endeavor, Rev. Francis E. Clark, Mr. John Willis Baer, Mr. C. E. Eberman, Gen. O. O. Howard, Mr. W. R. Moody, and many others, commenced its work by issuing an appeal to the ministry and members of the evangelical churches of the United States for engagement in a 20th Century Gospel Campaign for the promotion of the object in view. The appeal was sent to 30,000 ministers and many religious and secular newspapers. The Christian Endeavor World most nobly supported the movement, and brought it to the attention of a vast multitude of Christians. The Young Men's Christian Association, the International order of King's Daughters and Sons and other great Christian organizations generally united in responding to the appeal, as well as a very large number of ministers and churches throughout the United States. Ministerial associations were personally addressed at many points by members of the Central Committee, and the appointment of a National Canadian Committee was secured with headquarters at Ottawa, Canada. We regret that our limited time will not permit more extended reference to the work and results already achieved by the Committee, but subsequent issues of the Christian Endeavor World will doubtless bring to your attention such further appeals and plans of the Committee as may be issued from time to time. It is as Chairman of the National Central Committee of the 20th Century National Gospel Campaign that I appeal to all Christian Endeavorers to join with us in this mighty movement, firmly believing that if a general response is accorded such appeal, we shall soon realize the power of evangelism in the mightiest revival in the history of the Christian Church. In conclusion, let us all realize that the greatest opportunity of all the ages for the advancement of Christ's Kingdom is now before us, and that if we each do our part in the work we may have the supreme honor of being among those who ushered in the new century for Christ and the Church!

> "He has sounded forth the trumpet
> That shall never call retreat
> He is sifting out the souls of men
> Before His judgment seat.
> Oh! be swift my soul to answer Him!
> Be jubilant my feet!
> Our God is leading on!"

"There is nothing in this world so precious as a human soul," was the text of Rev. H. W. Pope, one of the leaders of the Northfield Extension movement. He made a powerful plea for personal work, calling on all who had been instrumental in leading a soul to Christ to lift their hands.

Personal Work.

Rev. H. W. Pope, New Haven, Conn.

The Master has given to every one of us a commission to do this work. In John xv. 16 we read: "Ye have not chosen me, but I have chosen you, and ordained you, that ye should go and bring forth fruit, and that your fruit should remain." It is a very simple thing to show one how to become a Christian. On God's part it consists in giving; on our part, in receiving. But the thing given by God and received by us is not a thing at all, but a person, and that Person is Jesus Christ, the one essential. If you find a person who is willing to accept Jesus Christ, make sure that he believes that Christ has come into his heart and taken possession. Be sure that he is not trusting to feeling.

Again, I would cultivate what might be called "a passion for souls." Some people have a passion for money and some a passion for music; why shouldn't we have a passion for souls? David Brainerd used to say: "I care not where I go or what hardships I endure, if I can only win souls to Christ. All I think of by day and dream of by night is the conversion of souls." If you say your heart is cold and unsympathetic, and you can live among unconverted people and not feel disturbed about them, I want to say this: It is the mission of the Comforter to reproduce in us the veritable feelings of the Master. He had tenderness and sympathy and a burning passion of love. Yes, and it is the mission of the Holy Spirit to make hearts of flesh so full of sympathy and compassion that we would not recognize ourselves as we were five years ago. Further, let our work begin, continue, and be saturated with prayer. First of all, let us pray for all people. There are fifteen hundred millions of people on this globe, and by our prayers we can bring down definite blessings upon every one of them, and we can do it every day of our lives. It is a special Scripture command that we do this. Then I would suggest that we try to improve the opportunities that come to us day by day, and they come much oftener than we suppose. If you say that you don't have opportunities, just stop and count them for a single day, and you will be surprised to see how many people you come in contact with to whom you might say a word.

I believe that teachers have some of the grandest opportunities that God ever gives any one on earth. A college friend of mine told me a little while ago how he became a Christian. His teacher came along and dropped a note behind her on the seat, so that no one else could see it. He picked it up. It read: "Dear Charles, as you are especially good in mathematics, I want to propound the following problem: 'What shall it profit a man if he gain the whole world and lose his own soul?'" "That word put in that way led me to accept Christ," he said, "and my seat mate, whose name was Ripley, and who was the best mathematician in the class, came out for Christ about a year after, and this was the story he told. He said: 'I accidentally looked over your shoulder and caught the first line of that note, "Dear Charles, as you are especially good in mathematics." It raised all the jealousy in me, for I thought I was a better mathematician than you, and so I was just mean enough to look over your shoulder and read the rest of it. It went like an arrow into my heart, and I was never able to shake it out,'" and about a year after he accepted Christ, and told what it was that set him thinking.

One more thought: I believe the Spirit is constantly trying to use us, and in many cases he fails through our neglect or disobedience. God help us to listen to even the faintest whisper of the Holy Spirit, that he may not be disappointed in us or thwarted in his purpose when he tries to turn the attention of the unsaved unto the Lamb of God, that taketh away the sin of the world.

Marion Lawrance, the eminent Sunday-school worker, opened his address on the power of the Sunday school by quoting Ian Maclaren's answer to Mr. McRae, a newspaper man of Cincinnati, affirming that the Sunday school impressed him as the most potent thing in America. Mr. Lawrance defined the Sunday school as something more than a field to work in; it is a tool to work with. Speaking of the Sunday school as a civil power Mr. Lawrance said that the Sunday school is a mightier agency for righteousness than all the laws on our statute books. To illustrate the power of the Sunday school as a teaching agency, Mr. Lawrance read a hymn sung in Mormon Sunday schools:

> "I'll be a little Mormon,
> And follow Brigham Young."

Scarcely ever is a Mormon trained in these schools converted. The spiritual power of the Sunday school was fitly expressed by the words of John Wanamaker: "I'd rather be a Sunday-school teacher than anything else, because when you save a man or woman you save only one, but when you save a boy or girl you save a whole multiplication table."

Speaking on the uses of conventions, Dr. Wayland Hoyt, of Philadelphia, proved conclusively and beautifully from the laws of crystallization that like particles cannot help coming together. We have to hold conventions because of the inherent unity of Christian life. The witnessing of kindly, courteous lives on excursion-trains and in hotels and streets is one great use of conventions. The acquaintanceship of conventions is another blessed utility of theirs. Dr. Hoyt spoke tenderly of his gratitude to Christian Endeavor conventions for having made him acquainted with the lovely character of Maltbie D. Babcock. Conventions pay in all these and many other ways; and the false economy of those that object to the expense of Christian Endeavor conventions Dr. Hoyt compared to a man who stooped to pick up a pin and thereby spilled over his head a pail of molasses he was carrying on a stick over his shoulder.

Christian Conventions.

Rev. Wayland Hoyt, D. D., Philadelphia.

Did you ever think how intertwisted with the beginnings of Christianity the tendency to gatherings, to conventions is? There in that upper room in Jerusalem, the faithful eleven shut in from their loving Lord, while he opened his heart to them—the windows of which gracious and inexpressible precious disclosure for us are the Scriptures, the 14th, 15th, 16th and 17th chapters of John's Gospel. What was that but a convening? When the three thousand smitten into surrender to Christ by the masterful sermon of Peter on the day of Pentecost, and the three thousand almost immediately swelling into five thousand, found themselves flowing together naturally and easily—what was that but a convening? When new and difficult questions began to emerge, and the membership of the Church in Jerusalem met to discuss and decide these questions in the first Council at Jerusalem—what was that again but a convening?

The fact is that instantly you open the inspired and historic pages of the beginning of Christianity, almost the first thing you come on are these gatherings—conventions. There is a significant physical analogy for all this. Take the force and law of crystallization going on in nature. The centuries have drifted from the solemn pyramids of Egypt. But nature is a pyramid-builder. When water holding salt atoms in solution has evaporated, the salt atoms immediately arrange themselves in the precise order of those great stone pyramids. What is the basal fact of this law of crystallization? The attractive poles of the ultimate particles of matter seek each other out, and as they hold each other the various shapes of crystals appear and stay. So there is a social crystallization. It is according to the nature of things. There is nothing new or unnatural in Christian Endeavor conventions. The attractive force in its members—the force which the pledge means and binds—love to the Supreme Christ, to his Church, and, therefore, of love to all who themselves love him and what he loves, compels convening together.

And the uses of such conventions? The use of witnessing for our Lord: Nothing has been more phenomenal than the impressions our great conventions have made as evidence of the reality, vigor, pervasiveness of Chritianity. The use of patriotism: The gathering of young Christians from all sections of our vast country, their devotion to good citizenship, is having enormous and purifying political influence. The use of acquaintanceship: How delightful is the gathering together, the knowing of each other, by those in different fellowships, loving and trusting a common Lord, yet never demanding any disloyalty to denominational convictions. The use of incitement and instruction: One goes from a great Endeavor convention as from an electric tonic, energized for hope, faith, service, triumph.

CHAPTER XIX.

The Power of a Noble Life.

"In our official processions," said the chairman, Canon Richardson, "we always put our bishops and archbishops last." And then he called upon Booker T. Washington, who was received with a superb burst of applause. Never has this great man, a wonderful leader of his race, spoken with greater power than before that magnificent audience in Auditorium Endeavor.

The Power of a Noble Life.

Booker T. Washington, Tuskeegee, Ala.

The subject assigned me is one which I fear I cannot discuss with advantage either to myself or to this audience. My early life was spent as a slave, and later the influences of poverty and ignorance were not such as to fit me to be your instructor on this great occasion on "the power of a noble life." I do not believe, however, that in all of the history of the country there has ever been a time when the want was so great for strong, unselfish, pure, intelligent men as is true at the present time. There was never a time when our country was more in demand of men who would be willing to sacrifice ambition, position, fortune and comfort for the welfare of their fellow men, and I am glad to add that I do not believe that there has been a time in the history of the world when so many men were finding pleasure and satisfaction in an effort to help their fellow men. In a country where the population is composed of so many racial elements, it is specially important that the standard of life be high, that we learn not to live for our own individual comfort; not to live for our own community, our own state or for our own race alone, but that our sympathies and activities extend to all communities and to all races. No man can do the highest and best work whose sympathies and activities are bounded by race or color.

One of the most beautiful and satisfactory things in connection with the effort to educate our people at the Tuskeegee Institute in Alabama is the beautiful, self-sacrificing spirit exhibited by the graduates of that institution. After they themselves have received education, often at the price of working with their hands for ten hours in the day and studying for two hours at night, they count it a privilege to go out in the plantation districts, amidst poverty, ignorance and superstition, and give themselves almost without price and hope of material reward in an effort to lift up their unfortunate fellows. I have in mind at the present time a young woman who, by reason of some inability, failed to finish the entire course of training at Tuskeegee. But nevertheless she went out into a district where she found the people in debt, mortgaging their crops, paying exorbitant rates of interest on their advances, living on rented land in small one-room log cabins from hand to mouth; they had never had a school longer than three months and that was taught in a wreck of a log cabin where there was no comfort and nothing in the way of school apparatus. In this community not only the material but the moral and religious condition of the people was anything but encouraging. For nearly a year this girl toiled among these people and did not receive as much as $5 per month in cash for her services. She not only taught the people in the little log schoolhouse in the day, but at night in meetings she taught the older people better methods of agriculture. She taught them how to save their money, how to stop spending it for whiskey, snuff, cheap jewelry, for cheap, flashy, showy ribbons and many other articles which they could do without. She taught them how to work harder, how to stop wasting their Saturdays, how to begin the buying of land and the erection of neat, comfortable homes. Not only this, but she taught them how it was possible for them to save their money and build a schoolhouse, and very soon a neat, comfortable schoolhouse replaced the wreck of a log cabin which she found when she went there. In addition, after this was completed, she began an effort to extend the school term, and very soon through the guidance and inspiration of this woman the school term was extended from year to year until at the present time the school is in session eight months. Within the short space of six or seven years in the industrial, educational, moral and religious life of this community there has been a complete revolution. No one can go into that community and look into the faces of the happy and hopeful people, no one can go through their well cultivated farms, into their nice, comfortable homes, into their well regulated church and schoolhouse and Christian Endeavor Society without realizing at a glance the power of a noble, self-sacrificing life.

The privilege of teaching and lifting up a fellow human being is the highest privilege given any man. The longer I live and the more experience I have, the more I am convinced that after all the one thing that is worth living for, and dying for if necessary, is the opportunity to make some individual more happy and more useful. Wherever you and I find selfishness and race prejudice we must teach ourselves to rise upon stepping stones of our dead selves and crush out this prejudice. We must learn to take our places upon the high ground of unselfishness and helpfulness to all classes of all people. Only a few days ago a white man in the South said to me that he was ashamed of the life that he had formerly lived; that it had been a selfish life, a life filled with regard only for the members of his own race, but that henceforth he was resolved to live for the benefit of both races and not permit himself to be narrowed and cramped in his sympathies and aspirations.

One of the best examples of the power of a noble life is furnished by the late General S. C. Armstrong, the founder of the Hampton Institute, who, immediately at the close of the Civil War, refused to yield to the temptation which would have brought him wealth, high social or official position, but chose rather to cast his lot among the poverty-stricken people of the South of both races. At the Hampton institute he worked with the high purpose in view of not only doing something that could lift up the Negro but at the same time would help remove the burden of caring for the Negro from the shoulders of the white people of the South. As a result of his self-sacrificing example we have at Hampton one of the noblest and most useful institutions in the country. The influence of this institution is not only felt in every part of the South among the colored people but is felt among the white people in addition. Here we have an example of the power of one man whose work has touched the hearts and activities of almost an entire nation. Compare the influence of such a man with that of one who has lived only for himself, only for the accumulation of money for money's sake without regard to using money as a means of lifting up the unfortunate.

In Wilcox County, Alabama, there is one of the highest and best examples of noble living that it has been my privilege to know about. In that county there is a Southern white man, Mr. R. O. Simpson, a former slaveholder, who a few years ago made up his mind that he was not doing his duty regarding the education of the colored people in that county, many of whom were formerly his own slaves. He too had been cramped and limited in his activities by reason of the narrowing influences of race prejudice, but he resolved to throw off this influence, to be master of himself and to do his duty regardless of what criticism might come in regard to the unfortunate blacks in his community. Largely as a result of the unselfish efforts of this one Southern white man in a community where a few years ago there was ignorance, poverty and superstition, today there is a large school of nearly 400 black students, there are 13 industries, there are 18 instructors, there is an industrial, intellectual and religious influence going out from that institution into every part of the South through the medium of the students educated there that is fast helping to regenerate the entire South. When I am asked how the race problem is to be solved, I say that it is to be solved largely through the efforts of such strong, far-seeing, unselfish men as Mr. Simpson, and I believe that the time is not far distant when his example will be followed in nearly every county of the South. In a large meeting not long ago when the colored people were praising God for His goodness in setting them free from American slavery, I remember that Mr. Simpson arose and said, "My colored friends, in the midst of your rejoicing and thanking God for setting you free you forget that God was also good to me and my people in setting our race free." And so in this country we are all free, free to work for each other, free to sympathize with each other in everything that will promote our mutual interests.

In 1840 one of my race was sold from Virginia into Georgia. After serving his master in slavery for twenty years, seeing his children sold, his wife subject to the lash and other hardships, at the command of Lincoln he became a free man. Conditions reversed themselves. By industry and economy the ex-slave secures a comfortable home, educates and trains his children along industrial lines; he becomes prosperous and independent. In the meantime, his former master and mistress grow infirm, have reverses, going down till poverty and want are reached. The black man, the ex-slave, hears of the condition of his former owners, and at great expense and inconvenience finds his way to them. Grasping them by the hand, he lets them know that the past is forgotten, tells them of prosperity and future hopes. This black man brings his former owners to his own home, builds for them a neat cottage, nurses them, feeds them, warms and protects and cheers them into happiness and contentment. This, this, my friends, is an example of a noble life. Let white men. North and South, strive to match it, to excel it, if they can.

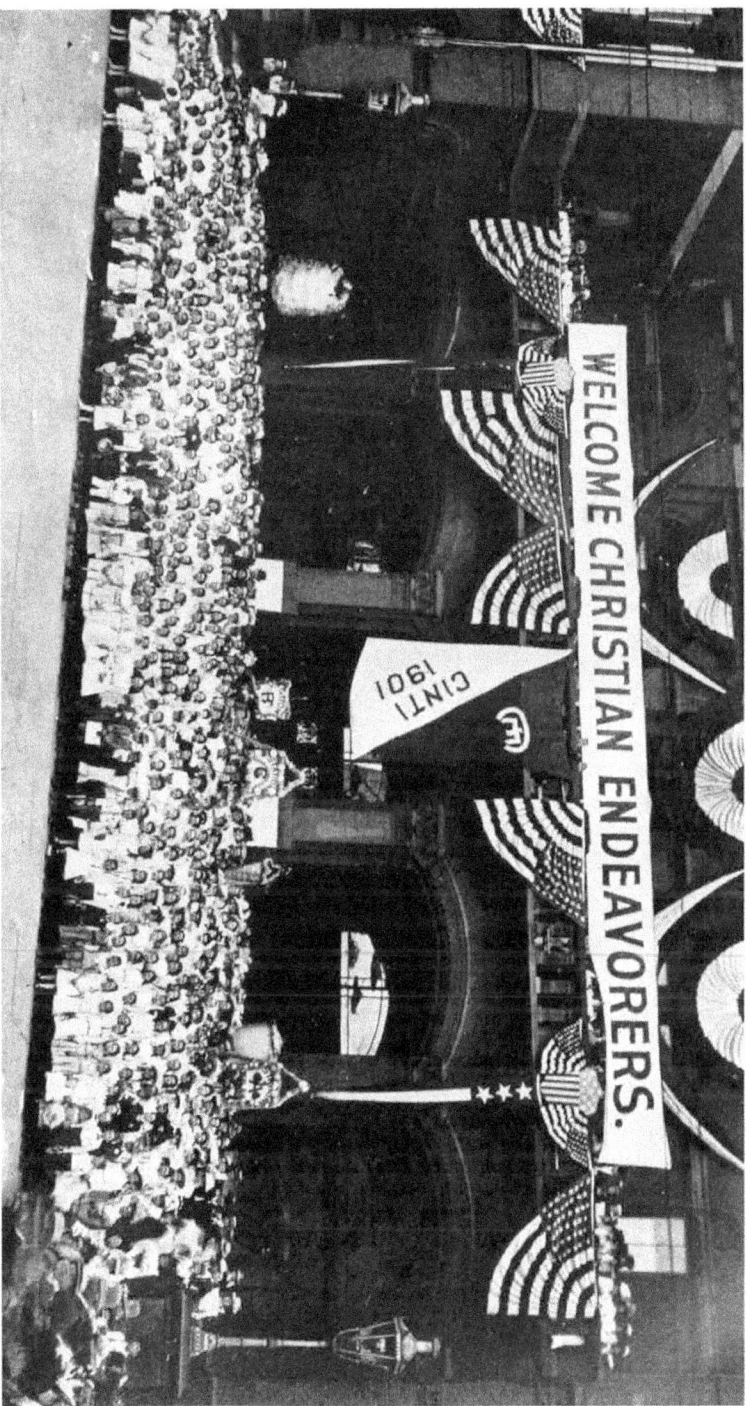

A PART (NOT HALF) OF THE CHILDREN THAT TOOK PART IN THE JUNIOR RALLY.

CHAPTER XX.

The Junior Rally.

This was the children's service, and the older Endeavorers had been told that they weren't wanted there. The great space of Auditorium Endeavor was packed long before the time for beginning, floor and spacious galleries to the roof, while the stage was a garden of beautiful child faces and gay colors.

How those Cincinnati Juniors can sing! Under the skilful direction of Mr. Palmer Hartsough they carolled their welcome song, and "There's a place in the ranks for me," and many another beautiful piece, with a brightness and readiness and accuracy that excelled all the Junior singing of our splendid Junior rallies of the past.

Treasurer Shaw, who presided, introduced our genial secretary by asking the children whether they had ever seen a menagerie. He was going to show them a bear. A bear with three cubs. A bear that liked to hug little boys and girls. Of course it was John Willis Baer, and he proceeded to give the children a very bright and sensible talk that held every one of their busy noddles from beginning to end. "Six P(ea)s in a Pod" was his subject, and the P's were Polite, Patriotic, Punctual, Practical, Persevering and Prayerful.

This year's Junior exercise was different from all its brilliant predecessors. It appealed in a thousand ways to the hearts of the vast audience. "Junior Endeavor Extension" was the title, and it was conducted by Mr. Henry Appleton, of Cincinnati. The first part was an exhibition of Cincinnati's institutions for the care and nurture of children, taken as representative of similar institutions the world around. It was a beautiful procession, eloquent of the blessed spirit of Christianity. Many times the stage was emptied, and many times it was filled again, but always with children,—children of the rich and children of the very poor. Pathetic little figures that know no father or mother. Children by the hundred, lovely bevies of girls with symbolic wreaths and flowers and banners and placards. Squadrons of boys in uniform. Comical children and solemn. Colored children and white. Children that sang (and better than we had imagined it possible for children, and especially boys, to sing). Children playing the zobo. A children's brass band, that made the big building ring. Children in many charming and appealing moods.

There was one of Cincinnati's great Sabbath schools; there was a splendid mission Sunday school; there were children from many Bethels and charitable institutions, and especially from the Cincinnati House of Refuge, whose inmates entertained us with a great variety of motion songs, delightfully rendered. The singing of "The Holy City" by a company of boys was a spirited performance. The public schools were represented by a chorus from the Newport schools, led by Professor Butler, their musical director. A military drill by a company of boys was executed with much accuracy and brightness. The German songs, sung by the German Protestant Orphan Asylum, were sweet and enjoyable.

The second part of the programme was brief, but full of point. It was a "conference" of Juniors, seated on the platform, who went through all the proper forms of a conference, electing officers, and hearing reports of committees. The present condition of the Junior work was exhibited in this unique way, and the splendid opportunities for Junior extension in all the institutions and schools shown in the first part of the programme.

This exercise held from beginning to end the closest attention of all, and had the rare merit of being practically suggestive as well as full of attractiveness and beauty.

CHAPTER XXI.

Twenty Years of Christian Endeavor.

The sessions of Wednesday morning gathered up some of the fruits of twenty years of Christian Endeavor. In Auditorium Endeavor Mr. George W. Coleman, the energetic advertising manager of the Christian Endeavor World, set a good example for those that attempted this all-but-impossible task. He told in a delightful way how our blessed Society has spread among soldiers and sailors. His reference to Ivory Soap, "It floats," was heartily appreciated by the Cincinnatians.

Christian Endeavor Among Sailors and Soldiers.

George W. Coleman, Boston, Mass.

Christian Endeavor has made a blessed record wherever it has gone, and not the least blessed thing about Christian Endeavor is that it never stops going. When it began its toddling steps in Portland, Me., more than twenty years ago, only its Father in Heaven knew what tremendous going power those little legs would soon develop. After spending an astonishingly brief time in its cradle, it walked down to Newburyport, Mass., one fine day and it has been steadily on the go ever since. It not only has become a noted globe-trotter, but being fully 99 and 44/100 per cent. pure, IT FLOATS—just as readily as it travels by land. You will find him down among the sailors and on the great deep, in the soldier's barracks, out among the life-savers and light-house keepers. But it is my especial privilege to tell you something about Christian Endeavor among the sailors and soldiers.

Miss Antoinette P. Jones of Falmouth, Mass., early in 1890, in reponse to a call for help, advised with Dr. Clark as to how Christian Endeavor methods might best be adapted to the sailor in his special environment. The United Society undertook to publish the literature necessary for the spread of the work and Miss Jones, simply as an earnest, loyal-hearted Endeavorer, entered into the work heart and soul. And from that day to this she has rendered a most noble and self-sacrificing service. The lives of hundreds of our sailor-lads have been ennobled and sweetened under her Christian influence and motherly care. Just to read some of her correspondence with these boys and thus witness the genuine nature of the Christianity they profess, would thrill you with gratitude to God for such a blessed work. But if Christian Endeavor made rapid progress on land, what shall we say of its floating capacity on the seas. Think of the sailor's reputation for wild living, remember the loneliness of his calling, his freedom from restraint when going ashore, and then let me tell you that over 150 floating societies of Christian Endeavor have been organized and more than 6000 sailor lads have taken their Christian Endeavor pledge. Now remember, too, a sailor's opportunity for meeting many peoples, and imagine, if you can, what a force for righteousness 6000 sailor-men can exert in the world. Societies have been organized on board the "Maine," "Olympia," "Indiana," "Oregon," and other battleships. Three loyal, true-hearted, Christian Endeavor sailor boys were buried with the "Maine" in the murky waters of Havana Harbor. One of them, Carlton H. Jencks, had already rendered notable service for his Master. having been largely instrumental in founding the Christian Endeavor Seaman's Home at Nagasaki, Japan. There is now in that home a memorial room furnished in honor of this Christian sailor through the contributions supplied by his friends and admirers. Ten other rooms have been furnished by Christian Endeavorers. There were twelve floating Endeavorers on the "Olympia" the morning Admiral Dewey sailed into Manila Harbor. A crew made up entirely of Christian Endeavor men were put in charge of one of the captured Spanish gunboats. There was a Floating Society of Christian Endeavor on board the "Oregon" when she made that magnificent run around Cape Horn. A Christian Endeavorer was among those killed at Cardenas, Cuba, where the first American blood was spilled.

But what about Christian Endeavor among our soldiers? If there is anything drearier than a sailor's life at sea it is a soldier's life in camp. Here it is that Satan finds all kinds of work for idle hands to do. Reckless living will decimate a regiment quite as ruthlessly as fire and sword. But the power and beauty of Christ make their appeal to the heart of the soldier boy quite as readily as to the sailor lad. And the great camps set up in our Southland in preparation for the advance on Cuba afforded a wonderful opportunity which Christian Endeavorers were not slow to take advantage of. In every great camp were found Christian Endeavor soldiers eager to co-operate with Christian Endeavorers from without in Christian work among the unconverted and in maintaining Christian Endeavor tents for the comfort and use of their comrades-in-arms. The record of Christian Endeavor among the soldiers is a noble one. I wish I might tell you of the work in the Philippines. Rev. Leonard P. Davidson, whose work among the soldiers there has counted for so much, and whose untimely death is so greatly lamented, was in close touch with the spiritual life of many of these Christian Endeavor soldiers. But I can only refer you to a future number of The Christian Endeavor World, which will publish extracts from the letters of these boys showing how earnest and practical they are in their Christian work. Notwithstanding I have not begun to cover the field in its relation to work among our sailors and soldiers, I have no time left in which to tell you about the Christian Endeavorers of the British Army and Navy, and of a certain Spanish Christian Endeavor soldier, and of the Christian Endeavorers in the Boer Army, and among the Boer prisoners in camp at St. Helena and at Ceylon. Neither is there time to tell you of the magnificent work done on behalf of sailors and soldiers by Christian Endeavorers in San Francisco, Philadelphia, and other great centers where our soldiers and sailors have congregated. I must in closing urge Endeavorers everywhere to take a hand in this work by sending literature, making comfort-bags and conducting Christian correspondence. It is literally like casting your bread upon the waters, but you shall certainly find it after many days.

The good word was then taken up by Rev. S. Edward Young, that long-time leader in Christian Endeavor work among life-savers and light-house keepers. Their lonely, heroic lives were depicted in sympathetic sentences, what our Society has already done among them was set forth, and an earnest plea was made for increased activity along this blessed line of service.

Christian Endeavor Among Life-Savers and Light-House Keepers.

Rev. S. Edward Young, Pittsburg.

Who will cheer the life-saver? Eleven thousand strong, he sentinels the coasts of Russia, Turkey, Austria, Spain, Denmark, Holland, Belgium, Germany, France, Great Britain, Canada and this Republic. Hale, stalwart soldier of the storm, whom neither icy blast, nor murderous billow, nor chasm of death can daunt, who times beyond reckoning have brought the life-boat or life-car, who breeches-buoy from wreck to shore, rescuing, how vast a multitude, eternity alone may tell! This unknighted chivalry lay down their lives for others. They ennoble human nature. They do honor to our race. But no school, no church, no comfortable lodging greets the life-saver. His family must live distant from the station. He is underpaid. His calling and his health are enemies. Governments provide chaplains and pensions for soldiers, whose business is to take life—none for the man whose task it is to save life. How shall Christian Endeavorers better the life-saver's condition? By transforming each life-saving station building into a chapel for the isolated group of surfmen, fishermen and laborers within attending distance. With what gladness they have welcomed religious services ever since a stage-load of Endeavorers sang and prayed and spoke the Word at a New Jersey station ten years ago this summer, until scores of societies along lake and ocean know the blessedness of bearing the Gospel to these most heroic, most neglected of mankind!

Who will cheer the lighthouse keeper? About thirty thousand guard all seas and lakes and rivers, giving guiding light yearly to the something like fifteen thousand million dollar traffic of the waters and to human beings, seafaring millions in number. What is the loneliest life beneath the skies? Is it not to be a hermit in the bleak, still tower far from the haunts of men, patiently, ceaselessly tending the great light, thinking how every ship out there hopes some day to make harbor, but the light-keeper never? Many keepers receive no visitor the whole year. Mail comes, may be, once a month. Counting the army of constructors, and allowing five to a family, and remembering the fishermen and heterogeneous population somehow immediately connected, there are probably half a million people to be reached by the International Committee of Christian Endeavor in work in life-saving stations, light-houses and light-ships, and these Christianized completely could give the Christian tone to the shipping relations of the whole planet. This is home and foreign missions combined. Is there a work more pleasing? Is there any organization to do it as Christian Endeavor can?

One of the editors of the Christian Endeavor World, with his characteristic and interesting style, had collected splendid information about foreign Christian Endeavorers.

Christian Endeavor Among Our Foreign Population.

Rev. John F. Cowan, D. D., Boston.

Tony, the banana man, has just rung your door bell. How much do you owe him? Don't feel for your small change; you can't pay what you owe this son of Mark Antony in that coin. The account is too large. Here is the way it stands: His fathers, in the days of Constantine, carried the Gospel of Jesus Christ to your fathers in Britain; and so his forefathers made Christian Endeavor possible. What is Christian Endeavor doing to square accounts with Tony, the banana man? Something, I am glad to answer. In Newark, N. J., there is a thriving Italian Presbyterian society of forty members that has repeatedly won two local union attendance banners and a Bible prize. It has also presented an Italian banner to the Essex County Union. Most of its members are converts from the Roman Catholic Church. There is another Italian society in Roseta, Pa.; possibly there are others. There ought to be. We can never pay Tony what we owe him by dubbing him "Dago" and leaving him to the policeman and newspaper cartoonist. One society in Vermont brought an Italian minister from New York to work among the laborers a new railroad had brought to their town. There are Spanish-speaking societies in New Mexico and Colorado, with opportunities for more among the Spanish-speaking people along our southern border, from Florida to California. Probably the largest body of Endeavorers in America using a foreign tongue are the German-speaking Endeavorers, who have a Union and conventions of their own, and a German paper published in Buffalo, Der Mitarbeiter. They have been holding their annual Convention here in Cincinnati, and have manifested a spiritual fervor and aggressiveness that we all might imitate. We can help them to bring in the day when every German-speaking Protestant church in America shall have its Endeavor societies. Next to the German societies in number come the Chinese. No Endeavorers in this country have a prouder record than these dozen or more. Half of them are in California. There in San Francisco is the heroic band of givers, of whom Rev. Jee Gam is pastor. The forty-four present members of this Congregational Chinese society gave last year for missions over $1500; and they have planned this year to support three missionaries in Northern China. Prejudice compels them to come in at the back door of this country, and some of them earn their living by washing our soiled linen; but they put to shame the giving of the favored sons of America, to whom all the doors of opportunity and wealth are wide open. There are Chinese societies in Boston, in New York, in Philadelphia, Toronto, and scattering ones all over the country. There ought easily to be one hundred societies among the thirty thousand Chinamen in this country whom we can evangelize without fears of Boxers. No work pays better. These Chinese societies in America have furnished some of the bravest and most self-sacrificing workers for the Chinese mission fields, and the staunchest and most loyal Christians in the land. There are several Armenian societies, from Worcester, Mass., to Fresno, Cal. There are two Japanese societies in California and one in Honolulu, U. S. A. I am sure you will all join in pledging the forty societies in Japan, whom Rev. Mr. Miyaki has traveled across the ocean and a continent to represent, that we will see that all of his countrymen that come to our shores shall have Christian Endeavor presented to them.

In Quincy, Mass., there is a Swedish Congregational Society of thirty members, and in San Jose, Cal., a Baptist Swedish Society. They are citizens America is glad to welcome. There are French-speaking societies in New York and among the French Canadians in New England. In Wisconsin there are a number of Welsh societies that publish a little Christian Endeavor paper called "The Lamp." May its light never flicker. The Greek societies are in Massachusetts and the Bohemian in Pennsylvania. Christian Endeavor has a way of springing up in the most unexpected places. I should not be much surprised to hear of societies among the denizens of the midway at the Pan-American Exposition. There is at least one society of Cubans, at Tampa, Fla., in the Congregational Church of which Rev. Mr. Hernandez is pastor.

I have spoken of these various societies today as being of our foreign populations. But one of the things that Christian Endeavor will help to come to pass more quickly is their transformation from foreigners into English-speaking, true-blue American citizens. Then in the place of all their flags there will wave over Italian and Spaniard and Greek and French and Armenian and Chinese and Japanese and Swede and German, and all other nationalities whom America has welcomed to her shores, but one flag, the glorious banner of the free, the Stars and Stripes for ever.

Mr. Baer then introduced Rev. George W. Moore, that noted African teacher and leader, who spoke about Christian Endeavor in his race. He was instrumental himself in organizing the first Afro-American society,—one in Washington, in a most disreputable district, which that pioneer society cleaned up,—every saloon, every house of ill repute. From this splendid beginning the Society has gone on, till now it is a mighty factor in the development of the African race in this country.

Christian Endeavor Among Afro-Americans.

Rev. George W. Moore, Nashville, Tenn.

Christian Endeavor has been a vital force in the work of uplifting and regenerating Afro-Americans. You have welcomed us into your fellowship, councils and service. We have been made to feel that we are a part of the great movement. When the C. E. Society was organized, in the Lincoln Memorial Church, Washington, in 1885, the place of its location, "Hell's Bottom" was the most notorious section of the National Capital. There were seventeen saloons within two squares of our mission, and several gambling places were in full blast. There were more affrays, more police on duty, and more subjects for the hospital and station-house than in any other section of the District of Columbia. We have known of three murders in the community in a single night. This society, in 1891, aided the pastor in a crusade against dens of iniquity, which resulted in wiping out all of the saloons and gambling places, and the community became one of the best sections of the city. A large number of students, while receiving their training in the schools and colleges of Washington, became members of this society. They have since gone out as ministers, teachers, physicians, lawyers, business men and home makers, carrying with them the Endeavor spirit throughout the South. There are now more than a score of Christian Endeavor Societies among Afro-Americans in the District of Columbia.

Christian Endeavor was first introduced among the Afro-Americans in the South by Northern Endeavorers who came as missionaries under the American Missionary Association and kindred missionary organizations. There are now many hundreds of societies among us in churches and schools.

There met in the city of Washington, March 1 and 2, representatives of twenty agencies and religious denominations, all of whom have some official relations to the Christian training of the negro youth, for the purpose of considering the call for a congress of the young people of the race, especially those having to do with young people's Christian work, and looking to a forward movement which shall find tangible results in increased activity along those lines. It is felt that a greater effort should be made for a larger uplift in morality and piety. The Christian Endeavor movement has been a vital force in this direction. It has stood first of all for loyalty to Christ. It has been a training school in Bible study, the Sunday-school and in church work. It has promoted the missionary spirit. Our societies are evangelical in spirit, and aggressive in the evangelization and upbuilding of our people in both large cities and country places. The movement has spread so much among us that its influence is felt throughout the South and in Africa. They are developing strong men and women, and are teaching missionary activities throughout the nation and the world.

Next came a symposium by several trustees of the United Society of Christian Endeavor. Speaking as a representative on the Board for the Methodist Protestants, Rev. George E. McMaminau of Steubenville, O., said:

The religion of Jesus is the most splendid theory ever given to the world. It lays down principles and rules unlike any other theory of conduct. That is possibly the reason why so many people have used it as a pure theory in their personal relation to it. They have not remembered that over against this splendid theory there is an equally splendid practice. The greatest service Christian Endeavor has done for the religious world is in the emphasis placed on practical religion in sweet and sensible conjunction with the theoretical. She has shown them to be like the Siamese twins who could not be separated without the death of both. This has been done largely upon young minds, at that time in life when the impressed truths would have most weight, and leave long years in which to apply them.

In at least three ways is this already affecting the religious life of the world: First, in our conception of the office and work of the Holy Spirit. For generations the mass of believers appeared divided into two classes in their view of the work of the Spirit. One class held that He came to men for the sole purpose of giving them religious pleasure, ecstasy, good feeling. They looked not to Him for guidance, inspiration to labor, help in overcoming, but for pleasure. The other class apparently held that He called men to a Christian life, quietly pursuing them through a thousand failures, until they heard the call and became religious, after which He left them so irrevocably. Today we combine these views, and add to them. As much as ever do we look upon Him as the Divine Agent who calls men to repentance. We also look upon Him as a constant companion who gives man the ability, power and the disposition for service.

Second—there is a radical change in our viewpoint toward social problems. Under this combination of faith and practice we are surely being led to see that every social problem is a problem in which church and state are equally interested. We are learning to approach every one of these momentous questions in the spirit of the political reformer, in the deeper, broader, more comprehensive spirit of the Gospel, and there is also a radical change in the character of our source of ministerial supply. The minister of the Gospel of tomorrow is to be the Junior of yesterday and the active Endeavorer of today. Like Samuel, he will have been trained to the priesthood in the temple. The Christian Endeavor Society is the most powerful and influential theological seminary on earth at the present time. And this is true because it gets in its training first; it lays foundations. We may almost claim that a new type of character has been formed, and we might well call it the Christian Endeavor type. When, from veteran to volunteer, the host of religious teachers shall have come up through these channels we may expect them to lead the religious world to splendid victories in the practical fields of human life.

Dr. Gilby C. Kelly of Nashville, Tenn., representing the Methodist Episcopal Church, South, said that his grandfather was in the habit of stating his belief that in the antediluvian age a boy was not weaned till he was twenty years old; but now twenty years means more than a century then. Dr. Kelly declared that Christian Endeavor has become so firmly rooted that the world is no more likely to give it up than to give up the electric light or the telephone.

Bishop Alexander Walters, D. D., of the African Methodist Zion Church, told of the fifteen hundred Christian Endeavor societies in his church, with fifteen thousand members, and of the fact that not one Epworth League exists in the whole denomination of half a million members. He spoke eloquently of the benefit he had received personally, and his race collectively, from Christian Endeavor associations.

Dr. James L. Hill, one of the "original" Endeavorers, made an original speech, full of his breezy illustrations and characteristic illuminations. Describing the accurate surveys of Western States, he made the point that Christian Endeavor has always been true to its spiritual base-line. He showed the distinct advantage of our pledge, and the "leveling-up" tendency of the social life among Endeavorers. Among other things Dr. Hill said:

In crossing the bridge it is the custom to put the little elephants over the structure first. That is the plan adopted this morning. I want to communicate back to the big elephants that the bridge is safe. In a church in the city where our presiding elder has his home I once said to a young man, "If I outlive you, as is unlikely, as you are younger, I would like to write your epitaph, 'Here is a man who was always willing to take hold of the cold end of a prayer meeting.'" It is easy to participate after the spirits of everybody have risen. I am willing to take hold of the first end that comes to hand.

In the West any piece of land can be located by certain lines that have been surveyed. There is a line running north and south, which they call the meridian; and then comes a range west, for example, of the fifth principal meridian. The location north and south comes from a base-line, and I know of a house that stands facing what is called the base-line road. Now for twenty years the Society of Christian Endeavor has been permanently located with reference to a spiritual base-line. Did it ever happen to occur to you to inquire what might have come to pass if these young people had fallen to drifting spiritually, or had dropped from the standards, or gone off after strange gods? They are young, and twenty years have proved that they have been located with reference to a spiritual base-line that is measured from the foot of the cross.

Some one has mentioned a man who resigned his position as a street-car conductor and entered the ministry because he said he was tired of standing up. Our young people through twenty years have stood up for their principles. They have been avowed; they have been pronounced. I attribute this strength of Christian character to the presence of the pledge and to our practice of standing by it.

Our work, too, has had in a new sense its social side. After all is said, the best mark of Christian Endeavor for these two decades has been its process of leveling up. We have used a mutual method. Each one gradually develops toward the level of the best. The prayer of our colored brother in a meeting has been graciously answered. He exclaimed, "Lord, prop us up on our leaning side."

I give to you a recital just as it came to me. I do not affirm the truth of the narrative. I think, however, it is quite suggestive. Two men were being conducted toward an insane asylum, and one of them said to the other, "What are you committed for?" "Well," said he, "I am crazy on religion; I have great dread of the future; I have a deep apprehension of what is to come. What are you crazy about?" "Oh," he replied, "I am afraid of the responsibilities that the church is now placing upon its young people. I think they ought to be kept out of sight until they are old. I do not think that a horse ought to be trained or worked until he has got well into his years. I think the same of young people." "Is that the matter with you?" said the other. "Then you are not crazy; you are a fool." In the last twenty years, how many apprehensions have been suffered that never came to pass! How many fears have been expressed of ghosts that have never risen!

In electric lighting, if anything goes wrong, the system is repaired. When anything gets out of joint, they never say, "Now we shall have to give this up." I once heard the response that came from the electric lighting station when a telephone message had been sent down that there was some difficulty about the practical workings of the lighting apparatus. "We will send the trouble-hunter up." That is, if anything is wrong we shall have it fixed and go on. Twenty years have proved that if anything needs modification in the Society, or improvement, or readjustment, have it attended to, and go on.

A citizen was once asked, if he could have three wishes, what they would be. His first wish was that he might have all the liquor he could drink; the second, that he could have all the tobacco he could use; and third, "Well," said he, "I guess I will take more liquor." I conclude with three wishes. First, that time may prove that the Society of Endeavor was started in just the right century, that the twenty years already passed shall be but preparative for greater things and larger growth in the new century on which we enter. The second, that in the years to come all societies of young people may be gathered under our Christian Endeavor banner; and third, well, my wish is for greater prosperity for Christian Endeavor.

Christian Endeavor among the prisoners was the inspiring theme of that young Napoleon of this great work, Frederick A. Wallis of Lexington, Ky. His striking address was a noble plea for the submerged masses, and an earnest appeal to the Endeavorers that they should engage in this blessed service of our brothers in bonds. Mr. Wallis said in part:

Amid the submerged mass in the ocean of human life there are yearnings for better living. It has been the pleasure of the Prison Committee to listen to these and bring them to Jesus Christ. Today I bring you glad tidings from a great number of Christian Endeavorers who find it impossible to be at this meeting. They are here in spirit, but in the flesh they are far removed by prison walls, a great many serving a few months, some a few years and still a larger number are serving for a life time. Yet they are free indeed, for they have been brought by the instrumentalities of Christian Endeavor into the light of freedom, into the gospel of Christ. I wish I could point you to faces which tell of separation and unrest, of broken peace and unsatisfied longings, and then I would like to point out to you a picture of those who wear the smile of contentment, even though they are behind prison bars. A great number of them rise early and in the quiet of the morning observe the quiet hour before leaving their cells to go to the shop for their daily toil. If we keep on with this good work, it will only be a short time when our penitentiaries shall become simply places of reformature.

CHAPTER XXII.

What Has Made Christian Endeavor a Success?

THE ELEMENTS OF OBLIGATION.— THE POWER OF TESTIMONY.—
THE JOY OF SERVICE.—THE SPIRIT OF CONSECRATION.

The Element of Obligation.—A Factor in the Success of Christian Endeavor.

Rev. A. B. Curry, D. D., Birmingham, Ala.

In naming the factors which have entered into the marvelous success of Christian Endeavor, the Element of Obligation is rightly placed first. We live in an age when even Christian people have largely lost sight of the religious imperative. In quarters where a sense of moral obligation is strongest, the sense of religious obligation is often weak. Men readily recognize this moral obligation not to kill or steal or lie, but they do not grasp so fully the religious obligation to believe in Christ and confess him, to pray and read the Scripture daily, and to support in every way the ordinances of God's house.

For some reason, the "thus saith the Lord" of the decalogue has more authority with them than the "verily I say unto you" of the Sermon on the Mount. Some one has said there are four parties in the Christian church, viz: the attitudinarian, the latitudinarian, the platitudinarian and the lassitudinarian. The last is the largest class of all. The great need of the church in our day is to feel deep down in its soul the grip of the religious or spiritual imperative; to feel that when Christ says respecting anything, "you ought," he means, "you owe it;" i. e., it is a sacred debt, which cannot be left unpaid without sin; that the commands of Christ are not optional but obligatory; and that we cannot convert the "thou oughtest" of Christ into the "thou mayest" of our own convenience.

Christian Endeavor seeks to meet this need by emphasizing the spiritual imperative. It begins with the pledge and centers in it. The pledge is the frame-work of Christian Endeavor. All of its comely parts, viz: habits of daily prayer and Bible reading, the faithful church life, systematic and generous giving, missionary activity, good citizenship, all are built about the pledge. The pledge is simply a recognition of religious obligation and a solemn promise to meet that obligation. Christ says: "thou oughtest;" Christian Endeavor answers back in its pledge: "by thy help, O Christ, I will!"

And it is not afraid to pledge itself to this course; to say: "trusting in Him for strength I promise Him that I will." Some are afraid of this pledge, not because it is hard and unreasonable, for it only represents honest Christian living; but they do not wish to bind themselves to any religious duty. Men, who quite willingly take the pledge of lodge membership, of business compact, of military service, and even the solemn pledge of marriage, refuse to enter into compact with Christ. It is largely a matter of the heart. If a man dislikes a thing, he would better not pledge himself to it. If a man dislikes the lodge or the military service, to pledge himself to either is unwise. If a young couple do not love each other, they would better not take the pledge of matrimony; but if they love each other deeply and truly, they need not fear to plight their troth. So if one dislikes Bible reading and prayer and the church life, he is not ready to take the Christian Endeavor pledge; he needs a change of heart. But if one loves these things, and above all if he loves Christ with all his heart, he need not fear to pledge Him faithful service. His love will make the keeping of the pledge a delight, for "love is the fulfilling of the law."

Christian Endeavor is successful, because it strives to make religion mean something. The world is full of young people who admire earnestness in religion, even to the point of heroism. They admire the old Scotch Covenanters in the Greyfriars church yard, not only pledging themselves to support with property and life the national covenant, but pricking the veins of their good right arms for blood with which to sign that covenant. The church of today needs more iron in its blood. Christian Endeavor proposes to infuse it, and therefore lifts over its young people the banner of the pledge with this inscription: "I promise Him that I will!" Under this banner it has achieved its success.

Christian Endeavor is successful because it is its effort to take young Christians out of the malarious and joyless valley of lassitude, and place them upon the life-giving, joyful mount of beatitude, and thus fill the church with beatitudinarians.

It has been said, that "he only can make his word like the thunder, whose life is as the lightning." And it is because Christian Endeavor seeks to make the lives of young Christians as lightning that the thunder of its success has rolled around the world.

The Joy of Service.

Mr. Tracy McGregor, Detroit, Mich.

The God of the Christian is a being of joy and blessedness. The singing of the birds, the beauty of the light, the brightness of nature and the glory of the heavens add their testimony to that of the Scriptures in declaring this fact. The writers of the Old and New Testaments who were God's friends and hence knew His nature, found Him a being of joy and proclaim that "In His presence is fulness of joy," and that the only fitting garments in which to appear before Him are those of praise and thanksgiving. Again and again they repeat the call to serve the Lord with gladness and to come before His presence with singing. The first followers of Jesus so lacked the customary signs of fasting and self-inflicted sadness as to surprise and condemn their fellow Galileans and Judeans and the question was asked, "Why do the disciples of John and of the Pharisees fast, but thy disciples fast not?" And in explaining the change from gloom to gladness, Jesus spoke of His band as a Bridal Party; and all who have followed Him during the centuries since have found the "Joy of the Lord" to be a chief element in their experience. From the days when the young follower of Jesus truly begins to live for Him to the strong activities of the mature Christian, there is music in his life, and first and last, this is the "Joy of Service." Even the happiness of victory over sin is herein included, for He delivered us out of the hand of our enemies that we "Might serve Him without fear, in holiness and righteousness before Him, all the days of our life."

True service is first a quality of love by which one wills to spend himself for God and for his fellows. Its joy is the joy of loving. Love is humble. "Love vaunteth not itself, is not puffed up, seeketh not her own." There is a certain kind of I-want-to-be-seen activity (falsely called Christian service) which desires to take part in almost every thing that is going on. This ministry, however, is selfish. The sweetness of Christian joy is absent. The gladness of motherhood is the joy of loving. Her lullabys, her kisses and caresses reveal the happiness of a soul in which service is first a principle of life and afterwards a matter of outward manifestation. The "Joy of the Lord" is in part the joy of love. God so loved the world that He gave Himself. "It is more blessed to give than to receive and the giving of self is the most blessed of all giving." Self-giving is love and is the basis of service. The mere possession of this spirit fills the life with joy.

The joy of service is the delight of pleasing the Master whom we worship and trust and who is everything to us. He said that His passing into the heavens was like the departure to a far country of the man who

124 TWENTIETH ANNUAL CONVENTION

left his property to the care of servants. The absorbing interests of Jesus
in this world have been left to our care. Faithfulness to this trust is of
incalculable importance to Him and His "well done," when we meet Him,
will be at least one jewel in the crown of rejoicing to be received in that
day. "I'm so happy, mamma, to help you," said the little daughter. "I'm
so happy in doing for him" thought the wife as she prepared for the husband's return at evening time. And as he toiled in the heat of the day
and rejoiced, it was because he was working for those who loved and
trusted him.

The joy of service is the satisfaction of being useful. No life is happy
which is not useful. Misspent lives are cheerless and sad. The deepest
regret of a sinful life is on account of the wasted years which cannot be
recalled. During my experience with many thousand outcast men, some
of the bitterest of confessions to which I have listened have related to
their lost opportunities and to the worthlessness of their lives. To be un-
profitable is sin. Cast such a servant into outer darkness where there is
weeping and gnashing of teeth. If it be only the fulfilment of the common duties of life in a spirit of service to God, there is deep joy in feeling
that one's life is useful, that something has been accomplished. Those
days in which the work in hand was accomplished and finished are days
of abiding joy and the people who work hardest, if in a spirit of self-
giving, find the greatest joy in life. When one looks upon the past, personal attainments and culture secured, will not be the source of fullest
satisfaction, but rather the consciousness of having spent one's self for
others. And this will not be diminished though the former has been sac-
rificed. Year after year of faithful living renders this satisfaction deeper
and deeper and thus the joy of service is cumulative. It groweth more
and more unto the perfect day.

A further element of this joy is the comfort of being loved. For,
though not seeking this, it is nevertheless true that whoever serves will
be loved. "With what measure ye meet it shall be measured to you
again," is true in this as in other things. Love given to others will be
poured back into the bosom until it is filled and running over. Jesus was
refreshed when Mary broke the box of costly ointment at the Bethlehem
supper, and he was comforted by the presence of the faithful women and
others. Though "It is more blessed to give than to receive," yet it is
blessed to receive the loving trust of those for whom we have lived and
whom we have served.

Service restores joy. When there is depression and gloom, no remedy
is so efficacious as that of doing something for others. An evening of
amusement and entertainment may be helpful and right, but it will only
soothe. It will not cure the heart that is suffering. Do something for
God. A few words spoken in testimony, some sacrifice fulfilled, a call
upon a needy friend, prayer and effort for an erring comrade, will bring
back lost happiness.

The joy of service is a manifestation of soul health. The great commandments are re-expressed in the oft-repeated words of Jesus: "Whoso-
ever will lose his life shall save it." This declares service to be the condition of spiritual health and safety and welfare and hence of joy. It is
like the gladness of childhood. All alone, the baby will often play with his
toys for hours and those who take an occasional peep at him are charmed
by his sweet glee. Whence this fulness of joy? It is the overflow of a
nature in harmony with its surroundings and with God. Health of body
is joy giving; health of soul is more joy giving. This animating, life-
giving joy of service is a sufficient cause in itself to account for the far
reaching fruitfulness of these twenty years of Christian Endeavor success. The young people have been yoked to each other and to Jesus for
practical Christian ministries. Personal joy has resulted and each society
has found that esprit de corps which makes the organization strong.
Church life often becomes feeble and sluggish because there is failure in
finding something for each member to do. If you would make life worth
living for yourself, arise from this convention to be a minister. Jessica,
the little London waif, asked the English clergyman, "What is a min-

ister?" He replied: "A minister, Jessica, is a servant—God's servant and your servant, too." If you would insure the future success of Christian Endeavor, go home to find ministers for others. Your presence here places upon you this responsibility of leadership, whether or not you are officially a leader.

"So take Joy home,
And make a place in thy great heart for her,
And give her time to grow and cherish her;
Then will she come and oft will sing to thee,
When thou art working in the furrows, ay,
Or weeding in the sacred hour of dawn,
It is a comely fashion to be glad—
Joy is a grace we say to God."

"The Power of Testimony."

Rev. John Snape, Wilmington, Del.

Testimony differs from evidence. "Testimony is the declaration of a witness; evidence is the effect of that declaration on the mind." Testimony is open attestation—profession; evidence is the light which such profession affords.

It is supposed that the framer of my subject had in mind the Christian Endeavor pledge—that gracious Covenant, which, joining the strength of the Lord Jesus Christ to the trust of his disciples, holds for twenty years millions of young people in indissoluble union, and in itself contains the answer to the question: "What has made Christian Endeavor a success."

It is a two-fold covenant—the Lord Jesus Christ promising strength and the Christian Endeavorer promising eight things. On the human side it is a Covenant of Trusting—"Trusting in the Lord Jesus Christ for strength"; a Covenant of Doing—"I promise that I will strive to do whatever He would like to have me do"; a Covenant of Praying—"I will make it the rule of my life to pray"; a Covenant of Reading—"and read the Bible every day;" a Covenant of Loyalty—"and to support my own Church in every way"; a Covenant of Constancy—"throughout my whole life I will endeavor to lead a Christian life"; a Covenant of Fidelity—"I promise to be true to all my duties"; a Covenant of Testimony—"to be present at and to take some part, aside from singing, in every Christian Endeavor prayer-meeting, unless hindered by some reason which I can conscientiously give to my Lord and Master."

It is of the Covenant of Testimony I am asked to speak, and to give to you in ten minutes what you have been giving for twenty years. That Christian Endeavor has survived and advanced for two decades without decadence is proof positive of its unparalleled success.

In the search for the secret of this success, the power of testimony has been a powerful element. And by "testimony" I do not mean merely taking part in meeting, for testimony to be a power must be something more than simply saying, "Pray for me that in the coming month I may do whatever Jesus would like to have me do." It must have the testimony of life to be a testimony of power. Living Epistles are those that are known and read of all men. If the power of its future testimony shall exceed its past, it will do so by bearing in mind the secret of the testimony of three men familiarly known to every Bible reader.

1. It must have a testimony like that of Enoch,—who, before his translation, had this testimony, that he pleased God. How few of us can really claim to live lives that please our God. Only one man (the sinless Savior), has ever said with perfect truthfulness, "I do always the things that please Him." Now it is impossible to have Enoch's testimony without his faith and experience. He walked with God. He was—he must have been—a good man, for he was God's man. He was forgiven, for God's forgiveness is assured when God's companionship is granted.

In Amos 3:3 we read, "Can two walk together except they be agreed?" Now this may mean either of two things or both. It may mean, shall two walk together except they make an appointment,—that is, except they be agreed before the walk begins. Or, it may mean, how shall two walk together except there be agreement while they walk—except they be companionable. You may be sure God eagerly waits to make an appointment with every inquiring soul, and you may be equally sure He will not be a companion to a disagreeable person. There must be both appointment and agreement, if we expect, like Enoch, to walk with God, and have his testimony—that he pleased God. Delightful intimacy! He walked so long with God that he must have become like God, and walked so far with God that he never came back to die. It was not necessary. He was not "kissed to sleep by the lips of God," as Moses; nor carried to Heaven in a chariot of fire, as Elijah,—he was translated. But before his translation he had this testimony, that he pleased God. Let us strive to have Enoch's testimony.

2. We must also have a testimony like that of John. What sort of a testimony had he? The twenty-first chapter of his Gospel tells us—"This is the disciple which testified of these things, and wrote these things: and we know that his testimony is true." It was the testimony of truth.

Truth and truthfulness need no defending, and for one to attempt to prove his truthfulness is to reflect on his own integrity. "Truth is deeper than fact," and deep truth like deep waters is often stillest.

Be sure you are right, then don't say so. He is a hero who writes an earnest denial of unfounded charges, determines to vindicate his position with violent emphasis—prepares to make sunlight explanation of dark misunderstandings—and having done all, stands. The testimony of truth is of more value to him than the testimony of declaration, for the testimony of truth is the testimony of power, and this has characterized Christian Endeavor testimony in the past and helped to bring it to its present success. Our testimony may be rejected like Christ's in Judea (John 3 : 32), or like Paul's at Jerusalem (Acts 22 : 18), but that may be the best evidence of its truth. Christian Endeavor has been a success because it is pleasing to God and its testimony, like John's, is true.

3. But Christian Endeavor must have a testimony like that of Moses. The author of the Epistle to the Hebrews says this of him: "And Moses verily was faithful in all his house as a servant, for a testimony of those things which were to be spoken after." Ah! this, after all, has been, this will be the secret of successful Christian Endeavor and the first element in the power of testimony, viz., faithfulness.

To be faithful to Christ in all things ought to be the dominating aim of every young Christian. The word "faithful" is first used in the Bible in reference to Moses, when in Num. 12 : 7, God says: "My servant Moses is faithful in all mine house." And the last name with which it is coupled in the Bible is with the name of Him of whom the exiled seer of Patmos speaks when he exclaims in Rev. 19 : 11, "And I saw heaven opened, and behold a white horse; and he that sat upon him was called faithful and true."

To be faithful is to be like Moses of whom God said: "My servant, Moses, is faithful in all mine house." To be faithful is to be like Abraham, whom Paul calls in Gal. 3 : 9, "faithful Abraham." It is to be like David, testimony concerning whom before Saul the king cost Ahimelech, the priest, his life, when he said (I. Sam. 22 : 13): "And who is so faithful among all my servants as David?" It is to be like Daniel, who made his usual petition three times a day with windows opened toward Jerusalem while scheming satraps plot and lions roar. It is to be like Andrew, who, immediately after he came to Christ, brought his own brother to Jesus. It is to be like Paul, who could say when he had finished his course, "I have fought a good fight, I have kept the faith." It is to be like Tichicus and Silas and Epaphras and Onesimus and Antipas, who, as servants, brothers, ministers and martyrs in the Lord, are called in Scripture "faithful."

It is not required of a steward that he be found successful—it is required that he be found faithful. The faithful man must be willing to fail. He who stoops to conquer may win, but he who stoops to disloyalty has failed at the start. There is no reward for faith mentioned in the Bible, but there is a reward for faithfulness. "They that be wise shall shine as the brightness of the firmament, and they that turn many to righteousness as the stars for ever and ever."

In Acts 4 : 33 we read these words, "And with great power the Apostles gave their testimony to the resurrection of the Lord Jesus; and great grace was on them all." What was the secret of the power of their testimony? It was this—the power of Pentecost. The gift of the Holy Spirit, like morning dew on opened rose, is still upon them; and fresh from the touch of the Spirit's power they go forth to declare the resurrection of our Lord. The gift of tongues preceded the use of tongues—at Pentecost—for power is essential to testimony.

Let every Christian Endeavorer here go home from this great Convention determined that hereafter his testimony shall be given "not in persuasive words of wisdom, but in demonstration of the Spirit and of Power."

The Spirit of Consecration.

Rev. Henry T. McEwen, D. D., Amsterdam, N. Y.

In the light of twenty years of enlarged and enriched experience, Christian Endeavor now contemplates Consecration as a power in the past, and as a possibility in the present, and for the future. Sublime achievements are creations, as well as revelations, of supreme motives. Purpose and power condition in the spiritual, as well as in the material realm. The triumphs which defy computation and comparison are the place which Christ has obtained in the thought and the affections of men; and the transformation He has wrought in and through them. The rate at which the church of Christ wins adherents by far surpasses that at which the world gains in population. It is a story which numbers cannot tell. The spirit of Christ is today felt, where the name of Christ is scarcely known. "He is conquering and to conquer." "He shall see of the travail of His soul and be satisfied." Of that which awaits the doing, as well as of that already done, Consecration is the Key. To say that self-surrender precedes self-sacrifice is to exalt mere chronological order above contemplative, comprehensive thought. Christ's self-surrender anticipated and included self-sacrifice. With Him the Cross was sequence, not surprise. "He was the Lamb slain before the foundation of the world" for ages and ages, ere prophetic vision exclaimed, "Lo I come, in the volume of the Book it is written of me, I delight to do thy will, O God." Doing the Father's will, without which there can be no consecration, held Him in obscurity for thirty years. For those three years of unparalleled service and sacrifice, it absorbed, as well as controlled His powers. Knowing no other motive, He endured the fierce and furious ordeals of Gethsemane, the Judgment Hall, and Calvary. Christ's final coronation is due to His consecration. When in the final Judgment, every knee shall bow to Him, and every tongue confess His name to the glory of God the Father, then Christ, God's perfectly consecrated co-laborer, shall receive His crown. The great condition upon which crowns are offered to us is as consecrated laborers together with God. There can be no consecration to God until His will is as supreme as it is superior. The Apostles forsook Christ and fled because, for the time, their care for personal safety outweighed their loyalty to and love for His service. With Peter the crisis had already passed, when before the Sanhedrin, he exclaimed, "We ought to obey God rather than men." Paul began and completed his consecration in obedience to the heavenly vision. Consecration is not ecstatic condition. It is obedient, heroic, co-operation with God. Because it loves God with all! its heart, it can serve Him with all its might, at every cost.

CHAPTER XXIII.

What Has Been Gained in Twenty Years of Christian Endeavor?

The answers in Auditorium Williston to the question, "What has been gained in twenty years of Christian Endeavor?" were magnificent uses of a grand opportunity; for there is much to tell.

President George B. Stewart, D. D., of Auburn Theological Seminary, thought that nothing more important has been gained than this, that the young people have found themselves and the church has found the young people.

When the society at Williston was organized, the young people's hour struck. Dr. Stewart told how, when he was a boy, his pastor persuaded him to break the ice and speak in the church prayer meeting. His experience reminded him of Mark Twain's description of seasickness as first making one afraid he would die, and then afraid that he wouldn't die. And, after the agony was over, one of the deacons said to him, "George, that was a brave thing to do, but, if I were in your place, I would never try it again." And he did not.

What the Young People Have Gained.

Rev. George B. Stewart, D. D., Auburn, N. Y.

The period is short, but the gain is immense. This splendid gathering of young people would have been an impossibility twenty years ago. But this convention is only an expression of the change that has come in the concerns of the young people during these two decades. The change is a revolution. The young people have found themselves. The church has found her young people. This is their age. For them nothing is as it was. All things have become new. And the new is better, infinitely better, than the old. In every direction they have made marvelous progress. These years have been as "centuries, loaded, fragrant." Here are some of the gains the years have brought to the young people.

I. The Gain in Status.

At the beginning of our period the young people had the status which had been the same in the church throughout the generations. The church was the parent. The young people were the children. They were to be nurtured, instructed, amused, interested. They were a charge upon the heart and hands of the pastor and the church. The question was, What can be done for the young people? The answer was sociables, soirees, and fandangoes of various sorts to interest them; catechetical classes for their instruction; and here and there a young people's prayer meeting for developing their religious life. But whatever form the activity among the young people took it was uniformly an attempt, sometimes wise and sometimes otherwise, to answer this question.

The question now is quite a different one. It is, What can the young people do for the church? This reveals an entirely new status. They are an integral part of the church, with their responsibilities, obligations and opportunities. They are a part of the church's equipment for worship and service. In their way and place they are as distinct a part of the church as are the adults, and as valuable. General conferences and general assemblies now give them flattering attention. Missionary boards take them into account in making up the annual budget. Building committees ask their co-operation and consult their needs. Pastors reckon on their help in every good work. The activities of the church are multiplied in number and efficiency a hundred fold because of their zeal and labor.

This is a gain of large proportions in the interest of the church. But it is also a gain to the young people. They have found a place on which to rest their lever. A fulcrum is essential. They now have one. They have gained recognition. The ecclesiastical recognition, which they are now receiving from the highest bodies in ample measure, is the latest and has its value. But it is only a small part of the large recognition the church has come to accord the young people. Their standing is assured. They belong to the army of the Lord. They are laborers in his vineyard. They are not merely a part of the church's problem but a part of her power. They are still a portion of the field she is to cultivate, and they are also among the workers who are to till it. They have come into their inheritance.

II. The Gain in Opportunity.

Opportunity is one of our priceless possessions. Young people have never been without it. Indeed, it might be thought that they have been richer in this than in anything else. The market has been overstocked with it. But there was one sort of opportunity which the young people had in miserably meagre measure twenty years ago. It was the opportunity to be somebody and to do something in the church. When the Williston Society was organized the young people's hour struck. A career was opened before them. They began to have a chance. Their new status brought new opportunities.

The active participation of a young Christian in the social worship of the church was not possible a few years ago. Their inexperience and immaturity were insuperable barriers to their "taking part to edification." They were silent partners in the mid-week service. If a zealous pastor ventured to call out the young men, and if the young men had sufficient temerity to respond, the church gave little countenance to such a lessening of the dignity and dullness of the meeting. Now in their own meetings they may worship with none to molest or make them afraid. But, best of all the mid-week service is open to them. They are under obligation to be present. They have the privilege of participating in its worship and of making their contribution to its value.

Many doors are open to them into the work of the church. They are hands and feet and eyes for their pastor. They are his assistants. To no other class of persons in the church does he give so many chances for aiding in his high office. Their Sunday school invokes their help in advancing its interests. The poor and the sick and the shut-ins smile and bless God for the flowers and fruit and sunshine brought into their lives through these societies and their committees. The young people may now have their missionary in the home and foreign field.

Twenty years ago nobody expected the young people to do anything. Now everything is expected of them. Then they were criticised for attempting to make themselves useful. Now they are condemned if they do not achieve usefulness. Superb facilities are afforded them for their work. This noble society with its abundant and varied organization, the generous support, and cordial good-will of the rest of the church, the ample information about the work to be done and the numerous open avenues through which it may be done,—these are some of the facilities the church has provided her young people for making their lives count for the kingdom of God. They are her challenge to them to devote their strength to this service. They constitute the opportunity now offered Christian young people for high usefulness.

III. The Gain in the Ability to Serve.

Are you not impressed with the fact that there are today millions of young people who are trained workmen? Such was not the case twenty years ago. They know how to do things now as they did not then. Young

men and young women can creditably conduct a prayer meeting, plan and
carry forward committee work, do personal work among the unconverted,
manage a missionary campaign, revive a dying church, keep active a
pastorless church, and do a hundred other things that but a few years
ago were supposed to be within the exclusive domain of the clergy. They
have acquired skill in all this work that makes them the admiration and
the despair of their elders. They are not less docile or more conceited
because of this skill. But they are more useful, more capable, more
worthy.

The amount of the work that they are doing is in the aggregate enormous. Although most of them are poor yet they give large sums annually
to the missionary and benevolent work of the church. Thousands of young
people are added to the membership of the church as the result of the activity of these young people. It is not possible to guess the whole of their
wide, subtle and beneficent influence. Power potential has been trans-
muted into power actual. The young people have become available assets
for the kingdom. Their real worth and their market value have alike increased prodigiously.

IV. The Gain in Outlook.

The actual gains that have come to the young people are many and
large. But they are only a beginning. There are more to follow. The
end is not yet. I am reminded of Gerald Massey's famous couplet in
which he gave his opinion of this country as he was about leaving it upon
his first visit here.

"Everything is humming, but it isn't all hum;
Everything is coming, but hasn't yet come."

We see the possibilities in the young people as we have never seen
them. "They have their future before them," in the language of Artemus
Ward, "and not behind them." What that future is to be none may pre-
dict, but it is big with incalculable gain to the young.

The young people have seen the vision of their greatness. They know
they are called to the kingdom for a larger service than they have yet
rendered. Their horizon has widened. They hear calls of duty they have
never heard before and these calls are all the more imperative because
of their deep suggestion of other duties yet to claim their strength. They
somehow feel that graver tasks, larger opportunities, worthier service are
before them. Our young men and maidens are having visions as never
before. They are now the joy and strength of the church and in the
days to come the young people of those days will be the same, only more
abundantly.

These are some of the gains the young people have received during
the two decades just passed. But they are not all. We cannot recount
all. They have come into great possessions—untold riches. Thus far
they have used their wealth wisely and to the greater glory of God.
Under competent leadership so will they always do.

No one has had a better chance to observe what the church has gained
through Christian Endeavor than Rev. J. G. Butler, D. D. He said
that the church has gained trained workers, and he ought to know, for
he has been for fifty years pastor of the Luther Memorial Church, in
Washington.

"What the Church Has Gained."

Rev. J. G. Butler, D. D., Washington, D. C.

It is not possible to tell all that the Church has gained from the discovery of Christian Endeavor. It is a discovery, not an invention.

Christopher Columbus discovered America: that which has grown and
will grow out of this discovery no tongue can tell. The falling of an apple

suggested the universal law of attraction and gravitation, upon which all matter and life depend.

A venerable electrician, in introducing his lecture upon electricity said, "I am about to talk to you of electricity; but I do not know what electricity is." "I know," said the small boy in the audience. "What is it?" said the man of science. "Electricity is lightning."

What this mysterious force is no man knoweth. We talk of Franklin and his kite; of Morse and talking wires; of Edison with the telephone and the graphophone and how many other phones I do not know. Electricity is the great discovery among material forces in the century just past. It pervades earth and heaven; no man knows what it is; and we have but begun by invention to apply it to human uses. We touch a button and light our houses. We hitch Niagara to the life of a great city. The President of the United States on the Pacific Coast touches a button, and the thousand wheels of the Pan-American on the Atlantic seaboard move with grace and power.

There stood before the world's magnates, civil and religious, about four hundred years ago, a simple Augustinian monk, with the unchained, open Bible in his hand. The artist has never thrown, in all its sublimity, upon the canvas the scene at Worms. That man of faith and courage had discovered a new principle. He raises his voice in protest against ignorance and superstition and priestcraft and kingcraft. The protest principle of the Reformation, with which the names of Wyclif and Huss and Savonarola and Calvin and Zwingli and Knox and Luther are forever linked, gave birth to Protestantism and is filling France and Austria and Spain and Italy with civil and religious unrest and revolution today. It has given us our New Possessions, an object lesson that should open the eyes of the world to the unwarranted yet perilous assumptions of the Papal Hierarchy. The protest principle is yet to give to the world the civil and religious freedom for which the American Flag stands,—a thing of beauty and a joy forever.

Christian Endeavor, yet in its infancy, is a new discovery among religious forces, and is of limitless application. The Church of the Living God has always cherished childhood and youth; but it remained for this generation to make childhood and youth a trained force in the Kingdom of God. It supplements the work of the Christian home, and of the Sunday School, and of the Church itself, by organizing and equipping our boys and girls, our young men and young women for the "firing line," in the ever present battle for our God and His Christ against the powers of darkness. And there is no line of work for the Kingdom, whether in the home, in the State, in the Church, in Christian or in non-Christian lands, for which the Army of Christian Endeavor is not being prepared.

Three fundamental principles are emphasized.

1. It does not strike its tap root in the dogmatic, but in the spiritual and Christian life of our common Christendom. The polemics may fight along hair-splitting theological lines, whilst the true Endeavorer recognizes every man as a brother whom Christ accepts.

2. It emphasizes loyalty to one's own denomination. So strongly is this emphasized that we see no use for any organization of young people in any of the denominations other than Christian Endeavor. May we not cherish the hope that all our Churches will swell our ranks by falling into line with us?

3. It is hastening the answer to our Lord's prayer for the oneness of all believers, by cultivating interdenominational and international fellowship. We are all one in Christ Jesus. Close up the ranks. And with our slogan, "For Christ and the Church," we march to victory. "Christ for the World, we sing; the World to Christ we bring."

CHAPTER XXIV.

Christian Endeavor Fellowship.

Field Secretary Eberman has his own specialty, local and district unions. He illustrated the importance of union by telling of a little boy who defended himself for liking his father better than his mother by saying, "I'm awful sorry for you, mother; but we men must stand together."

City and District Unions.

Rev. Clarence E. Eberman, Boston, Mass.

It is and always has been true that the unit of value in Christian Endeavor is the individual member and the individual society, in close practical and spiritual relation with the pastor, official boards and the local church. This is the fundamental principle of our great organization. But units serve a double purpose. They stand for something vital, supreme in themselves. They also represent profound truths in combination with one another.

One is the root-basis of all arithmetic, but subsequent problems demand integral combinations. One coal may have the property of heat, and you may have a very small fire of one little coal, but the philosophy of fire teaches us that much better results will follow, when a whole lot of coals are gathered together, stirred by the same flame, wrought by the same force. Indeed, it is quite conceivable that one coal, taken from the fire and laid upon some domestic or ecclesiastical hearth might sputter for a while, and then, with a dying gasp, go out into black charred coldness.

Scripturally, we may regard this truth from another standpoint. The primal history of the human race began with the family, thus revealing, at the very beginning, the two-fold relation of man, first to God, and then to his fellow-man. "Thou shalt love the Lord thy God," that is the first command; and the second is like unto it, "Thou shalt love thy neighbor as thyself." Jesus Christ laid special emphasis upon this two-fold relationship and insisted upon it as the fundamental principle of the Kingdom of God. He supplemented His precepts by His own methods of Christian work. He gathered together disciples of various temperaments, types and occupations, and in association with them, and with one another, He manifested the type of His church organism.

The disciples carried this great ideal into their subsequent service, and lifted the thought of fellowship into a practical reality. What a picture of practical love we have in that company surrounding the Lord's Table, where rich and poor, learned and ignorant, patrician and plebeian, master and slave broke bread together, and touched their lips to the one cup.

All through these centuries the word "brotherhood" has been closely associated with the Fatherhood of God, and fellowship has not wholly been lost sight of. The words of Jesus have been pulsating in the hearts of His followers, "This is My commandment, that ye love one another, as I have loved you."

True, it might almost seem as if the division of the Church into various denominations has weakened rather than strengthened the ideal of fellowship, but more and more we are coming to see that the churches are so many regiments and brigades of the One great Army of the living God, holding aloft their own distinctive markers, but also rallying around the one great standard of the Cross of Jesus Christ. Sectarian exclusiveness is a thing of the past. Partition walls are crumbling, as new and open doors are constantly cut into them. The identity is marked by hedges, which are now flowering and sending their fragrance everywhither; but all hearts are most intent upon the sowing and the reaping of the harvest of souls, in the fields enclosed, and when we have entered heaven, I do not believe that we will ever be able to tell on which side of the hedges the garnered sheaves grew.

On of the great forces which has most materially contributed to this larger Christian fellowship has been and is, Christian Endeavor; and our city and district unions are not only manifestations of this, but also large contributors to its reality.

With as little machinery as possible, but sufficient cohesion to establish a point of contact, for even wireless telegraphy must have some mechanism, the Christian Endeavor Unions bring together different workers, formulate plans and methods, and furnish common ground where all who love the same Lord may also engage in a common service, without yielding a single essential feature of denominational church creed and polity.

In these Unions the great century-principles of organization and concentration are conserved and find their readiest expression. In the progress of Christian work, these Unions have not only been found feasible, but they are the true logical sequence to the interdenominational genius of Christian Endeavor. Individual members are trained to love their own church, and to be loyal to it. They are also led to regard others as their brethren and fellow-workers, and finding them interested in the same cause and the same Christian methods, a common bond is established, and thus young Christians move towards this common centre.

For the practical exemplification of this thought we have but to study and concrete care of a county or city union, and mark the glowing results of these years of organized service. Such a union of forces is no longer an experiment. This confederation of Christian workers is a present, practical reality. With officers, chosen from the various societies, meeting together, planning together, as Advisory Boards, or Executive Committees, with Committees chosen from the membership, and every denomination represented, working along practical lines, with meetings and conferences, which draw together the rank and file of the members, the Union, whether city, county or local, is a most feasible and blessed solution to the question, "On what basis can young people of our churches come together, and work together?"

"Is it feasible to bring together diversified creeds and different church polities?" We do not appeal to ecclesiastical logic to prove that. The best proof is the Christian Endeavor meeting or convention. I do not ask to what church you belong, and yet you are all members of some church, and it is right and proper that each one should have a church home; but what bond makes this meeting possible, makes it strong and inspiring? Are we not, at this moment, thinking of this meeting as a direct fulfilment of the Savior's earnest prayer, "That they all may be one," and in our inmost hearts we are feeling that, in reality, we are brothers and sisters, of different names, perhaps, but all bearing the one great family surname, "Christ."

These city and district unions have not only developed true and earnest work, but also tried and efficient workers, who are most nobly serving in different fields of service, and very much of the future success of our beloved cause is in their hands. Much has already been done, but much yet awaits consecrated effort and glowing application.

These Unions have latent possibilities and reserve powers, which will surely be translated into the actual, not only as it concerns the whole world, but as it affects every locality. The union idea of our movement will be turned more and more towards the local unions, with the thought of developing local and individual service.

Now that the International Convention will only be held biennially, the United Society officers will find it possible to assist State officers in the aggressive prosecution of the work, and a uniform effort will be made to unify these unions, to stimulate activity, to organize new unions and even new societies, wherever the opportunity presents itself, to foster and conserve all lines of influence and power.

Fellowship will be best conserved by making it an actual reality among the societies, and by bringing them in closest touch with one another.

It will be found helpful to hold occasional and frequent meetings and conferences, at which pastors and local workers can be heard, discussing local needs, and shaping the union of work and service according to those needs. It is by no means necessary to have large mass-meetings, or out-of-town speakers, in order to insure the success of these conferences. It will be more advisable to enlist the active co-operation of the pastors and lay-workers of the Union.

Such a union of society and service will surely conserve energy. In this day we are learning to see the great value of conservation of power, and the concentration of energy. We must also learn this lesson in all Christian work. Their fellowship of service will prevent waste, and will lead to a judicious investment of power and abilities. Many opportunities will arise, too large or too complicated perhaps for single effort, but possible for united energies, and these can be most gloriously grasped by the united evangelistic forces of the churches.

This broader fellowship will also inspire hope and courage. God be thanked for the great host of Christian young people who have enlisted under the one standard and who are obeying the commands of the one great Captain. There is highest joy in encouraging one another, and in speaking the word of cheer and hope to those who have grown discouraged. This is the esprit de corps among Christian Endeavorers, who love their own church, but who also take the time to work with those of other churches, and are always ready to extend the helping hand, and to realize their kinship in the kingdom of Christ's brotherliness.

The old Theban regiments fought with such desperation on the field of battle because it was the principle of Theban military science that those who stood next to each other in the ranks should always, if possible, be bosom friends.

So, in the great spiritual warfare, the Church Militant, marching towards the Church Triumphant, may all Christian Endeavorers, as the bosom friends of Jesus, be standing next each other in the ranks, inspired by the same hope, actuated by the same love, and following Him, whom they all love as their Lord and Master.

Our Interdenominational Fellowship.

Rev. Harland L. Freeman, Sheridanville, Pa.

There is nothing egotistic in saying, "Our interdenominational fellowship." Other evangelic agencies have done much in arousing Christian fellowship, but the Endeavor movement has had this from the start as one of its distinctive features and has attained to a splendid success.

Some years ago it was the custom in many of our towns and cities to have strong fences around the beautiful lawns, so that their beauty was difficult to see from the outside. Of later years in many of these places it has become fashionable to have the lawns open and of easy eyesight in enjoying and learning the owner's tastes and designs.

Christian Endeavor through one of its primary principles has made it fashionable among the churches to keep an open front and let the world know that while there is a differing of tastes and methods, it is the common purpose, "To see the King in his beauty and to behold the land of far distances."

Twenty years of this growing heavenly influence has made quarreling among the churches exceedingly unpopular. It has been discovered that a far deeper interest in one's own church and a more willing service is secured by an agreement on essentials with others, than by a disagreement on non-essentials.

It has been demonstrated that it is not necessary to pick a quarrel with a sister denomination in order to grow and teach love for one's own. This has been a schooling in Christian courtesy so that we have not only learned how to treat each other, but have taken delight in putting Endeavor etiquette, which is Christ-like love, into practice.

There were some of course who looked upon this as a freakish fad and expected it to soon spend its force and "Die no more."

Consequently it was felt, a duty to put out this glowing spark of Christly Brotherhood. But the flame was not to be quenched. It was protected by too much consecrated common sense and transparent charity. It was as the farmer's problem who visited one of our large cities and took lodging at a leading hotel.

Recounting his experience to his friends, he said, "Everything was splendid. But they kept the light burning in my room where I slept and it bothered me." His friends asked him why he didn't put the light out. Replied he, "I did try to, but the blessed thing was in a bottle and wouldn't blow out."

Thanks, be to God, our Father, today that this light of brotherly love wouldn't blow out and that it is lighting up Christendom with its warming rays.

The fair Andromeda of soul-unity is no longer threatened by boasts nor exposed to the dangers of unreasonable pride or intolerable prejudice. She is safe in the embrace of our interdenominational fellowship.

Interdenominational seems to have been too sweeping a word for most of our English dictionaries or perhaps a work of too much latitude and longitude for any one language. I am not acquainted with the vocabulary of Volapuk but I have imagined this word must be in the list.

The word signifies a world-wide mission and it has reached a worldwide result. Our fellowship has meant pentecostal refreshment.

There have been many divisions of tongues but much unity of soul.

Devout dwellers from almost every nation under Heaven have spoken forth the wonderful works of God through this medium. The members of the Christian world had been singing, "Blest be the tie that binds," to one another, but of later years they have been singing it with one another. The one hundred and thirty-third psalm has been incarnated and the seamless vote of Christ made redolent with saintly communion.

Not only a pleasant aroma of fraternal feeling has been diffused around the globe, but also an aggressive spirit of world enterprise has been aroused. The words so often in the mouth of the Lord Jesus, to describe God's regenerative force in and among men have been repeated with a startling emphasis.

The Kingdom of God has been magnified and its unity made more clearly manifest in the midst of diversity. This has been and is the signal service of interdenominational fraternity.

We ought to be thankful that an all-wise Providence, who is our Father, has led us to see, that denominational zeal when it collides with the interests of the Kingdom savors not of things that be of God, but those that be of men.

We are to be loyal and true, through and through, to our own household, but we must not build tabernacles for our own pleasure but listen to the voice of the Beloved and please Him.

The development of this principle of the society has laid before us some special opportunities. Christian citizens banded together from the various churches have learned what a mighty stroke can be wielded for good government.

We dare not allow this power to lie idle and dwindle away, while the accused dragon of drink sows his corrupting teeth broadcast in our land. For the sake of our country, fellow Endeavorers, we must cherish, we must cultivate, we must covet interdenominational fellowship.

Farther away than American shores has gone the impress and impetus of this knitted bond. The world has felt through this open door of heart-unity the throbbing of the pulse of peace and the quivering desire for Gospel witnessing.

There is an open door before us and we have seen that no man can shut it.

Through this door we behold the bride putting on the righteousness of the saints and making ready for Him in whose vesture is written "King of kings and Lord of lords."

It has been a door into a larger hope for the church, a stronger faith and a deeper love. "Let brotherly love continue." "United we stand, divided we fall." Let not sloth nor greed nor pride nor prejudice nor ignorance nor any other thing of the Lilliputian tribe close this door that has opened to a scene of such power and promise.

May it swing more widely open to admit a still greater number of the sons of men who have made it their supreme choice to seek first the Kingdom of God. Long live our interdenominational brotherhood.

Dr. W. S. Ament, of China, presented the international and interracial phases of Christian Endeavor fellowship. In China little is made of denominations. The native Christians have denominational names of their own. They call the Methodists the "handshakers"; the Presbyterians "the won't-let-women-speak-in-meeting society"; the Baptists, "the bathing society"; and the Congregationalists, "the one-man-as-good-as-another society."

Dr. Ament showed his faith in it by inviting the World's Convention to come to Peking in 1950.

Christian Endeavor is International and Interracial.

Rev. W. S. Ament, D. D., Peking, China.

The appeal which China makes to the world is pathetic and convincing. A great nation awakes and finds herself lagging in the race after her sleep of ages. Foreign soldiers are within her borders, and misunderstandings have arisen. Unfortunate impressions of Chinese character and aims are prevalent in the world. China recognizes the fact that great mistakes have been made for which she is now suffering and has long since shown penitence. The programme of reform which the leading Viceroys of the land have drawn up is an indication that a new era has dawned. Two years ago no such sweeping suggestions for reform could have been made with safety. Fourteen subjects are presented on which changes are desired. If they are inaugurated, the face of China will be set squarely towards a newer and better day. The men of thought are in earnest for progress. China can no more return to the old order of things than the growing youth can go back to infancy. Many things have contributed to this unfolding of China. Commerce for many years has done missionary work. Diplomacy has taught its valuable lessons. But the force which we believe has done the most to arouse from the inertia of the past and leaven with a quickening life is Christianity.

In the future three men are to control the destinies of men. The great political triumph for the century to achieve is the federation of the Anglo-Saxon race. The man of the future will be racial, rather than national. First—The Anglo-Saxon is to be the conservator and distributer of the great moral and political ideas for the regeneration of society. Standing side by side, but representing a different trend in human society, will be the Slav. The third man of destiny is to be one who will represent the millions of Asia. Is he to be a Hindoo or a Japanese or a Malay? After conversation with many men from many regions the general and almost unanimous conclusion is that a Chinese is to be the third man. He has given ideas in art and ethics to Corea, Japan, and all the nations south and west of China have felt his stimulating influence. A nation that has given so much to the world in the way of genuine and permanent improvements can not be said to be lacking in the essential qualities of greatness. All that China needs to bring her out into her heritage is the realization of God and a willingness to fall into line with the plans of God for her.

The Christian Endeavor Society, with its broad platform and world-embracing ideas, and all Christian forces should unite with an undivided front. National and theological boundaries can afford to be ignored in the struggle for the conquest of China for Christ. Co-operation is the watchword of the future. We must stand shoulder to shoulder and prove to all the real oneness of our faith. The Chinese work well when there is something definite for them to do. Christian Endeavor gives them the proper stimulus and direction for energies which are by no means exhausted. Out of the blood and sorrow of massacre is there a new China to be born. It will depend in good part whether or not the Christian Church rises to its privilege and lends a hand of help to the efforts of its representatives in that far-off land.

Dr. Clark gave a rapid and vivid sketch of world-wide Endeavor, and said that the time has come when, if the Society is to go much further, Christian Endeavor in America must give it wings. He asked his hearers to give to this work a part of the money that it would have cost them to go to an International Convention next year, had there been one. Pledge-cards were distributed, and a generous response was made.

In Auditorium Endeavor at the same time Treasurer William Shaw described the World's Christian Endeavor Union, its great task, and the easy way in which any Endeavorer and church-member may join; namely, by the payment of one dollar for life-membership. He gave a splendid review of our world-wide work, and especially of the recent advance movement for sending forth Christian Endeavor traveling secretaries. Following up the splendid record of the Congregational denominational rally in raising a thousand dollars for a field secretary for China, the Endeavorers present made an offering, in addition to their regular gifts to denominational missions, for this advancement of Christian Endeavor work.

The World's Christian Endeavor Union and Its Work.

William Shaw, Treasurer.

I rejoice in the privilege of speaking to this great gathering of twentieth-century Endeavorers concerning the work of the World's Christian Endeavor Union. The object of the Union is to unite the Christian Endeavorers in closer fellowship, and to promote and conserve the principles of Christian Endeavor throughout the world.

It holds a meeting quadrennially in connection with the annual convention of some one of the national unions or United Societies.

The World's Union was organized at the Boston '95 Convention, and held its first regular meeting at Washington '96. The second meeting was in connection with the great Convention in London, 1900.

There are two classes of members. First, a general membership consisting of all members of Christian Endeavor societies. Second, a certificate membership for which by the payment of one dollar any past or present member of a society of Christian Endeavor, or any member of an evangelical church, is eligible. This is a life-membership, and the names are enrolled by the World's Union and an engraved certificate is sent to each member. Voting-power is limited to the certificate members.

The officers consist of a President, a Secretary, and a Treasurer, who are elected by the certificate members and receive no salary, and one Vice-President from each national, State, provincial and colonial union.

The World's Union does not send out missionaries to the foreign field, but does what the United Society did in the early days of Christian Endeavor in this country; it stands back of the workers on the field, and gives to them such financial assistance as it is able to furnish and as the work demands.

The work is done and the workers are selected by the national unions of the several countries, which consist of the missionaries and native workers. And now for the fields so full of opportunity and promise.

I pass with a mere mention the splendid national unions in Great Britain and Australia, which are self-supporting, and the plucky little South African Union, which, in the midst of a bloody war that had divided their churches and brought untold sorrow and suffering upon the people, yet felt so impressed with the need of organizing the work, that they raised the money, and called George L. W. Kilbon as secretary, and put him into the field. All honor to the brave and generous-hearted Endeavorers of South Africa.

But the special field of work for the World's Union is at present among the scores of millions of our brothers and sisters in Continental Europe and the hundreds of millions in Asia and the island empires who need the living Christ, the practical methods of service, and the inspiring fellowship of Christian Endeavor. They feel the need, and realize the oppor-. tunity; and for years the Macedonian cry, "Come over and help us," has been ringing in our ears; but we did not feel able to respond to it. The call became so imperative, however, that we could not longer resist ·it, and I desire to tell you very briefly of some of the results accomplished and the still greater opportunities before us.

Under the devoted leadership of Secretary Frederick Blecher, Christian Endeavor is making magnificent progress in the great German empire. The land of Luther and the reformation has sadly degenerated in evangelistic fervor and spiritual power. From there comes the "higher criticism"; the head has been unduly exalted and the heart religion neglected. It is a most hopeful and significant fact that in answer to President Clark's call to prayer for a great spiritual awakening, issued last year, a list of over twelve hundred German Endeavorers was sent in, the largest number, proportionately, received from any field. The warm, earnest, evangelistic spirit of our movement is making itself felt, and consecrated pastors are giving it a cordial welcome.

Secretary Franklin S. Hatch has been at work for three months under the direction of the United Society for India, Burmah, and Ceylon. The reports received from him and from the missionaries are most encouraging. The field is white already to the harvest. The five hundred societies in India will be five thousand, and even now they are beginning to talk of a World's Christian Endeavor Convention in Calcutta, India, in 1904.

If I had time to tell you of the practical work done by these Endeavorers of the Orient, you would see that when we go there we shall get points on how to do things as well as give them.

Japan, that wonderful empire, well called the Sunrise Kingdom, has appointed Rev. I. Inanuma as field secretary to organize societies in all the churches. We have admired the beautiful work of the skilful Japanese artisans, and have coveted specimens of it for our homes. The day is coming when the same patient, skilful, laborious work will be put into fashioning the boys and girls of Japan into jewels that will flash in the diadem of our Redeemer. And the Society of Christian Endeavor will be the training-school for these workers.

These are the fields into which the contributions received by the World's Union have gone. But the amount has been altogether inadequate to meet the needs.

And what shall I say of China? Reaping, from within, the awful harvest of centuries of paganism, and the prey, from without, of jealous and grasping political powers. Her soil consecrated by the blood of the noblest army of martyrs the church has ever marshaled in the service of our Savior. The picture of Mr. Simcox of Pao-ting-fu, walking amid the flames of his burning house, hand in hand with his two little children, and their ascension to heaven in that chariot of fire, is but a prophecy of China's redemption. The church with her children, the Sunday School and Christian Endeavor, shall yet open heaven's gates to the millions of China.

The workers are now calling for financial help from us to enable the United Society of China to put a secretary into the field to organize and reorganize the work. They say the time is ripe, and not a year should be lost. Where think you has our President, Dr. Clark, seen the finest Christian Endeavor prayer meeting? In Massachusetts? In Pennsylvania? In Ohio? In Canada? In England? No. No. Not in these gospel-favored lands, but in Foochow, China, on his recent trip around the world. And the national Chinese convention held in that city with an attendance of about fifteen hundred delegates was one of the missionary marvels of the closing months of the great missionary century.

And what shall I say for Spain, to whom we sent millions of bullets in the recent war? Would that we might now send as many Bibles. Christian Endeavor is doing a splendid work there. And France and Italy and Norway and Sweden and Korea all stand with open doors, but needing our help that the work may be done.

Not one dollar will this work take from the missionary offerings to our regular missionary boards; but rather, I believe, those gifts will be multiplied and increased as the hearts of the young people are turned toward their brothers and sisters who sit in darkness and the shadow of death.

Endeavorers of this great free land of gospel light and privilege, will you do your part individually, that the blessings we enjoy may be shared by the millions of young people on the other side of the globe for whom Christ died?

CHAPTER XXV.

For Christ and the Church.

New York's able president, Rev. W. B. Wallace, with clear thought and an inspiring voice, gave out the watchword, "For Christ and the Church."

For Christ and the Church.

Rev. W. B. Wallace, Utica, N. Y.

Above the smoke and strife of Trafalgar, there floated the famous signal that Nelson flung to the breeze as he went forth to meet the foe, "England expects every man to do his duty." Inspired by these words the hearts of British sailors became "hearts of oak," the wills of British sailors, Gibraltars, and twenty French sails struck their flags ere the day was done.

At the mast head of the Christian Endeavor ship, there has been unfurled a watchword, the sight of which has ever inspired to action, loyalty to which explains the achievements of the past twenty years, the mention of which sends the blood tingling through the veins of the Christian warrior, makes his heart beat with valorous zeal and his will grow strong to do exploits.

Voice of God, inspiring to victory yesterday, voice of God inspiring to victory today, voice of God inspiring to complete and final victory in some glad tomorrow is the watchword of our society "for Christ and for the Church."

I.—FOR THE CHURCH.

What power to arouse to action here! The very name of the Church ought to act as the sound of martial music upon the spirit of the soldier, and "set us into quick step and forward march." How comes it that the light generated by the dynamo of Calvary's Cross shines on our lives today? Because that light has traveled along the wire of the Christian Church that spans the centuries that lie between the Savior's time and ours. How comes it that we drink of the waters of Scripture truth? Because the Church has been a sure and safe aqueduct through which these waters have flowed down the centuries to us. It is easy for man to criticise the Church of God, but let him remember that he owes a measureless debt of gratitude to that same Church for making him a sharer of the benefits of Christian civilization.

The name of the church ought to inspire us, too, because of its service in the art of noble living. Amid a multitude of influences that tend to rob man of his crown, and make of him a muck-rake soul, there sounds the bell-toned voice of the Christian Church, urging him to turn his back on vice, and woo fair virtue. If not the mother, the church is at least the birthplace of our spiritual life. Here we learn to love the name of Jesus, and our stammering tongues to speak the language of His Kingdom. We creep like babes at first, but by the aid of the church, its songs, its services, its supplications, its society, we grow toward the measure of the stature of the fulness of Christ.

The church is defender and advocate of all that is purest and best in the world. Do you love the home? The mightiest bulwark against those forces that would change the home into a harem or a hell is the church of God. Do you love freedom? The church of Christ is the champion of physical, social, intellectual and spiritual liberty. Do you love the flag?

The arm that is doing the most to guard the flag from dishonor, the voice that speaks the loudest in denunciation of those foes that would tear down the banner that you love in the church. Do you love the heroic? The church is a heroine who has stood her ground against opposing odds, and won victory in the face of apparent defeat.

> "Unshaken as the Eternal hills,
> Immovable she stands,
> A mountain that shall fill the earth,
> A house not made with hands."

Do you love philanthropy? Her teachings and her actions show the church to be a leader in philanthropic endeavor and the mother of our great philanthropic institutions. Do you love evangelism? City and State, Home and Foreign missions are the expression of the church's life. Carey, Judson, Paton, McKay, Clough and Livingstone are her offspring.

I want to say that the church ought to have your truest service because she is loved by the Master. I could do no harm to a common toy that was dear to my child. His affection for it, somehow, would make me love it, too. Jesus loves the church. He purchased her with His own precious blood.

For the church then!—The preserver of the sacred Scriptures and the Gospel story, the inspirer to noble living, the advocate of the truest and the best, the object of the love of Christ. Let this be the watchword to arouse us to highest enthusiasm, and to fill us with a steadfast purpose to support the church of God by prayer and purse, by lip and life, so hastening the day when she shall stand before the Bridegroom's throne, "a glorious church, without spot or wrinkle or any such thing."

II.—FOR CHRIST.

"The name of Christ, the one great word, worthy all languages in earth and heaven." At sight or sound thereof the Christian soul ought to be ablaze with holy zeal.

What a leader He is as to His person! He is King of purity. A searchlight of twenty centuries shines upon Him only to make it more manifest that He is the peerless man, the Son of God. There is, so entomologists tell us, an insect that has power to draw about itself a covering of air as a kind of diving suit, that protects its gossamer wings from all pollution when it descends into impure or stagnant pools in search of food. Christ was so enveloped in the atmosphere of holiness that though He mixed with men, and ate with Publicans and sinners, He was ever spotless pure. The verdict of those who have made most careful study of His life is that of Pilate, "I find no fault in Him at all."

And He is King of love. In the story of the Rough Riders we read of Captain McClintock lying wounded on the battle-field. A trooper comes and lies down between McClintock and the firing line. The Captain orders him away, saying that he has no right thus to expose himself to danger, but the trooper gives as his excuse, that he is wounded, too. As the direction of the enemy's fire shifts, the trooper drags his body here or there, so as to shield his captain. At length the hospital corps comes to carry the wounded from the field. As McClintock is being taken away, he whispers, "Bring the other." The reply is, "No use, he is dead." Oh, how the name of Jesus ought to inspire us to action. He came in between us and the firing line. On the Cross He hangs to shield us from the bullets of the foe.

Prince of leaders, too, is Christ, because of His power. He has power to comfort. A husband, mourning for his dead wife in the darkness of the night, hears the cry of his motherless child, "Papa, take my hand," and reaching out his hand, he clasps that of his little darling, and the little one goes off to sleep. Then he reaches up his hand to God, and cries, "Father in heaven, take the hand of Thy child," and finds his own soul comforted. How many in the stress and strain of life have felt the touch of the Master's hand, and so have been strengthened and cheered.

Christ has power to save from sin. You remember old Nelson in Connor's "Black Rock." He is a hard-hearted sinner who has deserted his wife and children, and in the West is living a life of drunkenness and shame. Mr. Craig, the preacher, tells him of the power of Christ to save. Nelson asks if he is "dead sure" that he is right. Craig answers "Yes," and Nelson, straightening himself to his full height, cries, "I'll try Him." At once his life becomes sweet and strong and serviceful. Wounded unto death in an effort to save a friend, he turns while dying to Mr. Craig and says, "You said He wouldn't fail me; He hasn't, not once, not once." Whenever a sinner, be he idolater, blasphemer, drunkard, cannibal or murderer, turns to Christ and says "I'll try Him," his verdict will be "He has never failed me, not once, not once."

Christ has power to save from the wages of sin, from death. He swings ajar the gates of pearl, and gives free entrance to an endless life. "Oh, Papa," sobbed the dying child, "the grave is so dark, won't you go with me?" "I cannot, darling," answered the broken-hearted father. "Then won't you let Mamma go?" "She can't go either, darling," the father was forced to sob out in his agony. The little girl turned her tear-stained face to the wall. She had heard of Jesus and she began to talk to Him, who said, "Suffer the children to come unto Me." Soon she turned with her face all radiant and said: "Papa, the grave is dark no longer, Jesus will go with me." The risen Christ has power to change the gloom of the grave into the glory of Paradise.

In Marion Crawford's "Via Crucis" there is a graphic description of Bernard's appeal to men to rescue the sepulchre from the hands of unbelievers. The Knights and their ladies are assembled in an open field, for there is no building large enough to seat the throng. Bernard stands before them and with an eloquence that makes him rank among the world's great orators, he pleads with them that as they would hasten to defend the resting place of wife, or child, or mother, so let them now defend from infidel hands the tomb of Christ. As he ends his burning speech with these words, "Be Knights of Honor, Knights of France, and Knights of God Most High," he holds aloft his arm garmented in white and in his hand the crucifix. All is silence for a moment, then as one man they all press forward and cry, "Crosses, give us crosses!" Crosses that had been prepared are fastened on the dress of the Knights, and of the ladies until they all are gone, and then Bernard makes the sign of the cross for those who still would be crusaders. One old blacksmith asks for the cross. Bernard replies, "I have not one, but will make a sign for thee." "Not so," cries the blacksmith, and going to his forge he heats a piece of iron to a white heat and baring his breast burns a cross upon his flesh.

Endeavorers, when you think what the church is, and what Christ is, the one cry of us all ought to be, "Crosses, give us crosses!" I do not mean the cross that dangles from the necklace or the watch chain, that is worn upon the dress or even branded upon the flesh. I mean the cross that manifests itself in loyalty to the church, and stands for death to ease, and selfishness and sin for the church's sake. I mean the cross that manifests itself in a life as loyal to Christ as French soldiers were to Napoleon, or English soldiers to Wellington, or American soldiers to Grant. I mean the cross whose wearer sings:

> "If Jesus Christ be a man,
>   And only a man, I say
> That of all mankind, I will cleave to Him,
>   And to Him I will cleave alway.
>
> "If Jesus Christ is a God,
>   And the only God, I swear,
> I will follow Him through heaven and hell,
>   The earth, the sea and the air."

The associate member was the subject of earnest and prayerful discussion. Rev. D. Frank Garland of Dayton, O., said, "As we go to the sea for fish and to the mountain for gold, so the Endeavor Society must go to the associate member for its trophies of victory." Among other things Mr. Garland said:

The Associate Member.

The conquest of America will be accomplished by the conquering army of children. The book of the future is in the hands of the children, and its pages will be written by them. Yesterday we looked into their smiling faces, and I said to myself, these children of Christian Endeavor will take America for Christ. You know that every reform movement, beaten back and battled, and hindered and opposed, looks with hope to the children, the growing children of the land. My Christian friend, you and I have entered the associate membership, but it is far, far too small. When I look into the faces of the Christian Endeavorers, and when I look into the records of the movement, I say Christian Endeavor is not making the progress that it should. There are great recruiting grounds, and all you have to do is to marshal the hundreds and thousands into the service of Christ if you will but go after them. The Christian Endeavor movement has today no grander and no more glorious opportunity than in giving itself to the training of workers for service in the Kingdom of Christ. There are more than twenty millions of young men and women, boys and girls, in this country. Do you know that not more than one-half of them are in our churches? If our Christian Endeavor Society is to do its God-given work, it must bring into touch with the church this great multitude of the unused host of God's children.

CHAPTER XXVI.

The Twentieth Century Outlook for Missions.

A NEW CENTURY OF HOME MISSIONS.— FOREIGN MISSIONS; ITS
BREADTH AND OUTLOOK.—SYSTEMATIC BENEVOLENCE
ESSENTIAL TO AGGRESSIVE WORK.

Dr. Charles L. Thompson, the famous home-mission secretary of the Presbyterian church, is a man of statesmanlike presence and impressive speech.

"The problem of home missions," said he, "is so to establish our national character that it will endure the test of coming time." "I believe," he asserted, "that there never has been a missionary march comparable to the march of the Christian church during the last hundred years, from the Alleghenies to the Pacific coast."

A New Century of Home Missions.

Rev. Charles L. Thompson, D. D., New York City.

Not often in the history of centuries has the transition from one to another been accomplished with such mighty transitions of thought and life as have characterized the passing of the nineteenth and the dawning of the twentieth century.

To America the new century is a century of beginnings—"Through the shadow of the globe we sweep into the younger day." To us Americans it is a day of new opportunities. The boom of guns has burst open gates we had not thought of entering but whose portals now await our feet. This fact holds politically, commercially, religiously.

I am to speak of that phase of new opportunities that relates to the great work of the evangelization of our country. We have a new sphere of influence. America today presents the most neglected missionary field, —from the expanse of our country to the northwest, from the opening of new opportunities in the new possessions in the southeast and in the various republics of the southern part of the continent. It has become a truism to say that as goes America so goes the world. How America shall go depends at last not so much on the plans of politicians and statesmen as upon the methods and work of the Christian Church.

I will briefly sketch in geographical order the home mission opportunities of the new century. In the Caribbean Sea lies our beautiful new island of Porto Rico. It was given to Latin Christianity four centuries ago by the discovery of Columbus. These centuries have been heavy ones for that emerald island. They mean only superstition, poverty and degradation. The coming of the Christian Church means new light to nearly one million people. With what joy they welcome our message; with what readiness they accept and copy our institutions. Every place opened for worship is over-crowded; every Christian school is full of pupils. In one of our missionary stations in a year and a half two large congregations have been gathered, one commodious church erected, one church organized with a membership of nearly one hundred, a medical mission established and a Christian school full of scholars. In another mission in fourteen months a half-dozen preaching stations have been opened, always crowded, a church organized into which over a hundred members have been received, a school established. plans matured for the erection of a large church building.

PART OF THE ORPHAN CHILDREN THAT TOOK PART IN THE JUNIOR RALLY.

THE ENDEAVORERS COMING FROM A MORNING QUIET HOUR.

The Evangelical denominations at work on the island have entered into the work not only in a spirit of fraternity but of co-operation. There will be no unnecessary duplication of Christian work in Porto Rico. Together we are striving to lift that Island into the light of Christian civilization and liberty. When so lifted it will be one of the gardens of the Lord.

What I have thus said of Porto Rico I might say of Cuba with its much larger population—not an integral part of the United States, but home missionary ground, because it is so contiguous and because by the commercial and social bonds it is being bound so close to our republic. There, too, interested crowds await the voice of the messenger of Christ. Cuba and Porto Rico are only two of a score of West Indian Islands that wait for the light of Christian education and Christian truth. It is our opportunity to bring these to them; because they are within our sphere of Christian influence—and within ours only—it is our solemn duty to give education and the Gospel.

Let us pass on to the next picture of our Christian opportunity. It is in the Appalachian mountains, home of a sturdy people who, neglected by North and South alike for a century past, and now suddenly reappearing, present one of the most hopeful fields of missionary endeavor. Schools, colleges and Christian churches are lightening the darkness of that beautiful region. Out of one of those cabins came Abraham Lincoln. Other Lincolns may be waiting there for the delivering hand of Christian education and it shall not be withheld, for that sturdy stock of Scotch and Scotch-Irish are worth redeeming. They will add Christian tone and vigor to all the States beautified by those mountains.

The Christian Church in the last twenty-five years has done much to brighten the shadows of our centuries of dishonor in our treatment of the American Indian. The Indian missionary heroes of Colonial days on the Atlantic Coast—the Elliots, Brainerds and Sargents—have had their worthy successors in latter times among the tribes of the West that had been pushed to the last verge of being. On the burning sands of Arizona one heroic missionary, Charles H. Cook, in the last thirty years has brought a thousand Indians into the Church of Christ and established them in churches where they are now adorning the doctrine of their God and Savior. In the far Northwest, a missionary presbytery of Nez Perces Indians attests the power of the Gospel first carried to those mountain canyons by the lips of Whitman and Spaulding and continued in its blessed force by those who have been their worthy successors. It is true the Indian is a fading race, but it is also true that they present yet a large and most pathetic field for missionary labor. At the present time twenty-five thousand Navajos are calling for some one to lead them out of the darkness into the light, while still scattered remnants down a hundred canyons and across a hundred prairies by mute appeal are signaling to the Church to give those whose title of earthly lands has passed away a title clear to mansions in the sky.

And far up in Alaska thirty thousand natives long left in squalor and degradation are sending their call to the American Church to lift them from their destitution and despair. I know of no more pathetic picture than that presented by the Klawack Indians, a tribe on the west coast of Prince of Wales Island, when our missionary visited them last year, begging him that some one might be sent to teach them the better life, and when he said, "You must pray," down on their knees on the sands of the Pacific went that whole tribe, imploring highest heaven that the hunger of their heart might be met. This very month a missionary and his bride from Park College are on their way to that remote station—the answer of the Church to the prayers of the Klawacks. Similar instances might be repeated.

One more picture of missionary opportunity. It is on the awakening Pacific Coast—that coast which from San Diego to Puget Sound feels the pulse of the new life which is realizing its ever closer connections with the Eastern States, which looks across the blue Pacific and sights rising

connections with Asiatic communities. Business feels the thrill and the
ship-yards are busy preparing great vessels to carry the commerce of the
new Pacific, to take our products to Asia and bring theirs to us. Let the
Church join in this great enterprise. Let the thin line of Christian heroes
there be reinforced. Let them hear the tread of an army of Christian
Endeavorers coming to their help, for Seward's prophecy is about to be
fulfiled on the Pacific Coast, where will be transacted the mightiest events
of human history. The Anglo-Saxon race gathered on these shores in pushing westward, meets Asiatic races coming eastward. Shall it be collision
such as was threatened in China? Or shall it be co-operation by which the
children of men shall become the children of God? Behold the opportunity
of the Christian Church of America! Never such came to a church before.
A new century of home missions! Shall we be equal to what it implies?
Shall we be God's men and women in a peculiar consecration? Shall we
give our sons and daughters to heed the call? Shall we open our treasuries without stint and pour them at the Master's feet to the end that ere
the sunset of a new century shall flash over the world there may be
flashed upon us the chariot wheels of Him Who shall be King of nations
as He is now King of saints.

Foreign Missions; Its Breadth and Outlook.

Hon. Samuel B. Capen, LL. D., Boston.

It may help us to realize the breadth and enlarging power of our Foreign Missionary work today if we take a hasty view of the narrowness
and feebleness of its beginning, and the conditions as they then existed.
At the time our first foreign missionary society was born, at the beginning of the last century, the United States had only recently obtained its
freedom from the mother country. France had been our ally, and French
atheism was very popular all over our country. We have always thought
of Yale and Princeton as centres of religious life, but at one time at this
period there was but one Christian student at Yale, and not a single one
at Princeton. The efforts of the American Board to secure a charter
from the Massachusetts Legislature was received with ridicule, the request being met with the remark that "we had no religion to export."
All those who showed any interest whatever in this thought of a needy
world were sneered at continually. It was only a counterpart of similar conditions in England, where William Carey, one of the pioneers of
modern missions, was called a "consecrated cobbler," that title being
given to him in derision.

There were a hundred years ago but seven foreign missionary societies,
employing only one hundred and seventy male missionaries. When the
first missionaries of the American Board went to India, they were or-
dered away by the East India Company with the remark that they would
prefer a shipload of devils to a shipload of missionaries. When Robert
Moffatt went to South Africa, the people stole his food and threatened
his life. Cannibalism and every form of horror was prevalent in the
islands of the sea. China and Japan were practically closed to the
world. It is less than forty years since an edict was proclaimed in Japan,
that if any Christian teacher, or even the Christian's God himself, dare
set foot in those islands, he shall pay the penalty with the loss of his
head. With no organized Christian work in America outside of the local
church, and with the conditions as they were in the far-away lands, the
beginning of the nineteenth century had far more darkness than light.

CONDITIONS AT HOME TODAY.

With this hasty glimpse at the past, let us note the great changes
at home since the beginning of the century. There has been the wonderful growth of Sunday schools, so that today we have in these United
States alone, 1,400,000 teachers and over 11,000,000 pupils. We have over

60,000 Christian Endeavor Societies in this country, with a membership of 3,500,000. There are Young Men's and Young Women's Christian Associations in our principal cities, and Christian colleges have sprung up all the way from the Atlantic to the Pacific. Then there is a revival of practical religious life in our universities and colleges, which has taken form in the Students' Volunteer Movement. Rev. Dr. McCosh has asked, "Has any such offering of living young men and women been presented in our age, in our country, in any age, or in any country, since the day of Pentecost?" What this means is voiced by an American Bishop who says, "If you save one college man for God, you place in this world a force which will counteract the influence of 1000 illiterate, vicious men." In contrast with what we saw at the beginning of the last century, in Yale university today 65 per cent. of its students are church members. The various denominations have organized for Christian work to reach every class of society.

We must not forget either what we may call the unconscious influence of the Gospel as seen in our country, which is working indirectly but practically, and permeating every branch of society. Great gifts for hospitals and libraries, and other forms of philanthropy are being made by men who have been touched by the unselfish spirit which Jesus Christ brought into the world.

CONDITIONS ABROAD.

I have sketched briefly the conditions of organized work as we see them all about us today in our own land, as a background to what I now wish to say, that there is a work equally as great across the sea which most of us have not seen. Instead of the seven foreign missionary societies a hundred years ago, there are today over 400 foreign missionary societies representing the Protestant churches, employing 13,600 missionaries, and 73,000 native helpers, with nearly a million pupils in the various grades of Christian schools. It was fitting that there should be held last year in New York the great Ecumenical Conference, the grandest foreign missionary meeting of the century, where this important work was reviewed, and where the world were compelled to see how much had been wrought. Instead of sneers and ridicule, as at the beginning of the century, words of hearty welcome were spoken by President McKinley, ex-President Harrison, and Governor Roosevelt.

I do not wish to detain you, however, with rehearsing the statistics which might be given. These are important in their place, but you might as well try to measure the influence of the sun with a yard stick as to measure what has been wrought in the world by foreign missionaries by any tables of figures. The breadth of work to which I especially wish to call your attention is that which has come in the character of the work itself.

BREADTH OF WORK.

In a recent report from a missionary station in India we find this significant passage, "The time has passed when the Bible and a sun hat were all that a missionary needs to equip him for his work. Whether for better or for worse, it is not ours to say here, but the fact remains that most universally the missionary has pressed into the service of missions every agency that can be used to arouse, elevate or bless the people for whom he labors. The school, the press, the surgeon's knife, the painter's art, the craftsman's skill and the inventor's genius have already become in greater or less degree the heralds of the tidings of good will to men." The one purpose, to reach and save men has always been, and always will be, the same; but we have found the value of using other means besides direct evangelical preaching, to reach the conscience and the will.

EDUCATION.

The second step in the broadening of missionary work was along the line of education. The native Christian can reach his own people as no foreigner can possibly do. There is a closeness of touch and sympathy, and a knowledge of their life, which cannot be gained by any European or American. Furthermore, it costs far less to maintain such native helpers than to support missionaries from this country. Not only the quickest success, but the largest economy is along the line of training preachers and teachers in every country to reach their own people.

This step was not taken without serious opposition. There were those who feared that in putting the emphasis upon educational work, it would be at the expense of the evangelistic; but when one sees the result of this Christian education upon young hearts and lives, and notes that almost all the graduates from the schools are Christians, all fears vanish. Every missionary in some respects is an educator, and the work of the preacher and the Christian teacher are no more in conflict than are the bread and water which together are essential to support the physical body.

WOMEN'S WORK.

There was a movement started about 50 years ago which has had a large influence in helping to solve our most serious Foreign Missionary problems. Women in all heathen countries are kept away from contact with the outer world. They are not allowed the same educational facilities as men, and in most of these countries the education of a woman has been supposed to be impossible. Under these conditions they are, of course, more bigoted than men, and yet in these countries, as in our own homes, their influence is the greater for they are the mothers of the children. Furthermore, it was found while we were christianizing the young men, there were no young women being similarly trained to provide proper wives for these Christian preachers and teachers. It was vital to reach the women or else missions would fail at the most important point, namely, at the home, and under Oriental conditions men could not do this work. I never realized the full importance of this until after a conversation a short time ago with a missionary from India, who said that of 6000 pupils, examined by officials for promotion to the government high schools, only four were women, and but two of these passed the examination. Hence the supreme necessity for this work of Christian women for girls.

When the educated young men of India with their ignorant wives call on the Christian young men with their intelligent Christian wives, and see the contrast, the effect is marvelous. It opens their eyes wonderfully to the real significance of our missionary work. To plant the Gospel of pure Christian homes has been a mighty work, and deserves to be emphasized as we are considering the broadening out of our methods.

MEDICAL MISSIONS.

The first missionary effort was to reach the heart. It was found, as we have already seen, that one of the best ways to reach the heart was through the head. Then it was ascertained that another step in the same direction was to care for the body, and hence the beginning of medical missions. The first medical missionary was Jesus Christ. His whole heart went out in compassion to all who were distressed, and he saw that by the gift of healing he could touch the deepest springs of life. So our missionaries found speedily when they faced conditions in these far-away lands. Love for one's kindred is not peculiar to America or England or Germany. The man with the black or copper colored skin loves his own and will often sacrifice much to save them.

There is no end of illustrations to show the practical value of it all. A Mohammedan judge had been bitterly opposed to Christianity and lost no opportunity to show his contempt for the medical missionaries, but one day, in the good providence of God, this judge's boy swallowed some poison, and with a father's love, he summoned the missionary. After working over the boy two hours, he restored him to life. Now witness the change. The next day when the missionary appeared in the market place, the judge greeted him with both hands, presented him to his friends; the victory was won.

All over our missionary field are scattered modern hospitals and dispensaries equipped with missionaries with their surgical instruments, and with trained nurses to care for the sick and the suffering. We can hardly conceive how much these modern hospitals mean to these people. They have been accustomed to the barbarities of their ignorant "medicine men" who burn them with hot irons, and beat their hideous drums to drive away evil spirits when the patient is burning up with fever. When we take people out of such conditions as these and put them into a modern hospital with its quiet, and when they find after they are restored to health that this is perfectly free to them if they are in poverty, no wonder they are impressed at its unselfishness, so different from everything which they ever experienced, and they call these missionaries, the "Jesus man who cares." Not only Corea and Japan, but other large districts have been opened to missionary work as a result of the skill of the medical missionary.

There is in Madura one of the greatest heathen temples in the world, and not far away is a splendid hospital with modern appliances which will accommodate about 100 patients. If I ask what built it, you might answer English sovereigns; not one. Then American dollars; not one. Every rupee which went into this building came from the natives themselves, and was presented to one of our missionary boards as a tribute of love to a medical missionary, for what he had been doing in that region. Dr. Clark told me that he visited not only this hospital, but the heathen temple, and that the priest in the latter told him that they had opened their great coffers and taken out money that had been offered there in idol-worship, and paid it over to help build this hospital because of their love for the men who were doing such noble work for their poor people. It must be noted that in these hospitals there are other missionaries and helpers, besides the surgeons, who talk with the patients while they are waiting, and afterwards go from cot to cot with the message of life. Multitudes are being reached in this way and we must give large place to the value of this work as we consider what our foreign missions are doing in the world.

MISSIONARY PRESS.

In this effort to reach the heart by training the mind and caring for the body, there is another means that has been used of great importance: I refer to the missionary press. In visiting the museum in New York which was open in connection with the Ecumenical Conference, the thing that impressed me most was the number and variety of books printed for use in missionary lands, and yet they were just a few representative samples. Do we realize that the missionary press and publishing houses a year ago in their 148 establishments printed 10,561,000 copies of books and pamphlets, with a total of 364,904,000 pages, or a million pages a day! There are also issued by our missionaries 366 magazines and papers, with a circulation of nearly 300,000 copies. We cannot overestimate the importance of this work. There are said to be 15,000,000 people in India who either are now under instruction, or have graduated from government schools, the vast majority of whom are not yet Christianized. It is splendid to know that these people are willing more and more to read the books that are being prepared by the missionaries. We cannot do too much for these men. Bismarck said of the German students, one-third break down, one-third rot down, and the other one-third govern Germany. In India, as in Germany, it is these educated young men that are to control ultimately the 300,000,000 population of that nation.

Of course we must not fail when we speak of the work of the press, to refer to the greatest work of all, the publication of the Bible. When our missionaries went to many of these far-away places there was often no grammar or written language. By listening to the sounds they slowly made a language. And even in countries where they found a beginning, there were no words to represent virtue and righteousness and holiness and truth. Yet, notwithstanding all the difficulties in the way, in less than 100 years the Bible has been printed in more than 400 languages and dialects representing a population of more than three-fourths of the globe. It is the greatest monument we have to the patience and untiring industry of our missionaries.

There is no end of illustration to show the value of the Bible in heathen countries. A wonderful story was recently told of a whole village in India, where no missionary had ever preached, which has been converted to God from the teaching of a little child who read and re-read to eager listeners the Gospel of Mark; 16 chapters of Mark and a little child, and God's spirit added the blessing to his own word in the transformation of this whole village to Jesus Christ. "My word shall not return unto me void."

INDUSTRIAL TRAINING.

In our missionary work which reaches the heart and head and body, there is one step further that is being taken in many places, viz: the education of the hand. Gen. Armstrong and Booker Washington found it essential for work among the Indians and colored people in our own land, so our missionaries have found it essential, if they would do their best work across the sea. In many of these countries when a man becomes a Christian he is practically excommunicated by his friends, who make it very difficult for him to get a livelihood. When, however, he has been taught to do something skillfully through his superior intelligence, his chances for caring for himself are greatly increased. Again, if teacher and preacher have a trade, they can often support themselves in part as Paul did nineteen centuries ago, and so can reach further into the interior districts. Furthermore, in many of these heathen countries it has been considered beneath a man to do any manual work; he has allowed his wife to do all that. We must teach the boys in our schools that labor is honorable, and where industrial training has been taught it has brought large results. We are trying to educate the whole man, his head, his heart, his hands, that in every place and everywhere he may show to the heathen about him the complete transforming power of the religion of Jesus Christ. The body is the temple of the Holy Ghost, and we are showing him as never before, how essential it is to care for this temple, the earthly home of the soul.

Such is the briefest possible outline of the breadth of this great foreign missionary work. In the whole history of this wonderful century there is nothing so magnificent as the missionary story. In the majesty of its conception, in the heroism of its leaders, in the greatness of its results, it stands without a peer. Material growth, great inventions, progress in science and art, are as nothing compared with this mighty work, born in the heart of God, and given to his children to work out in all the earth. Other things may be forgotten, but the triumphs of missions wrought in the name of Jesus Christ, will outlive the centuries.

SECOND—THE OUTLOOK.

History has been making rapidly during the last few years. Passing by the wonderful changes that have taken place in the islands of the Pacific, and the new hopes that have come because of recent events, let us, by way of illustration, look at three countries where missionary work has been sadly interfered with during the past few years.

First, Turkey: The fearful massacres in Armenia a few years ago, filled the world with horror, and for a time interfered seriously with our missionary work; and yet we begin to see now in clearer light that out of these awful conditions there is increased progress being made. It is said that more Gregorians were won to Christ by the brave sufferings of the Armenians in these massacres than there were by their words before these events occurred. The world also saw the wonderful bravery of our missionaries, and their wisdom and Christian fidelity received universal approval. When the Duke of Westminster asked the English Ambassador at Constantinople to name some one to distribute the relief fund raised in England for the suffering Armenians, he replied, "Send no one; employ the American missionaries. No one knows the people or their wants as well, and none are as capable." This confirms what was said years before by the late Earl of Shaftsbury of the American missionaries in Turkey, "I do not believe that in the history of diplomacy we can find anything to equal the wisdom and soundness of the men who constitute the American missions. They are a marvelous combination of common-sense and piety." Then the orphan children have been gathered into homes and are under Christian teachers, and in a few years they will be sent out as a result of the training which otherwise they never would have received, to do larger service as preachers and teachers.

Second, India: The transformation here has been greater even than in Turkey. We stand aghast at the awful famines, and sometimes wonder how it was possible that these things could be permitted, and yet we are beginning to see as a result of it all that the nation is being opened to Christian influence as never before. When the famine came, and water in many districts was exhausted, the people saw their old priests take their holy alligators and carry them off to a place of safety for themselves, leaving the people to starve. In contrast with all this they saw the missionary stand in his place, in full touch and sympathy with the people, and the American nation send over a million dollars to give food to the suffering. No wonder that they see in this the reality of the religion of Jesus Christ, that they are turning away from the old in disgust, and accepting the new. The latest tidings from India show that whole districts are turning to the Gospel. People are coming from long distances, and in great numbers, pleading with the missionaries to give them Christian teachers, for they recognize that there is something in the Gospel which they represent, and the civilization for which they stand, infinitely superior to anything they have had before. I heard a statement recently which came from an educated Brahmin, who acknowledged that he was an agnostic, but prophesied that Christianity would speedily sweep over India as the waters rush across the country when a dam gives way. It certainly is true that everywhere Christianity is undermining heathenism and it is crumbling to its fall. The missionary, followed as he is everywhere by the civilization of the West, with its railroad and its telegraph, is showing the people its superiority to the old. It has been well said that their little clay gods look very small when the great locomotive rushes by.

Third: And what shall we say of the tragedy in China? The record of the past few months has given us a story as wonderful as any chapter in the world's history. As we read some of the stories in the Old Testament they seem almost beyond belief, but there is not one of them which is hardly more wonderful, or which shows more the overruling hand of God than is seen in the story of the siege of Peking. It has been seen as never before what splendid men our American missionary societies have sent to this nation. With wonderful wisdom, with a bravery unsurpassed, they have stood at their posts. Many of them are today wearing the martyr's crown because of their fidelity to their trusts. And what shall we say of the native Christians themselves who have, as a rule, been willing to die rather than to deny their new faith in Jesus Christ. There is nothing in human annals more wonderful than the fidelity of these men. Furthermore, the diplomacy of the nation under the skillful guidance of Secretary Hay, has been the admiration of the world. Because of all this, the American nation and the American Protestant missionary never stood so high in China as today, and the men at the front believe that as a result of this terrible disaster the cause of Jesus Christ is to be advanced with a rapidity not seen in the past.

It is a glorious hour in the history of the world, and the outlook is magnificent. I had rather live the next twenty years than twenty centuries of some of the days that are gone. We are in the midst of two great conflicts:

First: The civilization of the West as represented by Europe and America, against that of the far-away East. Cannot we see the wonderful Providence that at this hour we have Japan with us? Suppose no missionary had entered that empire, and she stood where she did thirty years ago. Instead of having had her as our splendid ally, with permission for us to use her soil for the transshipment of ammunitions of war, and with her finely equipped army which is receiving the admiration of the world, we should have had her during the past few months as an opponent. God's hand has been most evident in the preparation of this wonderful people for the hour of conflict through which we have been passing.

Second: There is the contest between the Teutonic race, including the Anglo-Saxon, on the one side, and the Slav, represented especially by Russia, on the other. No one can have watched the course of the latter as she has been steadily crowding England, at every point, without feelings of suspicion. She has built her great railroad to within a few miles of Herat, the key of India. Not far away is an immense army which she can mobilize for service at a few hours' notice. She has stretched another great railroad across Siberia to the China seas. She has granted a Persian loan of twelve million dollars, and one item in the payment of the loan, is the income from the Persian ports on the Gulf. She has made impregnable her possessions at Port Arthur, and she has a strong foothold in Corea. We must believe that the Czar himself is a man of many kindly impulses, as illustrated by his calling together the arbitration conference at the Hague; the people are kindly; but the machine, called the Russian Government, is now, and always has been, an enemy of all missionary work. Russia treats Americans with most distinguished consideration, but her diplomacy is smooth and plausible, and her purpose to control Asia is most apparent. We saw her course in Armenia a few years ago; we remember the recent outrage perpetrated in Finland where she violated the most sacred obligations. The recent treatment of her students also shows how the government lives in the past.

Under these conditions it is a happy Providence to see the closer drawing together of England, Germany, and the United States who represent the spirit of religious freedom. It is a battle of the Occident against the Orient; it is the battle of religious liberty and Christianity, represented by the Anglo-Saxon, against religious bondage and the centralization of power, as represented by Russia. I do not believe the Chinese "yellow peril," so-called, is as much to be feared as the cold and steadily moving "Russian glacier."

America never had before such a glorious outlook for foreign missionary work as at this hour. Our nation is the one great power in the world that has been unselfish in its foreign relations; we do not seek the country of other nations. Because of this, our missionaries have advantages over all others. It is no time for hesitation; because we have done so much, we must do more. God's love is as wide as the world. There are great differences among us as to "imperialism" politically considered, but we must all be Christian Imperialists. The marching order of Christ, "Go," is the very spirit of Christianity. If a brother was in need at our side we should help him. Is his need any the less because he is 12,000 miles away in the far Orient? A question which the Savior answered nineteen centuries ago is still most pertinent, "Who is my neighbor?"

It is splendid to see how not only here at home, but as well upon the mission fields, Christians of every name are coming into closer harmony and working with fuller co-operation. Let us all care less for our denominational distinctions, and more for Christ; let us forget all our differences, and present a common front to heathenism. Christian Endeavor has done much and is to do more towards this great end.

Ex-President Harrison at the Ecumenical Conference in words of splendid eloquence told us that nothing so creates a panic in an army as to be fired into by their own men. With this wonderful outlook for Christian nations in all the world, let everything that is akin to denominational controversy be forever ended with the nineteenth century, and let us enter the new as one great army marching steadily together. As on the field of battle the regimental flags are put aside, and only the stars and stripes are visible from one end of the line to the other, so in our war for righteousness in all the world, let all denominational badges be sent to the rear, and nothing be seen at the front but the banner of the Cross.

Systematic Benevolence Essential to Aggressive Work.

Rev. A. A. Fulton, D. D., Canton, China.

The most gigantic system of idolatry in the world is sustained and fostered by a vast army of small givers. Every dollar given to idolatry is not only an absolute waste, but it is tightening chains of superstition and is a sin which casts out from the Kingdom of Heaven.

Today more than six hundred millions of immortal souls are worshipers of worthless idols of wood and stone. The worshipers of these idols are among the poorest nations in the world. They give vastly more to these delusive systems than all the churches in the world give to the propagation of a pure Gospel. How is this done? How can they out of their bitter poverty exceed the contributions of Christianity with its billions of wealth.

They all give something. They all give something systematically. They all give something systematically and continuously. Fas est ab hostibus doceri.

In the early years of itineration my attention was frequently called to long lists of subscriptions posted in conspicuous places in cities and market towns in China. I soon learned to read these lists, and found that they contained the names of subscribers together with the respective amounts contributed to idolatrous feasts, or to the building and repairs of temples. The vast majority of the subscriptions were in small sums, often less than five cents. But every gift was recorded. I found that these subscriptions were given yearly with unfailing regularity. In one city I found that men were deputed to make daily collections from every shop. By giving daily a cent the shops did not feel the demand, and at the appointed time the money was all in the hands of the treasurer. More money is given to lying, idolatrous worship in the city of Canton yearly than is given by the entire Presbyterian Church to the cause of missions throughout the world.

Today in our own land thousands of churches do not take up a single collection for foreign missions. Ten years ago the International Society of Christian Endeavor approved the two-cents-a-week plan of contributions to Foreign Missions. It is my purpose to present reasons why the universal adoption of that plan by Christian Endeavor Societies would have the most far-reaching results in the overthrow of idolatry, and the planting of Christian churches.

It is a practicable plan. The least practicable achievement is better than the most elaborate and complicated plans that promise, at most, probable results. It is within the power of every wage earner to give two cents a week to the neediest cause on earth. The objection to the plan most frequently made is that the amount asked for is too small, and that societies find it troublesome to collect the small amount. That is the fault of the Society, not of the system. I have frequently heard it said that it is impossible for some persons to give one-tenth of their income. With that assertion I have nothing to do, only that I never heard any one say that they could not give two cents a week.

Again, it is a simple plan. Some of the richest corporations in the world gain their riches through small sums. The great ferry companies find no difficulty in collecting two cents from millions of passengers. The millions of money passing almost monthly into the treasuries of street car companies is the aggregate of small fares. There is surely brain capacity in every Christian Endeavor Society to make so simple a matter as the collection of ten cents a month a perfect success. A simpler plan cannot be put into operation. Let every society appoint a person who will gladly solicit subscriptions. These subscriptions may be asked for as soon as the society adopts the plan. The money may be paid weekly or monthly. To what purpose the money is to be put is another matter, to be determined by the Church Officers and the Society.

Again, the plan is a potential one. The number of Christian Endeavor Societies is now more than sixty thousand. The membership is in the millions. The membership of the Christian Endeavor Societies in the Presbyterian Church North is more than two hundred thousand. Last year they gave less than fifty thousand dollars to foreign missions. The entire amount given by all our Sunday Schools and Christian Endeavor Societies was less than one hundred thousand dollars. This is less than one cent a week. Had the entire membership of the Presbyterian Church last year, including all the millionaires, given each two cents a week and nothing more, we would have had the largest contribution ever given by our Church to the propagation of the Gospel among these six hundred millions of idolatrous worshipers. The Christian Endeavor Societies of the Presbyterian Church, giving each two cents a week to Missions, would contribute more money than is now spent by the entire Presbyterian Church on the great work in China. The membership of the Christian Endeavor Societies, by the adoption of this plan, could raise nearly one-fourth of the entire amount spent on Foreign Missions by the entire Protestant world.

We can do all this. I affirm, we ought to do this. The desperate condition of the heathen world demands it. The condition of these hundreds of millions, so far as religious beliefs are concerned, is like that of the man by the road-side, stripped and half dead. No power on earth can help them apart from the Gospel. Railroads will never induce them to part with their false beliefs. The ineradical tendency to worship is there, and must be met by the substitution of the mighty, soul-saving truths of the Gospel. We have had twenty years of Christian Endeavor. Let us demonstrate its mighty fruitfulness by the universal adoption of this plan, and that plan thus adopted and carried out would forever demonstrate the right of Christian Endeavor to a place in every Church. Best of all, the plan, thus adopted, would inculcate a habit of giving in every individual that would never be limited to two cents a week, but increase with the habit until the mighty influence of Christian Endeavor will be felt in the remotest hamlet in the uttermost part of the earth. and thus greatly hasten that blessed day when "the wilderness and the solitary place shall be glad for them, and the desert shall rejoice and blossom as the rose."

CHAPTER XXVII.

More About Missions.

EVERY CHURCH A MISSIONARY TRAINING SCHOOL.—THREE MIS-
SIONARY WATCHWORDS.—HOW TO FIRE YOUNG MEN
WITH MISSIONARY ENTHUSIASM.

Dr. Wilton Merle Smith of New York City caught his audience at the first sentence, and held them gripped to the last word of his magnificent address on "Every Church a Missionary Training-School." Missions must be incarnated somewhere in any church that is to be a missionary church. You can be that incarnation, and irradiate from your life the mission interest of your church. Dr. Smith told how the humblest Christian could do great things for missions, and illustrated his theme with the quaint fiction of "Miss Toosey's Mission," and the remarkable story of the mission work in his own church, where fifty-two out of his fifty-five active Endeavorers are pledged givers of the tenth. Among other things he said:

Every church a missionary training school. I wish I could so write it on your hearts that you would go home and make your church a missionary training school. It must be admitted that very few have the knowledge they ought to have of the missionary training. I believe there are four influences that ought to be brought to bear on every church, and it is these four influences that I want to speak on.

Did you ever realize the power of inspired personality? Take for instance the carbon on one of your electric lights. The electricity is far away in the dynamo. But when the two come together there is a flash of light. Just so it is with truth and personality. The truth is hidden and unseen. But let some great truth inspire the man and he flashes out like a light in the world. Personality becomes living, burning eloquence when inspired by truth. It is within the power of every one of the Christian Endeavorers to fill your church with missionary eloquence. I tell you, Christian Endeavorers, that there is not one of you here but what could do a great many things to fill your church with missionary enthusiasm. What I want you to write on your hearts is that the power of inspired under-leadership can make the church what it wants to be in a missionary sense. When we have money in our pocket enthusiasm is bound to follow and then pledge yourself to give systematically to the church.

Three Missionary Watchwords.

Rev. George Darsie, Frankfort, Ky.

A watchword is a military term. It suggests camps and armies, battles and sieges, marches and campaigns. It enables the soldier to distinguish friend from foe, it thrills him with lofty sentiment, it makes directly and mightily for glorious victory.

The conquest of the world for Jesus Christ is in a true sense a military undertaking. It is for this very purpose that the Christian is a soldier and the Church an army. It is for this very purpose that it marches under the banner of the Cross, owns the Lord Jesus Christ as its Commanding General, and seeks to obey the orders issued to it from Headquarters. Prompt obedience is no more the chief requisite of the earthly soldier than it is of those who claim allegiance to Him who speaks from heaven.

It is hard to reconcile the delay of Christian conquest with any known theory of obedience to heavenly commands. If the English officer spoke truly who said that the English army alone could get a message from the Queen to every man, woman and child in all the earth within eighteen months, does it not shame the tardiness of Christ's great army that it requires centuries to get His sublime message to the world?

If, then, the conquest of the world for Christ is a military undertaking, if the order for it comes from Headquarters, and if that order must be obeyed promptly and faithfully, there are three great watchwords that should pass clear down the line, and that should be ceaselessly on the lips and in the hearts of all who march in the ranks of Christ's army.

1. There is the watchword, Rejoice! Who can lift up his eyes and look on the vast and ripened harvest fields of earth and not rejoice in the very privilege of participating in the reaping? Wonderfully in God's providence has the way of entrance into every quarter of the globe been opened up. Old barriers, that for centuries shut out the Gospel, have melted away as if by magic and disappeared forever. All nations are now willing for the truth to be proclaimed in their borders. Notwithstanding our tardiness in entering, there are more missionaries now in heathen lands, more money being expended, more converts being made, more schools and churches being established,—more everything that goes to make up the enginery necessary to the conquest of the heathen world for Christ, than were ever known before at any period in the whole history of the Church.

And what a chapter in the annals of human heroism have the missionaries written! If fifty years ago Theodore Parker could say that the production of one Adoniram Judson of itself fully justified the expenditure of every dollar given for foreign missions, he could today point to hundreds, yea thousands, of men and women in far-off heathen lands equally heroic. In fact, heroism is the very stock in trade of all missionaries, insomuch that their acts of devotion and sacrifice, coupled with their spirit of patience and fortitude, give to the record of their lives a dignity and character truly apostolic. Who does not rejoice in this sublime capacity of our human nature under the power of divine grace to do and dare and suffer? And what a demonstration has thus been given of the Gospel's power to save the lost? In no field has it ever been preached in vain. The most ignorant and degraded have yielded to its persuasions. Let croakers say what they will, but the success of foreign missions is the miracle of our age. And whose heart does not swell with thankfulness at this renewed evidence of the fact that Christ can reach the lowest and save the vilest?

And not less do we rejoice in the confident anticipation of final victory. The trophies already won are its certain guaranty. Notwithstanding the darkness which yet covers the earth, and the gross darkness which yet covers the people, the light which has begun to break will grow and spread till the beams of the Sun of Righteousness have girdled the globe with the brightness of a spiritual noonday. The heathen shall yet become Christ's inheritance, and the uttermost parts of the earth his possession. He shall yet have dominion from sea to sea, and from the river to the ends of the world. The place of His humiliation shall yet become the place of His exaltation. Where He was once crucified He shall yet be crowned Lord of all. The plaintive minors of Gethsemane and Golgotha shall yet give place to the triumphant strains of the world-filling chorus, "The kingdoms of this world have become the kingdoms of our Lord and of His Christ, and He shall reign forever and ever."

If we had no other or greater assurance of such a result, it would be enough to know that the embattled hosts are marching under the leadership of the all-conquering Son of God. What a fellowship is thus permitted us! What an uplifting association! Laborers together with God! Soldiers in the army of an almighty captain! Followers of His blood-stained banner! Sharers in the glory of a campaign whose final end must be to answer the petitions of our life-long prayer, "Thy kingdom come, Thy will be done on earth even as it is in heaven." Well indeed, therefore, may our first watchword be, Rejoice, Rejoice.

2. But our second watchword is the utterance of a great and pressing duty,—a duty that we are all more and more coming to feel and acknowledge,—a duty that as loyal subjects of our King we must bravely face and fulfil—a duty from which we turn away at our own deadly peril—a duty that I would urge today with all the earnestness of my soul—and that I do thus urge when I speak the watchword, Unite!

Nothing impedes the progress of missions like a divided church. Nothing paralyzes the power of the Gospel in heathen lands like religious rivalries. Nothing so confuses and discourages the heathen mind like contending parties. If our heroic missionary army out yonder on the firing line sends back one message more plaintive and urgent than another, it is this, "O Church of God at home, adjust your differences, reconcile your antagonisms, simplify your creeds, get together on some basis of union and cooperation, if you would remove the greatest of all stumbling blocks from our path, if you would increase a hundred fold the power of the work we seek to do."

Surely we cannot claim a wisdom beyond that of the Son of God. When He prayed that His people might be one, it was with a single purpose in view—"That the world might believe." Is it strange or mysterious that we find it hard to make the world believe in Christ when we so flagrantly ignore the very foundation on which His infallible wisdom declared it possible? I know it does and will go against the grain of our sectarian pride to acknowledge ourselves in an attitude of antagonism to one of the plainest utterances of our Lord and Master, and yet I frankly ask, Is it not true? Are we not guilty?

But there is at least one thing that we can sincerely thank God for, and that is, that we did not bring the present situation about. Divisions are a heritage from the past. Nor am I here to blame our fathers for them. I am by no means sure that they could have been avoided. But, however that may be, I do believe that the time has now come for us to wrestle manfully with this great problem. I believe that God is trying to lead His Church toward the goal of Christian union. And I believe, too, that one of His mightiest agencies for the accomplishment of this great end is the Christian Endeavor movement. Its ministry of blessing in this direction is already so manifest that he who runs may read. But, while God leads, it is ours to follow, it is ours to use the providential means which he affords, and to recognize the fact that a tremendous responsibility rests upon all of us who any longer consent to the continuance of a divided Church, lest haply we be found fighting against God!

In the presence of the awful fact of heathenism how small and how ridiculous are the things which Christians allow to separate them one from another! When Lord Macaulay had returned from India, and an effort was made to draw him into sectarian controversy, he remarked with withering scorn that he had lived too long in a country where people worship cows to care anything for the differences that part Christians from Christians. The more we are enlisted in the world's salvation the more will we hate and oppose the sectarianism which thwarts that salvation, and the more will we plead for the unity which hastens it.

Had the late, lamented Dr. Behrends known that the words he spoke at the recent Ecumenical Missionary Conference would be his last message to the world, they could not have been more true or timely. Said he: "Do not misunderstand me. I am not an iconoclast. I would not break up any existing ecclesiastical or missionary organization. But in this matter I am a Christian evolutionist. I believe that our present-day methods are utterly inadequate. And I cannot evade the conviction that foreign missions carry in them the swift doom of our petty sectarian divisions. I do not know how this co-operation is coming; but come it must and will. Let it come, whoever is crowded to the wall! Our creeds and our rituals must not stand in the way of the massing of Christian forces for the world's redemption. When that co-operation comes it will be free—the spontaneous expression of a Christian life that has burst through the bandages of ecclesiastial traditionalism. We are nearer to each other than our fathers were, and our children will keep up the converging march. I plead for the fullest liberty in Christ, no matter how multitudinous our forms of service. But I believe that liberty in Christ will some day bring in an irrepressible eagerness for co-operation at home and abroad. When it does come it will come like a resistless flood. And then look out for the tramp of the great host and the flaming feet of the Captain! That will bring the fufilment of the apocalyptic vision!" Let us ponder well these weighty words of this mighty man of God, who though dead yet speaketh in our ears.

3. And what could our third and final watchword be but the inspiring word, Advance! Is not the need of it great beyond expression? How little we have done and are doing compared with what we might do! We have sent out men, but we could have sent ten where we have sent one. We have given money to support and equip the workers, but how often it has been a grudging dole rather than a glad and willing sacrifice.

The drink bill of this nation is a billion dollars yearly. Its tobacco bill is six hundred millions. Its candy bill is seventy-five millions. Even its chewing-gum bill is twenty-five millions. But its bill for world-wide missions is a pitiful five millions. No wonder two-thirds of our race are yet without God. No wonder there are portions of India where there is but one missionary to four millions of people. No wonder there are a million villages in China where the Gospel has never been preached. No wonder Japan has one hundred and eighty-five times as many heathen temples as it has Protestant Christian workers. No wonder Africa, out of a population of a hundred and seventy millions, has only nine hundred thousand nominal Christians.

Is it not time, high time, for the great advance? Has not the day long passed when we should be satisfied with digging trenches, defending breastworks, or holding forts? Has not the day fully come when we should be content only to follow a standard "full high advanced," when the whole church of God should become an invading army, when it should inaugurate an unprecedented struggle to storm and capture the pagan strongholds of the world for our King?

In view of the open doors that beckon, of the success that has rewarded the efforts already made, of the needs of the nations that sit in darkness, of the absolute certainty of final victory, of the assurance of His presence who has promised, "Lo, I am with you alway, even unto the end of the world," shall we not advance and take possession of all lands in the name of our Lord? Napoleon once said that "impossible" is a word found only in the dictionary of fools. Certainly it is the last word to be found on the lips of those who set up their banners in the name of Jesus, and who like Judson believe that the prospects of seeing the world redeemed and saved are as bright as the promises of God.

Has not the church dawdled and dallied long enough over the duty of the world's evangelization? Shall it encamp forever at Kadesh Barnea? Shall it not make an immediate advance all along the line? Not boastingly, nor presumptuously, nor self-confidently, but humbly, trustingly, prayerfully, let it be made. Never does the church advance so surely and so rapidly as when it advances upon its knees, when it lifts its eyes to heaven and says, "Trusting in the Lord Jesus Christ for strength I promise Him that I will strive to do whatever He would like to have me do."

Christ is now waiting to see the nations submit to His authority. For "this man, after he had offered one sacrifice for sins forever, sat down on the right hand of God, from henceforth expecting till his enemies be made his footstool." Seated yonder on His throne today, His attitude is for that of expectation, confident expectation. And He will not be disappointed; for the day of His universal triumph is drawing on, when the whole human race, redeemed by His precious blood, shall verify His own prophetic utterance, "And I, if I be lifted up from the earth, will draw all men unto me."

Rejoice—Unite—Advance, are not these worthy to be the watchwords, the missionary watchwords, of the church of God? And shall they not be ceaselessly on our lips and in our hearts? Do they not contain in them the potency of world-wide conquest? And do they not point with unerring finger to the dawning of the day when the earth shall be filled with the knowledge of the glory of the Lord as the waters cover the sea?

Rev. A. Miyaki of Japan, speaking in his Japanese costume—told us what Christian Endeavor had done for his own land. One Japanese out of every twenty native Christians is an Endeavorer. The predominant characteristic of these Japanese Endeavorers is missionary zeal. One of his deacons, he said, spoke in prayer meeting one night, and said: "I can't be a fisher of men; I am not good at fishing. But, pastor, I'll go where the fish are, and drive them out where you can catch them." And that is what the Endeavorers are doing.

Rev. Charles N. Ransom, for years the Christian Endeavor superintendent of South Africa, is a vigorous, graphic speaker, and his message was a glowing view of missionary heroism, self-denial, and patience. Christian Endeavor, he said, has put South Africa in touch with the world.

How to fire young men with missionary enthusiasm—that was Dr. Cleland B. McAfee's important theme. "The weak point of our missionary work just now is with young men," he thought. "There is no definite enthusiasm that does not spring from a definite hearing and heeding of the call of Christ." The home must implant this enthusiasm first, and the pastors must help, and other young men also, and the final work must be done by the Holy Spirit of God.

CHAPTER XXVIII.

A Symposium by Missionaries from the Field.

THE EVIL OF THE LIQUOR AND OPIUM TRAFFIC IN MISSION FIELDS.

The Liquor Traffic in India.

Rev. J. P. Jones, D. D., India.

For many centuries the inhabitants of India were a sober people. Their climate, social order and religion favored abstinence. The coming of the Anglo-Saxon has brought a deplorable change to that land in this respect. Drinking and drunkenness are today not only permissible; by many they are regarded as marks of a certain distinction. I will not assert that drinking is as yet a great and all-pervasive evil in India as it is in our own country. There are greater evils in the land. But it is a growing curse. And as its growth is fostered under the most favorable of auspices it presents a very serious danger to the people—a danger to which it is our duty to call attention and, if possible, to avert.

I. The Evil.

So far as my observation goes in South India the drinking habit finds increasing prevalence among two special classes—educated Brahmans and educated Christians. Neither among the Hindu middle classes nor among the ordinary village Native Christians have I found the drinking habit a prevailing or a growing evil. And for this I am thankful. But the ruling class of educated Brahmans and those Native Christians who live at large centres and are in many respects qualified to be leaders of their community are seriously and increasingly tainted by this accursed habit.

Next to Madras, Combaconam is the place in South India where the largest quantity of European liquor is consumed. And that town is pre-eminently a centre of Brahman life, influence and culture. It is no secret today among the Brahmans themselves that the use of spirituous liquors is rapidly increasing among the educated members of their community and that it is ruining the characters and blasting the prospects of many a bright and promising life of their class. I have today in mind the sad condition of a Brahman friend who is dying a wretched drunkard's death. He is a university graduate of distinguished ability, of fine attainments in his legal profession and has had a commanding influence in the community. He has been a great friend of missions, though a Hindu, and is kindly disposed towards our Faith. Enamored of Western life he foolishly thought that the use of whiskey would initiate him into the joys and privileges of the West. With terrible speed has he fallen to the lowest depths of degradation. He dies a victim to the demon drink, an outcast among men and a wreck in body, mind and soul.

This poor fellow is not alone. Not a few of the brightest stars of Hindu society are losing all their light and lustre, their promise and hope through a growing slavery to the bottle.

The significance of this increasing habit among the Brahmans lies in the fact that they represent the glory of Hindu society. How easy for the lower classes to emulate their wretched example and to plunge after them into the deep pit of drunkenness! It is also singularly unfortunate that this class, which is really the official right hand of the government in this land should become thus the victim of so damning a habit and prove also recreant to the example and teaching of their ancestors. Must our much vaunted western civilization and culture be wedded to this demon drink so that the East cannot touch the one without becoming a victim of the other?

This same habit of wine bibbing, though perhaps not so prevalent, is more inexcusable and deplorable among a certain class of Native Christians. Owing to their exalted position and social advantages these might be expected to walk circumspectly before their less privileged Native brethren of the villages. Instead of this not a few of them nurse the vain and pernicious conceit that it is a fine thing to imitate the English by introducing the wineglass into their select social events. It is needless to say that for such an example they turn away from the missionary to the Anglo-Indian society man.

And out of this, to them, seemingly harmless custom is often born a passion for spirituous drinks and a habit which not rarely leads to a drunkard's grave. Though, as I have said, this habit has not spread largely among the lower classes of our Native Christian community it has gained a strong foothold among many of the aspiring ones, and will, if not speedily checked, spread in demoralizing and deadly power among the others. We must no less watch the sad tendency of such an evil as this than we must be awake to the havoc which it is already doing.

II. What are the causes of this growing drink evil in India today?

In the first place, and above all, stands the Anglo-Indian example. The Anglo-Saxon life and character in India has been, in many respects an untold blessing to that land. And even today the Britisher stands as a worthy and inspiring model to that people in official integrity and in many of the noble traits of a masculine character. But, as a lover of strong drink and as a slave to the accursed cup, his influence upon that subject people is deplorable. It was said some years ago by a flippant critic that if England should then be driven out of India the only evidence left of her past reign would be empty whiskey bottles. While this was a base slander it has this element of truth in it—it suggests that aspect of Anglo-Indian life which most impresses many of the inhabitants of that country. Not very far from where I live in India an Englishman died about fifty years ago. His death was sudden and he was buried in the wilderness. For many years the Natives of that region visited his grave and worshiped his departed spirit by offering to it, in all sobriety, that which they thought it loved most—whiskey and cheroots.

The Indian firmly believes that strong drink is dearer than all else to the Anglo-Indian heart. And I sometimes feel, when I see his misery when apart from his bottle, that the Indian is right. And it is sad to know that in most of the recent high class entertainments given by official Hindus to their English superiors, champagne and whiskey flow freely; and this even when the host abhors the stuff himself and on no other occasion brings it into his house. It certainly seems a sad commentary upon Native conception of Anglo-Indian tastes and needs. And it is at the same time a most seriously debasing influence upon the morals and ideals of the people of that land. It is also one of the most serious barriers which stand between the Anglo-Indian Christian and his missionary brother in India today.

The Indian government is likewise culpable in this matter. One hesitates to make any charge against a government which, in the main, so admirably seeks the public good and which constitutes infinitely the best regime that India has ever known. After an experience of nearly a quarter of a century I can heartily bear testimony to the excellence of its administration and to the loftiness of its ideals and methods. But I am compelled to condemn its excise laws and their administration so far as intoxicating drinks are concerned. In the first place the State has demeaned itself by reserving for itself the sole right of manufacturing and selling the spirituous liquors of the land. It would seem as if a business whose sole tendency and result was the physical and moral degradation of a people was the last one that its government should touch. And yet the government of India has chosen this abkary business as the only one which it conducts for itself and whereby it demoralizes and impoverishes its people. It maintains the sole monopoly of this accursed trade and thereby gives dignity and prevalence to a traffic which should be banned and to a habit which should be eradicated. The Archbiship of England wisely protested against this and eloquently urged that no government can afford to engage in any business which demoralizes its subjects. To sacrifice the souls of the people on the altar of public revenue is unworthy of any State much less of a Christian government in a heathen land. I am aware of the defence which the friends of the State present in this matter. But the purity of the liquor sold could be secured in other ways than by the State conducting the trade itself. The least thing that could be expected of a State which was not prepared to prohibit this traffic is that it decline to countenance it or to soil its skirts by the least contact with it. And yet the Supreme Government of 300,000,000 souls deliberately countenances, encourages, dignifies and maintains a vast business the only reason for the existence of which is that it furnishes a revenue. What blessing can be expected to accrue from such a blood-stained revenue?

The easy revenue which this department creates is really the chief, if not the only, argument in its behalf. In a land of great poverty like India where it is always extremely difficult for the powers that be to avoid bankruptcy, a source of revenue so great and so easily maintained as this is a serious temptation to the State. By a turn of the' screw a crore of rupees may be poured into an empty treasury without producing a complaint from a patient people; for they have not yet learned how destructive the whole traffic is to their life and morals. And thus the moral obligation of the State to the people is allowed to slumber while the financial leech sucks at their vitals.

I therefore charge this otherwise excellent government with a serious lapse at this point. It sacrifices the highest moral interests of the country to its own financial exigency. And this must be regarded not only as a crime against the people; it is also to the State itself a policy of suicide as time will reveal and emphasize.

III. What are the Remedies which must be Applied?

They are in the main implied in what I have said. The remedy, like the responsibility, lies at the door of Great Britain. So long as her life and sentiment at home are what they are they will be faithfully reproduced, yea exaggerated, in India. So long as temperance principles will be scouted, drunkenness be regarded as a harmless foible and total abstinence as a silly fad in Great Britain so long will that country send out to India men who will themselves dote upon their whiskey and who cannot see any evil in transforming the millions of that land into slaves to the demon of drink.

The leopard will not change his spots by going to India; but rather will the spots multiply there.

In like manner a government which prides itself upon the enormous revenue which it collects from the rum traffic in England will have no scruples in permitting or encouraging its Indian government in seeking and fostering a revenue from the same source. We need to appeal to Great Britain's highest moral and religious sense. We should pray God that England first cleanse her own augean stables of drunkenness so that the men whom she sends out to India may be pre-eminently free from this accursed habit and be anxious to foster among the people of the British empire in India habits of sobriety and abstinence. We should also pray that the government of that land be saved from the snare and temptation of sacrificing the best and highest interest of the people to a financial exigency.

The Church of God in India also has a growing debt of responsibility to its infant community as it has to the whole population of that land. Some missions in India already demand that all who join them shall first pledge themselves to total abstinence from all intoxicating drinks. We can hardly expect all missionaries to unite in this severe though safe rule. But we certainly should expect that the missions of that land take a definite and pronounced stand against the use of spirituous liquors by its Native Christian community and also that they take a strong, united stand against the whole traffic in India. If not prohibited the evil certainly

should be discouraged to the highest degree. This in the first place should
be done by missionary example. I am proud to say that American missionaries have in this respect a clean and worthy record in that land. I
am also delighted to bear testimony to a marked change among British
missionaries in India in this respect during the last two decades or more.
Total abstinence is today, if not universal, very largely prevalent among
the missionaries of the British Isles in India. The temperance sentiment
has grown mightily among the missionaries during the last generation.
And may it continue to grow and may the leaders of the Church in India
unite their forces more and more against the swelling tide of intemperance
and its ghastly train of evils in that land. Concerted effort today will do
much towards arresting the evil and towards assuring the people that the
life and customs of the West must be followed with discrimination if they
are to be a blessing and not a curse to the East.

The Evil of the Liquor and Opium Traffic in Missionary Fields.

Rev. George Hubbard, China.

If I may be allowed, I will place the ofttimes very significant letter "d"
before the second word. We then read our topic, "The Devil of the Liquor
and Opium Traffic in Missionary Fields." Now this devil is not one of the
tail-end of the procession kind of devils, of little importance. Nay, he is a
devil of the first water. He is the very devil himself.

In China processions are common; in every large city, any day and
every day, some mandarin or idol is being carried about in a sedan chair.
All the gang, glare and glitter, and gorgeousness are for the central figure
and the ensign of the great dragon which he wears. Alas! that there are
so many in Christian and heathen lands who do not recognize this devil of
the liquor and opium traffic as such. Yea "devil" is the word. Evil doesn't
go far enough. It is too abstract, too easily excused. The devil is personal,
and he uses persons as his agents. Opium and liquor are his right hand,
and once in that hand what mortal can escape? The devil possesses men,
takes away their will, drives them mad. The evil of the liquor and opium
traffic is devilish in its effects on both foreigner and native. Who can
count the millions of blasted homes in China through the use of opium by
one or more of the family. Back in the forties of the nineteenth century
an Englishman estimated that even then there were nearly a million vic-
timized persons in the empire. But today, if the whole of China is like the
parish of five hundred square miles where I have been working among a
population of 500,000, of whom one in ten is a victim, then the whole number in China must be between thirty and forty millions.

You cannot realize what this means of poverty, distress and living
death. I have been among the common people for fifteen years. I have
called upon the official, and was informed that he was smoking opium.
When he appeared his face proclaimed it. I have visited hundreds of villages and passed from house to house with tracts and Gospel while preaching and teaching, and I tell you the solemn truth when I say one-half the
smartest men in China are the victims of opium. The Manchus furnished
with government rations are rotten with its use. The literary men who
take not exercise find it the one medicine to soothe their pain. The poor
sedan and burden bearer, overloaded and worn out with the long, hard road,
smokes a pipe of opium. The head boatman, skilled to guide the boat down
dangerous rapids; the skilled mechanic, carpenter and mason, with larger
incomes, think they can afford to try the pipe. The ecstatic feeling produced captivates them, and by and by we see all these moving languidly
about, if at work, and obliged to go more and more frequently to the pipe
which is taking their life. The day's wages are insufficient for the pipes of
the day; their good clothes and ornaments go from their persons and
houses first; the chest and tables that held them are not needed now, and
off they go to pay opium debts. Their fields, gardens and houses are mort-
gaged; they even sell their wives and children for opium. Would that the

world might hear the cry of the women of the Orient, "Tell the women of Britain that we will take the skin off our bodies to make shoes for their feet if they will stop the opium traffic."

Ten years ago, in my great parish at the south of Min River, below Foochow, but few gardens were used for growing poppies. Now every spring time the poppy is the rule, and food crops the exception. To be sure, the rice and sweet potato crop acreage remains, for these are planted after the opium is gathered, but are not as fruitful as formerly, for the farmers use their fertilizers on the opium crop so largely they can not afterwards do their best by the food crops.

Men have lighted a fire which is spreading fast and furiously, far beyond the man's power to control. May God Almighty pity poor, old China and have mercy on the so-called Christian nations who have helped to increase her poverty and distress. And His answer comes, "Except ye repent ye shall all likewise perish."

The Evil of the Liquor and Opium Traffic in Mission Fields.

Rev. G. L. Wharton, Hiram, O.

Can the drink and opium traffic be a greater evil in the mission fields than at home? Can the cry of the widow and orphan of the drunkard be more bitter and hopeless in India and China than in America. I answer, yes. In the first place, only the cheapest, strongest and most maddening kinds of liquors are used by the masses in heathen lands. Most mission fields are in tropical and semi-tropical climates. The inhabitants are weaker in body and easily succumb to the influences of alcohol. The lack of education and moral training, in connection with the enervating effects of the climate, has weakened the will-power of most native races. Add to this the great fact that they are sunken in immorality and superstition. It stands to reason that the double-edged scythe of liquor and opium will mow a wider swath of ruin among these people. Our statistics give us some approximate figures of the national destruction by the traffic, but only the angels of God can tabulate the souls slain in Africa, China, India and the islands of the sea. For seventeen years I met face to face all the evils of Hinduism and Mohammedanism combined, and know something of their effects on the body, mind and character. But I tell you that the liquor and opium traffic is a combination of evils more detrimental, destructive and damning than all the curses of heathenism. It is doing what centuries of heathenism could not do—namely, robbing these people of their only hope— the power to learn, to know, to love and serve the true and living God. Do we comprehend the widespread character of this traffic in the East? It is side by side in the grain, fruit and vegetable market. At home we protect our children from drink, and opium is marked poison; but here the mother buys opium to quiet her child as she buys rice to feed it. This evil strides the whole earth. It is foremost in the world's commerce. It traverses every sea. It enters every port. It finds every island. It goes where neither ship, railway nor bullock-cart can go.

This is a traffic only—simply trade and commerce. It is not carried on in the interests of science, art, religion, education, civilization, government, politics or morality. It exchanges liquor and opium for money, with only one motive—the love of gain. Where has this great traffic originated? How has it developed? Who are its responsible agents? It is not the indigenous growth of heathen countries, races or religion. Its capitalists are not Orientals. Who is responsible for the liquor and opium traffic in India, China and Africa? Who is responsible for the shameful saloon business in Hawaii, Porto Rico and the Philippines? There is but one answer. Christian governments with their Christian rulers and people. The headquarters of this business is the most enlightened and Christian nations. It sails under such flags as the Union Jack and the Stars and Stripes. The armies, navies and police forces of the world protect it. The seeming connection that Christianity has with the liquor and opium traffic stares every missionary in the face at every turn. Liquor is loaded on the ship with his baggage as he starts. It goes with him to his station. It is unloaded on the railway platform in the presence of the heathen along with his Bibles and prayer books. When Christian nations and rulers say that the native races need protection, and then establish and carry on a trade more destructive than heathenism, war, famine and pestilence; when the heathen themselves cry out against such injustice and humanity; when the missionaries, like the venerable John G. Paton, leave their native Christians to plead with Christian rulers to abolish this traffic, is it not time for the Christian people of the whole world to unite as one man, and, in the power of God, stop this most hurtful of all evils?

CHAPTER XXIX.

Two Appeals for Home and Foreign Missions.

In Auditorium Endeavor Mr. Robert E. Speer of New York City spoke of the claims and opportunities of foreign missions. "People now speak of the north pole," said he, "as if it was likely soon to become a summer resort. A man is ashamed not to think beyond his own country."

The claims of missions, he declared, rest on the fact that if I have a good thing I am bound to share it. The man who has a boat while another is drowning doesn't need a policeman to compel him to go to the rescue.

The stagnant character of heathen religions constitutes a claim on Christianity. A religion that is not trying to subdue the world is not fit to subdue the life of one man.

Another claim is human relationship. An eminent German ethnologist has just made the announcement that the most distant human relationship possible is fortieth cousin. The lowest savage imaginable is your fortieth cousin.

Their nearness in point of space is a claim. We dare not say that the heathen are too far away, unless we admit that their lands are too far away to send us our coffee and spices and silks.

Phillips Brooks once said that a man who refused the claims of the heathen on the ground that there is need at home, reminded him of a parricide who should claim pardon on the ground that he was an orphan.

The plea is made that the country is being impoverished by money sent away to foreign lands. A few years ago the Chamber of Commerce of Cincinnati represented to Congress that eight billion of dollars were lying idle awaiting a chance for investment. And we had to gobble up some islands outside of North America in order to open up investments. A small portion of this eight billions would evangelize the world. Among other things he said:

The Christian Endeavor movement, although it has not reached all the young people of our own country, has caught too well the spirit of Jesus and of his cross. This spirit laid upon the hearts of men has made them feel that the whole world has claims upon their possessions. On what do these claims rest? Why the fact that I have a good thing leaves me under the obligation to give it to every man who does not have it. If I have bread to spare in the presence of a starving man, I need no process of law served on me to indicate my duty to share what I have. I ask you to think, in this midst of plenty, of all the destitution and then of all facilities for hearing the Gospel.

My friends, we live in the midst of a world whose needs are claims upon us, and these claims are no distant things. We are bound together in ties of one common, human relationship. God has made of one blood all the races of men who dwell upon the face of the whole earth. I know what men and women are saying in their hearts. They are saying, "They are so far away." My friends, where did the coffee come from that you drank for breakfast this morning? Where did the diamonds come from that some of the ladies wear? If Africa and South America is not too far away to bring ornaments and coffee from, are they too far off to reach with the word of the Lord?

"Now let us come home," exclaimed David James Burrell, D. D., of New York City, "there's no place like home." His theme was, "My Own, My Native Land." He mentioned as one of the factors of our national greatness our welcome to the oppressed of every land. But we must welcome them on the condition that they become Americans.

Our political equality was illustrated by the story of the American cab-driver who called for a noble foreign visitor with the inquiry: "Are you the man I am to drive? Then I am the gentleman that is to drive you." Of our universal sovereignty he said, "Every American male child, is born an heir apparent to the throne." Dr. Burrell said in part:

They say we Americans are a boastful people. Why not? There is not any country on God's footstool that is so worthy to boast of. We have three million, two hundred thousand square miles of territory with the islands yet to hear from. I do believe that it is one of God's countries. We are one of the great powers of the earth today. I want to name four of the factors that have entered into the problem of our national greatness. The four pillars on which rest the prophecy of our Republic's perpetuity. One of these is the universal welcome to all the oppressed of all the nations. We give a cordial welcome to all the nations of the earth, but if you are coming, you must. come under these conditions: You are bound to be Americans. There is no room here for Irish Americans, there is no room in America for Scotch Americans or German Americans. There is room infinite and boundless here for all Americans. Not that we love the old country less, but we are bound to give undivided fealty to the land of our adoption. Welcome to the land of the free. The second of the great premises is popular equality. This is the only country of which I am aware where there is a definite and formulated recognition of absolute human equality before the Lord. The third great pillar upon which our national fabric stands, is popular sovereignty. We know no sovereign in America but the popular will. We know of no expression of sovereignty in America except that which resides in the ballot. The fourth pillar is our common education. It was wisely foreseen by our forefathers in early colonial days, that the great danger the republic would confront in coming years, was ignorant franchise. The thing that was in the minds of these men was an ignorant suffrage. We have no king but king people. Every man born in our country is heir apparent to the throne, and it is obviously the function of the state to see that the princes shall be educated. The church cannot undertake the work which devolves upon the state by virtue of the natural right of self preservation. Stand on guard as long as you live at the doors of our public schools, see there is no arrogant assumption on the part of any church or any body of people, or, let me put it in the wise and considerate words of Archbishop Ireland of the Roman Catholic Church. "The state school," he said, "is the basis of our National Life, and the assurance of our perpetuity."

CHAPTER XXX.

Two Thrilling Stories.

THE STORY OF AN AFRICAN JUNGLE.— THE STORY OF THE SIEGE
OF PEKING.

The Story of an African Jungle.

Rev. Willis R. Hotchkiss, East Coast of Africa.

It is a law of human life that we form our estimates largely upon the
basis of comparisons. We take things as a matter of course, until suddenly we find those things taken from us, then we wake up to some sense
of appreciation of the thing. We saw its value through its loss.

"Strange we never prize the music
Till the sweet voiced bird has flown,
Strange that we should slight the violets
Till the lovely flower is gone."

I am asked to give you the story of the African jungle. 'Tis an all but
hopeless task amid such surroundings as these. We have been taken up
into the heavenlies; we have had glimpses of the new heavens and the
new earth; we have seen the great heart of our God in his wondrous love
toward us, the sons of men. That vision has become an ideal. Toward it
we toil, lifting our eyes through the murky atmosphere of the present;
holding our heads above the choking damp of worldliness in which we
move. What should we be without such a vision to lure us on—such an
ideal to lift us out of the dead level of the actual! Come with me a few
moments and I'll try to show you. Come from the mount of vision into
the valley where human need utters its thousand voiced cry. Come with
me into the African jungle and in its need read the story of an earthly
hell, in whose cavernous depths men and women are this day being griev-
ously tormented.

Look you, fellow Endeavorers, lying here in the bosom of plenty, look
you into the black dungeon of heathenism! See the struggles of these
prisoners toward the light, hear their anguished cries as they endeavor to
find an answer to the imperious question which is of world wide consciousness, "Where is the Lamb?" Listen! and from out of that darkness you
will hear the clank of chains and the crack of a whip as these prisoners
of the dark are driven to their labors by the taskmaster of souls.

The saddest thing I know of in this world is the fruitless effort of
Africa's multitudes to find a way to God. I've watched their dances,
their incantations, their fetichisms, until the smile of contempt has been
followed by a groan of pity. I've seen the women dance until oblivious to
all about them they gave themselves up to the spell of their awful delu-
sions and they seemed like the very demons they were trying to propitiate;
until from the swaying, leaping mass, there reeled forth a form more
devilish than human, who with an unearthly shriek fell in convulsions at
my feet. Did they pick her up, carry her aside, tenderly care for her?
Not they! Heathenism has no lessons to teach its blinded devotees in the
art of compassion. Here everything tends to seared conscience, blunted
susceptibility, paralyzed will. Do not ridicule these children of the night:
those very dances, vile and repulsive as they are, those very superstitions,
dark as they are, are nevertheless the voice of their need, finding utterance.

Will ye then tantalize them with a crumb when they ask for bread? Will ye give them but a drop from your brimming cup when they thirst so much? God help us! We revel in God's sunlight, we feast on God's bounties, we joy in God's salvation, yet to the cry of human lives adrift in the storm we answer with miserable nothings. Think of it! Africa over 300 times as large as the beautiful State of Ohio, and yet there are more ordained ministers in this little corner of God's universe than there are missionaries in all that vast expanse called the Dark Continent. Somewhere a gigantic blunder has been made, somebody has been guilty of a frightful crime!

But let us peer over the edge of this fearful need a little farther. Behold men and women in absolute nakedness! Bodies smeared with red clay and grease; eyebrows shaved off; eyelashes pulled out; teeth filed to a sharp point; ears pierced, and holes gradually enlarged until I've seen them put an ordinary tin can in the ear and use it as a pocket in which they carried their trinkets.

Go with me, crawling on your hands and knees into their little conical grass huts and see as many as eleven persons and seventeen sheep and goats huddled together in a hut fifteen feet in diameter. There they have been living for centuries, and do you marvel that they have become beastly? and that in this choking atmosphere the finer senses, love, affection, etc., shrivel and wither as the green grass under the hot breath of the Sirocco? Do you wonder that the beast leaps forth and shows his teeth in brutalized countenance and vicious life! Where women are bought and sold as goats; where marriage is a mere matter of barter; where a father can rent out his own daughter to shame by the week, you do not look for the fragrance of genuine affection, or the bloom of a holy love. There is no love in hell, and in its earthly type, heathenism, its features are marred and distorted almost beyond recognition! During my four years in Central Africa, I never saw a native kiss another, nor did I ever see a tear of pity or sympathy gather in a native's eye. Thus do they go unloved through life, and in death are flung into the bush to be a prey of wild beasts.

Nine-tenths of the dead are never buried at all. A rope is fastened about the ankles, the body is dragged into the bush, and at night there is a horrid carnival of wild beasts, the morning light reveals a few scattered bones which tell the tale of what had been the temple of an immortal soul. God help us! Did we hear what the Master said, "them also I must bring." Them also! yet through the centuries they have been stumbling blindly to their fate, and this splendid 20th century is ushered in amid a blaze of glory, yet in the sight of God there is the amazing spectacle of these multitudes still groping in the night, and God help us again! likely, still, to continue so for centuries to come if we do not rise to the emergency in Christ's own spirit of self abnegation and self loss. The man who refuses to leave his own little heaven of bliss to go down into this awful inferno of heathenism, bringing into its darkness, light; to its hopelessness, hope; is fit only for the hell to which his selfish spirit allies him.

Do not imagine, however, that as these savages are groping for the light, that they therefore hail the coming of the missionary in their midst. Like the Jews of old, they are unable to distinguish the true from the false, consequently the missionary frequently finds himself in peril of his life because of their unreasoning hatred of innovation. For months they, supposing me to be a government official, sought to get rid of me. Finally a huge palaver was held within sight of my temporary grass hut. In the evening they sent a deputation to me who solemnly informed me that they had decided to give me three days to leave. Failing to do this I was to be killed and my station destroyed. I felt that I was in the place of God's appointment, which is the safest place in the world, so replied that I was there to tell them about God, and I expected to stay. They threatened all manner of things, howling about the station by day and night, but held in check by the power of God, and their superstitious notion that I must be in league with evil spirits, they did not resort to actual violence. But they were not done yet. They tried to starve me out. An order went forth that anyone found bringing me food was to be put to death. As I was largely dependent upon native supplies for myself and native men, this course might have had the desired effect. But God interposed. An old woman passed my hut to and from her work in the fields, and every time she did so, she managed to drop a root of cassava before my door. This I roasted and it enabled me to eke out my slender supply of provision.

What was it that put it into the heart of this heathen woman under penalty of death if she were discovered, to drop that food before the despised and then hated white man's door? The same power that made the ravens bring the meat to the famished prophet by the brook Cherith. You see for every Cherith God has the ravens still.

"God moves in a mysterious way His wonders to perform," and nowhere is this more strikingly apparent than in the methods He uses to break down the stubborn oppositions of His foes. After their ineffectual methods to get rid of me, they gave me permission to build across the river, on the very spot where two months before they had sentenced me to death. I set to work making brick, working with the men in the clay pit. Beside this, I had considerable amount of medical work—crude, to be sure, but none the less effectual. But still the opposition died hard. One morning while attending to my patients, my boy Vui came up and exclaimed, "Bwana nimepiga Mkamba." (Master, I have hit an Mkamba). I looked up and a startling sight he was. From a huge, ragged gash in his head the blood was streaming down his face. "What is the matter?" said I. "The river bed is filled with men," said he, "and they are going to kill us all." Then he told me he had gone to get a bucket of water and a man had sprung upon him and beat him with a club; he had beaten his antagonist off with his club, and so escaped.

I asked him if he would go to the river with me. He replied that he would, and so we started off at once, I in my shirt sleeves just as I had been working. He looked at me, hesitated a moment, and then said, "Bwana usimepata bunduki yaku!" (Master, you have not taken your rifle!) "No," said I, "we are here on God's business, and He will take care of us, and besides we shall be safer without the weapon, anyway."

I never did use a weapon in defending myself from natives, first, because I do not believe in it, and second, because it would have been useless. The presence of a weapon would only have excited their suspicion, and as I was only one, and they many, they could have easily riddled me with arrows before I could have done much.

Arriving at the river, sure enough, the dry bed was occupied by a mob of 25 or 30 painted savages, evidently bent upon mischief. Decisive measures had to be taken at once, so I jumped into the midst of them from the bank above and began pushing them apart, meanwhile pouring a volley of questions at them as to why they wanted to kill me. I asked them if I had harmed them in any way; if I had not paid them well for everything I got from them; if I had not healed their sick and asked nothing for it; in short, if I had not proven that I was their friend.

Gradually the spears were lowered, the arrows were taken from their bows and restored to their quivers, and they stood silent, but sullen. Meanwhile I had worked my way to a water hole and bathed Vui's wound. Then catching the ring leader of the band, I pulled him to the water hole. They expected me to take my revenge upon him, but were so awed that they did not attempt to molest me. To their astonishment I began to bathe his wound. It was a new principle to them. They could understand how I could do so to my own servant, but why I should do the same kindness to this, my bitterest enemy, the man who had raised the mob to kill me, was entirely foreign to their ideas. Seeing the effect it had upon them, I said, "If you will go to the house with me, I will put some medicine in the wound." They followed me, completely subdued; I sewed up the wound, and from that day their attitude changed, the stubborn opposition gave way, and the work of God went on.

Many times I am asked incredulously if such beastly characters can really become Christians. To this question, thank God! we are able to reply that the things that are impossible with men are still possible with God, the arm of God is long enough to reach down even into the depths of this rubbish heap of creation, and His love is strong enough to lift up these bruised and battered masses of humanity, and by the unerring friction of His Spirit so transform them that they are new creatures indeed.

One incident will suffice to illustrate this fact. After one of my boys became a Christian, the other men began to taunt him by pointing to the holes in his ears—holes into which I could thrust my thumb—and say, "You are only an Mshensi—a bushman—look at the holes in your ears." He came to me greatly troubled and asked me if I could not stop this. I did not know what could be done, and it went on for some time. Then he came and asked me if I could not sew up those offensive holes. "No," said I, "it will do no good, and anyway it does not matter what the men call you so long as you do not live like a bushman. You are to please God rather than men." This seemed to satisfy him for a time, but only for a time. Back he came and besought me to sew up the ears. I could no longer refuse, so sat him on the floor with his head on my knees, and set about the task of obliterating those visible marks of his old heathenism.

Every jab of the needle hurt him, and the blood flowed down and dyed his shirt crimson. I finished one ear and then asked if he did not want me to stop. His answer was to roll his head over and beg me to sew up the other one. I did so, and the light in that countenance was worth seeing. But when the threads were taken out, alas! the holes were still there. His countenance fell, he seemed crushed in spirit. Then in a few days his face was beaming again. Those holes were closed once more. And how? He had hired a native to thrust thorns into the still sore, festering parts. Here was the stuff martyrs are made of. I said then, as I say now, "would God Christians in America were as willing to suffer something to get rid of the ear-marks of the old life which mar so many of our professions!"

But the battle for Africa's redemption has to be fought out against many a hindering thing. The obstacles are many and varied. Even famine, so familiar in India, here, too, stalks abroad in the land, and has to be reckoned with. During my last year and a half there, I had to provide food for my people and largely for myself by means of my rifle.

I find that a rifle may be consecrated to God's service as well as a Bible, when occasion demands. Game in bewildering variety swarmed the plains and bush, and roamed over the mountain ranges. There were thousands of antelope of various kinds; immense herds of zebra, brilliant in their striped coats; huge, lumbering rhinoceri; fleet footed, gay plumaged ostriches; long necked, curious giraffes; mean, sneaking hyena; streams swarming with hippopotami and crocodiles, and last of all, but above all, lions in abundance.

In my enforced hunting expeditions, these latter more than once nearly ended my career. But thank God, He who said, "Go," also said, "Lo, I am with you," and with that assurance the jungle of Africa is as safe as the streets of Cincinnati. Coming toward my station one afternoon, accompanied by a brother missionary from an adjoining tribe, we got within three or four miles of the station, when we wounded an antelope. The herd ran over a ridge, we followed, but when we reached the place, they were nowhere to be seen. Not wishing to be caught in the bush at night, we turned toward the station. We had only gone about 150 yards, when we discovered what we thought were the antelope in a depression about 200 yards ahead. We knelt to fire, but we quickly rose to our feet when we discovered to our dismay, that instead of antelope, we had run into a lot of lions.

Eleven of them—six full grown, and five cubs there proved to be. They started for us: we wanted to run, I frankly confess, but knew it was the worst thing we could possibly do, so walked back. We did not dare run; to fire upon them would have been madness. In a zig-zag course they made for us, their hoarse growls going through us at every step. We gained the crest of the ridge, and they were then within 90 yards of us.

By this time we had reached a clump of little scrubby trees, so small, that two of us could not get into one, so I crawled into one, and my companion into another. High as we could get, we yet stood only eight feet from the ground, from which the lions could easily have pulled us had they reached us. They stopped on the crest of the ridge to devour the antelope which they had pulled down prior to our appearance. We did not dare to get out of the trees because one or the other of them kept watch of us; we could not shoot, because they were partially screened by the bushes; and our great fear was, lest they keep us there until nightfall, when our case would have been hopeless. But we prayed, while they fought and roared over the carcass. Finally they came to the charge: in a solid body, led by the largest of the pack. Still we did not dare to fire, as my companion could not see them until they had advanced some distance, owing to some bushes which obstructed his view.

With terrible deliberation they advanced, heads erect, noses bloody, jaws open, until they were within 70 yards. We fired, and the leader dropped. This checked them and before they could recover themselves a second shot brought down another. This was too much for them, and they turned and dashed back into the bush from which they had come. A third one was badly wounded before they had quite disappeared. As the last one ran into the bush we hastily swung ourselves from our dangerous perches, and made for the path and home. Five minutes afterwards it was so dark we could not see the path before us. But as the mountains are round about Jerusalem, so the Lord is round about His people from this time forth—and even unto the end of the 20th century.

I have tried to show you the desperate need that confronts us: I have tried to show also, that the "Lo, I am with you," is a blessed reality wrought out in the daily experience of the missionary, and now briefly let me touch upon the spirit in which this mighty work must be performed.

Nothing less than the very spirit of Christ will suffice. We must get beyond doing the convenient thing and do the necessary thing. We must learn as we have never learned it that the spirit of Jesus Christ is inseparable from the spirit of sacrifice. The one thing is the natural visible expression of the other. "He that hath not the spirit of Christ is none of His." These are solemn words, and they search deep down into the secret motives of your heart and mine. Those only have learned the blessedness who have learned the lesson of sacrifice for others.

For fourteen months I had tasted no bread; then I raised a little crop of wheat. I put into its cultivation all the energy born of those fourteen months' abstinence from bread. I watched it grow up, head out, and grow golden under the sunlight. It was reaped a handful at a time, beaten out with sticks, and I had between nine and ten bushels of beautiful grain, worth its weight in gold to me. Visions of bread in plenty came up before me: I reveled in the delicious prospect of such a luxury. Then there came a vision of human need that staggers imagination. For months I had been stumbling over the bodies of famine victims, lying in my path in the last awful contortions of death from starvation. Now the wretched remnants of humanity came crawling upon my station. Emaciated, skeleton-like forms, gaunt, wolfish, hungry eyes looked out from hollow sockets in terrible appeal. They did not need to tell me their need. Those skeleton forms, those big hollow eyes, spoke the mute but eloquent appeal of suffering. My precious wheat rose before me. There was a need: here was a supply. But what about my desire? Which shall it be? My desire, or their need? My luxury or their necessity? Then came a vision which settled forever those questions for me, and the wheat went. I could afford to do without bread a few months longer, but I could not afford to look into those eyes which closed in death for me, into those scars which were the price of my redemption, and hear Him say, "I was hungry and ye gave me no meat, I was thirsty, and ye gave me no drink, naked, and ye clothed me not." "But Master, when saw I thee ahungered or athirst and ministered not unto thee?" Then would He say, "Inasmuch as ye did it not unto one of the least of these, ye did it not unto me." I could stand anything but that!

Between our heaven of blessedness and this hell of Africa's woe and want and wretchedness, there is a great gulf fixed—a gulf of selfishness, a gulf of indifference, a gulf of ignorance. And I see no hope of bridging the chasm, until we get beyond missionaries, and missions and human appeals and get one clear vision of Jesus Christ.

Fellow Endeavorer, I do not ask you to pity the heathen, but I do beg of you that you simply treat Jesus Christ right! Is it right to accept the gift of life at the price He paid for it, and then give Him only the spare change you happen to have left after your luxurious tastes are satisfied? Is it right to give Him only the odds and ends, the spare moments, the convenient service, the thing that costs you nothing? Is it right to grudge Him even so small a portion as the tenth of your income for the advancement of His cause? Shall we forever crucify the Son of God on the cross of convenience?

It was an afternoon of the romances of missions. After this thrilling story of African heroism came the siege of Peking, told by Rev. Courtenay H. Fenn. It is an old story now, but ever new and fascinating. Mr. Fenn, like all other eye-witnesses who tell the story, believes that not the rifles of the marines, nor the sandbags of the intrenchments, but the prayers of the Christian world, saved the legations.

Mr. Fenn said that, while he heard many legation attaches say, "If ever we get out of this, you'll never catch us in China again," he heard not a single missionary say so. There is no more defeat in the catastrophe in China than there was in the crucifixion of Jesus.

The Marvelous Providence of God in the Siege of Peking.

Rev. Courtenay Hughes Fenn, of the Peking Mission.

When the allied forces reached the city of Peking and raised the siege of the diplomatists, business men and missionaries shut up there for eight long weeks, among their number was the British Chief of Engineers, Col. Scott Moncrief. When he had completed his tour of inspection he pronounced the system of barricades truly marvelous, considering all the circumstances of their construction. "Marvelous indeed they are," replied a companion; "but after all, how do you account for it that this mere handful of men, women and children has been able to hold out against such fearful odds?" Said Col. Moncrief: "But you must remember that probably never in the history of the Christian Church did such a volume of prayer ascend to Almighty God on behalf of any body of men in peril as ascended to Him this past summer on behalf of these people." These memorable words of the British engineer give forceful expression to the feelings of the majority of the besieged, that without special divine interposition, in answer to the prayer, it would have been impossible for any to obtain deliverance. So clearly manifest was the hand of Providence in our escape that the siege in Peking deserves to rank among the great miracles of history. The first thing in this wonderful Providence was the long period of warning given of impending trouble. All recall with distinctness that remarkable series of progressive edicts which followed one another in rapid succession from the imperial palace during the summer of 1898, and startled the civilized world. But there was growing up at the same time the society of the "I He Chuan," or Boxers, an organization with a history of more than two centuries. Originally for the mutual protection of the inhabitants of neighboring villages against the attacks of marauders, it assumed, in recent development, a patriotic attitude, with the war cry: "Establish the Empire; exterminate the foreigner." The American people will never appreciate the tremendous provocation unless they picture to themselves their own beloved land in the position occupied by China during the past few years. Should Japan seize San Francisco as a coaling station, China take Tacoma as indemnity for outrages against Chinese subjects, Great Britain appropriate New York and several adjacent counties, and Russia absorb New Orleans "that they might be better able to protect the United States," it requires no vivid imagination to forecast the result. And as to the railroads, the Chinese were not sufficiently far-sighted to see in them anything more than a foreign imposition, which threw thousands out of employment.

The rapid progress of the "Boxer," and "Big Sword," societies, due in large measure to the sanction and encouragement received from the Empress Dowager, was due also to other causes—its patriotic war cry, its promise of unlimited foreign loot. As the movement grew in numbers and courage its destruction of property and life became more frequent and terrible. Dividing "foreigners" into three classes, they fell upon the nearest and most defenceless, the native Christian, first. Refugees began coming into the city in large numbers. Though we could not assure them of protection, we took them in. For months the foreign Ministers had been urged to make such representations to the Chinese government as should compel the suppression of this fanatical society; but they did not realize to the full the gravity of the situation and peremptorily demand immediate action. In response to their protests, the government issued edicts. When matters had reached this stage, we knew that hundreds of Boxers were practising openly and unhindered while the general attitude toward us was growing more menacing. Not only were we warned, but we were given time to prepare for defence before the storm broke. We must do more than shoulder rifles and take our places on the walls of the compound, and on the roof of the great church side by side with the twenty marines assigned to us by the American minister. The work of fortification began almost at once. The able-bodied native refugees were organized for labor; all the brick walls and some useless inner walls were utilized as material for barricades on the neighboring streets or about the church.

It was well that the warnings which we had received were so effective, for the storm finally burst suddenly, and itself served as a warning that yet more awful things were planned. On the evening of June 13, the cry of fire was raised. Quickly yet calmly we hurried our ladies and children into the church, while we took positions on the walls and roof. Our twenty marines charged out through the narrow street, on which the mission was located. Meeting a mob of Chinese rushing down our way, they charged them with such vigor as to force them to hastily retreat. One after another we saw our homes, with all of our personal possessions, our schools, chapels, churches, hospitals and dispensaries, and the homes of our native Christians, burst up in fierce conflagration. Our native Christians, and all connected with the foreigner in any way, had been thoroughly black-listed in advance, and were diligently sought out by the human bloodhounds. The number slaughtered was not far from eighty per cent. of our native church. It was well for us at this juncture, as at many a later time, that our heads and hands were, of necessity, busy about many things, else our sorrow might have proved unendurable. On the 19th of June began a series of events which constituted our final warning. The ministers received warning from the State Department to leave Peking within twenty-four hours, as the Taku forts had been demanded in surrender by the foreign admirals. In the face of what seemed certain massacre on leaving the city, the ministers asked the Chinese government for means of transportation. On the morning of the twentieth the German minister set out for the Yamen to arrange the matter. We gathered together to do the only thing possible, to pray. Hardly had we left the room of prayer when there was brought into our court a man who had dragged himself to our lines and there fallen exhausted. He proved to be the German interpreter, bringing the horrible tidings that the German minister had been foully murdered by Chinese soldiers. The whole aspect of affairs was changed in an instant. It awoke the ministers to a realization of the gravity of the situation. There was no longer any thought of departure from Tientsin. We tried to induce the American marines to procure our food and clothing. They are not to be blamed for refusal; it was an awful risk, and none then knew how indispensable these things would prove. After a light lunch, however, Rev. W. S. Ament of the American Board, brave almost to rashness, took with him one Chinese servant, walked over to the mission, found everything yet untouched. What one could do, more could do; so gathering fifteen or twenty missionaries, fifty or sixty Chinese, with ropes and poles for carrying, and with spears and rifles for defense, we returned to the mission, saving more than half of what we had stored there. Before the work was completed, the Chinese had begun their attack on our northern line; and that evening "the war was on," and the Chinese rifle and cannon fire was almost incessant for four long weeks.

Our position could hardly have been better, had we been given our choice in the city. We supposed that two or three days would bring the end of the siege through the arrival of the long expected reinforcements. No one imagined that we should or could be there for eight weeks. The amount of food which our foresight had provided was insufficient for our whole company of foreigners and Chinese for a single week. In no other quarter of that city, of equal extent, could we have found what we needed in such quantity and variety. Even the imperial granaries would have provided but rice. Within the lines held we had no less than three foreign stores, with fair stocks of canned goods, milk, butter, sugar and cooking utensils. An even greater Godsend, however, was found in several Chinese grain shops within our lines. Here we found several thousand bushels of rice and from five to eight thousand bushels of new wheat. The 4,000 by the Sea of Galilee were no more divinely fed. We had also an excellent supply of meat, in the more than one hundred horses and mules connected with the various foreign establishments in the city. We had also a few sheep, most of which were eaten by the wounded and the sick. The few chickens furnished broth for the children. Such a water supply could not have been found elsewhere. Peking is simply saturated with filth; but three of the eight wells in the British legation contained water which we could drink unboiled, and the supply seemed inexhaustible. Within our walls were also several native coal shops. A serious problem which presented itself was that of clothing and bedding for the native Christians. We found and opened up stores piled high with readymade clothing and quantities of bedding, enough to fit out the whole company of refugees. Marvelous as was the provision thus made for us it hardly surpassed the wonders of God's defence. One of our worst enemies would naturally have been the North China summer. June is usually very hot with very dry heat; but last June was neither hot nor dry. July is usually very hot with a very wet heat; but last July was neither hot nor wet; and August followed July's good example. Thus sanitary conditions which would ordinarily have been productive of fearful pestilence did little harm. It is estimated that the Chinese fired at us no less than two million rifle-balls. The attack was almost incessant, day and night, for four weeks. The Chinese cannon tore up our roofs, penetrated our buildings, passing through rooms where persons lay sleeping, without harming them. But two persons were killed and two injured. We became accustomed to the whistling of bullets and the shrieking of shells. The attacks of our enemies grew in fierceness as their desperation increased. But one of the almost ninety missionaries was struck with a bullet, and even his wound was not serious.

From the 14th of June until the 16th of July we were absolutely without word from the outside world. Then came the strange telegram for Major Conger, to which he made a reply which startled a rather incredulous world. Soon after a messenger succeeded in reaching Tientsin, and returning with word of its siege, the capture of Taku, and the preparation for our relief. The Chinese troops went north to help defend the gates attacked; and when the British and Americans reached the southern gates they found few defenders, soon shelled open the gates or climbed over the

wall, and were in the city. Most timely proved this arrival, for, on opening up the Imperial Carriage Park on our northwest, it was found that
from one of the buildings of this park the Chinese had dug a mine 100 feet
in length, extending to some of our largest buildings, and almost ready for
the firing. Forty-eight hours more would have seen much of the legation
wrecked, and our lives, possibly, at the mercy of our enemies. Our food
supply in many lines was low; our ammunition was almost exhausted;
the ranks of our defenders were depleted and sadly fatigued; and to God's
loving Providence we owe it that ourselves and so many of our native
Christians were delivered from the hands of the Empress Dowager, and
from all the expectation of the Chinese.

After suffering the loss of all worldly possessions and many loved
ones, and, for the most part, uncomplainingly, our native Christians had
done most of the hard work of ditch-digging, barricading, bag-filling,
food-gathering and milling, often under fire, while many of them also
served as volunteer soldiers. And, be it said, by direct appointment of
Sir Claude Macdonald, the chairman of all the committees, and most of
the active members of those committees, were missionaries.

Rev. W. S. Amert, D. D.

Rev. A. Miyaki.

Tracy McGregor.

Rev. Cleland B. McAfee, D. D.

Rev. George W. Moore.

Rev. J. G. Butler, D. D.

Rev. Howard W. Pope.

Rev. Richard W. Lewis.

Rev. G. L. Wharton.

William R. Moody.

Rev. A. J. Lyman, D. D.

Booker T. Washington.

SOME OF THE CONVENTION SPEAKERS.

CHAPTER XXXI.

The Farewell Meetings.

Long before the time of beginning, every seat in Music Hall was filled, in both the immense auditoriums, on the closing evening of the Convention. The central hall, Auditorium Endeavor, was an especially magnificent sight,—by far the finest Convention meeting-place Christian Endeavor has yet enjoyed. Rank upon rank, up to the lofty ceiling, rose the solid galaxies of young faces, eloquent of happiness and at the same time of a serious, earnest purpose.

For this closing meeting was to be a purpose meeting. We had been celebrating the two decades already accomplished. Now for a hopeful and courageous forward look over the decades of a new century. What may they not contain of beautiful living and fine achievement!

Nevertheless, the meeting began with two looks backward, which were also looks forward. Dr. Teunis S. Hamlin of Washington, D. C., spoke of the cosmopolitan character of Christian Endeavor. We are becoming citizens of the world, as Christ was a citizen of the world. Dr. Wayland Hoyt, of Philadelphia, reckoned among the noblest achievements of Christian Endeavor its great International Conventions, testifying to the fact that our religion is not a waning but a waxing one, promoting acquaintance among the denominations, promoting acquaintances among the young and old, arousing patriotism, and inciting to better Christian service.

Always the most enthusiastic and enjoyable hour of our Conventions is the annual roll-call, with its admirable miscellany of song and testimony.

Japan was represented by Mr. Miyaki, who came forward in rich costume, unfurled a beautiful Japanese banner, and sung a stanza of "Stand up, stand up for Jesus," in his own language.

China was well represented by President Hubbard, head of the Chinese Christian Endeavor Union, and by Mr. Fenn, of Peking, who unrolled the large dragon flag of China with the meaningful quotation, "And the great dragon was cast out, that old serpent. . . . And I heard a loud voice saying in heaven, Now is come the kingdom of our God. . . . And they overcame him by the word of their testimony, and they loved not their lives unto the death."

Three African missionaries, Ferris of the Congo, Ransom of Natal, and Hotchkiss of East Central Africa, stood up for the Dark Continent. Their speaker urged more definite prayers for missionaries, and sung a Christian song in the native tongue.

Mr. Marsh, of Australia, in doubt whether other Australians were in the house, gave the shrill cry of the bush, "coo-ee," which was answered by other "coo-ees" until three Australians stood together. Their message was based upon Lord Roberts's famous question, "Can they stand fire?" and was, "Watch ye, stand fast in the faith, be strong."

For India there strode forward a gigantic fellow in the brilliant native costume, a Hindoo Endeavorer from Detroit, who told how he had been converted by a Christian Endeavorer, and had been disowned by his father, mother, brothers, and sisters; but now he looked around, and he found he had thousands of brothers and sisters right before him. Three missionaries to India stood with our Hindoo brother. "God be with you till we meet again" was sung in Tamil, and our dear brother Endeavorer, Rev. J. P. Jones, D. D., spoke a brief farewell message before his return to the five hundred Endeavor societies of India.

Turkey was represented by a Christian Koord, born under the shadow of Ararat, who sung a quaint native song, and also by an Armenian, who gave his testimony from one of the galleries.

Some cablegrams and telegrams were then read: from Spain, "Come over and help us"; one from California; one from the Twentieth-Century Chautauqua Association; one from the State union of New South Wales, Australia; and one from Berlin, Germany: "Christ, Victor."

Very fittingly, there came next the response of the American German contingent. They rose from the front seats, more than 150 of them, and they sung most magnificently that grandest of German hymns, "Ein feste Burg ist unser Gott."

A Persian native: "Let us never be ashamed of the name of Jesus."

Helpful responses from the District of Columbia, from Florida, from North Dakota, from Oklahoma (represented by two young women who spoke most manfully), Nebraska, Utah ("Trusting, striving"), California ("Study to show thyself approved unto God"), Texas (a verse of "Texas for Christ"), Iowa, Nevada, New Hampshire ("Ever forward for Christian Endeavor"), Colorado, Vermont, ("God forbid that we should glory, save in the cross of Jesus Christ").

Virginia gave a new interpretation to "F. F. V.,"—"Forever faithful and valiant for Christ."

Kentucky rose in a splendid phalanx, whose size aroused delighted applause. President Danley emphasized the prominence given to the home during the Convention, and the ever-beautiful State song, to the tune of "My Old Kentucky Home," was sung even more finely than at any previous Convention.

The prison societies were called next, "and most fittingly after Kentucky," said Dr. Clark. This started a laugh, and our president had to make prompt explanation, telling about Kentucky's unequaled work for prison Endeavor. Various messages from prison societies were read, and a Utah delegate excited amusement by the proud announcement that the largest Christian Endeavor society in this State is in the penitentiary. "They were not Endeavorers before they went there," Dr. Clark put in the caveat.

The goodly company from Illinois put together two texts: "Lord, what wilt Thou have me to do? I can do all things in Him who strengtheneth me."

Maine's delegation, through President Crane, expressed its pride in coming from the birthplace of prohibition and of Christian Endeavor, "the State that was once the home of Father Endeavor Clark, Forward Endeavor Clark, Forever Endeavor Clark." They gave a beautiful bouquet to Mrs. Clark and the doctor, and they won great applause by bringing to the front five members of the original Williston society, who stood up, flanked by Dr. Clark and Rev. Dwight M. Pratt, two of their former pastors. "Three cheers for Williston!" was proposed, and they were heartily given.

"Kansas," said Dr. Sheldon, speaking for his State, "appeals for her Endeavorers to join in her undismayed fight for the extirpation of the saloon in America, and our motto for the whole century is this: 'Do all things to the glory of God.' "

Pennsylvania was irrepressible with its taking song, "Keep on the sunny side," and the Cincinnati Endeavorers, represented by the noble choir, sung for us that sweet and purposeful hymn, "Just to say what He wants me to say."

One of the most stirring moments of the Convention was the presentation of two banners given to the United Society by foreign lands in order to stimulate interest in Christian Endeavor in America! One of these was presented by an Intermediate society in Foochow, China, and is to be given each year to the city or State that does the most to bring into the Christian Endeavor work all the young people of all ages. The banner is exquisitely painted by hand, and represents two Christian Chinese preaching to one heathen Chinaman, pointing him to the cross. Philadelphia is to hold the banner for the next year, and Chicago for the year following.

The other banner was a beautiful blue affair with white lettering in cabalistic characters, and was sent by the local union of Osaka, Japan. It will be presented at our next Convention to the State that makes the best all-round gain in the formation of new societies.

The enlivening roll-call was at length completed, with its inspiring glimpses of Christian Endeavor all over the globe. Then we reached the closing half-hour, and the Convention sermon.

Dr. Floyd W. Tomkins of Philadelphia, whose beautiful services throughout the Convention in the Quiet Hours so greatly endeared him to the Endeavorers, took for his text those tender words of the One Hundred and Nineteenth Psalm, "I opened my mouth and panted, for my delight was in Thy commandments." "Is there one of us," he asked, "who does not long to draw near to that perfect Christ, who does not pant after Him? This aspiration is the most hopeful thing in the world. The man who is satisfied with himself is spiritually dead. The man who cries, 'My heart has no rest, nor can it rest until it rests in Thee,' is the man who is alive.

"And how we long to get our lower selves under our feet! Do we not open our mouths and pant for a holiness without which we cannot live? Pity the man who does not want to be a better man.

"If we go out from this Convention with these two desires, it will not be in vain that we have met upon this mountain-top. But on the morrow shall we still feel these longings? Shall we be inspired with the duties that 'crowd upon us? Shall we pant after noble service? Woe to us if our blessings end with the end of this service. No man receives a blessing without receiving also a responsibility.

"It's a cold world outside. A world of sin. A world of hardness. Shall we go forth into it driven by a sense of fear? weakened by unworthy fears? or shall we long after it, pant for it, agonize to make it better? If you are a Christian, a real Christian, you cannot help it. You will feel a hunger for souls. You will pant with a longing for souls.

"Then, we shall pant to purify the world. We have been fooling about it long enough. The church has only within the last twenty years begun to learn that Christianity is in the world to save the world. Have you ever done anything for temperance? What are you doing for the awful matter of social impurity? Are you guarding yourself with a sanctity that comes pure from God Himself? Have you ever gone to your fallen brothers and sisters and tried to lift them up? The man who tries to save himself merely, is a man who hasn't a soul worth saving. What are you doing about gambling, policy-shops, the dishonest ways of making money?

"Ah, there lies the world in sadness, longing for something, she knows not what. Will you go out, with a great, panting desire that you cannot resist, to make this world God's world? First, will you pant after God? Then, will you pant after service?

"God grant us grace so to long after Him here that we shall know Him hereafter."

The closing words, spoken by Dr. Clark, were an earnest appeal for a wise use of the splendid opportunities of the Convention. "Will you carry this Convention to others? Will you make much of it, as a talent given you by God Himself?"

High praise, and none too high, was given by our president to the Committee of 1901, as noble and efficient a committee as ever served Christian Endeavor; also to the self-sacrificing choir, who had rendered such faithful service, though from the choir seats not a single address could be heard; also to the ushers, and more sensible, modest, and manly ushers no convention ever enjoyed. He spoke a word of gratitude for the weather, so perfect in spite of its fierce preamble. He was proud of the attendance, so remarkable under the circumstances. He took up again the note of home religion, so prominent in the sessions, the new plans for better citizenship, the enlarged designs for world-wide Endeavor.

There was a tender and hopeful prayer. There rose the strains of our parting hymn, "God be with you till we meet again." Vice-chairman Dawson led us in the Mizpah benediction. The buckeye gavel fell, and our twentieth Convention was at an end.

THE CLOSE IN WILLISTON.

In Auditorium Williston, which was thronged, Treasurer Shaw's opening words were: "This will go down into history as the Convention of Expansion. Our hearts have all rejoiced over the forward movements in Endeavor for Germany, Scandinavia, China, and other countries."

Among the striking messages in answer to the roll-call was that of North Carolina's quartette of sweet singers.

"Tennessee for Christ," rung out grandly from a chorus of tuneful voices.

Georgia elicited hearty applause by uplifting a banner with a great, luscious watermelon painted on it.

"Michigan, my Michigan," was beautifully sung by the Wolverine Endeavorers.

Missouri was much in evidence, but Indiana was an army with banners and trumpets, and a voice like the sound of many waters.

Connecticut had a State song to the tune of "Stand up for Jesus."

West Virginia kept "step with the Master" in beautiful song.

New Mexico was represented in the singular number, but it was a case where one is equal to a thousand.

Canada, led by sturdy Canon Richardson, sung "God save the King." That brought Rev. G. Campbell Morgan to his feet, and then the whole audience came up, and a stanza of "America" was followed by "Blest be the tie," amid waving flags and handkerchiefs.

When Mr. Shaw, who presided, had exhausted the list of foreign countries, he said, "There is one more foreign country to be heard from— New Jersey."

When Ohio rose, it seemed as if no one was sitting down. They were a splendid body.

After Australia came the mother country. Dr. Morgan and the Canadians stood and sung "God save the King." The whole audience again arose and joined in.

"Three cheers for King Edward," proposed Canon Richardson at the close. Right heartily were they given. "Three cheers for President McKinley!" he next proposed, and with hearty good will rung out four thousand voices. "A tiger!" said some one, and a rousing tiger it was.

"What's the matter with Emperor Wilhelm?" called out Mr. Shaw.

"He's all right!" responded the German Endeavorers in a body.

"Now let us sing to the King of kings," suggested some one, and the strains of "All hail the power of Jesus' name" rung out with intense devotion. It was a climax of enthusiasm such as has rarely been reached in International Conventions.

Miss Myers responded in fitting words for Ceylon.

"Haven't we had a splendid meeting?" said Mr. Shaw, as the responses ended; and the fusillade of hand-clapping that followed showed that the whole audience was in hearty accord with him.

"Some people ask what Christian Endeavor has done," he continued. "I can remember when such a meeting as this had never been dreamed of. The man that suggested it as a possibility would have been called a fool, or worse."

Softly and sweetly, with bowed heads, the audience sang, "Nearer, my God, to Thee," and Rev. G. Campbell Morgan was introduced to speak on "Our Marching Orders."

Speaking of the first order, that we face the foe, Mr. Morgan said that there is a threefold peril,—atheism, animalism, abjectness.

The atheism of today isn't delivering lectures and saying smart things against the Bible, but it is manifesting itself in apathy.

The recent simultaneous missions in London, the most magnificent religious movement since the days of Wesley, brought to light the fact that there are thousands of men who are torpid as concerns God and spiritual things. This is the appalling atheism we must face today.

Then, there are masses of people who live to tickle their nerves and gratify their ambition for material things.

The last degree of this antagonism to Christ is abjectness. It is the fruit of the saloon and of vice.

We are to oppose atheism with a new theism. We are to oppose animalism with a new spiritual life. And we are to oppose abjectness with a new courage.

This new theism means a new realization of the presence of God.

Concerning the new spirituality, he said it is a word that needs to be rescued from abuse. It is not ascetism. It is not Pharisaism. It does not consist in taking life out of everyday relations and putting it into some uniform or institution. It is not some ecstatic, visionary life that looks down with contempt on others. We need to show the world that spiritual life is the broadest and best and most helpful life possible.

Telling a story of his little girl's capture of a bread-knife, he said, "I'm afraid you won't see the point of this story; for your knives have no edge, but ours have." The mother hastened to take the sharp knife from the hand of the little girl, and, to compensate for the disappointment over the loss of the glittering treasure, she placed a golden orange there. That is what God does with our lives. He takes the edged, hurtful things out, and puts in their place the golden fruit of the liberty of sons of God.

Mr. Morgan's last word was one of hope. He said he was eager for the conflict. He believed in the ultimate victory of Christ.

And thus ended, seriously and blessedly, one of the best-balanced and most uplifting closing meetings Endeavor has ever enjoyed.

CHAPTER XXXII.

The Power of the Bible in the Twentieth Century.

Rev. A. J. Lyman, D. D.

Will you permit me to waive formality in the interest of courtesy, and instead of an introduction substitute the payment of a debt? The debt, if put into the form of a promissory note, would read something like this, perhaps: For value received I promise to pay to Francis E. Clark, or order, a principal sum of heart-felt thanks and fraternal honor for the beautiful service rendered to me and my church by the Christian Endeavor Society during recent years.

I have long wished to get even with Dr. Clark on this debt, and this is a magnificent opportunity. Here's my hand—both hands—on it, Doctor!

"Beautiful" seems to me just the word for this service which your society has thus rendered. It is a service which has been most healthful, helpful, and blessed.

In earlier days some good saints were timid about trusting the young people with an organization of their own, as though two factions might be created in the church, the young and the old. As well employ the term faction to describe a single department in the one army, or a single organ in the human body.

I love to think of the Christian Endeavor organization as one department of the church itself. Our Endeavor Society is riveted fast to the Sunday school on the one hand and to the adult church organization on the other. It is our normal school in which those who are to become officers in the church are trained,—and if you want a first class junior deacon, make him out of a senior Endeavorer.

You strike new notes on the old church bells, but you do not invent new bells. It is the old gospel, ever new; it is the old church, ever young, whose methods you seek to readapt to current conditions in the actual life of the age. You have signalized the close of one century and the opening of the next by striking three such notes; the notes of "Missionary Enthusiasm;" the "Tenth Legion;" the "Quiet Hour." These are not the notes of factions; they are the spontaneous outpourings of the inmost spirit of the church universal, showing that the "Endeavor" movement is not a provincial or temporary response to casual demands for novelty, but is naturally integral in the church, and walks midrank in that mighty march by which Christ is leading His church onward to an everlasting dominion.

Twenty-five minutes is the time assigned for this address, including my debt-paying salutation. Twenty minutes is long enough in these crowded sessions. My first duty is not to overstep this limit. "The Power of the Bible in the 20th Century" is my subject. Only the whole century and the entire Bible to talk about in twenty minutes! No elaboration then, no side-track dallying, but just a simple statement, strong and swift as I can make it, of one or two convictions, not so much upon the general academic question concerning the power of the Bible in the 20th century, as upon the specific question; how that power relates itself to the work of this great society in the new age.

Exceedingly simple is the general thought I would present. It is that the Bible is not a book merely, but an incarnation. It is a life in a book; it is God in a literature. And the power of the Bible is the power of that life in that book reproduced in other lives and going forth in forms of service suited to the current age. Two lives with one book between them, connecting them; this is the true idea. Not the book, as a book alone, considered as a relic, a missal, a chart of texts; but as the incarnation of life, of divine life in the human life.

With this general thought in mind, I venture to say a word as to four departments of influence,—terraces if you please to call them such, rising one above the other, illustrating what I believe to be the characteristic power of the Bible in the new age, and as to the relation of each of these departments to the younger members of our churches.

First. The power of the Bible in the 20th century as an intellectual power. It is the power of genius, the power of a very high order of literary inspiration.

"The Bible as literature" is now a current phrase and a good one, provided we remember that literature means more than fine writing. It means choice, supreme, immortal writing. We insist upon our right to apply this word inspiration to the nobler activity of the human brain. We agree with the philosophic intuition which from Plato to Hogel affirms that the human intellect shines with something of the light of God. With this agrees also the deeper logic of the doctrine of evolution. Genius is a gleam from the eternal, so that we look beyond the "Banks and braes of Bonnie Doon" to find the source of Burn's wild music, and beyond the meadows of the Avon for the secret of enchantment woven into the dream of Shakespeare's "Midsummer Night."

So when Coleridge worships in the vale of Chamouni, or voyages with his "Ancient Mariner" amid the emerald ice of the Antartic world, when Spenser passes yonder with his faery bells, or Calderon of Spain, or that stern Florentine whom alone we name with Homer and Shakespeare, the three monarchs of song, we drop for the moment our literary measuring line, and exclaim, "This in very truth is the inspiration of the Almighty!"

Now the power of the Bible upon the 20th century mind is this power of supreme genius embodied in an immortal literature. It is an intellectual fascination and ascendency. For the Bible is literature.

One does not wish to overstate the point. Not all of the Biblical writing is of this very high quality, but it is fair to say that the narratives, the histories, the dialogues, poems, parables, dramas, which make up our Bible, clustered as they are about one progressively unfolding religion, set forth the ideas of that religion with a literary energy and splendor certainly equal with the average level of the pagan classics. There are passages in the Psalms and the Minor Prophets which outsweep Homer, and above these even is such a work as the book of Job, an archaic masterpiece, at least on a par with the highest summits of Greek tragedy; and still above these, unmatched in human language for their depth and for their truth to life, are the parables and maxims attributed to Jesus. Nothing in Plato is more exquisitely simple and profound.

Here, then, in this field of clear intellectual power and charm is exhibited the mastery of the Bible over the modern mind.

One practical conclusion from this is evident. It is this—the Endeavor Society will match the new age by being alive to this intellectual quality in the Biblical writings. Possibly something might be done to further this. A closer connection might perhaps be established between the Endeavor work and the higher class of Biblical study in our Sunday schools. The Sunday school is the place to inaugurate the intellectual impulse with reference to the Bible which shall go on to pervade the Christian Endeavor Society, and fix its attitude towards these immortal writings, apprehending and using them not as a string of beads, a series of isolated texts, even though each bead were a pearl; but as a glorious library of God, a series of writings in which the Eternal Genius inspired human genius for a spiritual end—writings in which Mind immortally calls to mind.

Second. The power of the Bible upon the mind of the present and coming age is in the second place distinctively a moral power. This form of influence represents a terrace one step higher than that of the intellect alone. It is the terrace or field of what we may accurately call the moral inspiration of the Bible. Here, also, we maintain the scientific use of the word inspiration. In the human conscience is the reverberation of the Eternal. The ancient classic world had its Socrates and its Epictetus,

China its Confucius, India its Vedas, Rome its Marcus Aurelius, Islam its Koran. Many of these writings are endued with what John Milton called the ' Sanctity of reason;" they are the world's Bibles.

But on this scale of moral supremacy, our Biblical writings, most of them, stand unquestionably first, and the proof of this is that the Bible and the Bible alone has mastered the master nations. Wendell Phillips once made this reply in a Boston coterie where some had said, "Jesus was amiable, but not strong." "Not strong!" replied those never blanching lips. "Test the strength of Jesus by the strength of the men whom he has mastered."

The Bible is the moral athlete of history, because it has conquered the conquerors. Why! even to lay your hand on the Bible and think what it has done, is like laying your hand upon a great hot cannon.

Take the Biblical thought of the Diety, gradually unfolded, indeed, but at last standing complete—one vast personal Energy, transcendent yet immanent, in the depths of whose limitless life dwells an Eternal Father-hood, a Divine Sonship, a Holy Spirit quickening all things; take the Biblical thought of man, that God's own son, noble, erring, lost, saved; take its tremendous conception of sin, which makes Aescuzlus seem pale; take its wonderful and thrilling message of rescue through suffering; take the glowing light and final flash of its vision of immortality—and you have an assemblage of moral ideas by the side of whose instant might all other books seem tiny and thin. Mohammed's Koran seems well enough when one reads it by the creak of the "Sakiah" as he drifts on the Nile, but the Koran is verbose, is petty, when set beneath the colossal arches of Isaiah or of Job. Marcus Aurelius is impressive when read in the ruined Roman forum, but the ethics of Aurelius compared with the ethics of Paul are like the Matterhorn in the pallor of evening compared with the same Matterhorn when standing amid the "golden candlesticks" of the morning sunrise.

Here, then, is the second ground of permanent ascendency of the Biblical writings upon every age, and especially upon our own age. These writings are the supreme articulation of the human conscience. And here again we find an immediate and an imperative practical lesson. If the Endeavor Society desires, as it does, to represent the distinctive power of the Bible, it must be by reaffirming its ethical note, and not only by af-firming it but by embodying it in personal character. The Christian En-deavorer must incarnate the Biblical ethic—and let us remember that the ethical note of the whole Bible is unique. It is not justice merely, but justice clothed upon with generosity. It is integrity radiant with charity. It is law set to the music of love. It is duty blossoming into beauty, as the very rocks underlying your city burst at their summits into your beautiful parks and gardens and emerald lawns.

The Christian Endeavor Society, I repeat, must incarnate something of this ethical ideal in personal character if it would be a spokesman for the Bible to the modern age. To speak is well, to act is better, to be is best of all. I love this rich red word "incarnate." Do you remember that we employ the same Latin root in our glowing word "incarnadine"? Christian Endeavor must incarnadine the pale, conventional morality by a richer exhibition of moral force, of ethical chivalry, of a spiritual daunt-lessness allied with the very grace and tenderness of the Master. Thus shall you reincarnate the very life of the Bible and maintain its hold upon the conscience of men.

Third. The third terrace or field of Biblical ascendency in the modern world is still higher. It is distinctly spiritual and superhuman. It derives its power from certain examples of clearly demonstrable superhuman in-spiration in these marvelous writings. Beyond the remarkable literary inspiration, beyond the supremely remarkable moral inspiration, the mod-ern mind is aware of something more in the Bible,—namely, gleams here and there,—not everywhere, for I am wishing to claim only what is clearly demonstrable,—but here and there gleams of an insight so transcendent into the spiritual nature of man and his spiritual ideals as to be clearly beyond the unaided human power which produced these writings in that little strip of rocky upland east of the Mediterranean in those fierce and dark or jaded and brazen ages.

How can I possibly account for the spirituelle loveliness of the Gospel of John by anything I can find in the Syria of Herod, or even in the Roman Empire of the early second century? As well look for a spray of Syrian lilies bursting from a stack of Roman spears. There are passages in the Book of Job, in the Psalms, in the letters of St. Paul and of St. John which exactly match and meet the finest aspirations of the present age twenty centuries after. What magic had the fishing nets of Galilee thus to anticipate the summit centuries of Europe and the New World?

Now the modern mind, the twentieth century mind, is alive as no other mind ever was to these high lights of Biblical inspiration, and a Christian man or church or society which desires most finely to enforce the Bible upon this age, must bring forward the Bible in its own spiritual perspective.

This more modern way of using the Bible which the modern mind appreciates, and to which it responds, reaches its highest note in emphasizing with chief accent the incomparable picture which the New Testament writers give of Jesus. So far as we know Jesus left no memorial of Himself, save the shifting impressions made upon the rocking brains of a small group of frightened fishermen who had fled in cowardly terror from the scene of His execution. A few decades later these exquisite Gospels appear, so unapproached in their beauty, in the spiritual symmetry of the figure of Jesus which they present. How could a lot of terrified fugitives create a literary masterpiece which 2000 years later, at the peak and pinnacle of a civilization then undreamed of, should be recognized as the supreme spiritual idyll of the world? As well might you expect a dozen common quarry-men, all hammering together, to chisel out the Apollo of the Vatican.

Here is the culminating point of the power of the Bible upon the twentieth century, in its delineation of the beautiful and holy Nazarene. And here, therefore, must be the point of chief stress on the part of any society which would represent the Bible. Employing the first tremendous syllable of your title alone, your society must be the Christ-Endeavor Society. For in this rendition of Jesus upon the New Testament page is the final demonstration of a higher than human hand upon the record.

To recognize this spiritual perspective and the true authority of the Bible as based upon it is the new errand of modern Protestantism, and therefore of young Protestant Christians. The question then is, will the Christian Endeavor genius maintain itself in true alignment with this profound movement of the Protestant mind in our day? If it could not do this, or should not do this, then possibly the days of the Christian Endeavor Society as a vitally effective force in the modern Christian world would be drawing towards a close.

But I believe exactly the contrary. I believe that the Christian Endeavor spirit so truly voices what is vital in the church that it cannot but align itself with what is best in the modern development of Christianity. I believe that these coming years will witness a wonderful new awakening of the Christian Endeavor hosts to this more intellectual and more spiritual way of regarding the Bible; not only as a superb religious literature, not only as a supreme moral code, not only as a series of isolated texts, however precious; but, in the fuller apprehension of its true spiritual perspective, its real summits of divine and final authority.

Fourth. The fourth and final field or terrace of fact and of thought upon which the power of the Bible in the twentieth century will be illustrated is less easy to state, but it follows in the same chain of logic, and without it that logic would not be complete. It is in a word this: there are so many of these high lights of superhuman inspiration in the Bible and they are so distributed that they become interpretative over all the remainder of the Biblical writings.

In other words, the Bible as a whole, and here is its unique and divine distinction, becomes self-interpreting, self-adjusting, self-corrective with reference to the partialness of its separate writings, and so becomes, when taken as a whole, practically infallible, if employed by the full roused intelligence and spirit, as a guide to duty and to God.

This is rational infallibility—the infallibility of infallible self-correction. Of course there is no time now for illustrating this in detail. I am attempting to follow only the heart of the argument, and that at railroad speed, but here is the flash at the finial. We want an infallible Bible, and we have it, but not a petty infallibility, suited to keep men children, but a rational infallibility, suited to make children men. God's infallibility in the Bible matches his infallibility in nature, an infallibility that calls out the utmost energy of the free intellect in reverent study, makes such study necessary, and then rewards it. Men seem not to have grasped the truth that the modern critical movement in Biblican study is itself a product of the deeper study of the Bible, and the final result thereof will be a freshened and mightier faith in a divine-human Bible, infallible as a whole, because as a whole self-interpretative to the mental mood which it itself kindles and maintains.

Here, if I mistake not, is the secret of the final mastery of the Bible upon the modern mind. We need the whole Bible in order to interpret any word in it, but the whole Bible taken together does interpret every word in it, and this total impression leads me to the gates of life, leads me to the bosom of the Father.

This position lies beneath thé critical discussion as to the date and authorship of various documents or parts of documents. It does not tell me who wrote Genesis, but it keeps me reasonably quiet while the critics are finding out who wrote Genesis.

Now to grasp this, to enunciate this, to stand for this rational infallibility of the whole Bible is the high and noble office of any society that in our age is building a Christian future.

Saying this I "rest my case," as the lawyers say, and close with my glad comrade cry of God-speed, good cheer, and again God-speed. Can we, without loss of the ancient sanctity and spiritual power of the Bible, merge the traditional views of it in a sane, large, vital way with this more rational view to which the Spirit of God in our age is leading the church? That is the living question. It is the peremptory question. It is the instant question of modern Protestantism. It is your instant question. Oh, great Endeavor Army! No more vital challenge is flung upon you as you wheel out into the splendid open of the twentieth century than this: What attitude will you take toward the Bible?

The Bible is the incarnatioh of a living God in the whole of a supreme literature, in which certain turret tops of living light furnish view point and lens from which and by which all minor statements may be understood, all local limitations adjusted, all personal equations balanced, all casual inaccuracies, if there be such, corrected.

I love to recall my clear faith that the genius of this noble society will be endued by God's grace with that union of practical wisdom, of intellectual honesty, of spiritual passion which, all at once alive, and all working together, shall take the Bible in this larger, living way, so fulfilling the ancient Scripture, "holding forth the word of life" along the entire scale of consecrated intellect and chivalrous devotion in a spirit at once knightly and sacramental, in service to humanity in God's name.

CHAPTER XXXIII.

The Happiest Peace on Earth.

Rev. Ira Landrith.

God leads his leaders. He manages the surrendered minds he has made. Let the too materialistic Christian believe if he will that the universe is but a monster machine set a-going at creation and fated to be controlled by inexorable laws with which even Omnipotence cannot in the slightest degree interfere; but some of us must be allowed to believe that God does sufficiently interrupt the course of affairs to require his servants to produce great ideas for great crises. Four years ago in San Francisco the Lord used the brain, pen and voice of Dr. Francis E. Clark to give expression to such an idea. It was a thought born for such a time as this:

"In seeking a closer walk with God, let us give more attention to family religion. A multitude of Christian Endeavorers have, within the past sixteen years been set together in families. As the years come and go other millions will enter these same relations. The Endeavorers of America can within the next decade distinctly raise the tone of the religious life of the nation. Why not carry our Endeavor principles into the family? Let us promote family religion by making more of daily household worship, and by having, at least once a week, family Christian Endeavor worship, in which every member, even to the lisping four-year-old shall have some personal participation. Let the children of Christian parents grow up as confessing, outspoken disciples of Christ in the family, making their choice of Him early, and never remembering the time when they did not love Him. . . . The family for Christ."

Let us now make the suggestion a permanent part of the Christian Endeavor movement. It would be putting first things first to carry Christian Endeavor into the most important business on earth, home making. Underestimating nothing which the Young People's Society of Christian Endeavor has done it is still insisted that family religion is of vaster value than any other of its practical endeavors. It is better than denominational loyalty, for domestic loyalty is prime preparation for every other kind. It is better than interdenominational fellowship, for he who is supremely happy in his own home will be happy in his church and joyful in the fellowship of other churches. It is better than Christian citizenship, for when the home is right the citizen will do right. It is better than Tenth Legions or Macedonian Phalanxes, or Comrades of the Quiet Hour, or even consecration meetings, piedges, and committee work. All these are good but every one of them would be better as a result of a needed revival at the heart of all religious life, the family circle. In these twenty years Christian Endeavor has transformed many of our churches and has blessed all of them. Let it now set itself to the task of transforming and blessing our homes. Ring it out in your conventions, let it echo and re-echo in our echo meetings, give it the first place on the programmes of your local unions and individual societies, print it large in your literature —Christian Endeavor stands for Christianity in the home. Let the Board of Trustees and the executive officers of the United Society adopt as the first new movement of Christian Endeavor for the twentieth century, The C. E. Home Circle, or some fitter name to be suggested by the inventive genius of the Boston office. Let there be a certificate of membership to adorn the walls of our homes, a pledge, and suggestive and helpful literature about family worship and domestic Christian service in general.

If this movement needs any justification find it in the fact that the Juniors in the first Christian Endeavor societies are fathers and mothers now, while the older members then are grandparents today. Shall not Christian Endeavor continue to be a blessing to its first friends? Shall it be guilty of the suicidal policy of losing from its ranks and from the circle of its influence the men and the women whom it has trained and to whose labors it has the right to lay claim, and to bless whose lives it is still its first duty? Properly promoted this would give immortality to the Christian Endeavor movement. It would cover with confusion the cynic who is trying, by telling it to others, to persuade himself that Christian Endeavor is dying out. Are there not four millions of us? Are we not, to use the characteristically delicate and expressive language of Dr. Clark, being set together in families? Has not the croaker from the beginning declared, in effect, that it was a matchmaking society, and that the initials C. E. stand for "courting everywhere?" Cheerfully let us accept the sneer as a compliment, and make the most of it. Certainly if there are in all the world any two people who should be "set together" in a family a devout young Christian Endeavor man and a consecrated young Christian Endeavor woman are those twain. Forbid not the bans, but rather let these young people go from the marriage altar pledged not only to mortal fidelity but also as Christian Endeavorers to the sublime duty of devout homemaking.

But there is another sufficient reason for the prompt inauguration of this new idea in Christian Endeavor. The home itself which should be the source, normal and abounding, of all true righteousness and patriotism, culture, and happiness is threatened by a hundred enemies. It is of the utmost importance that something should be done to set the world agog about the home, its duties and its dangers; for when people think, they are reasonably safe. There would be immeasurable meaning in the fact that 60,000 Christian Endeavor societies are engaged in considering the conditions which contribute to the ideal Christian Home. There would be abundant reason for the new birth of hope for the future of the church and the state, if, with its splendid organization, its matchless machinery, and its superb literature, the whole Christian Endeavor movement should be set to this task, among others—the labor of discovering and destroying the foes of the fireside, and of finding and enthroning the influences that should reign in the realm domestic.

Chief among the hazards of the home today is the fact that we have grown too busy for household duty and joy. Have you read "A Plain Talk with Young Men and Women Who Work," a capital book by the wizard of Christian Endeavor, Prof. Amos R. Wells? In it is a fable which is remarkable for being more nearly true than is most history. It is the story of a lithe-limbed young farmer who went out in the early morning to plow. In the crisp air of the new day you might have heard his cheery voice as he bade his beast go on, urged forward by the keen crack of a whip which the sturdy youth wielded above his back the ox moved forth across the field. Noontide came and the plowman but bent lower over his task. The evening shadows grew long but the absorbed worker was all unmindful of the vanishing day. Deaf to the melody of day-long bird songs, and blind to all the beauty about him, the worker thought only of his task, and plodded painfully on. Suddenly the bent shoulders felt the cruel cut of the whip, and glancing down made the astounding discovery that the hands with which he had grasped the plow handles had turned to hoofs, and that instead of driving he was now drawing the plow, and being driven by the ox. It is not a fable it is a photograph. Ours is a too strenuous age. We have too little time from our toil to devote to our homes. Even those of us who are Christian workers are not at this point the least guilty—some of us, alas, are the chief of sinners. We have succeeded in persuading ourselves that old heresy is orthodox—that God requires some men to neglect their own homes and children in order to serve Him, as if there were anywhere service more divine than is the training of those who are of one's own flesh and blood. We need to be reminded that every child in the world has a native right to the constant influence and training of both a father and a mother, masculine and feminine culture. It was God's plan for making men more refined and considerate and women in every way more stalwart and sturdy. It would be a calamity incalculably great if the present generation of children should be exclusively mother-reared; yet are we not rapidly drifting in our too-hurried lives toward the point where a man is the head of his home only in his wife's name? The time has come—it ought to have arrived sooner—when we must spend as much time studying home-making as we ever spent pondering the problems of success in business. The proposition of a current magazine has in it more of the elements of earnestness than jest: that our schools for girls should establish chairs on husband and home-keeping. Our schools for boys might do well not to be outstripped in this suggested educational progress. What with the business which keeps us away from home all day, and the club-life and social demands which lure us from our firesides at night, there is little opportunity for our children to share with us any good thing which we might be or do; and now that our wives have also discovered the club and are insisting upon such a declaration of "independence" as will make them our competitors in business and professional life it begins to look as if we were about to have to do by proxy all our work at home and with our children.

But the kind of homes in which we live are not the least of the dangers that threaten the households within. The crowded flat, with its plausible pleas for co-operative housekeeping, greatly increases the difficulties; while the boarding house is positively fatal to true home life. We must be reasonable, of course, and there may be conditions under which it is impossible for a family to live apart from other families, and when a boarding house may be a financial necessity; but certainly there is great loss when a child cannot live in a house which deserves the honored name of home, and somewhere about which there is a plat of green grass all his own. Laziness and stinginess have no right to deny to childhood these inherited domestic privileges.

Perhaps the greatest dangers menacing the home are those growing out of what has been aptly denominated the industrial heresy that every woman should be a wage earner, and as a result of which there are among the five million American bread-winning women so many who ought to be home-keeping women. All honor to the woman who works at a trade or in some other lucrative pursuit because she must to keep the wolf from her own door or from the portal of some other's home; but let us not be in haste to glorify the woman who seeks a salary merely to be "independent" of those upon whom she has the natural and moral right to be dependent. The only truly independent woman is the home-making woman, and the woman who most deserves and should most surely have the largest attainable earnings is she who gladdens a home for the worthy toiler who is its head, her husband or her father. It is no evidence of progress, the advanced woman to the contrary notwithstanding, that one-twelfth of all the women and girls of this country are at work for wages, nor is it a mark of progress that, whereas forty years ago only twenty trades and professions were open to women, there are now 360, so that a woman may be a butcher, a baker, a candle-stick maker, or anything else which her brother or her husband might aspire to be. If there were fewer avocations open to working women fewer women who do not need thus to toil for value received would leave their homes uncared for while they elbowed their deserving and needy sisters in competition until the average income of working women is but four dollars and fifty cents a week, considerably less than half the average sum paid to men who work in the same relations. The most womanly of American women has declared truly, "Home is woman's climate, her native air, her vital breath," and in full sympathy with this sentiment of Frances E. Willard is the pleasing prophecy of Flora McDonald Thompson, "The twentieth century will witness the splendid spectacle of prodigal wives returning to the domestic sphere under the stern tyranny of the truth they have learned about themselves." Call not that sphere narrow, O thou new woman, for thy views are destined to undergo a happy change as soon as thou dost become some worthy man's old woman. It is estimated that 80 per cent. of the crime committed in our cities is chargeable to people who never knew the benefits of genuine home life. Some one has said that a woman has the right to do whatever she can do well, adding that a woman ought to do whatever she can do better than a man; and it is true, but it is only half the truth, the other half being, a woman must do whatever only a woman can do. A woman can do a great many things as well as a man, but only a woman can make a home. Even better than a woman a man can build a house, but it is only a house, until under the alchemy of a woman's touch it is transformed into a home. Note this, too, oh ye women ambitious for "careers." Everywhere else in relation to men, women are competitors; in homes they are queens of realms exclusively their own.

The world's great need, then, is not tariff reform, nor currency reform, nor even temperance reform, necessary as either or all of these and a hundred others like them may be—the world's chief need is home reform. To that end, no woman is too noble, and none too wise, to sit and serve at the cradle-side of her own babe; for

"The night hath a thousand eyes, and the day but one,
But the light of the whole earth dies with the setting sun.
The mind hath a thousand eyes, and the heart but one,
But the light of the whole life dies when love is done."

My time is out and I have but just reached the point where I could begin to speak on my appointed theme, "The Happiest Place on Earth." If I owe an apology for thus departing from the topic assigned me, allow me to make it by humbly saying that I have been no less than half conscious of a divine call to diverge. It is my prayer that when this morning's session, devoted as it is to The Twentieth Century Home, shall have closed, it will be impossible for the Christian Endeavor movement ever more to be rid of the duty of espousing "Christianity in the Home" as chief among the cardinal principles governing the society and its individual members.

To make our homes the happiest places in the world they must be of all places the holiest. No other temple is so sacred as that wherein the husband and father is the high priest; and no altar is so worthy of seraphim guards as is the one at the fireside; and verily if there were more such altars in the home there would be fewer skeletons in the closet. Of course I had meant to say that the home should be the dwelling place of mutual love and confidence; that it should be the best and brightest of all schools, and the most desirable of clubs. Of course I meant to add that into it should be brought every pure amusement, and that no other kind should be allowed to exist anywhere. It was my further purpose to insist that the cheeriest and dearest of all the playmates of our children should be their own fathers and mothers, and that a man who is too stiff and dignified to let his lusty four-year-old son convert him into an Arabian horse, tangling chubby fingers in that horse's mane, ought to be bald without hope of the successful application of hair restorers. I would have been glad to insist at length upon making our homes the playhouses of our own and our neighbor's children.

All this and more I had planned to say about "The Happiest Place on Earth," which of course is the home where there are children, for what is home without a baby? But it is now too late, and I shall tax your time no longer, if you will but allow one of the sweetest of our Southern singers, Frank L. Stanton, to express for me the sentiments which I have not the gift of worthy words to utter:

"Des a li'l' cabin, en a white road leadin' ter it;
I follers up de furrer, en I hoe de cotton fer it;
    Chillun on de flo',
    En a woman in de do',
Singin' en singin' in de mawnin'

"Des a li'l' cabin in de shadder er de pines,
Frame wid honeysuckles en de mornin'-glory vines;
    Li'l' spot o' groun'
    Wid de chillun playin' roun',
Singin' en singin' in de mawnin'.

"Des a li'l' cabin whar de firelight I see,
Twinklin' er a welcome 'cross de cotton-fiel's ter me:
    Sayin', 'Whar you roam,
    Heah's yo' home, yo' home, yo' home!'
Singin' en singin' in de mawnin'.

"Des a li'l' cabin; yit it frequent 'pear so high
Dey kin hear what we a-sayin' in de mansions in de sky!
    Dis word de sweet word said:
    'Give us our daily bread!'
Singin' en singin' in de mawnin'.

"Des a li'l' cabin whar de blue smoke rise en curl
Kin hal' enough er happiness ter reach eroun' de worl'!
    Dey tells me dat I po'—
    But de woman's in de do'
Singin' en singin' in de mawnin'."

CHAPTER XXXIV.

The Special Meetings and Conferences.

THE PASTORS' MEETING. — PERSONAL EQUIPMENT CONFERENCES. — PERSONAL WORKERS' CONFERENCES. — THE MISSION WORKERS' CONFERENCE. — THE JUNIOR WORKERS' CONFERENCE. — THE DAILY QUIET HOURS. — THE DAILY BIBLE TEACHING MEETINGS.

The Pastors' Meeting.

More than three hundred pastors gathered in Auditorium Ohio on Monday afternoon,—a splendid and inspiring company. They came together to ask questions, and the person at whom the multiplied queries were fired was the one man best fitted to answer them, best fitted by wide experience, native genius, and broad human sympathies,—Charles M. Sheldon. Here are some of the questions and replies:

"How can a young minister help in the spread of the Kingdom by his pen?"

Dr. Sheldon told how some young Kansas ministers had obtained from near-by editors the use of several columns in their papers, and employed the space as they thought best for the community.

"What suggested to you the writing of 'In His Steps?'"

"When I went to my parish, I found myself in a sparsely settled district; and I found, too, that I didn't know enough to preach two sermons on Sunday. Moreover, I found that the young people would come out to hear a story, and I didn't want the business men to come out on Sunday evening, since I found that their home life needed them then. So I wrote 'In His Steps' sitting out on the porch with the thermometer for days 104 degrees in the shade."

"How do you conduct your Sunday evening services?"

Dr. Sheldon described his plan: a ten-minute prayer service in his study with the Endeavor prayer-meeting committee and leader; an hour's Christian Endeavor meeting, the pastor present or in his study; at eight he enters the room and speaks on the Christian Endeavor subject just as long as he pleases, sometimes an hour; finally, a social hour and Christian Endeavor committee meetings, so that often he is with his young people three hours on Sunday evenings. He has found ninety-five ministers in Connecticut who are already pursuing this plan.

"Does this plan reach the unsaved?"

Dr. Sheldon expressed his belief that evangelistic work should not be relegated to the evening service. "Every preaching service should be evangelistic." He can always make an appeal to sinners in connection with the Christian Endeavor topic, and he always does.

"Why don't you preach on the street corners?"

"I am going to."

"How do you reach the young men?"

"I get acquainted with them, play ball with them, visit them, get them to visit me, try to be one of them."

"What plan of raising money do you approve?"

"I think the only plan worth the name is to put one's hands in his pocket and pull out the money."

"How do you conduct your midweek meetings?"

"We are going to have more of a program. Last winter we spent two months talking about the family and its dangers. This fall we are going to have three months of Bible study, everybody bringing his Bible."

"How much time do you give to prayer?"

"Sometimes all the time."

"How long does your prayer meeting last?"

"As long as we want it."

"Suppose a prominent State official, a church member, openly espouses the cause of the saloon. Should the pastors criticise him openly and by name in their sermons?"

"Yes, after faithful private remonstrance."

From a colored pastor: "What do you think should be the attitude of the pastors towards the lawlessness and mob violence of the present day?"

"It is our duty as prophets to preach against every wrong."

"Will you not kindly define a sermon?" (This from G. Campbell Morgan.)

"A sermon is anything that puts God's truth into the hearts of men."

"Do you always write your sermons?"

"Very seldom."

"When do you have the most conversions?"

"I think that conversions should come all the year round."

("Hear! Hear!" from G. Campbell Morgan.)

"How do you choose your themes for sermons?"

"By what happens among the people during the week. I go out among them every afternoon of the week."

"Do you get definite results in conversions from the Sunday school?"

"Yes, I believe we preach too much to the old people. I don't believe any preacher could do better than to preach for two solid months, every Sunday morning, solely to the children of the Sunday school."

MISS KOCH'S CONFERENCES.

One feature that deserves prominent notice was the daily "personal equipment" conference, conducted by Miss Margaret Koch, of Waterville, Me. Out of her large experience as a teacher, the leader gave valuable suggestions for training the voice, the body, and all the powers for the largest use in Christian Endeavor work.

Her topics were unique and profitable, such as, "Bodily and Vocal Development an Aid to Power in Christian Endeavor Work," "The Relation of Expression to Power in Christian Work," "How to Read the Bible." Since Endeavor emphasizes serving Christ with all there is of the man or woman, these conferences were of a most helpful nature, and the many that attended them felt amply repaid.

THE PERSONAL WORKERS' CONFERENCES.

A crowded house to hear prayer discussed is a spectacle that excites no comment in a Christian Endeavor convention, especially when Dr. R.

A. Torrey, of Chicago, is the speaker. The Bible study conferences which he conducted daily were a feature much talked of, and eagerly attended by hundreds. One young man was overheard to say, "This lay-out of fat things keeps me on the jog, but I'll miss dinner before I'll miss Torrey's meetings." Never before was the Bible teaching on prayer so succinctly and profitably set forth. The practical hints of Rev. H. W. Pope, one of the promoters of the Northfield extension movement, were golden nuggets to those desirous of becoming personal workers. The hour a day spent in this school of inspiration and methods may easily mean untold development of latent evangelistic forces in thousands of lives.

"The Importance of Prayer."

Rev. R. A. Torrey, D. D., Chicago, Ill.

The apostles regarded prayer as the most important business of their lives. All the mighty men of God outside the Bible have been men of prayer. They have differed from one another in many things, but in this they have been alike. But there is a still weightier reason for this constant prayer. It occupied 'a very prominent place and played a very important part in the life of our Lord. Again, praying is the most important part of His present ministry. Christ's ministry did not close with His death. What His great present work is, by which He carries our salvation on to completeness, we read in Heb. 7:25: "Wherefore He is able also to save them to the uttermost that come unto God by Him, seeing He ever liveth to make intercession for them." This verse tells us that Jesus is able to save us unto the uttermost, not merely from the uttermost, but unto the uttermost, unto entire completeness, absolute perfection, because He not merely died, but because He also "ever liveth."

Prayer is the means that God has appointed for our receiving mercy, and obtaining grace to help. Heb. 4:16 is one of the simplest and sweetest verses in the Bible,—"Let us therefore come boldly unto the throne of grace, that we may obtain mercy, and find grace to help in time of need." These words make it very plain that God has appointed a way by which we shall seek and obtain mercy and grace. The next reason for constant, persistent, sleepless, overcoming prayer is that prayer in the name of Jesus Christ is the way Jesus Christ Himself has appointed for His disciples to obtain fullness of joy. He states this simply and beautifully in John 16:24, "Hitherto have ye asked nothing in My name; ask, and ye shall receive, that your joy may be fulfilled." "Made full" is the way the Revised Version reads. Who is there that does not wish his joy filled full? Well, the way to have it filled full is by praying in the name of Jesus. Again, the reason for constant prayer, in every care and anxiety and need of life, with thanksgiving, is the means that God has appointed for our obtaining freedom from all anxiety, and the peace of God which passeth all understanding. "Be careful for nothing," says Paul, "but in everything by prayer and supplication with thanksgiving let your requests be made known unto God, and the peace of God which passeth all understanding shall keep your hearts and minds through Christ Jesus." (Phil. 4:6, 7.) Prayer is the method that God Himself has appointed for our obtaining the Holy Spirit. Upon this point the Bible is very plain. Jesus says, "If ye then, being evil, know how to give good gifts unto your children, how much more shall your Heavenly Father give the Holy Spirit to them that ask Him?" (Luke 11:13.) If we would only spend more time in prayer, there would be more fullness of the Spirit's power in our work. Many and many a man who once worked unmistakably in the power of the Holy Spirit is now filling the air with empty shoutings, and beating it with his meaningless gesticulations, because he has let prayer be crowded out.

THE MISSION WORKERS.

The daily mission workers' conference, conducted by Mr. J. Lawrence Thurston of Whitinsville, Mass., was a centre of interest. Here the cream of the Convention might be found. The prominent missionaries in the Convention gravitated hither. If one wanted to grasp the hand of Willis R. Hotchkiss, the hero of East Central Africa, or have the privilege of a word with Dr. Ament, of Boxer-persecution fame, this was the best place to come.

Mr. Thurston's level-headed, vigorous management ensured a successful conference. Fuel was piled on the missionary fire that will make it burn warmer in many a society.

THE JUNIOR CONFERENCE.

At the conferences there was a full and free discussion of some of the problems that perplex the Junior superintendents. Mrs. Clark presided at these conferences, and among the Junior workers who took part in the discussion were Miss Kate Haus, Mrs. M. L. Hageman, Miss LeBaron, Miss Travis and many others whose names are familiar to Endeavorers. Here are a few of the questions and answers:—

"How has the pledge helped your boys and girls?"

"They are reading their Bibles more regularly and more thoughtfully than they would have done if they had not signed this pledge.". "They pray more, and more sincerely."

"How do you guard the pledge, and make sure that the children know what they are doing when they sign it?"

"Hold little special prayer meetings with those who wish to sign it." "Talk over each promise of the pledge separately." "Let the children practice the pledge for a few weeks before they promise." "Give each child five or six questions on the pledge to be answered in writing." "Talk with the parents before their children sign it." "It ought to mean the beginning of the Christian life to those who have not already begun it." "The pastor ought to have something to say about it when a child signs the pledge and begins the Christian life."

"The pastor ought to sign the pledge and be an active member with the Juniors; though not perhaps taking part in every meeting, yet he ought to be there and know what the Juniors are doing, that he may know how to help them." (This from a pastor.)

"How do you secure reverence in the meetings?"

"Teach the children to remember that they are in God's house." "Never have a prayer offered till the room is perfectly still." "Wait till every head is bowed and every eye closed before praying." "Ask the pastor to preach a children's sermon on reverence." "Ask the pastor to preach to the older people about reverence." "Cultivate a spirit of reverence among the older Endeavorers." "Take some of the Juniors to the older Christian Endeavor meeting, and ask the Endeavorers to set them an example of reverence." It will be good for the older Endeavorers, too.

DR. CARSON AND MR. MORGAN.

One of the most interesting characters of the Convention was Rev. G. Campbell Morgan, and the place of his daily special meetings was a Mecca toward which eager feet pressed every morning. The purpose of these meetings, in which Dr. J. F. Carson, of Brooklyn, was Mr. Morgan's powerful and wise associate, was to unfold the Bible doctrine of the Holy Spirit. Mr. Morgan's tall, spare figure, his rugged, striking features, and his refreshingly original though entirely unaffected manners, give great piquancy to his thoughtful utterances. Mr. Morgan is an animated speaker, but not a nervous one. When he reads the Scriptures, he does not read with his lips alone, but with his whole body. He emphasizes words not only by his flexible voice, but by nods and shakes and tossings of his head, by pursing his lips and by his uplifted eyebrows. For the most part, the expression on his face is the seriousness of a man tremendously in earnest over heart-burdening problems. But now and then his homely features are so transfigured by a smile that a beauty almost unearthly irradiates them. When Mr. Morgan approaches a climax, sometimes he crouches like a gladiator who is about to hurl himself forward in some supreme effort, as if he would add the momentum of his body to the power of his message. He springs forward with the climacteric word, literally projecting himself, his personality with his words. And that is one of the secrets of his tremendous influence. He puts all of himself into his work. And the work of those precious hours of contact with him will mean unutterable good to the multitudes that listened.

THE QUIET HOURS.

"If God is not real to us—anything short of that is practical atheism." This was the opening thought of Dr. Cornelius Woelfkin's series of Quiet Hours in the Ninth Street Baptist Church. The theme that ran through all four of the luminous and uplifting services was "The Inner Man,"— "strengthened with might by His Spirit in the inner man," "for it is God that worketh in you."

There also ran through all the sessions the thought of Dr. Woelfkin's opening parable, the striking story of King Thelema, given a realm by a great Emperor on condition of loyalty, who had for his assistants a notable judge, a master artist, merchantmen of enterprise and skill, a musician of beauty and force, a wise scholar, a sacristan or librarian. The parable told of the King's revolt, of how the judge was a faithful remonstrant, but was silenced, of how the artist fell away from his ideals, of how all the other rulers of the King's council dropped with the King from their former glory and nobility. Sorrowful experience, a final return to fealty, and the long instruction of the loving Emperor leading Thelema and his associates back to their lost power and skill,—this completed the story. It was a story of the soul. Thelema is the will, assisted by Artist Imagination, Musician Love, Scholar Thought, Merchantmen Desires,· Judge Conscience, and Memory, the Master of the Rolls.

Following out this parable, Dr. Woelfkin, on successive mornings, gave a series of talks that searched every heart, fired every will, and purified every life of the many Endeavorers whose privilege it was to hear him.

The theme which Dr. Floyd W. Tomkins chose for the Quiet Hour meditation that he led, in the Second Presbyterian Church, was a vital and attractive one: "Our Best Friend; confessing Him, walking with Him, having Him within us."

The morning sunlight streamed in through the colored windows in rainbow tints, upon an audience that prized as a precious boon every seat on floor or in gallery, and even the standing-room around the wall.

Speaking of confessing Christ publicly, Dr. Tomkins said that a church notice of an eighth of an inch in a newspaper that elsewhere displays a page advertisement of a department store illustrates the meagreness of our confession of our need of Christ as compared with our consciousness of our need of temporal things.

As a means of walking with this best Friend, Dr. Tomkins suggested printing plainly some of the principles that controlled the life of Jesus and pasting them on the dressing-mirror. Speaking of duty, he said, "Don't serve God as a duty. Don't say, 'I must go to church, I must pray.' You don't say, 'I must kiss my loved one.' What kind of kiss would that be? God hates the word 'must.' He wants us to be glad to walk with Him." The Quiet Hour address of both Dr. Woelfkin and Dr. Tomkins, as well as those which Dr. Chapman had intended to give at Cincinnati, have all been nicely printed in cloth-bound volumes, and can be had from the United Society of Christian Endeavor at a cost of only 35 cents each volume.

THE LOVING-CUP

Presented by the Trustees to Dr. Clark.

CHAPTER XXXV.

Two Surprises Not on the Programme.

A pleasant surprise was sprung on Dr. Clark at the trustees' dinner to the local committee, speakers, and State officers. Dr. Teunis S. Hamlin, in words of generous appreciation, presented a large silver loving-cup, on behalf of the trustees.

The cup had three handles, and in acknowledging the gift, Dr. Clark asked Mr. Baer and Mr. Shaw to come forward and take each a handle, saying that the number must have been made three purposely, since it was to these two associates of his, as much as to himself, that the success of Christian Endeavor is due, recognizing always that all the blessings enjoyed through it came from above.

Once again, he said, he wished to express his obligations to another helper, out of whose Mizpah Circle had really sprung the first society, and he had Mrs. Clark join him in holding the cup.

Had there been scores of handles, instead of but three, he would have been glad, he said, to have all the trustees, and the others that had done so much to advance the movement, take hold with him.

The happy event closed by a presentation of the Committee of 1901, whose self-sacrificing efforts had kept the Convention running so smoothly without a jar or a break.

A Memorial Presented to President Clark at the Congregational Rally.

Hon. S. B. Capen, LL. D.

Dear Dr. Clark:—

It is more than twenty years since, in the far-away city of Portland, you, as pastor of the Williston Congregational Church, organized among your own people the first Christian Endeavor Society. The little seed which you planted there in simple faith, and with no other thought than the honor of Jesus Christ, He has taken and blessed until the leaves of this tree have been for the healing of the nations. Not only in America, Europe, and Australia, but in India, Africa, Turkey, China, and Japan, there have grown up strong, vigorous societies, which are moulding the young life for righteousness. It is one of the great movements of the last century, and millions, for as many years as there are in time and eternity, will thank God for the inspiration that has come to them from what God has wrought through you.

At this Congregational Rally it has occurred to some of us to present to you a memorial. We have not chosen to put it in the form of a gift, which could easily have been done, but in a way which we think will be far more pleasing to you,—just a simple letter to which we have subscribed our names. The letters which I have received show with what love and affection you are regarded by your friends. Back of these names you can feel the warm hearts of loving friends, who most gladly bear this testimony of admiration for the modesty and Christlike spirit with which you have led these hosts of young people in service for the King.

We desire also to say that we have made no attempt to get a larger number of signatures to this memorial letter. If we had, tens of thousands would have rejoiced to be included upon such a roll. We have rather chosen to take a few men in the different States and of all professions and callings to represent these multitudes. In addition, then, to these names, remember those others, from Maine to California, whom we could not reach, but whose hearts will respond with ours in glad joy when they read what is being done here.

We have also, for today only, limited the names to those of our own Congregational polity. We rejoice to know that the Presbyterians at their late General Assembly gave a section of their denominational exhibit to Christian Endeavor, with photographs of many of the leaders, of the birthplace of the movement, and of the little stone church where you were baptized. While this great sister denomination is thus recognizing this great work, we can do no less than take this special notice of you whom God has so signally used in marshaling the young life of the world for aggressive Christian work.

We glory continually, however, in the thought that no one denomination can hold you, but that you are leading a movement which is helping more and more to break down narrow sectarianism and unite in practical fellowship the followers of Christ in all the world.

May the Lord spare your life for many years still to lead the hosts to nobler achievement and more glorious service.

Rev. Francis E. Clark, D. D., President United Society of Christian Endeavor.

Dear Friend:—At the first International Christian Endeavor Convention of the new century, will you permit us in this gathering of Congregationalists to present to you this letter signed by a few of the thousands who, if opportunity had offered, would gladly have joined in this message of love and good will? It seems to us most fitting that at this gathering those who have no official connection with the movement, but who have watched with interest its growing power, should thus express their appreciation of you and the work God has wrought through you. It is now a little over twenty years since you organized the first society in the Williston Congregational Church, Portland, Me. Thus the movement has special claims upon Congregationalists. It was begun by a Congregationalist in a Congregational church, and the first news regarding it was given to the public through one of our denominational newspapers, The Congregationalist. The societies have found a place in the work of more than five-sixths of all Congregational churches.

These things we believe it has done:—

First, It has federated millions of young men and young women in common service for Jesus Christ. It has been one of the mightiest forces in the closing years of the century in developing healthy and real Christian character.

Second, In connection with Young Men's Christian Associations, it has been a large factor in helping to bring about closer fellowship with those of other denominations. It has contributed much to destroy the spirit of narrow sectarianism.

Third, It has inculcated a proper denominational loyalty, especially to the missionary work of our denomination. You and your associates have been unceasing in urging benevolence as a proof of discipleship, and all our missionary boards have been enriched thereby. Through the "Tenth Legion" you have made this most practical.

Fourth, You have helped to educate our young people to understand the history and principles of missionary work, and thus have aided materially in training up a generation of intelligent givers.

Fifth, The movement has helped to make manly, stalwart Christians, who in the college and the place of business have gladly worn the "C. E." pin, and honored that for which it stands.

Sixth, You have led young people along the lines of true Christian citizenship. It was Robert Ross, of Troy, a Christian Endeavorer, who defended the ballot-box by the sacrifice of his life; and because of the inspiration of your words, young men all over the land are more and more entering into the battle for civic righteousness.

Seventh, It has recognized the importance of child life, which has too often been sadly neglected in our churches. Through the Junior societies it has sought to teach our little children the great truths that centre around the cross.

Eighth, While Christian Endeavor has required a definite pledge, which is very important if we would have our young people properly appreciate that there is something vital and real in the Christian life, yet it allows the greatest flexibility, so that any pastor can adapt the movement to local conditions. It cares not for the form, but for the substance. It insists on that which will help to make heroic, Christian character.

Ninth, Its great conventions have been a continual surprise. To these gatherings the greatest and wisest of our leaders have gladly come from all over the world, that they might instruct, mould, and fire this young life. These enthusiastic young people have been a mighty help to every community where meetings have been held.

As you enter the new century you may rightly have great courage and hope. With the splendid group of men working with you, we believe that, under the blessing of God, you will be able to lead us on to still larger things. You will be ready with large plans to meet the new emergencies which the coming years will bring. Holding to all that is best in the past, we feel sure you will gladly accept the new light that comes, for the great work of Christian Endeavor is not yet complete. May the Master continue to lead you day by day in all the future years.

Very sincerely yours,

EDUCATORS.

Pres. William J. Tucker, New Hampshire; Pres. Jas. B. Angell, Michigan; Pres. John K. McLean, California; Pres. Wm. D. Hyde, Maine; Pres. C. F. Thwing, Ohio; Pres. W. F. Slocum, Colorado; Pres. M. H. Buckham, Vermont; Pres. C. D. Hartranft, Connecticut; Pres. Jas. W. Strong, Minnesota; Pres. E. D. Eaton, Wisconsin; Pres. W. G. Sperry, Michigan; Pres. Stephen B. L. Penrose, Washington; Pres. Thomas McClelland, Illinois; Pres. C. F. P. Bancroft, Massachusetts; Pres. J. H. Sawyer, Massachusetts; Prof. Egbert C. Smyth, Massachusetts; Prof. George F. Moore, Massachusetts; Prof. F. K. Sanders, Connecticut; Prof. Williston Walker, Connecticut; Prof. A. L. Gillett, Connecticut; Prof. E. K. Mitchell, Connecticut; Prof. A. R. Merriam,

Connecticut; Prof. C. J. H. Ropes, Maine; Prof. C. A. Beckwith, Maine; Prof. G. Frederick Wright, Ohio; Prof. H. C. King, Ohio; Prof. E. I. Bosworth, Ohio; Prof. Franklin W. Fisk, Illinois; Prof. H. M. Scott, Illinois; Prof. Graham Taylor, Illinois; Prof. W. Douglas Mackenzie, Illinois; Prof. George Mooar, California; Prof. C. S. Nash, California; Pres. James G. Merrill, Tennessee; W. R. Moody, Massachusetts.

CIVIL LIFE.

Judge David J. Brewer, Washington, D. C.; Gov. W. Murray Crane, Massachusetts; Hon. O. Vincent Coffin, Connecticut; Gen. O. O. Howard, Vermont; Joseph Cook, New York.

EDITORS.

Rev. Lyman Abbott, New York; Rev. William Hayes Ward, New York; Rev. A. E. Dunning, Massachusetts; Rev. H. A. Bridgman, Massachusetts; Rev. E. F. Williams, Illinois; Rev. E. H. Merrill, Wisconsin; Rev. J. A. Adams, Illinois; Rev. Simeon Gilbert, Illinois.

MISSIONARY WORK.

Rev. Judson Smith, Massachusetts; Rev. Joseph B. Clark, New York; Rev. A. F. Beard, New York; Rev. C. H. Daniels, Massachusetts; Rev. C. J. Ryder, New York; Rev. G. H. Gutterson, Massachusetts; W. B. Howland, New York; Rev. Harlan P. Beach, New Jersey; Rev. Henry Fairbanks, Vermont; Rev. Joshua Coit, Massachusetts; Rev. L. H. Cobb, New York; Rev. G. A. Hood, Massachusetts; Rev. E. E. Strong, Massachusetts; H. W. Hubbard, New York; Rev. Washington Choate, New York; Rev. Geo. M. Boynton, Massachusetts; Rev. D. W. Waldron, Massachusetts; Rev. George R. Merrill, Minnesota; Rev. W. H. Willcox, Massachusetts; F. H. Wiggin, Massachusetts; M. C. Hazard, Massachusetts; J. H. Tewksbury, Massachusetts.

PASTORS.

Rev. George C. Adams, California; Rev. Theodore T. Munger, Connecticut; Rev. E. C. Moore, Rhode Island; Rev. Asher Anderson, Connecticut; Rev. Alexander McKenzie, Massachusetts; Rev. S. H. Howe, Connecticut; Rev. Charles Ray Palmer, Connecticut; Rev. John De Peu, Connecticut; Rev. S. M. Newman, Dist. of Columbia; Rev. J. R. Thurston, Massachusetts; Rev. H. H. Kelsey, Connecticut; Rev. W. E. Park, New York; Rev. H. P. Dewey, New York; Rev. Frederick A. Noble, Illinois; Rev. Wm. H. Davis, Massachusetts; Rev. D. M. Pratt, Ohio; Rev. W. A. Waterman, Indiana; Rev. Frank S. Fitch, New York; Rev. J. W. Bixler, Connecticut; Rev. Arthur Little, Massachusetts; Rev. Wm. E. Griffis, New York; Rev. S. H. Virgin, Massachusetts; Rev. T. B. McLeod, New York; Rev. C. P. Mills, Massachusetts; Rev. A. W. Hazen, Connecticut; Rev. A. Z. Conrad, Massachusetts; Rev. Willard Scott, Massachusetts; Rev. Reuen Thomas, Massachusetts; Rev. DeWitt S. Clark, Massachusetts; Rev. Charles E. Jefferson, New York; Rev. James G. Vose, Rhode Island; Rev. C. M. Southgate, Massachusetts; Rev. Samuel E. Herrick, Massachusetts; Rev. Charles H. Richards, Pennsylvania; Rev. James W. Cooper, Connecticut; Rev. Henry A. Stimson, New York; Rev. W. E. Barton, Illinois; Rev. Cyrus Richardson, New Hampshire; Rev. Judson Titsworth, Wisconsin; Rev. Dan F. Bradley, Michigan; Rev. W. T. McElveen, Massachusetts; Rev. Richard Cordley, Kansas; Rev. A. H. Bradford, New Jersey; Rev. L. H. Hallock, Minnesota; Rev. R. T. Hall, Connecticut; Rev. N. A. Hyde, Indiana; Rev. N. Dwight Hillis, New York; Rev. A. W. Ackerman, Oregon; Rev. C. W. Hiatt, Ohio; Rev. C. H. Patton, Missouri; Rev. G. R. Leavitt, Wisconsin; Rev. D. N. Beach, Colorado; Rev. Sidney Strong, Illinois; Rev. W. H. G. Temple, Washington; Rev. E. P. Ingersoll, New York; Rev. F. L. Goodspeed, Massachusetts; Rev. Smith Baker, Maine; Rev. E. N. Packard, New York;

Rev. A. H. Plumb, Massachusetts; Rev. A. G. Upton, Idaho; Rev. E. M. Vittum, Iowa; Rev. C. M. Sheldon, Kansas; Rev. P. S. Moxom, Massachusetts; Rev. W. B. Thorp, Illinois; Rev. J. B. Gregg, Colorado; Rev. M. Burnham, Missouri; Rev. A. J. Lyman, New York; Rev. Henry Hopkins, Missouri.

BUSINESS MEN.

Edward Whitin, Massachusetts; Dr. L. C. Warner, New York; A. Lyman Williston, Massachusetts; Charles A. Hopkins, Massachusetts; W. H. Wanamaker, Pennsylvania; H. H. Proctor, Massachusetts; Charles A. Hull, New York; Henry M. Moore, Massachusetts; Herbert J. Wells, Rhode Island; J. M. W. Hall, Massachusetts; G. Henry Whitcomb, Massachusetts; N. P. Dodge, Iowa; C. Henry Hutchins, Massachusetts; Frederick Fosdick, Massachusetts; W. W. Mills, Ohio; Lewis N. Gilbert, Massachusetts; David Fales, Illinois; S. C. Darling, Massachusetts; A. S. Johnson, Massachusetts; Frank Wood, Massachusetts; F. P. Shumway, Massachusetts; E. H. Pitkin, Illinois; William H. Rice, Illinois; David C. Bell, Minnesota; and many other pastors and laymen.

CHAPTER XXXVI.

Special Interesting Features.

THE EVANGELISTIC MEETINGS.—THE VETERANS' MEETING.—THE GERMAN CONVENTION.—THE STATE RALLIES.—THE MUSEUM.

THE EVANGELISTIC WORK.

The noonday evangelistic meetings were a vital feature of the Convention, and we are to have a full account of them written by Dr. C. L. Work, chairman of the evangelistic committee. The headquarters of this committee was one of the nerve centres of the Convention. It was a recruiting-office for the King's yeomanry. There were more volunteers than could be used in the dozen or more meetings held daily. The Philadelphia delegation assumed entire responsibility for one meeting. Some of the best speakers at the Convention gave their services. The larger manufacturing establishments, the railroad shops, and the parks and markets were used. On Sunday the asylums, homes, houses of refuge, and the prisons were visited. An especially interesting meeting was held in the jail.

THE VETERANS' MEETING.

"Just an informal little meeting," said President Clark. The veterans were those who have been ten years or more connected with Christian Endeavor societies. They filled the elegant amphitheatre of the Odeon. They were ready for any suggestion Dr. Clark might throw out for the good of our movement, recognizing that they are very largely responsible for Christian Endeavor success.

We veterans can become honorary members, honorable honorary members, honorary members that keep their pledge with reference to the older church-work. We can form Intermediate societies, so that all the young people may be set to work. We can bring about in some churches the separation of the society into two or more divisions, like the fourteen Christian Endeavor societies in Dr. Conwell's church. A pleasant emulation springs up among these divisions, and every one is thus set to work.

The oldest society in the world, the Williston society of Portland, Me., has just formed a Veterans' Association. Thus they will keep up the traditions, and hold for Christian Endeavor the love and wisdom of the old-time members. There will be correspondent members, also, since the old members are scattered all over the United States.

The Veterans' Association of the State officers of Massachusetts was described by Rev. W. P. Landers, and then the questions and suggestions flew thick and fast. "In our society we urge the older members to keep in the background." "In our society we urge every older Endeavorer to work himself out of the society, but only as he works some one else in."

The meeting will have a strong and healthy influence, and will do much toward the regeneration of many societies.

CONVENTION DER DEUTSCHEN VEREINE.

Comparatively few of the delegates knew that a second Christian Endeavor convention was in session at Cincinnati, its sessions running parallel to ours, but all in the German language. Beginning in Philippus Kirche on Sunday evening, this German convention held sessions throughout Monday and Tuesday in Zion's Kirche. With the exception of an address through an interpreter by Dr. Clark, every speaker was a German, and all the exercises, songs, and addresses were conducted in the rich German tongue.

We looked in on one of their sessions, and though we could not listen intelligently, we could readily translate the thronged church, the registration-book with its more than two hundred names, the bright decorations, the unique badge which they pinned on my coat, the earnestness of the speakers, and the evidently pleased attention of the strong-faced German men and sweet-faced German lassies.

It is certain that from this gathering will go forth a powerful influence in favor of Christian Endeavor among the Germans. The speakers were men of weight,—influential pastors, theological professors, editors, and Young Men's Christian Association secretaries. The themes were comprehensive. The discussions were marked by German thoughtfulness and by German practicality. We may confidently count on the Germans to bring from them practical results.

STATE SOCIABILITY.

Tuesday evening was given up to general jollification. It was a welcome period of relaxation from the prolonged attention required by our immense and campact programme. Nineteen of Cincinnati's noble churches, down-town, over on the Kentucky side, and in the wealthy hilltop suburbs, had been thrown open during the past week to delegates from all over the land. Their spacious auditoriums were adorned in many tasteful ways. Their prayer meeting and class rooms had been transformed to registration-booths, rest-rooms, committee-rooms of all kinds. The homes of the congregations had been exercising a beautiful hospitality. Thousands of pleasant acquaintances had been formed, acquaintances that often will ripen into true friendship. All this delightful intercourse, in which, after all, much of the value of our conventions consists, was caught up together on Tuesday evening, and bound into golden sheaves at the State rallies.

These rallies gave opportunity to hear the noted Convention speakers in their most familiar, informal moods. Scores of less-known speakers were also introduced, speakers of equal brilliancy and force. Many a Christian Endeavor orator has been discovered in these easy-going sessions.

Everywhere the churches were crowded, in many places crowded to their utmost capacity. All sorts of pretty souvenirs were given out to the guests, and refreshments were charmingly served by the most charming of young hostesses. Nor was the practical forgotten, and in many places the State officers used the opportunity most wisely to promote their work for the advancement of Christian Endeavor.

THE MUSEUM.

Between the sessions thousands found their way to the Christian Endeavor Museum, which occupied a long space in one of the corridors. Here was displayed the wonderful collection which by a fit providence has gravitated toward Mr. Merritt B. Holley, of Michigan. Counter after counter was weighed down with interesting articles; great masses of them hung against the wall or depended from the ceiling.

What was not there? Here were photographs of Endeavor societies in all parts of the world. Yonder were topic cards and pledges in a babel of languages. Then followed a collection of outlandish objects sent by Endeavorers of Africa, China, India, all creation. Behold the evolution of this paper, from the old blanket form of The Golden Rule, through all the many changes of cover, form, and type, down to the Cincinnati Convention number. Note the collection of rare Convention reports, from foreign lands and our own,—a very valuable set.

Many of the exhibits deserved prolonged study. "It requires consecrated thought," said a paragraph, "to prepare a heading. Examine these carefully." The collection showed some of the best headings devised by various Christian Endeavor unions. In the same way were classified all kinds of Christian Endeavor helps, committee aids, convention advertising, banners,—indeed, a truly bewildering variety, from the most cursory inspection of which one gained a profound respect for Christian Endeavor's versatility, its grasp on the world, its practicality, and its abounding enthusiasm.

The Cincinnati Prison Conference.

Frederick A. Wallace, Prison Superintendent of the Kentucky Christian Endeavo Union.

The Convention meeting in the interest of Christian Endeavor work for prisoners was a grand success. The Odeon was crowded even to the gallery, and the programme was carried out to the letter. Mr. Landrith, in his inimitable way presided, and Mr. Hillis in his own enthusiastic manner conducted the music. The solo of the latter, "The Bird with a Broken Pinion," was pathetic and beautiful, and the audience seemed deeply moved.

Dr. R. A. Torrey and Dr. Cornelius Woelfkin spoke on the "Christian's Responsibility to Their Brothers in Bonds," and I do not believe there was a soul in that large audience but felt that it was a duty to minister to these unfortunate men behind prison bars. Both of these speakers showed the audience very clearly that by ministering to these men they were ministering to Christ Himself. If the meeting had gone no further than this, it would have been a grand success.

And then, when Rev. H. W. Pope spoke, it seemed to me that the audience was even more deeply impressed; but the climax came when Dr. Charles M. Sheldon spoke upon "What Would Christ Do for the Prisoner of Today?" He first said that Christ would visit them. He dwelt at length upon this thought. He said also that Christ would improve the places of imprisonment, both in our county and State prisons, and he pleaded with Endeavorers to see that old and young prisoners were not confined together, so that young lives might not be brought into touch with hardened criminals. He then preached the need of repentance, and showed that sin is not a disease, refuting the sentimental idea that sin is a hereditary weakness alone.

Speaking of the possibilities of regeneration, Dr. Sheldon read a letter from a man who had been imprisoned seventeen times and who had broken nearly every law upon the calendar; yet he had became converted through the kindness of Christian workers, and is today a living monument of God's mercy and of the kindness of those who carried the gospel into prison walls.

Dr. Sheldon pleaded that devout Christian men might be in charge of the prisons, and not men who are as bad as the prisoners themselves, and who have been put in office simply through political "pull" and chicanery. The speaker closed his remarkable address by saying that Christ would seek to remove the cause that brought men to prison, and that the first thing that Christ would do would be to strike out the saloon. The official records of our State prisons today show that ninety per cent. of all imprisonment is due, directly or indirectly, to the cause of drink. From the saloon and from the tenement-houses is made the prison population. While Dr. Sheldon was passing through the slums of Cincinnati the evening before, the street-car had an accident and they were delayed for a short time, and all over the hot, dirty streets and sidewalks the little ragged, dirty-faced children were playing; and there was not a tree or a single spot of grass in sight, and many of them, no doubt, by their environment and by the example of the older ones about them, were being trained for the penitentiary. He said that he had never heard such oaths as these little children used. In this dark and barren region there was not a thing in sight to inspire these children to a thought beyond shame, poverty, and degradation; and then he went on to prove that the men who live in fine, luxurious homes, and own these tenement-houses, and huddle together this class of people with no inspiration toward spiritual, mental, or physical development, are greater criminals in the sight of God than many confined within prison walls. He dwelt at length upon this tenement question, and the audience was moved to feelings of deepest emotion. He said that if he had no other message to the Convention, he believed that the one he was now speaking was the one that God had sent him to deliver. I believe that it will be the beginning of a new crusade in and against the tenement districts of our cities.

The meeting closed with a very enthusiastic prison conference, several being on the floor and trying to speak at the same time, and we all left believing that prison work had been given an impetus that would soon establish it in every State in the Union.

CHAPTER XXXVII.

The Denominational Rallies.

Disciples of Christ.

Rev. John E. Pounds, D. D., Cleveland, Ohio, Chairman.

The large auditorium of Central Christian Church was crowded with enthusiastic Endeavorers, at the rally of the Disciples of Christ, and the programme was worthy of the occasion. Rev. F. D. Power, of Washington, D. C., always happy in his addresses to young people, was at his best in speaking of "The Endeavorers' Debt to America." Mrs. Helen E. Moses, Secretary of the Christian Woman's Board of Missions, was prevented from attending the Convention, but she sent her paper on "The Endeavorer Girl's Future." Rev. Charles S. Medbury, of Angola, Indiana, moved the audience deeply as he spoke with eloquence and power of "The True End of Endeavor Training." Benjamin L. Smith, Secretary of the Home Missionary Society, and representative of the local committee from Minneapolis, urged Endeavorers to attend the National Convention in that city next October, especially as a great Christian Endeavor rally is to be heled on Saturday night. R. H. Timme, who is partly supported by the Endeavorers in his work among the Germans, was introduced to the audience, and made a happy speech.

The most touching part of the service was the farewell to F. M. Rains, Secretary of the Foreign Society, who is about to depart for a visit to the mission stations of the world, and the introduction of returned missionaries. As E. E. Faris, from the heart of Africa, and G. L. Wharton and M. D. Adams, after long years of service in India, came before the audience, the spirit of heavenly fellowship seemed to enter every heart, and from every tongue came, with new meaning, the words, "Blest be the tie that binds."

The United Evangelical Church Rally.

Rev. U. F. Swengel, York, Pa., Chairman.

The rally of the United Evangelical Church was held in the Fergus Street Christian Church. Miss Carrie A. Parker presided at the organ and Mr. H. N. Stauffer offered prayer.

The chairman spoke of the royalty of Christ, the purity and loyalty of the Church as suggested by the purple and white which have been adopted as the colors of the Keystone League of Christian Endeavor.

Rev. N. W. Sager spoke on the Christian Sabbath and the duty of Christian Endeavorers in reference to it.

Miss Mabel L. Givler delivered an excellent address on "Spirituality in Our Meetings." She emphasized the responsibility of the devotional committee, the importance of the study of the topic as well as the fact that the leader should be a religious teacher and guided by the Holy Spirit. Three things should be observed, reverence, faith and enthusiasm.

Rev. H. C. Stephen spoke on the Christian Endeavorer's part in making the world better.

Mr. A. E. Stauffer spoke of the importance of taking an interest in the business meeting. A parliament on this topic brought out many helpful suggestions.

Rev. N. W. Sager called attention to the importance of having echo meetings of this great Convention of 1901 to spend its blessings far and wide.

A very interesting letter from Rev. C. N. Dubs, Missionary Superintendent in Hunan, China, was read by Rev. H. C. Stephen.

Representatives were present from Pennsylvania, Ohio, Indiana and Illinois. The meeting closed by singing, while all hands were joined, "Blest be the tie that binds," and the Mizpah benediction.

The Methodist Episcopal, Methodist Episcopal South and Canadian Methodist Joint Rally.

Rev. Forrest J. Prettyman, Washington, D. C., Chairman.

In opening the rally Mr. Prettyman said that Methodists should feel at home in a Christian Endeavor Convention, as all Endeavor plans were Methodist plans. That the very idea of pledged service was John Wesley's and that the Endeavor movement was but the adaptation of Wesley plans.

Rev. C. Lee Gaul of Philadelphia, Pa., spoke on the topic, "Is Methodism Meeting the Demands of the Twentieth Century in the Northern States?" He said, among other pertinent things, "We are looking after our young people in the North. They have a place in the Church. They are being developed for the responsibilities of the Kingdom. We are taking them at an earlier age than ever before. Our baptized children are being looked after as the wards of the Church. Our Sabbath School pupils are regarded as the lambs of the flock. The young converts are receiving instruction to an extent they never did previously. Pastors who give systematic instruction to probationers are being sought after to shepherd the largest congregations."

Rev. Gilby C. Kelly, D. D., of Nashville, Tenn., spoke on the question, "How is Methodism Meeting the Demands of the Twentieth Century in the Southern States?" In the course of his address Mr. Kelly said that some very hopeful signs were apparent. That the missionary conference of the Southern Methodist Church in New Orleans last May was the most enthusiastic and vital meeting that church had ever held. That inspiration from it had gone through all the connection. That out of the Woman's Missionary Board Conference recently held will doubtless come the organization of Deaconess work and the establishing of an industrial school for colored youth at Augusta, Georgia. That the Twentieth Century fund of one and one-half million dollars had been more than subscribed. He said he believed that as Endeavorers "we in this rally stand for something Methodism has always stood for."

Mr. A. T. Cooper, of Ontario, Canada, spoke in response to the question, "How is Methodism Meeting the Demands of the Twentieth Century in Canada?" He said that in evangelistic work the Methodist Church in Canada had always been in the forefront. The observance of the Quiet Hour in their recent conference had made it one of the best ever held. Their general conference has granted them the privilege of working under either the Epworth League or Christian Endeavor form of organization, and they have combined the names and call themselves Epworth Leagues of Christian Endeavor, and they are living to make their church a power in the land.

The rally voted to send the following message to the Epworth League Convention soon to be held in San Francisco:

"The Methodist Christian Endeavorers attending the International Convention at Cincinnati, July 6-10, 1901, assembled in our denominational rally, extend our most cordial and fraternal greetings, and our most hearty and earnest prayers to our brethren and sisters soon to assemble in the Epworth League Convention in San Francisco, with the strong desire for their success along all lines which have made our beloved Church so great. See John 17: 20 and 21."

The following persons also took part in the rally: Miss Mamie Bays, chairman press department North Carolina Christian Endeavor Union;

Mr. George M. Paul, president Philadelphia Christian Endeavor Union;
Mr. Robert J. Jessup, Salt Lake City; Mr. W. T. Young of Oklahoma;
and Rev. George M. Hammell, of Harriman, Tenn.

The United Presbyterian Rally.

Rev. A. M. Campbell, Princeton, Ind., Chairman.

The United Presbyterian Rally was held in the First Church of that
denomination on Walnut Hills, and was largely attended. Representatives were present from New York, Pennsylvania, Virginia, Ohio, Indiana,
Illinois, Kansas, Texas. The principal speakers were from Indianapolis,
Oxford, Allegheny, Hamilton, Ohio. A full recognition was made of the
debt of all Young People's societies to the Christian Endeavor movement.

A parliament was held on the question of whether the societies are
becoming simply prayer-meetings, and the concensus was "no."

Another parliament was engaged in by very many as to the ages of
boys and girls in the Junior and Intermediate societies, and what means
of passing them on from the first to the second ranks.

After two hours of enjoyment in such a meeting, the young ladies of
the local church became hostesses, and a happy hour was had in a social
way in the handsomely decorated church and everybody was made at
home with others and refreshments were served.

The Reformed Episcopal Rally.

Bishop Sam'l Fallows, D. D., Chicago, Ill., Chairman.

The Reformed Episcopal Rally was held at the Lincoln Park Baptist
Church. Brief addresses of cordial welcome were made by Dr. Eugene
Swope, Miss M. Solloman, and Miss Emma Fensten in behalf of the
Young People's Baptist Union.

Bishop Fallows gave the first address on the increasing power and enlarging influence of Christian Endeavor in the new century. He said he
believed that it would be the hand of Christian Endeavor which would
place the crown of all the earth upon the brow of Christ. For He could
not reign supreme until its principles of an all-embracing Christian fellowship and a thoroughly united Christian service prevailed.

Mr. A. N. Burnham of Chicago spoke on the increasing importance of
Christian Endeavor in its manifold activities to the individual churches.

Miss Elizabeth Dencer of Chicago spoke briefly in the same direction.

The Protestant Episcopal and Church of England Rally.

Rev. Canon J. B. Richardson, London, Ont., Chairman.

There was a good attendance of visiting delegates and members of the
church belonging to the city, also a number of clergy.

A short liturgical service was conducted by Rev. F. H. Nelson,
Rector of Christ Church, who afterward extended a cordial welcome to
those present and gave some incidents of the good work of Christian Endeavor which had come under his observation.

The chairman briefly explained the objects and operations of the Christian Endeavor movement and showed how pre-eminently suitable it was
to the Episcopal Church. The pledge, Bible study and consecration meeting harmonized exactly with church institutions.

Rev. W. G. Marsh, of Adelaide, Australia, spoke with warm enthusiasm. At first he had been opposed to the Endeavor Society, but from
a happy experience of what it had done among the people of his own
parish of St. Luke, Adelaide, he had become an earnest convert to the
cause. His Bishop strongly favored it and recommended him to accept
any office in which he might promote it.

Rev. Dr. Floyd W. Tomkins, Rector Holy Trinity Church, Philadelphia, showed the necessity which exists in the Episcopal Church of some organization to hold the young people of the church when they leave the Sunday school. They cannot be held by sociables, literary associations, musical clubs and such like, but only by such societies as have a purely religious basis. By the Christian Endeavor Society the young men and maidens are brought together and united in the Lord. He strongly urged the adoption of Christian Endeavor in every parish.

Rev. Arthur Murphy, of Toronto, thought that the problem of how to keep the young people was solved in the Endeavor movement. He gave a short Bible reading from Gen. xxii. and St. John xiii., showing the two great principles, prayer and service, as underlying all true Christian Endeavor. A short conference followed in which several questions and suggestions were offered. Some of the clergy present promised to adopt the society into their parishes.

The United Brethren Rally.

Rev. H. F. Sharpe, Dayton, Ohio, Chairman.

The largest, cheeriest, and most enthusiastic rally in the history of the United Brethren Church's connection with Christian Endeavor, was held in the First United Brethren Church. Miss C. E. (Christian Endeavor) Scott was elected secretary. Rev. H. J. Fischer in words, and the choir, in a grand German song, welcomed the one hundred and thirty delegates, representing the different States.

Rev. C. W. Brewbaker, secretary of the denominational union of young people's societies, spoke of the growth and meaning of the movement. Dr. J. P. Landis, president of the young people's union, from observations gathered from attendance at conventions in various States, declared that the young people's work is not waning in the United Brethren Church. Prof. G. A. Funkhouser of the United Brethren Theological seminary, declared that the greatest need was pastors in downright earnest.

A dozen short talks on the topic "Christian Endeavor and the United Brethren Church," added interest, while the songs in English and German were greatly appreciated. At the conclusion a photograph of the audience was taken.

The Baptist Rally.

Rev. Henry W. Sherwood, Kingston, N. Y., Chairman.

The Baptist rally met in the Ninth Street Baptist Church, with Mr. Percy S. Foster of Washington, D. C., in charge of the music. The attendance was large and the meeting was helpful and inspirational.

The Rev. Warren G. Partridge, D. D., pastor of the church, welcomed the speakers and delegates in a happy and hearty address to which Mr. Sherwood responded. The Rev. Johnston Myers, D. D., of Chicago, formerly pastor of the church, gave an encouraging review of the progress of the Baptist cause in Cincinnati since he began work here. Brief, vigorous addresses followed by Doctors Wayland Hoyt of Philadelphia, Cornelius Woelfkin, Brooklyn, J. W. Weddell, Davenport, Iowa, and Reverends Frank Dixon, Hartford, Conn., and W. B. Wallace, Utica, N. Y. Dr. Hoyt urged that all Baptist Unions become Baptist Young People's Unions of Christian Endeavor, that in addition to denominational loyalty, the inspiration and helpfulness of interdenominational fellowship might be enjoyed. This utterance was received with the heartiest applause.

Excellent solos were rendered by musical directors Percy S. Foster and F. H. Jacobs. At the close of the rally, Mr. W. Luther Parker of Cincinnati invited the speakers and some others to take a ride in a special chair trolley car through the extensive and beautiful suburbs of the city.

The Methodist Protestant Rally.

Rev. C. H. Hubbell, Chairman.

The Methodist Protestant rally was an enthusiastic one. Rev. G. W. Haddaway of Crisfield, Md., was to have presided, but was detained on account of the funeral services of a member of his church. Rev. C. H. Hubbell was elected chairman pro tem.

Prayer was offered by Rev. S. K. Spahr, of Tomkins Cove. At the roll call of unions, eleven responded. The report of the secretary and treasurer was given by Miss Moall. Words of welcome were spoken by the pastor of the church, Rev. Mr. Ganes.

Prof. Amos R. Wells brought greetings from The Christian Endeavor World, the organ of the societies, on which, said he, Dr. Cowan and others play rich tunes. It is like a postage stamp, sticking to its duty. It is Methodist Protestant, for it has method and it protests against all evil. It protests against five cents spent for soda water, and one for the church. It protests against a town having eight churches, when it is large enough for but two. It protests against calling temperance people saloonatics. It protests against resolutions on paper, that are not passed in the congress of the heart.

Rev. J. F. Cowan, D. D., brought greetings from the Christian Endeavor Headquarters, and said the newly appointed Field Secretary for Japan was a Methodist Protestant. He gave this watchword, More Work, More Societies, and Better Ones.

Miss Tei Morita of Japan, told of the work there. Miss Mary Moall spoke of "What We are Doing" and it was voted to continue to support the Christian Endeavor missionary in China.

Rev. Lee Anna Star represented the home missionary work, and Miss Margaret Kuhns the foreign, both interesting the audience in their work. Rev. G. E. McManiman, a trustee of the United Society, made a stirring address on "What We Might Do."

Rev. Dr. Anna Shaw was introduced and said she was glad to be a Methodist Protestant. She was a pastor without a church, a minister without a congregation, and a missionary without a field, but was working all the time, visiting on an average, two hundred and fifty cities a year.

A few words were spoken by Miss Hodges, a missionary elect, and the following officers were elected. President, Rev. C. H. Hubbell; vice-president, Rev. H. L. Feeman; secretary-treasurer, Miss Mary Moall; Junior superintendent, Mrs. J. W. Zirckle; additional members of the executive committee, C. R. Strayer, C. O. Harvey, Mrs. C. L. Ellis.

The Christian Church Rally.

Rev. H. F. Burnett, Chairman.

The Christian Church rally held in the Richmond Street Christian Church, was largely attended and very enthusiastic. Rev. M. W. Butler conducted the praise service. The devotional services were led by Rev. Dr. S. Q. Helfenstine of New York. The rallying hymn was written by Rev. John G. Dutton, the newly elected denominational secretary of Christian Endeavor.

The Rev. J. G. Bishop of Ohio, spoke on "Christian Endeavor and Missions." The address was packed with good wholesome thoughts. One of the principal things urged was the missionary library in connection with the regular work.

Prof. John N. Dales, of Kingston, Ontario, spoke on "Christian Endeavor and Education." He said Christian Endeavor and education go hand in hand. To have consecrated effort we must study to show ourselves workmen of God. We are to press forward and not forget. The times of sacrifice are times of spiritual building and education.

"A Message from the South" was responded to by Rev. W. Wicker of Newport News, Va. What we need, he said, as a people is better organization. The Christian Endeavor means organization and education. A man does not have to go to a university to learn how to do Christian work. Let him follow out the plans laid down in the great literature of the Christian Endeavor Society. Again we need enlargement in giving and going.

The Round Table was enriched by responses from Vermont, Michigan, New York, Ohio, New Jersey, Illinois, North Carolina, Virginia, Iowa, Indiana, and Ontario, Canada. The missionary idea was prominent throughout the rally.

The Southern Presbyterian Rally.

Rev. A. L. Phillips, D. D., Nashville, Chairman.

The rally of Southern Presbyterians was held in Westminster Presbyterian Church, on Price's Hill. Representatives were present from Kentucky, West Virginia, Virginia, Georgia, Alabama and Tennessee. Encouraging reports were made from the regions represented, especially from Birmingham, Ala. A slow but real growth in the young people's work was manifest. Addresses were made by Rev. W. C. Clark of Kentucky, by Rev. A. B. Curry, D. D., of Birmingham, Ala., by Prof. James Lewis Howe of Lexington, Va., and by Rev. A. L. Phillips, D. D. of Nashville, Tenn., all bearing on present conditions and methods for future work. A determined purpose was formed to push the work of development and organization wherever it was prudent, and where conditions were not ripe for Christian Endeavor to aid in organizing Westminster Leagues.

The Congregational Rally.

Rev. D. N. Beach, D. D., Denver, Col., Chairman.

The church was packed. "Remember Plymouth and Portland" was the motto, and the meeting did so. Dr. Leonard Bacon's "O God Beneath Thy Guiding Hand" was sung. Dr. James L. Hill, of Salem, Mass., read the triumphant CXXVI Psalm, and prayed to match hymn and Psalm.

Rev. Dwight M. Pratt, pastor of the church (formerly from Williston Church, Portland), told of the historic spot on which Walnut Hills Church, founded by Dr. Lyman Beecher, stood—one block from Lane Seminary where Dr. Beecher taught and the general scene of "Uncle Tom's Cabin." He welcomed the Congregational Endeavor hosts to a spot so sacred.

Mr. Will R. Moody said the best way to answer the first question on the programme—"How can the denomination in which Christian Endeavor began, best serve it?" was to produce the highest type of Christian living among Congregational young people.

The Rev. George W. Moore of Nashville, answered that the best way to serve Christian Endeavor was to "carry it on." He told of organizing the first Endeavor society of Afro-Americans in the world; of the great work for his people that it and Congregationalism had done; and by his eloquent words—for he was born a slave—set the pace for what followed.

The Congregationalist by Rev. W. P. Landers, The Advance by Mr. Goodspeed, and The Christian Endeavor World by the chairman, were commended under the head, "The Christian Endeavor World and a denominational paper in every family."

The Hon. S. B. Capen, president of the American Board, propounded the second question on the programme, namely, "Is the Time Ripe for the Denomination—as a Thank Offering (for the Christian Endeavor Movement's beginning within it) to Undertake Some Special Christian Endeavor Task? If so—What?" He thought the time was ripe. He wanted to suggest the answer to the question. Endeavor societies were springing up rapidly in China before the massacres; many Endeavorers unflinchingly suffered martyrdom; the survivors were rallying, and the work, under the inspiration of suffering, was ripe for large expansion. A secretary of the United Society of China, with prerogatives like Mr. Baer's, and following on Mr. Hatch's similar undertaking for India, was the need of the hour. He did not, as president of the board, hesitate for one moment to advocate such a thank offering. For one dollar thus given by Endeavorers, ten he felt sure would flow in to the Board's treasury. Miss Morrill's and Miss Gould's saintly martyrdom, and that of other missionaries and natives in China, called for this memorial.

Dr. Clark said that this was the very thing the United Society at home longed for; and with wit, reason and impassioned earnestness, he pointed out how such a solution of the question propounded would meet not only a great need, but further the evangelization of the Martyr Empire as almost nothing else.

Then Dr. Ament, the hero of Peking, described, as only an eye witness of the opportunity could do, the possibilities of such a secretaryship.

Upon this Mr. Capen moved that here and now the Congregational Endeavorers of America determine to raise two thousand dollars this year and annually for this purpose. The motion was instantly seconded, and Mr. Hubbard of China, Dr. Jones of India, and Mr. Ransom of Africa, all Christian Endeavor leaders on their fields, in rousing brief talks, advocated the measure. The motion was carried by an enthusiastic rising vote.

Before the vote was taken, Mr. Moody, who had another engagement, but who, scenting the battle, had waited for a chance, said "Two thousand dollars, or twenty-five hundred dollars, or three thousand dollars for such a memorial and such a cause, were a mere bagatelle," and asked the privilege of offering for the little society at Northfield, twenty-five dollars as the first pledge. When the applause had ceased, Mr. Capen said that the society at Jamaica Plain, he felt sure, would endorse his action, and he wanted to offer on its behalf fifty dollars as one of the first pledges.

The scene that followed beggars description. Dr Jones pledged twenty-five dollars from India. Dr. Ament pledged ten dollars from the Endeavorers of the South Church, Peking. Mr. Hubbard from China, and Mr. Ransom from Africa, pledged for their fields. With trembling voices, classmates, or friends, of Miss Morrill and Miss Gould rose and made memorial pledges. Endeavorers rose in all parts of the house, waiting their turns to pledge their societies. In sums of five, two and a half, to fifty dollars—with an Afro-American Jubilee song by Mr. Clark, a Christian Endeavor pastor from Charleston, South Carolina, while people took breath, nine hundred and twenty-two dollars were offered on the spot toward an annual two thousand dollars for a secretaryship of the United Society of the Chinese Empire, to be known as the "Christian Endeavor Martyrs' Memorial." Dr. Clark, Mr. Shaw and Mr. Capen were empowered to name a standing committee who should complete the fund. Subscriptions to it and moneys for it may be sent to Mr. William Shaw, Tremont Temple, Boston, whom the meeting appointed treasurer of the fund.

This seemed enough, but Mr. Capen rose and projected another precious surprise—the address to Dr. Clark signed by hundreds of leading educators, missionaries, editors, jurists, and business men of our churches. Dr. Clark with deep feeling responded. To receive the loving cup and this loving address, in one afternoon, were such experiences as few men in any age have known.

Then Dr. Sheldon and Dr. G. Campbell Morgan followed, the former with a few lines of impromptu verse and a plea for the Christliest living in the Endeavor ranks, and the latter with a tribute to the honor and love in which English Congregationalists hold Dr. Clark.

A telegram of greeting by Dr. Ryder for the American Missionary

Association Headquarters, whose work extends from Porto Rico to Alaska; the five delegates from the Christian Endeavor Society of the Williston Church, Portland, received an enthusiastic welcome, and prayer, Mizpah, and benediction by Dr. Clark, closed a never to be forgotten and an epoch making rally.

The Presbyterian Rally.

Rev. Cleland B. McAfee, D.D., Chicago, Ill., Chairman.

A beautiful afternoon, a large audience, a long list of crisp speeches, hearty singing, plenty of applause, a few tears, much enthusiasm—what more does it take to make a great rally? Add to all that the traditions and service of the church and its young people, and you may know that the Presbyterian rally was inspiring.

The theme was "Presbyterians at Work." Dr. J. F. Carson of Brooklyn, led an informal devotional service, quoting the Scripture instead of reading it and pointing out the three requisites for good work; 1st, a clear conception of the work to be done; 2d, thorough equipment for the work; 3d, power. All are found in Acts 1: 8. That gave a solid foundation for the rally.

Then came the inspiring greeting from the Cincinnati Presbyterians, voiced by Dr. C. L. Work, with its resume of Presbyterian history and achievement, and the greeting from the United Society, voiced by the well-known Presbyterian elder, Secretary Baer, who declared that the Endeavor Society owed much to Presbyterians, however much obligation might appear on the other side. A large chart showing the growth of the society in the Presbyterian church illustrated the welcome. There are 9000 societies with 500,000 members, putting this church in the lead.

Rev. E. F. Hallenbeck of Albany, said the word of response, pledging the present young people to loyalty to traditions of the past and prophecies of the future.

Then began the real study of Presbyterians at work. Dr. Teunis S. Hamlin of Washington and Dr. H. T. McEwen of New York spoke of "The Presbyterian Pastor and His Society," Dr. Hamlin accenting the pastor, and Dr. McEwen the society. Dr. Hamlin urged the pastors to 1st, Sympathy; 2d, Active Co-operation; 3d, Guidance. Dr. McEwen urged the societies to 1st, Recruit; 2d, Serve; 3d, Pray.

Then our minds went afield. Dr. J. A. Worden of Philadelphia had "come all the way for ten minutes of chance to lay a burden on the young people." As superintendent of Sunday School work, he announced the purpose of the Board to assign special work to special parts of the Church. Cuba, the Mountaineers of the South and the Great West are the three sections assigned. One of the features of the rally was the silent prayer for which Dr. Worden called as he concluded.

Then a message came straight from the field in the word of Rev. Dr. C. Humble, one of our Southern Sunday School missionaries. There were some tears near by when he told of those who could not go to hear him preach, but who sat up late into the night to hear him pray, of those who had descended from heroic ancestry and had heroic possibility yet. Mrs. F. D. Palmer of the Freedmen's Board took up the story, urging larger attention to the negroes. Only six hundred of the nine thousand societies gave last year. She told thrilling incidents of heroism in present day life among them. But, naturally, high tide of home missions was reached in the address of Dr. C. L. Thompson, Secretary of the Home Board. He laid on the hearts of the young people the work in Porto Rico, especially the much-needed hospital at San Juan, where the young medical missionary, Miss Grace Atkins, is already called "The Angel." Forty thousand dollars were given by the Presbyterian C. E. Societies last year for home missions through the Home Board. Dr. Thompson urged greater things another year. They will be forthcoming.

Before we could go across the sea, what was more natural than that the rally should adopt a message of love to be sent to Dr. J. Wilbur Chapman, whose sickness has been so much thought of. A prayer was offered, and Dr. Maltbie D. Babcock's fine setting of the hymn "O Lamb of God Still Help Me" was sung. It was like a rest by the wayside to think heavenward for a moment.

But Presbyterians are in "the uttermost parts," and Mr. Robert E. Speer told the story of their work. "No other church but this has its work on all the continents and fronting all the world." "No other church is so well adapted as this to deal with the greatest problem of missions today, the Mohammedan problem." Naming the countries where our work is being done, Mr. Speer thrilled our hearts. Two college classmates were put side by side before us. One is in Korea and is laying foundations for a new civilization. The other is "pottering about in the Massachusetts Legislature." But the life of the one is going toward the crown, the other is fulfilling personal ambition. The church's resting time will not come until the world is won. Until then a Christian's best crown is more work.

Who should put before us the "Two-Cents-a-Week Plan" but Rev. Dr. A. A. Fulton of China, who inaugurated it? It is all implied in the name—an effort to reach the many small givers. It would more than double the missionary gifts of the young people if such a plan were generally adopted. Dr. Fulton told that he had baptized one thousand adults in China in ten years.

"The Tenth Legion" originated in the church of Dr. Wilton Merle Smith of New York, who told us the story of the great missionary movement which has made that church famous. Out of the founding of that Legion came the supporting of five home and seven foreign missionaries, the quickening of the spiritual life of the whole church and the enlarging of all its work. It was Dr. Smith also who said the closing word, a plea for fullest surrender, for utter abandonment of ourselves to Christ. This, he urged, is at the root of all real work for the Church, and for it he led in the prayer which closed the rally in the very presence of God.

Friends' Rally.

Mr. Albert J. Brown, Indianapolis, Ind., Chairman.

The first part of the meeting was devoted to business, consisting of the report of the Secretary and Treasurer. The Secretary's report was made up of the statistics of the Union and an account of the work and plans of the several yearly meeting Unions. One of the important things in the report was that a Christian Endeavor Union has been formed in London and Dublin Yearly Meetings. Hitherto the young people have been organized under a Young People's Fellowship Union.

A nominating committee made up of delegates officially appointed by the Yearly Meeting Unions selected the following officers for the coming year, which was ratified by the meeting:

President, Elwood O. Ellis, Richmond, Ind.
Vice-President, Alfred T. Ware, New Haven, Conn.
Secretary, Myrtle S. Lightner, Sabina, Ohio.
Treasurer, Samuel Purviance, Smithfield, Ohio.
Missionary Superintendent, Mr. Edwin McGrew, Newberg, Oregon.

The subjects under discussion were:—How to make the Friends' Christian Endeavor Union most effective in, 1st, Spiritual Things; 2d, Bible Study; 3d, Personal Meditation and Prayer; 4th, Personal Work and Soul Winning. Richard Haworth, Marion, Ind., presenting the first subject, thought the only way was to let the Spirit of Christ come into our lives. Levi Mills, Wilmington, Ohio, said the best way to make Bible study effective was not to consider it a book of comfort especially, but a text book for equipment and qualification. Mr. Lewis E. Strout spoke of the Quiet Hour as the most effective for personal meditation and prayer. He said it was an old Friends' idea, and we were simply coming back to the principles taught by our forefathers. Mr. Edgar Stranahan, Sabina, Ohio, gave four plans for effective use in personal work and soul winning: 1st, Study the methods of George Fox and his coadjutors; 2d, Study the lives of the immediate followers of Christ; 3d, To examine carefully the methods of Christian Endeavor upon the subject; 4th, Study the great soul winner and worker—Christ Himself. Rev. Willis R. Hotchkiss gave an account of work that is being done for Foreign Missions among Friends. He said the Unions average 46 cents per member for missions. Miss Ruth Farquhar, Wilmington, Ohio, said to make Junior work effective among Friends is to never criticise it, always praise it, to talk and teach it, praise and preach it wherever you go.

Free Baptist and General Baptist Rally.

Mr. Harry S. Myers, Hillsdale, Mich., Chairman.

The Free Baptists and General Baptists met in a pleasant joint denominational rally presided over by Mr. Harry S. Myers, Hillsdale, Mich. Miss Ruth Chappell of Oakland City, Ind., spoke on "Ways to Help the Pastor." Prof. G. W. Lawrence of Midway, Tenn., spoke of the great opportunities for home mission enterprise among the mountain whites. General Secretary Harry S. Myers spoke of the present needs of co-operation, evangelization and missionary work in our societies.

Rev. W. E. Dennett of Pascoag, R. I., gave a stirring address on the hopeful things of our work.

The attendance was good and Christian Endeavor increased its grip on our people.

The Lutheran Rally.

Rev. Millard F. Troxell, D. D., St. Joseph, Mo., Chairman.

The rally of the Lutherans was held in the First English Lutheran Church. The pastor of the church, Rev. Dr. J. M. Ziegler, gave an address of welcome which was responded to by the veteran Endeavorer, Rev. Dr. J. G. Butler, of Washington, D. C.

"Endeavor and Lutheranism for Each Other" was the topic on which Rev. Dr. S. S. Waltz, of Louisville, Ky., spoke in an eloquent way, giving as three pointers showing their fitness one for the other, their mutual loyalty, mutual piety, and mutual worshipfulness in the service of God in the church.

"The Lutheran and the Quiet Hour" was the subject from which Miss Celia Lyday of Newton, Iowa, at present State Secretary of Iowa Endeavor work, made an ideal address, rich in Bible quotation and other allusions helpful in the morning watch with God.

Miss Grace Beelman, of the Lutheran Society in the First Church, Dayton, Ohio, who so charmed the large audiences in Auditoriums Endeavor and Williston with her cornet solos, gave the Lutheran Rally the benefit of her presence and sweet music.

Another specialty was the genial presence at the rally of Rev. Marion J. Kline, of Bethlehem Lutheran Church, Harrisburg, Pa., just elected President of all the Endeavor hosts of the Keystone State in place of Rev. C. E. Eberman, just promoted to the position of Field Secretary. President Kline received enthusiastic congratulations from his Lutheran Endeavorers over his promotion to the Presidency of Pennsylvania.

Sister Keturst, a deaconess of the Lutheran Church, was introduced to the rally and spoke a few ringing words concerning service and consecration.

"The Lutheran and Missions" was handled by Mr. George W. Lubke, Jr., of St. Louis, in a practical way, and he developed the fact that seven native helpers are being supported in foreign fields by the societies represented at the rally.

In the home field, Rev. W. B. Lahr, of the Endeavor Memorial Mission at Cleveland, Ohio, told of his excellent growing work and said there was now another missionary in the city and there were fields for several more if they could be properly supported. The sentiment of the rally favored the centreing of all Endeavor home mission work in Cleveland and helping there until the churches reach self support.

The Lutheran Endeavor Gatling-Gun was touched off by President Troxell, and a fire of questions and answers centred about the target personal topics, "What Is Your Society Doing?" and "What Will You Do More?"

This, with fellowship, prayer and praise, closed one of the most successful Lutheran rallies ever yet held. The officers elected for the next two years are Rev. Millard F. Troxell, St. Joseph, Mo., President, and Rev. Charles W. Leitzell, Newton, Iowa, Secretary.

Welsh Rally.

Rev. John Hammond, Columbus, Ohio, Chairman.

The Welsh are nothing if not enthusiastic, so the singing and speaking and handshaking at this rally were full of enthusiasm. Rev. D. E. Jones spoke on "Saved to Serve." Rev. J. D. Jones, Ripon College, Wis., "Called to Rescue Others." Rev. D. I. Jones, Cincinnati, spoke of "The Spirit's Power in the Christian Endeavor Machinery." Rev. W. A. Powell, D. D., Toledo, "Rooting Down by Branching Out."

The church where the rally was held has no Christian Endeavor Society, but one will soon materialize as the outcome of our meeting.

The Reformed Church in the United States.

Charles E. Wehler, Dayton, Ohio.

The Reformed Church in the United States held an enthusiastic rally in the Salem Reformed Church. There were three hundred in attendance coming mainly from Ohio and Pennsylvania, though other States were also fairly represented. After a brief devotional service, the programme was heartily entered into by all present.

Among the leading features of the programme was a stirring address by the Rev. J. P. Moore, D. D., of Japan, who with eighteen years of experience in the foreign field, was abundantly able and well qualified to give much needed information. Good results will follow this address. "The Denominational Reading Course" was the subject of a paper by the Rev. C. E. Miller, of Dayton, Ohio. Steps were taken looking to the outlining of a course of reading, comprising the subjects of the History, Biography and Educational works of the denomination.

Perhaps the most spirited part of the rally was the discussion on the feasibility of organizing a Heidelburg League of Christian Endeavor (denominational). After a well directed conference on the subject, it was decided to remain in the ranks of the great United Society without the attachment of a distinctly denominational name.

A pleasant feature of the rally was the singing of the rally song, specially composed for the occasion. The young people of the Reformed Church have lost none of their love and enthusiasm for the movement which has for its watchword "For Christ and the Church." All are hopefully looking for rich results from this Twentieth Century Rally.

The Mennonite Rally.

Rev. H. J. Krehbiel, Trenton, Ohio, Chairman.

The Mennonite Rally was held in the Lyceum Hall. After the invocation by Mr. J. King, the chairman made a few opening remarks. "The Future Mission of the Church" was the subject of a paper written by V. Strubhar of Washington, Ill., read by Miss Martha Augspurger. "Unification of the Different Factions of Our Denomination" was discussed in a paper by Rev. H. P. Krehbiel of Newton, Kansas, read by Mr. Edward Mosurian. The next topic was "What the Christian Endeavor Society Has Done for Our Young People," by Mrs. J. C. Mehl of Goshen, Ind. "What Our Denomination Has Done in the Mission Work" was the final topic, written by I. A. Sommers of Berne, Ind., and delivered by Miss Lydia Augspurger. After the regular programme a short "Open Parliament" was held during which the topic "What Benefit Have We Derived from Attending the Christian Endeavor Convention?" was considered.

The African Methodist Episcopal and African Methodist Episcopal Zion Rally.

Bishop B. W. Arnett, LL. D., Wilberforce, Ohio, Chairman.

This joint rally was held in Allen Temple A. M. E. Church, which was tastefully decorated with the Christian Endeavor and national colors, and many delegates were present. Chaplain B. W. Arnett, M. A., opened the proceedings by announcing the familiar hymn, "In the Cross of Christ I Glory." Rev. O. E. Jones, B. D., Oakland, Cal., offered prayer. At the conclusion of the prayer, Prof. G. F. Woodson, D. D., of Payne Theological Seminary, Wilberforce, Ohio, read the Scripture lesson.

Dr. I. N. Ross, pastor of the local church, delivered a brief but most hearty address of welcome to the visitors from other cities and States. Bishop Alexander Walters, M. A., D. D., of the African Methodist Episcopal Zion Church, was the first to respond to the welcome address. He was followed by Chaplain B. W. Arnett, M. A., General Secretary of the Christian Endeavor Societies of the African Methodist Episcopal Church. He accepted the cordial greeting in behalf of his denominational Endeavorers of the United States, the West Indies and of the West Coast and South Africa and spoke of the growth of the Christian Endeavor Societies in his denomination. Chaplain Arnett was followed by Rev. E. D. W. Jones, pastor of Avery Chapel, Allegheny City, Pa.

Rev. J. W. Jeffries of Pittsburg, Pa., made a stirring address and emphasized the importance of Junior work. Booker T. Washington in an eloquent address referred to the elements which must enter into all permanent work for Christ. Bishop Arnett closed with a speech full of the warm spirit of denominational loyalty and urged greater zeal for the accomplishment of the larger purposes for which Christian Endeavor now stands.

This rally was the most enthusiastic and also the largest and best ever held. Delegates were present from twelve States and the District of Columbia. The music was under the direction of Prof. I. N. Quarles, of Allen Temple A. M. E. Church.

Churches of God.

Rev. C. I. Brown, Chairman.

The rally of the Churches of God was conducted on the plan of a Round Table talk. "More Trained Workers" was the subject, and the educational needs were especially emphasized, trained in the home, trained in the Endeavor Society, and trained in our schools.

Moravian Rally.

Rev. W. H. Vogler, Indianapolis, Ind., Chairman.

At the Moravian Rally, the following resolution was unanimously passed:

"We, the representatives of our American Moravian Christian Endeavor Societies at this International Convention, assembled in Cincinnati, July 9, 1901, herewith place on record our heartfelt gratification over the appointment of our brother, the Rev. C. E. Eberman of Lancaster, Pa., to the responsible and honorable position of Field Secretary of the United Society of Christian Endeavor. We congratulate the Endeavor host on the man whom God has called to this office; we rejoice that the honor has come to our own dear Moravian Church; we invoke the Savior''s constant and daily ministrations of the Holy Spirit for our brother as he enters on the new office of great responsibilities and great possibilities in which office we have the fullest assurance that God will grant him 'the largest measure of success."

INDEX FOR REPORT U. S. C. E.

ILLUSTRATIVE ANECDOTES.

GREETINGS, RESOLUTIONS, PRESENTATIONS, ETC.

SOME CONVENTION INCIDENTS.

ILLUSTRATIONS.

THE ROUND TABLE.

REPORTS AND STATISTICS.

OPEN PARLIAMENTS.

PERSONNEL.

www.ingramcontent.com/pod-product-compliance
Lightning Source LLC
Chambersburg PA
CBHW031953040426
42448CB00006B/336